MARRIOTT'S
Practical
Electrocardiography

NINTH EDITION

Galen S. Wagner, M.D.

Associate Professor
Department of Internal Medicine
Duke University Medical Center
Durham, North Carolina

SANS TACHE

Williams & Wilkins

BALTIMORE • PHILADELPHIA • HONG KONG
LONDON • MUNICH • SYDNEY • TOKYO

A WAVERLY COMPANY

Editor: Jonathan W. Pine, Jr.
Associate Editor: Molly L. Mullen
Copy Editors: Klementyna Bryte and Janet Krejci
Designer: Norman W. Och
Illustration Planner: Wayne Hubbel
Production Coordinator: Barbara J. Felton

Copyright © 1994
Williams & Wilkins
428 East Preston Street
Baltimore, Maryland 21202, USA

Accurate indications, adverse reactions, and dosage schedules for drugs are provided in this book, but it is possible that they may change. The reader is urged to review the package information data of the manufacturers of the medications mentioned.

Printed in the United States of America

Chapter reprints are available from the publisher.

First Edition, 1954
Second Edition, 1957
Third Edition, 1962
Fourth Edition, 1968
Fifth Edition, 1972
Sixth Edition, 1977
Seventh Edition, 1983
    Reprinted 1984, 1985, 1986, 1987
Eighth Edition, 1988

Library of Congress Cataloging-in-Publication Data

Wagner, Galen S.
    Marriott's practical electrocardiography.—9th ed./Galen S. Wagner.
        p.   cm.
    Rev. ed. of.: Practical electrocardiography / Henry J. L. Marriott. 8th ed.
c1988.
    Includes bibliographical references and index.
    ISBN 0-683-08604-9
    1. Electrocardiography.   I. Marriott, Henry J. L. (Henry Joseph Llewellyn),
    1917–   Practical electrocardiography.   II. Title.
    [DNLM: 1. Electrocardiography.   WG 140 W133m   1994]
    RC683.5.E5M3   1994
    616.1'207547—dc20
    DNLM/DLC
    for Library of Congress   93-30277
                                                                          CIP

                                            94   95   96   97   98
                                    1   2   3   4   5   6   7   8   9   10

Henry J. L. Marriott

The ninth edition is dedicated to Henry J. L. (Barney) Marriott, M.D., for conceiving *Practical Electrocardiography,* nurturing it through eight editions over 34 years, and graciously assisting me with this edition.

Preface to the Ninth Edition

Barney Marriott created *Practical Electrocardiography* in 1954 and nurtured it through eight editions. After assisting him with the eighth edition, I enthusiastically accepted the challenge of writing the ninth edition. Barney has graciously assisted me with this edition of *Marriott's Practical Electrocardiography.*

We initially agreed upon a revision of the chapter order. There have been many recent insights into problems of waveform morphology, especially regarding ischemic heart disease. These chapters were expanded and grouped together in Section II prior to the consideration of the cardiac arrhythmias in Section III.

Attention to the details of ECG waveforms has so challenged diagnostic skills that there are now efforts to present the frontal plane leads in an orderly sequence similar to that used for the leads in the transverse plane. A display of the orderly sequence of single cardiac cycles in both sets of six leads is presented beneath the classical display of four groups of three time aligned leads for many of the example ECGs in Section II on Abnormal Wave Morphology. This provides the reader with the ability to observe serial progression and regression of ECG waveforms. Olle Pahlm and his colleagues in Lund, Sweden, where routine display of the "Cabrera sequence" of frontal plane leads originated, have been most helpful.

The first three chapters provide an introductory orientation to electrocardiography. One of the strengths of *Marriott's Practical Electrocardiography* has been its lucid foundation for understanding the basis for ECG interpretation. I have added concepts of my own and adapted innovations from other authors.

Thaler's *The Only EKG Book You'll Ever Need,* Dubin's *Rapid Interpretation of EKG's,* and Netter's *The Ciba Collection of Medical Illustrations* have provided novel visualizations of the relationships between cardiac electrical events and their depiction on surface ECG recordings. Both reproductions and adaptations of these authors' illustrations have been integrated into my revised text in an expanded initial section of the ninth edition. Rick White's magnetic resonance images of the heart in situ have provided the orientation to the relationship between the cardiac structures and the body surface ECG recording sites.

The second section of eight chapters considers abnormalities of the ECG waveforms. Barney Marriott recognized the unique contributions of Mauricio Rosenbaum to the understanding of the problems of intraventricular conduction. His Tampa Tracings published the English version of *Los Hemibloques* and he incorporated Rosenbaum's principles into *Marriott's Practical Electrocardiography.*

The Duke University Medical Center has been the source of many of the advances in the understanding and treatment of ventricular preexcitation during the past 25 years. I have relied on this experience for my reorganization of this chapter.

I have expanded presentation of myocardial ischemia and infarction into four chapters. As new clinical methods for treatment of ischemia and limitation of infarct size have evolved, we have gained new insights into quantitative changes in QRS complexes, ST segments, and T waves. Ron Selvester has been my mentor during 20 years of research into understanding these changes, and I have relied heavily on his guidance throughout this section. His understanding, derived from his simulation of normal and abnormal human ventricular activation, has transformed an old qualitative tool into a modern quantitative one. I have also incorporated Barry Ramo's practical clinical insights into my presentation of infarction, and Mitch Krucoff's unique experience with continuous monitoring into my presentation of ischemia.

Barney Marriott's greatest contribution has been his innovative approaches to understanding the arrhythmias during the era of continuous bedside and ambulatory ECG monitoring. As soon as I had conceptualized my presentation of the final section of this edition, I invited him to Durham for some brainstorming. This was the highlight of this book for me. It must have been difficult for Barney to hear an upstart challenge his many time-proven concepts, but he graciously and patiently parried every thrust and led me into practical compromises. His remarkable chapter on aberrant conduction remains intact from the eighth edition.

I relied heavily on years of co-teaching the arrhythmias to practicing nurses and physicians and co-authoring texts for Churchill Livingstone and FA Davis with Bob Waugh, Barry Ramo, and Marcel Gilbert. Many illustrations that originated and evolved during these joyous interactions are included throughout the arrhythmia section of this edition. Andy Wallace spawned this Duke group, which also includes Fred Cobb, Jim Dorsey, John Gallagher, Mike Rotman, Rick Schaal, Tsuniaki Sugimoto, Menashe Waxman, and Doug Zipes during the late 1960s and early 1970s. I also relied on Stan Anderson who ascended into this Duke group from Australia in the early 1970s. He continued to ascend from time to time as I wrote the arrhythmia section and provided the basis of the chapter on artificial cardiac pacemakers from his vast experience.

I have been fortunate to have had many excellent mentors in practical electrocardiography in addition to those who helped directly with this edition. Fred Hunter of Connellsville, PA, taught the basic geometric principles, Duke's Harvey Estes provided the understanding of vectorcardiography, and Don Hackel, the visualization of cardiac anatomy and pathology. Albert Jablonsky, Don Bortz, and Henry Lewis of Greensburg, PA, introduced me to using the ECG in community practice, and Ed Orgain and Joe Greenfield provided the academic understanding in their Duke Heart Station. The use of one-on-one interaction to teach arrhythmia interpretation to a group came from Louis Katz's course with Alfred Pick and Richard Langendorf at the Michael Reese Hospital, and the use of the coronary care unit as an ECG learning laboratory came from Bernie Lown at the Peter Bent Brigham Hospital.

I have also been fortunate to have an excellent production crew for this edition of *Marriott's Practical Electrocardiography.* Law student Michele Klaassen descended from the Netherlands to become both my editor and my guinea pig. When she returned home at my halfway point, premed students Cara Gambill and Michelle Wilkins assumed the editor/guinea pig roles. The ninth edition is really Michele's, Cara's, and Michelle's in so many ways. They made me change the words until they could understand them, and then they made Williams & Wilkins alter the production until they were satisfied.

Scott Scheirman of Hewlett-Packard provided the majority of 12-lead ECGs and Sousin Leggett and Phyllis Sewell of the Duke Heart Station provided the others. Scott went above and beyond to obtain recordings from the HP files. Francine Mehler did the original drawings for all of the new figures.

Jonathan Pine has been my guiding light from Williams & Wilkins. He has been patient with my many expanded "deadlines" and my reasonable and unreasonable requests. His superb team, including Molly Mullen, Wayne Hubbel, Barbara Felton, Norman Och, Wilma Rosenberger, Klementyna Bryte, and Janet Krejci have been remarkably helpful, creative, and flexible.

With this publication of the ninth edition, we launch our work on the tenth edition. This will be a 5-year effort to produce an interactive computerized textbook. Barney Marriott has mastered both the personal classroom interactive method and the textbook didactic method of teaching practical electrocardiography. He and I will be working with Williams & Wilkins toward combining these methods for a tenth edition of *Marriott's Practical Electrocardiography* to be published in 1999.

Preface to the First Edition

Books on electrocardiography seem to possess one or more of several disadvantages for the beginner: the introductory chapters on electrophysiology are so intricate and long-winded that the reader's interest is early drowned in a troubled sea of vectors, axes, and gradients; or only certain aspects of the subject are dealt with, for example, the arrhythmias may be entirely omitted; or illustrations are deficient and frequently situated uncomfortably far from the descriptive text.

For several years I have been attempting to introduce fourth year students to the comparatively easy technique of interpreting electrocardiograms. During this period I have been unable to recommend any single text that deals with the subject quickly and simply and yet is sufficiently comprehensive. This book is an attempt to supply such a manual. Its aims are: (1) to emphasize the simplicities rather than the complexities of the electrocardiogram; (2) to give the reader only those electrophysiologic concepts that make everyday interpretation more intelligible without burdening him with unnecessary detail; (3) to cover all diagnostically important electrocardiographic patterns; and (4) to provide adequate illustrations and in every instance to have the illustration conveniently situated to the reader as he reads the descriptive text. To achieve this last desideratum, the publishers have generously waived publishing conventions and given me a free hand in the arrangement and spacing of illustrations and text.

This book is designed for those approaching electrocardiography from the point of view of the clinician. It is hoped that it will enable the beginner to acquire a rapid but thorough grasp of a sophisticated yet simple discipline.

H.J.L.M.

Contents

I. Basic Concepts

II. Abnormal Wave Morphology

I

BASIC CONCEPTS

CHAPTER 1

Cardiac Electrical Activity

ANATOMIC ORIENTATION OF THE HEART WITHIN THE BODY

 The position of the heart within the body determines the "view" of the cardiac electrical activity that can be observed from any site on the body surface. The *atria* are located in the top or *base* of the heart, and the *ventricles* taper toward the bottom or *apex*. However, as can be seen in Figure 1.1, the right and left sides of the heart are not directly aligned with the right and left sides of the body. The long axis of the heart, which extends from base to apex, is tilted to the left and anteriorly at its apical end. Also, the heart is rotated so that the right atrium and ventricle are more *anterior* than the left atrium and ventricle.[1,2]

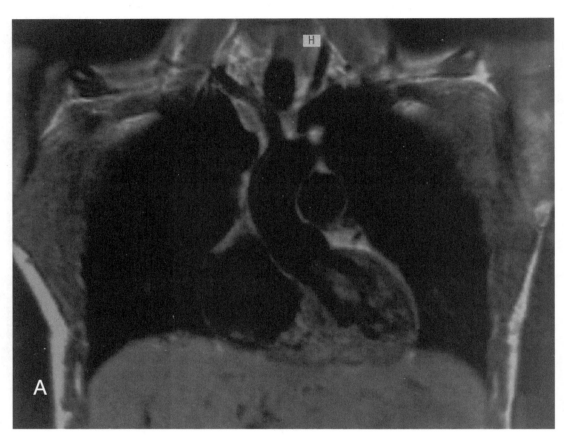

Figure 1.1. Magnetic resonance images of the heart within the thorax, viewed from the front in the frontal plane (**A**) and from above in the transverse plane (**B**). Note that the apex is tilted to the left and that the interventricular septum is rotated counterclockwise. The right ventricle is orientated more anteriorly than the left ventricle.

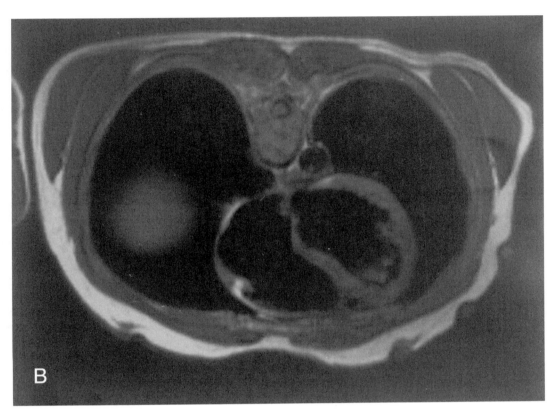

Figure 1.1B

THE CARDIAC CYCLE

The mechanical pumping action of the heart is produced by myocardial cells that contain contractile proteins. The timing and synchronization of contraction of these cells are controlled by cells of the *pacemaking and conduction system*, which is described below. Impulses generated within these cells create a rhythmic repetition of events called *cardiac cycles*. Each cycle is composed of electrical and mechanical activation *(systole)* and recovery *(diastole)*. The terms commonly applied to these components of the cardiac cycle are listed in Table 1.1. Since the electrical events initiate the mechanical events, there is a brief delay between the onsets of electrical and mechanical systole and of electrical and mechanical diastole.

Table 1.1. Terms Describing Cardiac Cycle

	Systole	Diastole
Electrical	Activation	Recovery
	Excitation	Recovery
	Depolarization	Repolarization
Mechanical	Shortening	Lengthening
	Contraction	Relaxation
	Emptying	Filling

The electrical recording from inside a single myocardial cell as it progresses through a cardiac cycle is illustrated in Figure 1.2. During electrical diastole, the cell has a baseline negative electrical potential and is also in mechanical diastole with separation of the contractile proteins. An electrical impulse arriving at the cell allows positively charged ions to cross the cell membrane, causing *depolarization* of the cell. This movement of ions initiates electrical systole, which is characterized by an *action potential*. This electrical event then initiates mechanical systole in which the contractile proteins slide over each other, thereby shortening the cell. Electrical systole continues for a period of time until the positively charged ions are pumped out causing *repolarization* of the cell. The electrical potential returns to its negative resting level. This return of electrical diastole causes the contractile proteins to separate again. The cell is then capable of being reactivated if another electrical impulse arrives at its membrane.

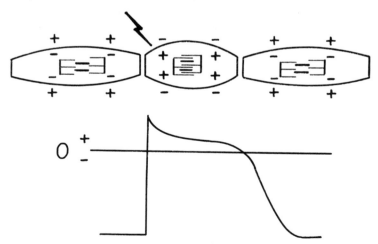

Figure 1.2.   An electrical current initiates the progression of a single myocardial cell through a cardiac cycle that includes both systolic and diastolic states. Below the cell is a representation of an internal electrical recording. The *horizontal line* indicates the level of zero potential, with positive values above and negative values beneath. (Modified from Thaler MS. The only EKG book you'll ever need. Philadelphia: JB Lippincott, 1988:11.)

The electrical and mechanical changes in a series of myocardial cells as they progress through a cardiac cycle are illustrated in Figure 1.3. In *A*, the four representative cells are in their resting or repolarized state. Electrically, the cells have negative charges, while mechanically their contractile proteins are separated. An electrical current arrives at the second myocardial cell in *B*, causing electrical and then mechanical systole. The wave of depolarization in *C* has spread throughout all the myocardial cells. In *D*, the recovery or repolarization process begins in the second cell, which had been the first to depolarize. Finally, the wave of repolarization in *E* has spread throughout all of the myocardial cells and they await the coming of another electrical current.[3-6]

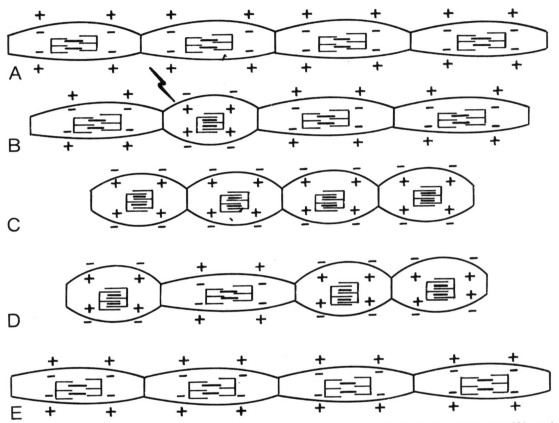

Figure 1.3. A series of four myocardial cells is represented in their resting state (**A**), and then in their progression through a cardiac cycle (**B–E**). An electrical current is depicted in **B** as initiating depolarization in the second of the four cells. (Modified from Thaler MS. The only EKG book you'll ever need. Philadelphia: JB Lippincott, 1988:9.)

In Figure 1.4, the relationship between the intracellular electrical recording from a single myocardial cell presented in Figure 1.2 is combined with an electrocardiogram (ECG) recording from the body surface. The ECG recording is formed by the summation of electrical signals from all of the myocardial cells. When the cells are in their resting state, the ECG recording produces a flat baseline. The onset of depolarization of the cells produces a relatively high frequency ECG waveform. Then, while depolarization persists, the ECG returns to the baseline. Repolarization of the myocardial cells is represented on the ECG by a lower frequency waveform in the opposite direction from that representing depolarization.

The process of production of the ECG recording by waves of depolarization and repolarization spreading toward an electrode on the body surface is presented in Figure 1.5. In *A*, the first of the four cells has been electrically activated and the activation has then spread into the second cell. This spread of depolarization toward the recording electrode produces a positive deflection on the ECG. All of the cells are in their depolarized state in *B*, and the ECG recording has returned to its baseline level. In *C*, repolarization has begun in the same cell in which depolarization was initiated, and the wave of repolarization has spread into the adjoining cell. This produces the oppositely directed waveform on the ECG recording.

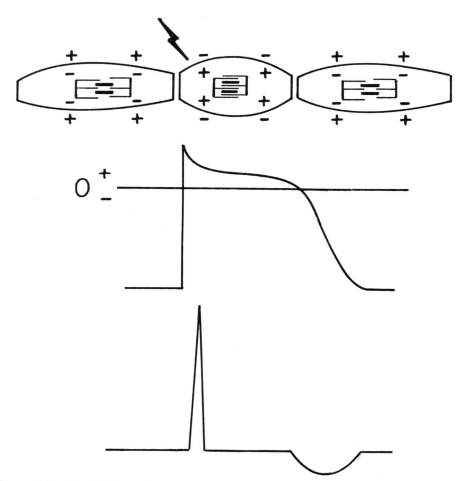

Figure 1.4. The ECG waveforms representing the summation of electrical activation and recovery of all of the myocardial cells are shown in relation to the activity within a single cell presented in Figure 1.2. (Modified from Thaler MS. The only EKG book you'll ever need. Philadelphia: JB Lippincott, 1988:11.)

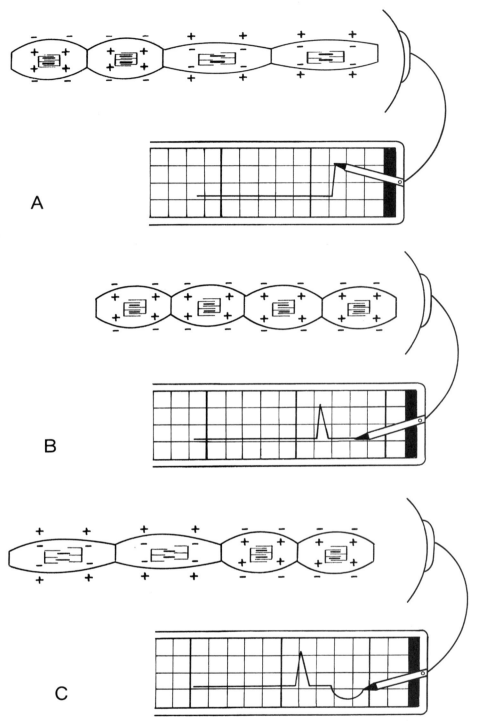

Figure 1.5. An electrode has been placed on the body surface and connected to a single channel ECG recorder. Depolarization and repolarization are spreading from left to right toward the recording electrode. An old-fashioned recorder with a mechanical stylus activated by a galvanometer has been used to best illustrate the process. As the ECG paper moves from right to left, the waveforms are recorded by the stylus, which is free to move in an upward (positive) or downward (negative) direction. (Modified from Thaler MS. The only EKG book you'll ever need. Philadelphia: JB Lippincott, 1988:29,31.)

CARDIAC IMPULSE FORMATION AND CONDUCTION

 The electrical activation of a single cardiac cell or even a small group of cells does not produce enough current to be recorded on the body surface. Clinical electrocardiography is made possible by the activation of atrial and ventricular myocardial masses that are of sufficient magnitude for their electrical activity to be recorded on the body surface.

Myocardial cells normally lack the ability for either spontaneous formation or rapid conduction of an electrical impulse. They are dependent for these functions on special cells of the cardiac pacemaking and conduction system placed strategically throughout the heart (Fig. 1.6). These cells are arranged in *nodes*, *bundles*, *bundle branches*, and branching networks of *fascicles*. They lack contractile capability, but are able to achieve spontaneous electrical impulse formation (act as pacemakers) and to alter the speed of electrical conduction. The intrinsic pacemaking rate is most rapid in the specialized cells in the atria and slowest in the cells in the ventricles. This intrinsic rate is altered by the balance between the sympathetic and parasympathetic components of the autonomic nervous system.[7-10]

Figure 1.6 illustrates the anatomic relationships between the cardiac pumping chambers and the specialized pacemaking and conduction system. The *sinoatrial (SA) node* is located high in the right atrium near its junction with the *superior vena cava (SVC)*. The SA node is the predominant cardiac pacemaker, and its highly developed autonomic regulation allows the heart to alter its pumping rate to meet the changing needs of the body. The *atrioventricular (AV) node* is located low in the right atrium adjacent to the interatrial *septum*. Its primary function is to slow electrical conduction sufficiently to synchronize atrial and ventricular pumping. Normally, the AV node is the only structure capable of conducting impulses from the atria to the ventricles.[11-13]

In the atria, the electrical impulse spreads through the myocardium without the need for specialized conduction bundles. However, rapidly conducting bundles with branches and fascicles are present in the ventricles so that activation of the myocardium at the base can be delayed until the apical region has been activated. Since the pulmonary and aortic outflow valves are located at the base of the ventricles, this sequence of electrical activation is necessary to achieve the most efficient level of cardiac pumping.

The intraventricular conduction pathways include a common bundle *(Bundle of His)*, which leads from the AV node to the summit of the interventricular septum, and its right and left bundle branches, which proceed along the septal surfaces to their respective ventricles. The left bundle branch fans into fascicles that proceed along the left septal surface and toward the two papillary muscles of the mitral valve. The right bundle branch remains compact until it reaches the right *distal* septal surface, where it branches into the distal interventricular septum and toward the *lateral* wall of the right ventricle. These intraventricular conduction pathways are composed of fibers that contain *Purkinje cells* with specialized capabilities for both pacemaking and rapid conduction of electrical impulses. Fascicles composed of Purkinje fibers form networks that extend just beneath the surface of the right and left ventricular endocardium. The impulses then proceed slowly from *endocardium* to *epicardium* throughout the right and left ventricles.[14-16]

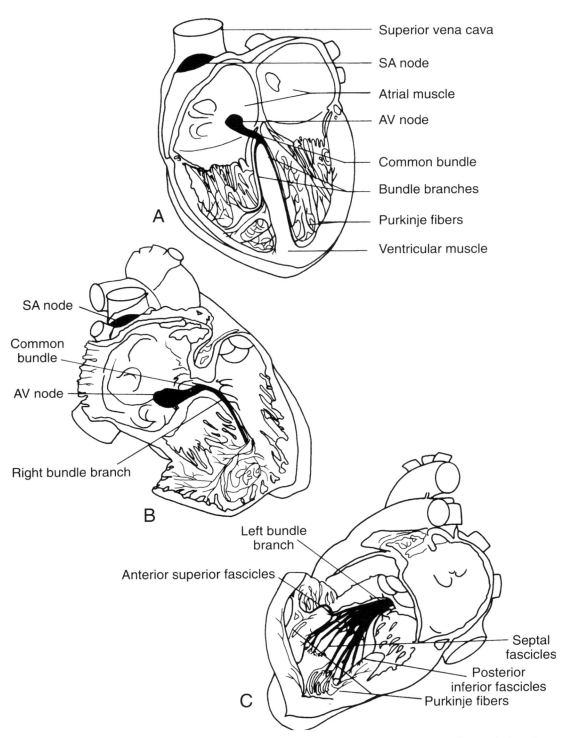

Figure 1.6. Three views of the anatomic relationships between the cardiac pumping chambers and the structures of the pacemaking and conduction system are displayed. **A.** From the left anterior precordium parallel to the axis of the interatrial and interventricular septa. **B.** From the right anterior precordium looking onto the interatrial and interventricular septa through the right atrium and ventricle. **C.** From the left posterior thorax looking onto the septa through the left atrium and ventricle. (Modified from Netter FH. In: Yonkman FF, ed. The Ciba collection of medical illustrations. vol 5. Heart. Summit: Ciba-Geigy, 1978;13,49.)

RECORDING BASE TO APEX CARDIAC ELECTRICAL ACTIVITY

The optimal body surface sites for recording base to apex electrical activity are located where the extensions of the long axis of the heart intersect with the body surface (Fig. 1.7). A negative *electrode* on the right shoulder and a positive electrode on the left lower chest produce predominately upright *waveforms* on the ECG, as will be discussed in Chapter 2, "Recording the Electrocardiogram."

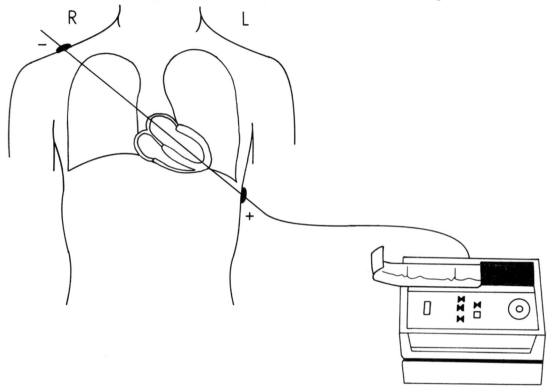

Figure 1.7. A schematic view of the heart in the thorax similar to the orientation depicted in Figures 1.1*A* and 1.4 is presented. The positive electrode on the left lower thoracic wall and the negative electrode on the right shoulder are aligned parallel to the interatrial and interventricular septa and attached to a single channel ECG recorder. The typically positive P waves, QRS complexes, and T waves recorded by electrodes at these positions are indicated on the ECG.

The initial wave of a cardiac cycle represents activation of the atria and is called the *P wave* (Fig. 1.8). The first part of the P wave represents the activation of the right atrium. The middle section of the P wave represents completion of right atrial activation and initiation of left atrial activation. The final section of the P wave represents completion of left atrial activation. The AV node is activated by the middle of the P wave, and this activation proceeds slowly toward the ventricles during the final section of the P wave. The wave that represents electrical recovery of the atria is usually obscured by the waves representing ventricular depolarization.

The next group of waves recorded is the *QRS complex*, which represents the activation of the ventricles. On this base to apex recording, the P wave is entirely upright and the QRS complex is predominately upright. Minor portions at the beginning and end of the QRS complex may appear as downward or negative waves. The QRS complex may normally appear as one *(monophasic)*, two *(diphasic)*, or three *(triphasic)* individual waveforms. By convention, a negative wave at the onset of the QRS complex is called a *Q wave*. The predominant portion of the QRS complex recorded at this base to apex site is normally positive and is called the *R wave*, regardless of whether or not it is preceded by a Q wave (Fig. 1.9). A negative deflection following an R wave is called an *S wave*. When a second positive deflection occurs, it is termed *R′*. A monophasic negative QRS complex should be termed *QS*. Occasionally, more complex patterns of QRS waveforms occur, as will be discussed in Chapter 3, "Interpretation of the Normal Electrocardiogram."

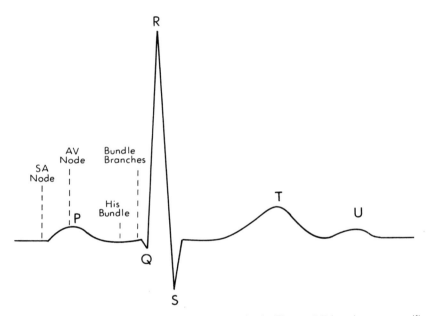

Figure 1.8. The recording from the base to apex site in Figure 1.5 has been magnified. The visible waveforms represent activation of the atria and ventricles and recovery of the ventricles. The timing of activation of the structures of the pacemaking and conduction system is also indicated.

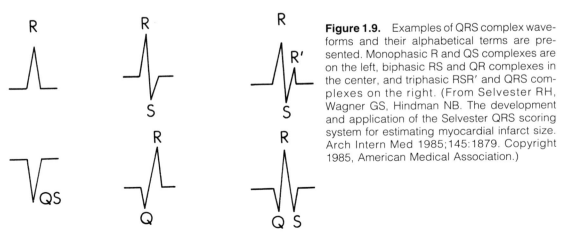

Figure 1.9. Examples of QRS complex waveforms and their alphabetical terms are presented. Monophasic R and QS complexes are on the left, biphasic RS and QR complexes in the center, and triphasic RSR′ and QRS complexes on the right. (From Selvester RH, Wagner GS, Hindman NB. The development and application of the Selvester QRS scoring system for estimating myocardial infarct size. Arch Intern Med 1985;145:1879. Copyright 1985, American Medical Association.)

The wave in the cardiac cycle that represents recovery of the ventricles is called the *T wave*. Since recovery of the ventricular cells (repolarization) causes a counter-current to that of depolarization, one might expect the T wave to be inverted in relation to the QRS complex. However, epicardial cells repolarize earlier than endocardial cells, thereby causing the wave of repolarization to spread in the direction opposite depolarization. This results in a T wave deflected in a similar direction as the QRS complex (Fig. 1.10). The T wave is sometimes followed by another small upright wave (the source of which is uncertain) called the *U wave*.

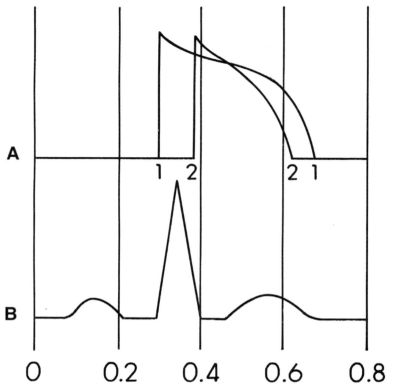

Figure 1.10. Schematic recordings from ventricular myocardial cells on the endocardial (*1*) and epicardial (*2*) surfaces are depicted in **A**. Note that the total duration of activation is much longer at the endocardial than at the epicardial site. A schematic of the ECG waveforms is presented in **B**. The *numbers below* refer to the sequential time lines (0.2 seconds, etc.)

The time from the onset of the P wave to the onset of the QRS complex is called the *PR interval*, whether the first wave in this complex is a Q wave or an R wave (Fig. 1.11). This interval measures the time between the onsets of activation of the atrial and ventricular myocardium. The designation *PR segment* refers to the time from the end of the P wave to the onset of the QRS complex. The *QRS interval* measures the time from beginning to end of ventricular activation. Since activation of the thicker left ventricle requires more time than the right ventricle, the terminal portion of the QRS complex represents only left ventricular activation.

The *ST segment* is the interval between the end of ventricular activation and the beginning of ventricular recovery. The term ST segment is used regardless of whether the final wave of the QRS complex is an R or an S wave. The junction of the QRS complex and the ST segment is called the *J point*. The interval from the onset of ventricular activation to the end of ventricular recovery is called the *QT interval*. This term is used whether the QRS complex begins with a Q or R wave.

At low heart rates in a healthy person, the PR, ST, and TP segments are at the same level and form the *isoelectric line*. This line is considered *baseline* for measuring the amplitudes of the various waveforms. The TP segment disappears at higher heart rates when the T wave merges with the following P wave.[17-19]

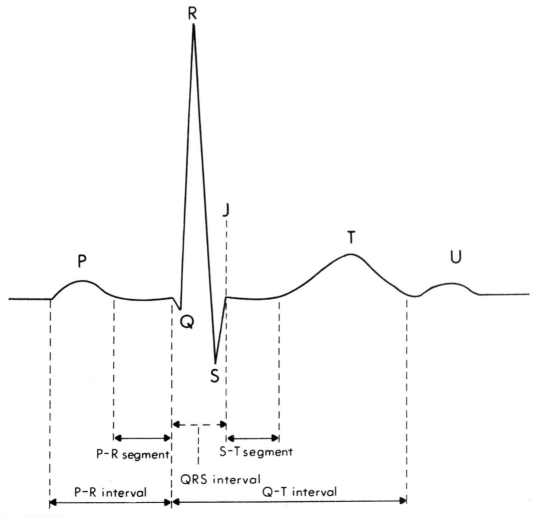

Figure 1.11. The magnified recording from the base to apex site in Figure 1.6 is presented with the principal time intervals indicated.

RECORDING LEFT VERSUS RIGHT CARDIAC ELECTRICAL ACTIVITY

  It is often important to determine if an abnormality originates from the left or the right side of the heart. The optimal sites for recording left versus right cardiac electrical activity are located where the extensions of the short axis of the heart (which is perpendicular to the interatrial and interventricular septa) intersect with the body surface (Fig. 1.12). A positive electrode on the right anterior thorax and a negative electrode on the left posterior thorax produce waveforms similar to those indicated on the ECG recording.

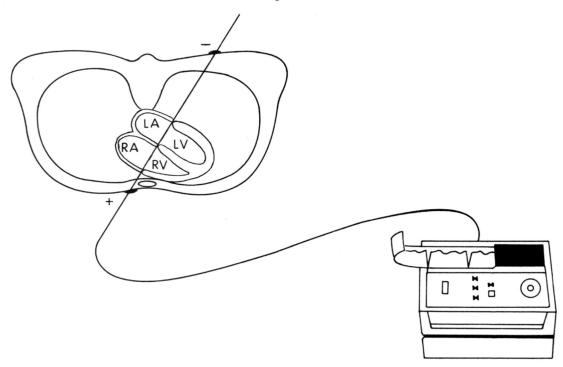

Figure 1.12. A schematic view of the heart in the thorax similar to the orientation depicted in Figure 1.1B is presented. The positive electrode at the fourth intercostal space to the right of the sternum and the negative electrode to the left of the spine are aligned perpendicular to the interatrial and interventricular septa and attached to a single channel ECG recorder. The typically diphasic P and T waves and the predominately negative QRS complex recorded by electrodes at these positions are indicated on the ECG.

These ECG waveforms are magnified in Figure 1.13. The initial part of the P wave representing right atrial activation appears positive at this site because of progression of the electrical activity from the interatrial septum toward the right atrial lateral wall. The terminal part of the P wave representing left atrial activation appears negative because of progression from the interatrial septum toward the left atrial lateral wall. This activation sequence produces a diphasic P wave.

The initial part of the QRS complex represents the progression of activation in the interventricular septum. This movement is predominately from the left toward the right side of the septum, producing a positive (R wave) deflection at this left versus right recording site. The midportion of the QRS complex represents progression of electrical activation through the right and left ventricular myocardium. Since the posteriorly positioned left ventricle is much thicker, its activation predominates over that of the anteriorly placed right ventricle, resulting in a deeply negative deflection (S wave). The final portion of the QRS complex represents the completion of activation of the left ventricle. This posteriorly directed excitation is represented by the completion of the S wave.

The left versus right recording sites are very useful in identifying enlargement of one of the four cardiac chambers and localizing the site of a delay in ventricular activation. Right atrial enlargement produces an abnormally prominent initial part of the P wave, while left atrial enlargement produces an abnormally prominent terminal part of the P wave. Right ventricular enlargement produces an abnormally prominent R wave, whereas left ventricular enlargement produces an abnormally prominent S wave. A delay in the right bundle branch causes right ventricular activation to occur after left ventricular activation is completed, producing an R' deflection (Fig. 1.9). A delay in the left bundle branch markedly postpones left ventricular activation, resulting in an abnormally prominent S wave.

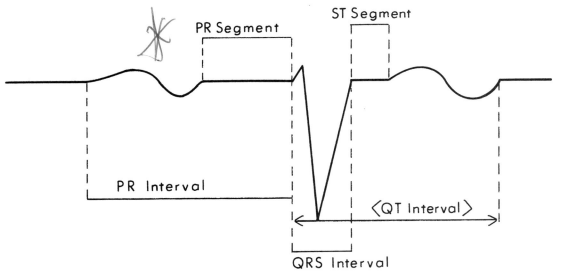

Figure 1.13. The recording from the left versus right site from Figure 1.10 has been magnified with the principal time intervals indicated.

GLOSSARY

Action potential: the positive electrical potential recorded from within a cell as it is activated by an electrical current or impulse.

Atrium: a chamber of the heart that receives blood from the veins and passes it along to its corresponding ventricle.

Anterior: located toward the front of the body.

Apex: the bottom of the heart where the narrowest parts of the ventricles are located.

Atrioventricular (AV) node: a small mass of tissue that is situated in the inferior aspect of the right atrium adjacent to the septum between the atria. Its function is to slow the impulses traveling from the atria to the ventricles, thereby synchronizing atrial and ventricular pumping.

Base: the broad top of the heart where the atria are located.

Baseline: see isoelectric line.

Bundle branches: groups of Purkinje fibers that emerge from the common bundle (His); the right bundle branch rapidly conducts electrical impulses to the right ventricle, as does the left bundle branch to the left ventricle.

Cardiac cycle: a single episode of electrical and mechanical activation and recovery of a myocardial cell or of the entire heart.

Common bundle (His): a compact group of Purkinje fibers that originates at the AV node and rapidly conducts electrical impulses to the right and left bundle branches.

Cardiac pacemaking and conduction system: Groups of modified myocardial cells strategically located throughout the heart and capable of either formation of an electrical impulse and/or of particularly slow or rapid conduction of impulses.

Depolarization: a condition in which there is minimal difference between the electrical charge or potential on the inside versus the outside of the cell. In the resting state, the cell is polarized, with the inside of the cell markedly negative in comparison to the outside. Depolarization is then initiated by a current that alters the permeability of the cell membrane, thus allowing positively charged ions to cross into the cell.

Diastole: the period in which the electrical and mechanical aspects of the heart are in their baseline or resting state: electrical diastole is characterized by repolarization, and mechanical diastole, by relaxation. During mechanical diastole the cardiac chambers are filling with blood.

Diphasic: consisting of two components.

Distal: situated away from the point of attachment or origin; the opposite of proximal.

Electrode: an electrical contact that is placed on the skin and is connected to an ECG recorder.

Electrocardiogram (ECG): the recording made by the electrocardiograph depicting the electrical activity of the heart.

Endocardium: the inner aspect of a myocardial wall adjacent to the blood-filled cavity.

Epicardium: the outer aspect of a myocardial wall adjacent to the pericardial lining that closely envelopes the heart.

Fascicle: a small bundle of Purkinje fibers that emerges from a bundle or a bundle branch to rapidly conduct impulses to the endocardial surfaces of the ventricles.

Inferior: situated below and closer to the feet than another body part; the opposite of superior.

Isoelectric line: a horizontal line on an ECG recording that forms a baseline; representing neither a positive nor a negative electrical potential.

J point: junction of the QRS complex and the ST segment.

Lateral: situated toward either the right or left side of the heart or of the body as a whole.

Monophasic: consisting of a single component, being either positive or negative.

P wave: the first wave depicted on the ECG during a cardiac cycle; it represents atrial activation.

PR interval: time from the onset of the P wave to the onset of the QRS complex. This interval represents the time between the onsets of activation of the atrial and ventricular myocardium.

PR segment: the time from the end of the P wave to the onset of the QRS complex.

Purkinje cells or fibers: modified myocardial cells that are found in the distal aspects of the pacemaking and conduction system; the common bundle, the bundle branches, the fascicles, and individual strands.

Q wave: negative wave at the onset of the QRS complex.

QS: a monophasic negative QRS complex.

QRS complex: the second wave or group of waves depicted on the ECG during a cardiac cycle; it represents ventricular activation.

QRS interval: time from the beginning to the end of the QRS complex, representing the duration required for activation of the ventricular myocardial cells.

QT interval: time from the onset of the QRS complex to the end of the T wave. This interval represents the time from the beginning of ventricular activation to the completion of ventricular recovery.

R wave: the first positive wave appearing in a QRS complex; it may appear at the onset of the QRS complex or following a Q wave.

R' wave: the second positive wave appearing in a QRS complex.

Repolarization: condition in which the inside of the cell is markedly positive in relation to the outside. This condition is maintained by a pump in the cell membrane, and it is disturbed by the arrival of an electrical current.

Sinoatrial (SA) node: a small mass of tissue that is situated in the superior aspect of the right atrium adjacent to the entrance of the superior vena cava. Its function is to be the dominant pacemaker that forms the electrical impulses that are then conducted throughout the heart.

ST segment: the interval between the end of the QRS complex and the beginning of the T wave.

Septum: a dividing wall between the atria or between the ventricles.

Superior: situated above and closer to the head than another body part.

Superior vena cava: the large vein that empties into the right atrium.

Systole: the period in which the electrical and mechanical aspects of the heart are in their active state: electrical systole is characterized by depolarization, and mechanical systole, by contraction. During mechanical systole, blood is being pumped out of the heart.

T wave: the final major wave depicted on the ECG during a cardiac cycle; it represents ventricular recovery.

Triphasic: consisting of three components.

U wave: a wave on the ECG that follows the T wave in some individuals; it is typically small and its source is uncertain.

Ventricle: a chamber of the heart that receives blood from its corresponding atrium and pumps it out into the arteries.

Waveform: electrocardiographic representation of either the activation or recovery phase of electrical activity of the heart.

REFERENCES

1. De Vries PA, Saunders. Development of the ventricles and spiral outflow tract of the human heart. Contr Embryol Carneg Inst 1962;37:87.
2. Mall FP. On the development of the human heart. Am J Anat 1912;13:249.
3. Hoffman BF, Cranefield PF. Electrophysiology of the heart. New York: McGraw-Hill, 1960.
4. Page E. The electrical potential difference across the cell membrane of heart muscle. Circulation 1962;26:582–595.
5. Fozzard HA, ed. The heart and cardiovascular system: scientific foundations. New York: Raven Press, 1986.
6. Guyton AC. Heart muscle; the heart as a pump. In: Guyton AC, ed. Textbook of medical physiology. Philadelphia: WB Saunders, 1991.
7. Rushmer RF. Functional anatomy and the control of the heart, Part I. In: Rushmer RF, ed. Cardiovascular dynamics. Philadelphia: WB Saunders, 1976:76–104.
8. Langer GA. Heart: excitation-contraction coupling. Ann Rev Physiol 1973;35:55–85.
9. Weidmann S. Resting and action potentials of cardiac muscle. Ann N Y Acad Sci 1957;65:663.
10. Rushmer RF, Guntheroth WG. Electrical activity of the heart, Part I. In: Rushmer RF, ed. Cardiovascular dynamics. Philadelphia: WB Saunders, 1976.
11. Truex RC. The sinoatrial node and its connections with the atrial tissue. In: Wellens HJJ, Lie KI, Janse MJ, eds. The conduction system of the heart. The Hague: Martinus Nijhoff, 1978.
12. Hecht HH, Kossmann CE. Atrio-ventricular and intra-ventricular conduction. Am J Cardiol 1973;31:232–244.
13. Becker AE, Anderson RH. Morphology of the human atrioventricular junctional area. In: Wellens HJJ, Lie KI, Janse MJ, eds. The conduction system of the heart. The Hague: Martinus Nijhoff, 1978.
14. Meyerburg RJ, Gelband H, Castellanos A, Nilsson K, Sung RJ, Bassett AL. Electrophysiology of endocardial intraventricular conduction: the role and function of the specialized conducting system. In: Wellens HJJ, Lie KL, Janse MJ, eds. The conduction system of the heart. The Hague: Martinus Nijhoff, 1978.
15. Guyton AC. Rhythmic excitation of the heart. In: Guyton AC, ed. Textbook of medical physiology. Philadelphia: WB Saunders, 1991.
16. Scher AM. The sequence of ventricular excitation. Am J Cardiol 1964;14:287.
17. Graybiel A, White PD, Wheeler L, Williams C, eds. The typical normal electrocardiogram and its variations. In: Electrocardiography in practice. Philadelphia: WB Saunders, 1952.
18. Netter FH. Section II, The electrocardiogram. The CIBA collection of medical illustrations. vol 5. New York: CIBA, 1978.
19. Barr RC. Genesis of the electrocardiogram. In: Macfarlane PW, Veitch Lawrie TD, eds. Comprehensive electrocardiology. vol I. New York: Pergamon Press, 1989:139–147.

CHAPTER 2

Recording the
Electrocardiogram

EVOLUTION OF FRONTAL PLANE LEADS

Examples have been provided in Chapter 1 ("Cardiac Electrical Activity") of two sites for recording the cardiac electrical activity, from base to apex and from the left versus right sides of the heart. The standard electrocardiogram (ECG) used for clinical diagnosis includes these two plus 10 other viewpoints. Each view is provided by recording the electrical potential difference between a positive and a negative body surface electrode, referred to as a *lead*. Six of these leads provide views in the *frontal plane* and six in the *transverse (horizontal) plane*. The device used for recording the electrocardiogram is called the *electrocardiograph*.

In the early 1900s, Einthoven and colleagues[1] placed recording electrodes on the right and left arms and the left leg and an additional electrode on the right leg to ground the "elektrokardiogramme" (EKG). Three leads (I, II, and III) are produced using a pair of the limb electrodes, one serving as the positive and one as the negative pole (Fig. 2.1). The positive poles of these leads are located to the left or inferiorly so that the cardiac waveforms appear primarily upright on the recording. For lead I, the left arm electrode is the positive pole and the right arm electrode is the negative pole. Lead II, with its positive pole on the left leg and its negative pole on the right arm, provides a view of the cardiac electrical activity similar to that of the base to apex site presented in Figures 1.7–1.11. Finally, lead III has its positive pole on the left leg and its negative pole on the left arm.

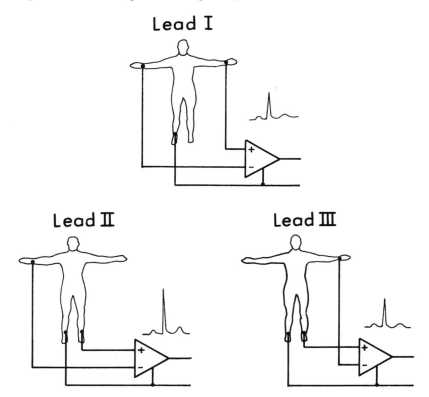

Figure 2.1. The method of ECG recording of Einthoven's three original limb leads is illustrated along with an example of a typical recording of each. An electrode placed on the right leg is used to ground the system. The distal limb sites for positive and negative electrodes are indicated. (Modified from Netter FH. The Ciba collection of medical illustrations. vol 5. Heart. Summit: Ciba-Geigy, 1978:51.)

These three leads form the *Einthoven triangle* (Fig. 2.2A), a simplified model of the true orientation of the leads in the frontal plane. Consideration of these three leads so that they intersect in the center of the frontal plane, but retain their original orientation, provides a triaxial reference system for viewing cardiac electrical activity (Fig. 2.2B).

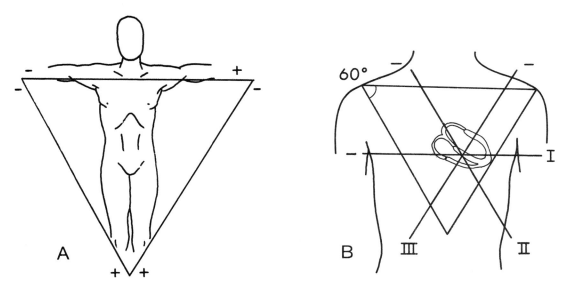

Figure 2.2. The relationships of the original three limb leads are illustrated. In **A**, the equiangular (60°) Einthoven triangle formed by leads I, II, and III is shown with positive and negative poles of each of the leads indicated. In **B**, the Einthoven triangle is shown in relation to the schematic view of the heart presented in Figure 1.7. Leads I, II, and III are also presented as a triaxial reference system that intersects in the center of the ventricles.

The 60° angles between leads I, II, and III create wide gaps among the three views of cardiac electrical activity. Wilson and coworkers[2] developed a method for filling these gaps by creating a *central terminal*, connecting all three limb electrodes through a 5000-ohm resistor. A lead using this central terminal as its negative pole and an exploring electrode at any site on the body surface as its positive pole is termed a *V lead*. When the central terminal is connected to an exploring electrode on an extremity, the electrical signals are small. The amplitude of these signals in the frontal plane may be increased or augmented by disconnecting the attachment of the central terminal to the explored limb. Such an augmented V lead is termed *aV*. For example, aVF measures the potential difference between the left leg and the average of the potentials at the right and left arms. The gap between leads I and II is filled by lead aVR, between leads II and III by lead aVF, and between leads III and I by lead aVL (Fig. 2.3). Leads aVR, aVL, and aVF were introduced in 1932 by Goldberger and colleagues[3].

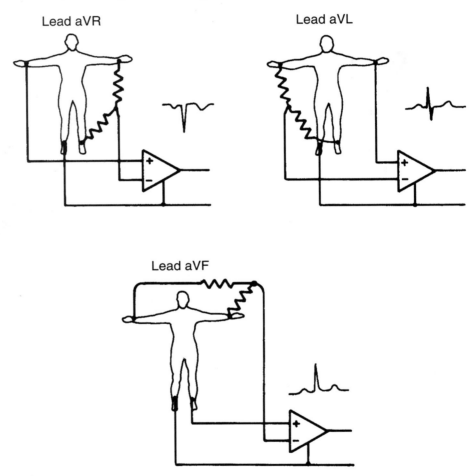

Figure 2.3. The method of ECG recording of the augmented limb leads is illustrated along with an example of a typical recording of each. The alternating lines indicate the connections between two of the recording electrodes that produce the negative poles for each of the aV leads. (Modified from Netter FH. The Ciba collection of medical illustrations. vol 5. Heart. Summit: Ciba-Geigy, 1978:51.)

Addition of these three aV leads to the triaxial reference system produces a hexaxial system (Fig. 2.4) for viewing the cardiac electrical activity in the frontal plane with the six leads separated by angles of only 30°. This provides a perspective of the frontal plane similar to the face of a clock. By convention, the degrees are arranged as shown. Using lead I (located at 0°) as the reference, positive designations increase at 30° increments in a clockwise direction to +180°, and negative designations increase at the same increments in a counterclockwise direction up to −180°. Lead II appears at +60°, aVF at +90°, and III at +120°, respectively. Leads aVL and aVR have designations of −30° and −150°, respectively. The negative poles of each of these leads complete the "clock face." Most modern electrocardiographs use digital technology. They record leads I and II only and then calculate the remaining limb leads in real time based on Einthoven's law: I + III = II[1]. The algebraic outcome of the formulas for calculating the aV leads from leads I, II, and III are:

$$aVR = -1/2(I + II)$$
$$aVL = I - 1/2(II)$$
$$aVF = II - 1/2(I)$$

thus

$$aVR + aVL + aVF = 0$$

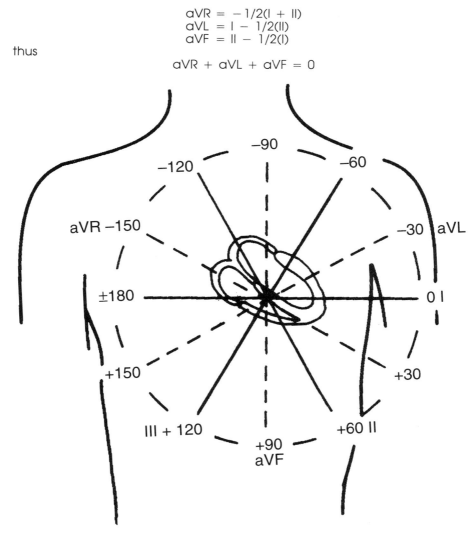

Figure 2.4. Leads aVR, aVL, and aVF have been added to the triaxial reference system presented in Figure 2.2 to produce the hexaxial reference system. The locations of the positive and negative poles of each lead around the 360° of the "clock face" are indicated. The names of the six leads appear at their positive poles.

TRANSVERSE PLANE LEADS

The standard 12-lead ECG includes these six frontal plane leads and also six leads relating to the transverse plane of the body. These leads, introduced by Wilson[4-8], are produced by connecting the central terminal to an exploring electrode placed at various positions across the chest wall. Since the sites of these leads are so close to the heart itself, they are termed *precordial*, and the electrical signals have sufficient amplitude so that no augmentation is necessary. The six leads are labeled V1 through V6 because the central terminal connected to all three of the limb electrodes provides their negative poles (Fig. 2.5). Lead V1, with its positive pole on the right anterior precordium and its negative pole in the center of the chest, provides a similar view of cardiac electrical activity as the site for distinguishing left versus right cardiac activity presented in Chapter 1. The sites of the exploring electrode are determined by bony landmarks on the anterior and left lateral aspects of the precordium, and the angles between the six transverse plane leads are smaller and more variable than those between the six frontal plane leads.

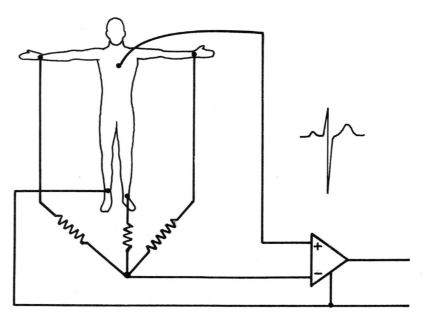

Figure 2.5. The method of ECG recording of the precordial leads is illustrated along with an example of lead V2. The alternating lines indicate the connections between the recording electrodes on the three limb leads that produce the negative poles for each of the V leads. (Modified from Netter FH. The Ciba collection of medical illustrations. vol 5. Heart. Summit: Ciba-Geigy, 1978:51.)

The precordial leads are placed in accordance with the designated bony land-marks of the chest (Fig. 2.6). The clavicles should be used as a reference for locating the first rib. The space between the first and second ribs is called the first *intercostal space*. Lead V1 is placed in the fourth intercostal space just to the right of the *sternum*, V2 in the fourth intercostal space just to the left of the sternum, and V4 in the fifth intercostal space on the *midclavicular line*. Placement of lead V3 is then halfway on a straight line between leads V2 and V4. Leads V5 and V6 are positioned directly lateral to V4, with V5 in the *anterior axillary line* and V6 in the *midaxillary line*. In adult females, leads V4 and V5 should be positioned on the chest wall beneath the breast.

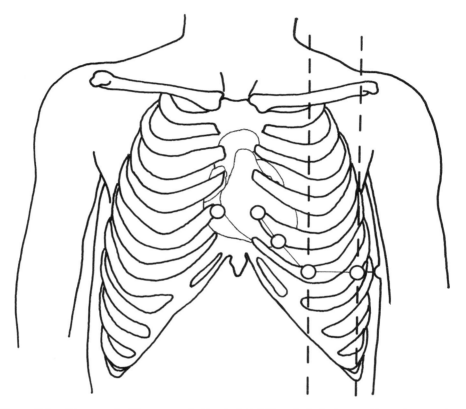

Figure 2.6. Placement of the precordial leads (V1–V6) at their designated bony landmarks. The position of lead V6 is indicated by the semicircular indentation to the left of the V5 position. The *dashed vertical lines* signify the midclavicular (through lead V4) and anterior axillary (through lead V5) lines. (Modified from Thaler MS. The only EKG book you'll ever need. Philadelphia: JB Lippincott, 1988:41.)

INCORRECT LEAD PLACEMENT

 An accurate electrocardiographic interpretation is possible only if the recording electrodes are placed in their proper positions on the body surface. The three frontal plane electrodes (right arm, left arm, and left leg) should be placed at mid or distal positions on the designated extremity. When more proximal positions are used, particularly on the left arm,[9] marked distortion of the QRS complex may occur. The mid or distal limb positions provide "clean" recordings from a resting subject, but produce too much movement *artifact* to be used for continuous electrocardiographic monitoring. As is discussed later in this chapter, proximal limb or torso positions are required for this special electrocardiographic application.

The most common error in frontal plane recording results from reversal of two of the electrodes. One example is reversal of the right and left arm electrodes, as illustrated in Figure 2.7A. In this instance, lead I appears inverted, leads II and III are reversed, leads aVR and aVL are reversed, and lead aVF is correct. Another example that produces a characteristic pattern is reversal of the right leg grounding electrode with one of the arm electrodes. Extremely low amplitudes of all waveforms appear in lead II when the grounding electrode is on the right arm, and in lead III when the grounding electrode is on the left arm (Fig. 2.7, B and C). These amplitudes are so low because the potential difference between the two legs is almost zero. It is also possible for the positions of the precordial electrodes to be reversed, as illustrated in Figure 2.7D.

However, a more common error in transverse plane recording involves the failure to place the individual electrodes according to their designated landmarks. Precise identification of the bony landmarks may be difficult in adult females, obese individuals, and those with chest wall deformities. Even slight alterations of the position of these electrodes may significantly distort the appearance of the cardiac waveforms. Comparison of serial ECG recordings relies upon precise electrode placement. This can be facilitated by the use of an indelible marker to indicate the correct sites for electrode placement.

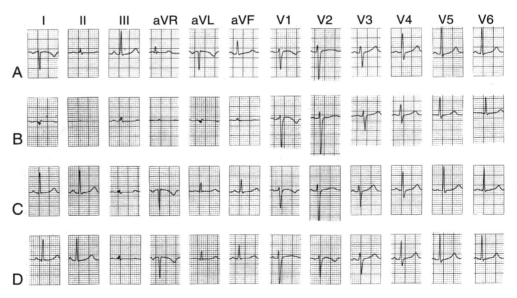

Figure 2.7. **A.** Reversal of the right arm and left arm electrodes, resulting in inversion of lead I and reversal of leads II and III and leads aVR and aVL. **B.** Reversal of the right arm electrode and right leg grounding electrode, producing extremely low amplitudes in lead II. **C.** Reversal of the left arm electrode and the right leg grounding electrode, producing extremely low amplitudes in lead III. **D.** Reversal of the V1 and V2 electrodes, resulting in lack of progression of R and S wave amplitudes from V1 to V3.

OTHER PRACTICAL POINTS FOR RECORDING THE ECG

Care should be taken to insure that technique is uniform from recording to recording. The following points are important to consider when preparing to record an ECG:

1. Electrodes should be selected for maximum adhesiveness and minimum discomfort, electrical noise, and skin-electrode impedance. The standards for electrodes published by the American Association for Advancement of Medical Instrumentation[10] should be followed.
2. Effective contact between electrode and skin is essential. Sites with skin irritation or skeletal abnormalities should be avoided. Hair should be parted or shaved. The skin should be cleaned with gauze soaked in alcohol to remove substances that increase impedance or decrease adhesiveness. Mild abrasion of the skin with ultrafine sandpaper may be required when applying electrodes for continuous ECG monitoring. Poor electrode contact may produce instability of the baseline of the recording, termed *baseline wander* (Fig. 2.8A).
3. Calibration is typically 1 mV = 10 mm. When large QRS waveform amplitudes require the use of a calibration of 1 mV = 5 mm, this should be noted to facilitate interpretation.
4. ECG paper speed is typically 25 mm/sec, and variations used for particular clinical purposes should be noted. A faster speed may be used to provide a clearer depiction of waveform morphology, and a slower speed to provide visualization of a greater number of cardiac cycles to facilitate rhythm analysis.
5. Electrical artifacts may be external or internal. External artifacts introduced by line current (50 or 60 Hz) may be minimized by disconnecting other nearby electrical devices. Internal artifacts may result from muscle tremors, shivering, hiccups, etc. as illustrated in Figure 2.8, *B* and *C*.
6. It is important that the patient be in a supine position during the ECG recording. If another position is clinically required, notation of the altered position should be made. Lying on either side or elevation of the torso may change the position of the heart within the chest. A change in body position may have an effect on the accuracy of an ECG recording[11] similar to a change in electrode placement.

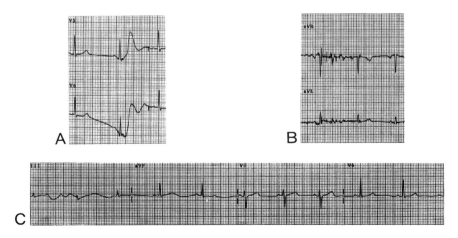

Figure 2.8. Examples of ECG artifacts produced by patient movement are shown. In **A**, a wandering baseline is produced by slight body movement. Shivering is shown in **B** and hiccups in **C**.

ALTERNATIVE LEAD PLACEMENT

There are several situations that require alternative sites for placement of ECG electrodes.

1. The standard sites are not available due to patient pathology (e.g., amputation or burns) or other impediments (e.g., bandages). In these instances, the electrodes should be positioned as close as possible to the standard site, and the alternative site should be noted on the recording.

2. The standard sites are not in the optimal position to detect a particular cardiac waveform or abnormality (e.g., P waves obscured within T waves or *dextrocardia*). Detection of P waves requires sufficient time between cardiac cycles to provide a baseline between the end of the T wave and the beginning of the QRS complex. In the presence of a rapid cardiac rate *(tachycardia)*, alternate lead placement might record recognizable atrial activity (Fig. 2.9*A*). This may be accomplished by any one of several methods: (*a*) move lead V1 one interspace above its standard site; (*b*) use this site as the positive pole and the *xiphoid process* of the sternum as the negative pole for lead I; or (*c*) record from a *transesophageal* electrode.

   When the congenital position of the heart is rightward (dextrocardia), the right and left arm leads should be reversed and the precordial leads should be recorded from rightward oriented V leads progressing from V1R (standard lead V2) to V6R (Fig. 2.9*B*). *Right ventricular hypertrophy* and *infarction* may best be detected via an electrode in the V3R or V4R position. In infants, where the right ventricle is normally more prominent, standard lead V3 is often replaced by lead V4R.

   Experimental studies have used multiple rows of electrodes on the anterior and posterior torso to identify specific abnormalities. This provides improved capability for diagnosis of clinical problems such as *left ventricular hypertrophy* or various locations of myocardial infarction[12].

3. The standard sites produce a recording obscured by artifacts (e.g., skeletal muscle potentials during ambulatory monitoring). When alternative sites are used, there should be careful notation on the recording.

   Continuous monitoring of the cardiac electrical activity may be useful for evaluating abnormalities of *rhythm* or of myocardial blood flow. Monitoring may be performed in three different situations: (*a*) at the bedside; (*b*) during exercise stress testing; or (*c*) during routine ambulatory activity. Each situation may require particular alternative electrode placement.

Bedside

When monitoring for disturbances of rhythm, to allow easy access for clinical examination of the heart and possible use of an external defibrillator, placement of electrodes in the left parasternal area should be avoided. A modified lead, *MCL*₁, with the positive electrode in the position of V1 and the negative electrode near the left shoulder, usually provides good visualization of atrial activity (Fig. 2.9*C*). Since this lead provides the optimal view of left versus right cardiac activity, as presented in Figures 1.12 and 1.13, it may be useful for multiple cardiac diagnostic purposes.

The detection of alterations indicative of ischemic changes is more readily accomplished by the placement of the positive electrode at or near the V6 position. The use of multiple leads enhances the capability of *ischemia* detection.

When monitoring for evidence of cardiac ischemia, a complete set of 12 leads may be preferred. Krucoff and coworkers described the usefulness of continuous ST segment monitoring over 12 leads during various unstable coronary syndromes. Some of its major applications include: detection of reoccluded coronary arteries after *balloon angioplasty*,[13] detection of *reperfusion* and *reocclusion* in acute myocardial infarction[14,15] and surveillance during *unstable angina*. For this ST segment monitoring, a modification of the *Mason-Likar*[16] system has been developed.

Exercise Stress Testing

The single lead that is most useful during exercise stress testing has its positive electrode positioned at the V5 level. The negative electrode may be placed in a variety of distant positions. A second useful lead has an orientation similar to aVF with its positive electrode on the left midaxillary line over the lowest rib.

Monitoring of all 12 ECG leads during exercise necessitates moving the limb electrodes from standard distal to more central positions. Alternative torso sites for the right and left arm and left leg electrodes are placed on bony prominences that are close to the base of the respective limbs (Fig. 2.9D). Ideally, these sites would: (a) avoid skeletal muscle artifact; (b) provide stability for the recording electrodes; and (c) record waveforms similar to those from the limb sites. The Mason-Likar[16] designations of torso sites are commonly used. The resultant recording, however, has some features that differ from the standard 12-lead recording.

Routine Ambulatory Activity

The method of continuous monitoring and recording of cardiac electrical activity is referred to as *Holter monitoring*[17] after its developer. Originally, only one lead was used. When monitoring for cardiac rhythm abnormalities, the American Heart Association (AHA) recommends use of a "V1-type" lead, with the positive electrode in the fourth right intercostal space 2.5 cm from the sternum and the negative electrode below the left clavicle. Currently, a second or even third lead is added to facilitate interpretation and to assure recording of some information if one electrode is detached. These are placed at the V5 and modified aVF positions, as indicated for use in exercise stress testing (Fig. 2.9E).

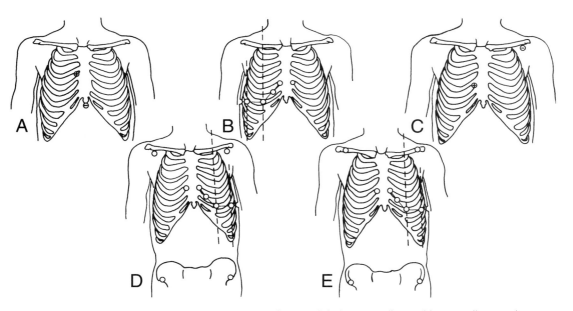

Figure 2.9. Alternative sites used for special electrocardiographic recording as shown on the same schematic torso as seen in Figure 2.6. **A.** Detection of atrial activity. **B.** Evaluation of right ventricular hypertrophy, right ventricular infarction, and dextrocardia. **C.** Typical bedside monitoring—a modification of lead V1 termed MCL₁. **D.** Electrode placement as recommended by the AHA for exercise stress testing. **E.** Electrode placement as developed by Krucoff for ischemia monitoring. Locations of positive and negative poles of a single ECG lead are indicated for **A** and **C**. Locations of the electrodes for each of the precordial V leads (1–6) are shown in **B**, **D**, and **E**. Torso locations of RA (right arm), LA (left arm), RL (right leg), and LL (left leg) positive electrodes are shown in **D** and **E**. The right midclavicular line is indicated in **B**. Both the left midclavicular and left anterior axillary lines are indicated in **D** and **E**.

DISPLAY OF THE 12 STANDARD LEADS

 The 12-lead ECG is typically presented via a three-channel recording with the two groups of frontal plane leads preceding the two groups of transverse plane leads. The six precordial leads are presented in their orderly sequence (V1 through V6), but the six frontal plane leads are typically presented in the groups in which they were historically developed (I, II, and III; then aVR, aVL, and aVF). These leads have been presented in their "orderly sequence" by Cabrera: aVL, I, −aVR, II, aVF, and III (Fig. 2.10). Note that lead aVR is inverted to −aVR to provide the same leftward orientation as leads I and II. There is sufficient space along the length of an 11-inch page to display a single cardiac cycle from each of the 12 standard leads, as illustrated in Figure 2.10A. The orderly sequence of frontal plane leads followed by the transverse plane leads provides a *panoramic display*[18] of cardiac electrical activity proceeding from left (aVL) to right (III), and then from right (V1) to left (V6). The Swedish version of the panoramic display is shown in Figure 2.10B. There is the disadvantage of lack of continuity between the two planes, but the advantage of vertical alignment allows comparison of the beginning and end of the individual ECG waveforms.

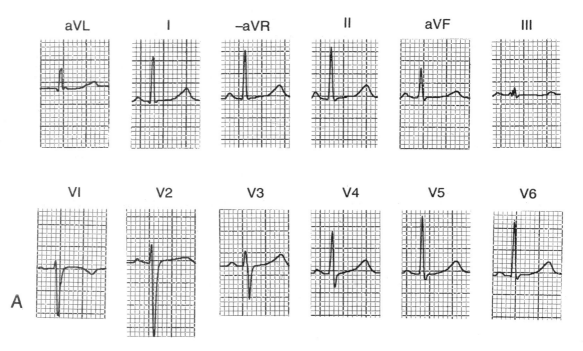

Figure 2.10. The panoramic display of the 12 standard leads is presented in their orderly sequences in both the frontal (aVL–III) and transverse (V1–V6) planes. Lead aVR is included in its position as −aVR. All 12 leads appear in a single horizontal display in **A**, and the six limb leads and the six precordial leads appear in parallel vertical displays in **B**. The *vertical lines* in **B** indicate the completion of the QT interval (see Fig. 3.12).

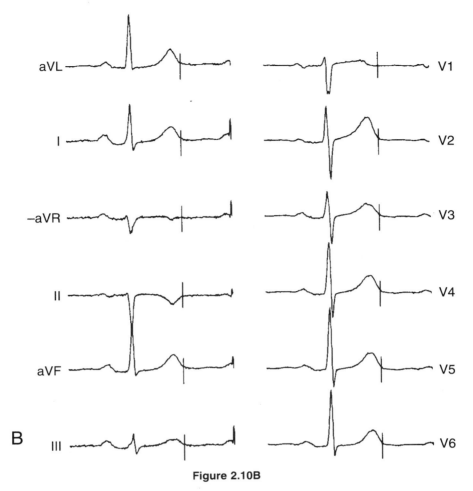

Figure 2.10B

GLOSSARY

aV lead: an augmented V lead (see below); it uses a modified central terminal with inputs from the electrodes on two other limbs as its negative pole and the electrode on that limb as its positive pole.

Angioplasty: a procedure using a balloon-tipped arterial catheter to break up atherosclerotic plaques.

Anterior axillary line: a vertical line on the thorax at the level of the anterior aspect of the axilla, which is the area where the arm joins the body.

Angina: angina pectoris, referring to precordial pressure or pain caused by cardiac ischemia or lack of blood flow to the heart muscle.

Artifact: an electrocardiographic waveform that arises from sources other than the myocardium.

Baseline wander: a back and forth shift of the isoelectric line or baseline, inhibiting precise measurement of the various ECG waveforms.

Central terminal: a terminal created by Wilson and colleagues that connects all three limb electrodes through a 5000-ohm resistor so that it can serve as the negative pole for an exploring positive electrode to form a V lead.

Dextrocardia: an abnormal condition in which the heart is situated on the right side and the great blood vessels of the right and left sides are reversed.

Einthoven triangle: an equilateral triangle composed of limb leads I, II, and III that provides an orientation for electrical information from the frontal plane.

Electrocardiograph: a device used to record the electrocardiogram (ECG).

Frontal plane: a vertical plane of the body (also called coronal) which lies perpendicular to both the horizontal and sagittal planes.

Hypertrophy: increase in muscle mass; most common in the ventricles when compensating for pressure or systolic overload.

Infarct: an area of necrosis in an organ resulting from an obstruction in its blood supply.

Intercostal: situated between the ribs.

Ischemia: an insufficiency of blood flow to an organ which is so severe that it disrupts the function of the organ; in the heart it is often accompanied by precordial pain and diminished contraction.

Lead: a conductor that connects the body surface with an electrical recording device or ECG.

Mason-Likar: alternative lead placement system used for recording the limb leads while the patient is moving about or exercising; the electrodes are moved from the limbs to the torso.

MCL$_1$: a modified lead V1 used to enhance visualization of atrial activity.

Midaxillary line: a vertical line on the thorax at the level of the midpoint of the axilla, which is the area where the arm joins the body.

Midclavicular line: a vertical line on the thorax at the level of the midpoint of the clavicle or collarbone.

Panoramic display: the typical display of the precordial leads in their orderly sequence from right to left and an innovative display of the frontal plane leads from left to right (aVL, I, −aVR, II, aVF, and III). Limb lead aVR is inverted to obtain the same positive leftward orientation as the other five limb leads.

Precordial: situated on the thorax, directly overlying the heart.

Reocclusion: a recurrence of a complete obstruction to blood flow.

Reperfusion: a reopening of a complete obstruction to blood flow.

Rhythm: the pattern of recurrence of the cardiac cycle.

Sternum: the narrow, flat bone in the middle of the anterior thorax; breastbone.

Tachycardia: rapid heart rate; above 100 beats/min.

Transverse plane: horizontal plane of the body which lies perpendicular to both the frontal and sagittal planes.

V lead: an ECG lead that uses a central terminal with inputs from leads I, II, and III as its negative pole, and an exploring electrode as its positive pole.

Xiphoid process: the lower end of the sternum that has a triangular shape.

REFERENCES

1. Einthoven W, Fahr G, de Waart A. Uber die richtung und die manifeste grosse der potentialschwankungen im menschlichen herzen und uber den einfluss der herzlage auf die form des elektrokardiogramms. Pfluegers Arch 1913;150:275–315. (Translation: Hoff HE, Sekelj P. Am Heart J 1950;40: 163–194.)
2. Wilson FN, Macloed AG, Barker PS. The interpretation of the initial deflections of the ventricular complex of the electrocardiogram. Am Heart J 1931;6:637–664.
3. Goldberger E. A simple, indifferent, electrocardiographic electrode of zero potential and a technique of obtaining augmented, unipolar, extremity leads. Am Heart J 1942;23:483–492.
4. Wilson FN, Johnston FD, Macloed AG, Barker PS. Electrocardiograms that represent the potential variations of a single electrode. Am Heart J 1934;9:447–471.
5. Kossmann CE, Johnston FD. The precordial electrocardiogram. I. The potential variations of the precordium and of the extremities in normal subjects. Am Heart J 1935;10:925–941.
6. Joint recommendations of the American Heart Association and the Cardiac Society of Great Britain and Ireland. Standardization of precordial leads. Am Heart J 1938;15:107–108.
7. Committee of the American Heart Association for the Standardization of Precordial Leads. Supplementary report. Am Heart J 1938;15:235–239.
8. Committee of the American Heart Association for the Standardization of Precordial Leads. Second supplementary report. JAMA 1943;121:1349–1351.
9. Pahlm O, Haisty WK, Edenbrandt L, Wagner NB, Sevilla DC, Selvester RH, Wagner GS. Evaluation of changes in standard electrocardiographic QRS waveforms recorded from activity-compatible proximal limb lead positions. Am J Cardiol 1992;69:253–257.
10. A Report for Health Professionals by a Task Force of the Council on Clinical Cardiology, AHA. Instrumentation and practice standards for electrocardiographic monitoring in special care units. Circulation 1989;79:464–471.
11. Sutherland DJ, McPherson DD, Spencer CA, Armstrong CS, Horacek BM, Montague TJ. Effects of posture and respiration on body surface electrocardiogram. Am J Cardiol 1983;52:595–600.
12. Kornreich F, Rautaharju PM, Warren J, Montague TJ, Horacek BM. Identification of best electrocardiographic leads for diagnosing myocardial infarction by statistical analysis of body surface potential maps. Am J Cardiol 1985;56:852–856.
13. Krucoff MW, Parente AR, Bottner RK, Renzi RH, Stark KS, Ahmed SW, DeMichele J, Stroming SL, Green CE, Rackley CE, Kent KM. Stability of multilead ST-segment "fingerprints" over time after percutaneous transluminal coronary angioplasty and its usefulness in detecting reocclusion. Am J Cardiol 1988;61:1232–1237.
14. Krucoff MW, Wagner NB, Pope JE, Mortara DM, Jackson YR, Bottner RK, Wagner GS, Kent KM. The portable programmable microprocessor-driven real-time 12-lead electrocardiographic monitor: a preliminary report of a new device for the non-invasive detection of successful reperfusion of silent coronary reocclusion. Am J Cardiol 1990;65:143–148.
15. Krucoff MW, Croll MA, Pope JE, Pieper KS, Kanani PM, Granger CB, Veldkamp RF, Wagner BL, Sawchak ST, Califf RM. Continuously updated 12-lead ST-segment recovery analysis for myocardial infarct artery patency assessment and its correlation with multiple simultaneous early angiographic observations. Am J Cardiol 1993;71:145–151.
16. Mason RE, Likar I. A new system of multiple-lead exercise electrocardiography. Am Heart J 1966;71:196–205.
17. Holter NJ. New method for heart studies. Science 1961;134:1214–1220.
18. Anderson ST, Pahlm O, Selvester RH, Bailey JJ, Berson AS, Barold SS, Clemmensen P, Dower GE, Elko P, Galen P, Greenfield JC, Haisty WK, Kornreich F, Krucoff MW, Laks M, Marriott HJL, Macfarlane PW, Okamoto N, Page RL, Palmeri ST, Rautaharju P, Tolan G, White R, White T, Wagner GS. A panoramic display of the orderly sequenced 12 lead electrocardiogram (submitted for publication).

CHAPTER 3

Interpretation of the Normal Electrocardiogram

For every ECG there are nine features that should be examined systematically:

1. Rate and regularity;
2. P wave morphology;
3. PR interval;
4. QRS complex morphology;
5. ST segment morphology;
6. T wave morphology;
7. U wave morphology;
8. QTc interval;
9. Rhythm.

Rate, regularity, and *rhythm* are commonly grouped together. However, to accurately assess rhythm, it is necessary to consider not only rate and regularity, but also the various waveforms and intervals.

Determination of cardiac rate and regularity requires understanding of the grid markings provided on the ECG paper (Fig. 3.1). There are thin lines every 1 mm and thick lines every 5 mm. The thin lines, therefore, form small (1-mm) squares and the thick lines form large (5-mm) squares. These vertical lines facilitate measurements of time such as the cardiac rate and the various intervals. At the usual paper speed of 25 mm/sec, the thin lines are at 0.04-sec (40 msec) intervals, and thick lines at 0.20-sec (200-msec or 1/5-sec) intervals. The horizontal lines facilitate measurements of waveform amplitudes. At the usual calibration of 10 mm/mV, the thin lines are at 0.1-mV increments and the thick lines at 0.5-mV increments.

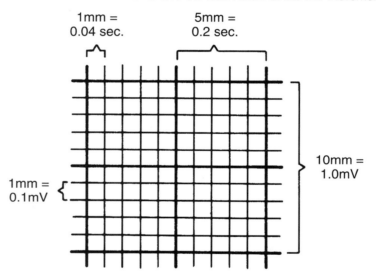

1mm =
0.04 sec.

5mm =
0.2 sec.

1mm =
0.1mV

10mm =
1.0mV

Figure 3.1. The time intervals indicated for the *vertical grid lines* are appropriate for the standard paper speed of 25 mm/sec; the amplitudes indicated for the *horizontal grid lines* are appropriate for the standard gain of 10 mm/mV.

Much of the information provided by the ECG is contained in the morphologies of the principal waveforms: the P wave, the QRS complex, and the T wave. It is helpful to develop a systematic approach to their analysis:

A. Examine their contour;
B. Measure their duration;
C. Measure their maximal amplitude;
D. Estimate their direction in each of the two planes.

The guidelines for measuring and estimating these four parameters for each of the three principal waveforms are presented below. The definitions of the various waveforms and intervals have already been presented in Chapter 1 ("Cardiac Electrical Activity") in the context of describing ECG recordings of base to apex and left versus right cardiac activity.

1. RATE AND REGULARITY

The cardiac rhythm is rarely precisely regular. Even when the cardiac electrical activity is initiated normally in the sinus node, the rate is affected by the autonomic nervous system. When the individual is at rest, minor variations in the autonomic balance are produced by the phases of the respiratory cycle. A glance at the sequence of cardiac cycles is enough to determine whether the rate is essentially regular or irregular. Normally, there are the same numbers of P waves and QRS complexes, and either may be used to determine cardiac rate and regularity. When, in the presence of certain abnormal cardiac rhythms, the numbers of P waves and QRS complexes are not the same, the atrial and ventricular rates and regularities must be determined separately.

If there is essential regularity, the cardiac rate/minute can easily be determined by counting the number of large squares between cycles. As there are 300 fifths of a second in a minute (5 × 60), it is necessary only to determine the number of fifths of a second (large squares) between consecutive cycles and divide this number into 300. It is most convenient to select a prominent ECG waveform that begins on a thick line and then count the number of large squares before the same waveform recurs in the following cycle. When this interval is only one-fifth of a second the rate would be 300 beats/min; if two-fifths, 150; if three-fifths, 100; etc.

When the rate is less than 100 beats/min, it is sufficient to consider only the large squares. When the rate is greater than 100 (tachycardia), however, small differences in the observed rate may alter the assessment of the underlying cardiac rhythm, and the number of small squares must be considered (Fig. 3.2). Since there are 5 small squares in each large square, the number of small squares between successive waveforms of the same type must be divided into 1500. Rate determination is facilitated by the use of "rate rulers," which are easily obtained from pharmaceutical representatives.

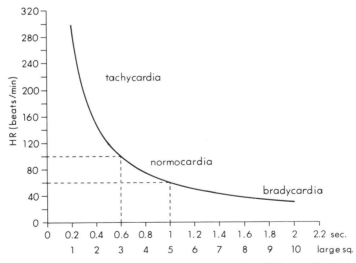

Figure 3.2. Use of time intervals between successive similar ECG waveforms to estimate the cardiac rate. This illustrates the importance of considering the thin (0.04 sec) time lines rather than the thick (0.2 sec) time lines for estimating rates in the tachycardia range, where small differences in the number of intervals between cardiac cycles result in large differences in the estimated rate.

If there is irregularity of rate, the number of cycles over a particular interval of time should be counted to determine the average cardiac rate. Many electrocardiographic recordings conveniently provide markers at 3-sec intervals. A simple and quick method for estimating rate is to count the number of cardiac cycles in 6 seconds and multiply by 10.

2. P WAVE MORPHOLOGY

   At either slow or normal heart rates, the small, rounded P wave is clearly visible just before the taller, more peaked QRS complex. At more rapid rates, however, the P wave may merge with the preceding T wave and become difficult to identify.

A. The P wave contour is normally smooth, and it is either entirely positive or negative (monophasic) in all leads except V1 (Fig. 1.8). In this view, which best distinguishes left- versus right-sided cardiac activity, the divergence of right and left atrial activation may produce a diphasic P wave (Fig. 1.13). The contributions of right and left atrial activation to the beginning, middle, and end of the P wave are indicated in Figure 3.3.

B. The P wave duration is normally less than 0.12 sec.

C. The P wave amplitude is normally less than 0.25 mV in all leads.

D. The P wave normally appears entirely upright on leftward and inferiorly oriented leads such as aVL, I, II, aVF, and V4–V6. It is negative in aVR, because of the rightward orientation of that lead, and variable in the other standard leads. Its direction, or *axis* in the frontal plane, should be determined by the same method indicated below for the QRS complex. The normal limits of P wave axis are between 0 and +75°.[1]

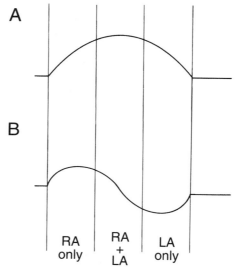

 Figure 3.3.   The typical appearance of a normal P wave in a base to apex lead such as II (**A**) and a right versus left lead such as V1 (**B**) are shown. The times of activation of the right and left atria are indicated by the *vertical lines.*

3. PR INTERVAL

The PR interval measures the time required for the impulse to travel from the atrial myocardium adjacent to the SA node to the ventricular myocardium adjacent to the fibers of the Purkinje network (Fig. 1.11). This duration is normally from 0.10 to 0.22 sec. A major portion of the PR interval reflects the slow conduction through the AV node, which is controlled by the sympathetic-parasympathetic balance within the autonomic nervous system. Therefore, the PR interval varies with the heart rate, being shorter at faster rates when the sympathetic component predominates, and vice versa. The PR interval tends to increase with age:[2]

Normal PR interval duration	0.10–0.22 sec
In childhood	0.10–0.12 sec
In adolescence	0.12–0.16 sec
In adulthood	0.14–0.22 sec

4. QRS COMPLEX MORPHOLOGY

 A. The QRS complex is composed of higher frequency signals than are the P and T waves, thereby causing its contour to be peaked rather than rounded. Positive and negative components of the P and T waves are simply termed positive and negative deflections, while those of the QRS complex are assigned specific labels such as Q wave, etc. (Fig. 1.9).

1) Q Waves. In some leads, V1, V2, and V3, the presence of a Q wave should be considered abnormal; in all other leads (except III and aVR), a "normal" Q wave would be very small. The "upper limit of normal" for such Q waves in each lead is indicated in the table and illustrated in Figure 3.4.[3]

Limb Leads		Precordial Leads	
Lead	Upper Limit	Lead	Upper Limit
I	<0.03 sec	V1	Any
II	<0.03 sec	V2	Any
III		V3	Any
aVR		V4	<0.02 sec
aVL	<0.03 sec	V5	<0.03 sec
aVF	<0.03 sec	V6	<0.03 sec

Modified from Wagner GS, Freye CJ, Palmeri ST, Roark SF, Stack NC, Ideker RE, Harrell FE Jr, Selvester RH. Evaluation of a QRS scoring system for estimating myocardial infact size. I. Specificity and observer agreement. Circulation 1982;65:345.

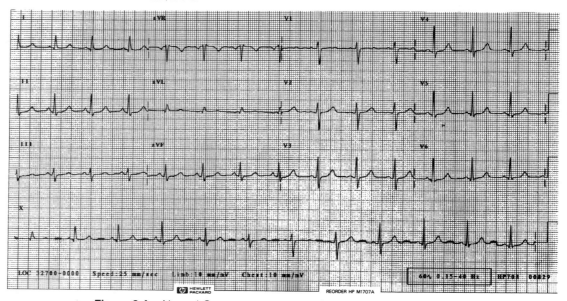

Figure 3.4. Normal Q waves are apparent in leads *I, II, aVL, V4, V5,* and *V6.*

The absence of small Q waves in V5 and V6 should be considered abnormal. A Q wave of any size is normal in III and aVR because of their rightward orientations (Figs. 2.5 and 2.6). Q waves may be enlarged by conditions such as local loss of myocardial tissue (infarction), enlargement (hypertrophy or dilatation) of the ventricular myocardium, or abnormalities of ventricular conduction.

2) R Waves. Since the precordial leads provide a panoramic view of the cardiac electrical activity progressing from the thinner right ventricle across the thicker left ventricle, the positive R wave normally increases in amplitude and duration from V1 to V4 or V5 (Figs. 2.10 and 3.5). Reversal of this sequence with larger R waves in V1 and V2 can be produced by right ventricular enlargement, and accentuation of this sequence with larger R waves in V5 and V6 can be produced by left ventricular enlargement. Loss of normal R wave progression from V1 to V5 may indicate loss of myocardium in the left ventricular wall, for instance after myocardial infarction.

3) S Waves. The S wave also has a normal sequence of progression in the precordial leads. It should be large in V1, larger in V2, and then progressively smaller from V3 through V6 (Figs. 2.10 and 3.5). As with the R wave, alteration of this sequence could be produced by enlargement of one of the ventricles.

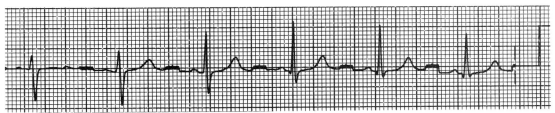

Figure 3.5. The typical panoramic display of the precordial leads illustrating the progression and regression of R and S wave amplitudes from a normal individual.

B. The duration of the QRS complex is termed the QRS interval, and it normally ranges from 0.07 to 0.10 sec (Fig. 1.11). It tends to be slightly longer in males than in females. The QRS interval is measured from the beginning of the first appearing Q or R wave to the end of the last appearing R, S, R', or S' wave. Figure 3.6 illustrates the use of three simultaneously recorded leads to identify the boundaries of ventricular activation. Such multilead comparison is necessary since either the beginning or end of the QRS complex may be isoelectric in any single lead, causing underestimation of QRS duration. The onset of the QRS complex is usually quite apparent in all leads, but its ending at the junction with the ST segment is often indistinct, particularly in the precordial leads. The QRS interval has no lower limit that indicates abnormality. However, QRS prolongation may be caused by left ventricular enlargement, an abnormality in impulse conduction, or a ventricular site of origin of the QRS complex.

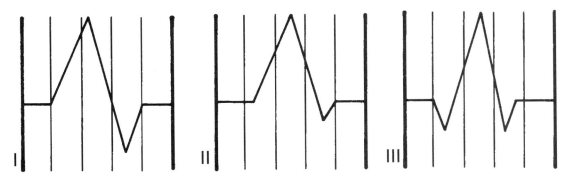

Figure 3.6. Magnified schematic of QRS complexes recorded simultaneously via limb leads I, II, and III are presented on a grid of thick (0.2 sec) and thin (0.04 sec) time lines. Only *lead I* reveals the true QRS duration (0.12 sec). An isoelectric period of approximately 0.01 sec is apparent in *lead II* at the beginning of the QRS complex, and an isoelectric period of similar length is apparent in *lead III* at the end of the QRS complex.

The duration from the beginning of the earliest appearing Q or R wave to the peak of the R wave in several of the precordial leads has been termed the *intrinsicoid deflection* (Fig. 3.7). Electrical activation of the myocardium begins at the endocardial insertions of the Purkinje network. The end of the intrinsicoid deflection represents the time of arrival of the electrical impulse at the epicardial surface located beneath the recording electrode. It is called intrinsic when the electrode is on the epicardial surface and intrinsicoid when the electrode is on the body surface.[4] The intrinsicoid deflection for the thinner walled right ventricle is measured in leads V1 or V2 (upper limit, 0.035 sec), and for the left ventricle in leads V5 or V6 (upper limit, 0.045 sec). This time is prolonged by either hypertrophy of the ventricle or intraventricular conduction delay.

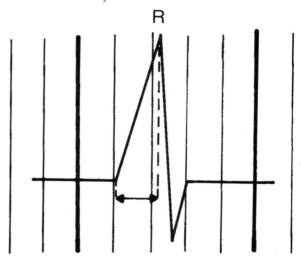

Figure 3.7. Magnified schematic of a QRS complex presented on a grid of standard ECG time lines. The length of the *arrow* indicates the duration (0.05 sec) of the intrinsicoid deflection as measured from the beginning of the QRS complex to the peak of the R wave.

C. The amplitude of the overall QRS complex has wide normal limits. It varies with age, increasing until about age 30 and then gradually decreasing. The amplitude is generally larger in males than in females. Overall QRS amplitude is measured between the peaks of the tallest positive and negative waveforms. It is difficult to set an arbitrary upper limit for normal voltage. Amplitudes as much as 30 mm are occasionally seen in normal individuals. Factors that contribute to higher amplitudes include youth, physical fitness, slender body build, intraventricular conduction abnormalities, and ventricular enlargement.

Abnormally low QRS voltage is present when the overall QRS amplitude is no more than 5 mm (0.5 mV) in any of the limb leads, and no more than 10 mm (1.0 mV) in any of the precordial leads. The QRS amplitude is decreased by any condition that increases the distance between the myocardium and the recording electrode such as a thick chest wall or various intrathoracic conditions that cause impedance of the electrical signal.

D. Estimation of the direction of the QRS complex requires consideration of both the frontal and transverse planes. In the frontal plane, the full 360° circumference is provided by the positive and negative poles of the six limb leads (Fig. 2.4). Therefore, it is possible to determine the QRS direction or axis, which represents the average direction of the spread of electrical activation throughout the right and left ventricles. The identification of the axis would be easiest if the frontal plane leads were displayed in their orderly sequence, as illustrated in Figure 2.10. A simple method for identifying the frontal plane QRS axis using the orderly sequenced limb leads is illustrated in Figure 3.8.[5]

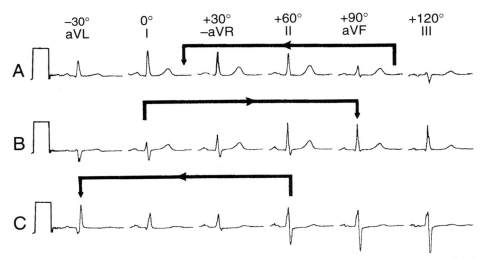

Figure 3.8. The *vertical line without an arrow* indicates the location of the frontal plane QRS transitional lead. Note that there is no transitional lead in **A**, indicating that the QRS transition is located between leads aVF and III. The *long horizontal line* contains an *arrow* indicating movement to 90° away from the transitional lead in the direction of the tallest R wave. The *vertical line with an arrow* indicates the location of the axis: +15° in **A**; +90° in **B**; and −30° in **C**.

When the typical display is used, there is a three-step method for determining the frontal plane axis:

1. Identify the *transitional lead*, as defined by positive and negative components of the QRS complex of approximately equal amplitudes. The positive and negative components may be of any size, varying from quite prominent to minuscule.
2. Identify the lead that is oriented perpendicular to the transitional lead by using the hexaxial reference system (Fig. 3.9, *top left*).
3. Consider the predominant direction of the QRS complex in the lead identified in step 2. If the direction is positive, the axis is equal to the positive pole of that lead. If the direction is negative, the axis is equal to the negative pole of that lead.

The frontal plane axis is normally directed leftward and either slightly superiorly or inferiorly: between $-30°$ and $+90°$ (Fig. 3.9, *top right*). Therefore, the QRS complex is normally predominately positive in both leads I (with its positive pole at 0°) and II (with its positive pole at $+60°$). If the QRS is positive in lead I but negative in II, the axis would be deviated leftward between -30 and $-120°$. However, if the QRS is negative in I but positive in II, the axis would be deviated rightward between $+90$ and $\pm180°$. The axis is rarely directed entirely opposite to normal with predominately negative QRS orientation in both leads I and II.

The frontal plane axis is typically rounded to the nearest multiple of 15°. If it is directly aligned with one of the limb leads, the axis is designated as $-30°$, $0°$, $+30°$, $+60°$, etc. If it is located midway between two of the limb leads, it is designated as $-15°$ $+15°$ $+45°$ $+75°$, etc. (Fig. 3.9, *top left*). Examples of patients with various frontal plane QRS axes are presented in Figure 3.9, *bottom.*

The normal frontal plane QRS axis is rightward in the neonate, moves to a vertical position during childhood, and then moves to a more horizontal position during adulthood (Fig. 3.10A).[7] In normal adults the electrical axis is almost parallel to the anatomical base to apex axis of the heart, in the direction of lead II. However, they are more vertical in thin individuals and more horizontal in heavy individuals. A QRS axis more positive than $+90°$ in an adult should be designated *right axis deviation (RAD)* (Fig. 3.10B); and an axis more negative than $-30°$ at any age should be designated *left axis deviation (LAD)* (Fig. 3.10, *C* and *D*). Right ventricular enlargement may produce right axis deviation, while left ventricular enlargement may produce left axis deviation. An axis between -90 and $+180°$ should be considered *extreme axis deviation (EAD)* without designating it as either rightward or leftward (Fig. 3.10E).

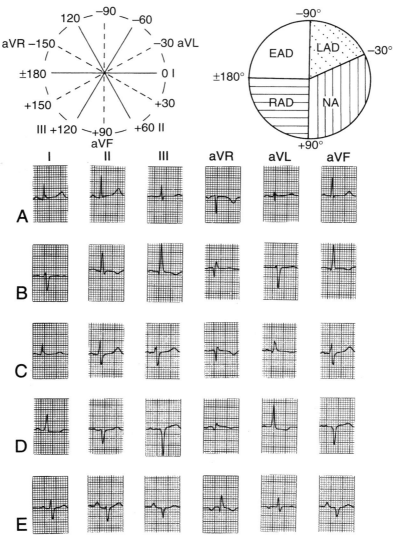

Figure 3.9. At the *top left*, the frontal plane hexaxial reference system is presented as in Figure 2.4. At the *top right*, the sectors indicating the various designations of frontal plane QRS axis in adults are identified: normal axis *(NA)* from −30° to +90°; right axis deviation *(RAD)* from +90° to ±180°; left axis deviation *(LAD)* from −30° to −90°; and extreme axis deviation *(EAD)* from −90° to ±180°. At the *bottom*, examples of various frontal plane QRS axes are shown: **A**, +60°; **B**, +120°; **C**, −30°; **D**, −60°; and **E**, −150°.

The limited arc provided by the six precordial leads and the varying angles between the leads preclude use of a hexaxial reference system required to locate the QRS axis. However, the QRS waveforms usually appear in transition from predominately negative to predominately positive in one of the six precordial leads, which is termed the *transitional lead*. Obviously, there could be a positive to negative transition located 180° away from this lead. However, the site of the negative to positive transition is that which is commonly considered in ECG analysis. The transitional lead is normally rightward (toward V1) in the neonate and moves leftward during childhood to the vicinity of V3, where it remains throughout adulthood.[6] The transitional lead also moves to the right with enlargement of the right ventricle and to the left with enlargement of the left ventricle.

5. ST SEGMENT MORPHOLOGY

The ST segment represents the period of time when the ventricular myocardium remains in an activated or depolarized state (Fig. 1.11). At its junction with the QRS (J point), it typically forms a nearly 90° angle and then proceeds horizontally until it curves gently into the T wave. The length of the ST segment is influenced by factors that alter the duration of ventricular activation. Points along the ST segment are designated with reference to the number of milliseconds beyond the J point such as "J + 20", "J + 40", "J + 60", etc.

The first section of the ST segment is normally located at the same horizontal level as the baseline formed by the PR segment discussed above and the TP segment that fills in the space between electrical cardiac cycles (Fig. 3.10A). Slight up-sloping, down-sloping, or horizontal depression of the ST segment may occur as a normal variant (Fig. 3.10B). Another normal variant appears when there is early repolarization in epicardial areas within the ventricles.[8] This causes displacement of the ST segment as great as 1 mm in the direction of the following T wave (Fig. 3.10C). Occasionally, there may be as much as a 4-mm ST elevation in leads V1–V3 in young males, particularly in young black males (Fig. 3.10D).[8] The appearance of the ST segment may also be altered during exercise or when there is an altered sequence of activation of the ventricular myocardium (Fig. 3.10E).

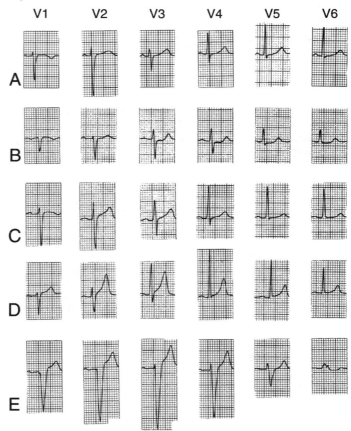

Figure 3.10. Variations of normal in the appearances of ST segments in the precordial leads V1 to V6. **A.** Typical horizontal position along the baseline formed by both the PR and TP segments. **B.** Minimal (<0.1 mV) horizontal depression. **C.** Minimal up-sloping elevation of early repolarization. **D.** Marked up-sloping elevation of early repolarization occasionally seen in young black males. **E.** Marked up-sloping elevation typical with left bundle branch block.

6. T WAVE MORPHOLOGY

A. The smooth, rounded shape of the T wave resembles that of the P wave. However, there is greater normal variation of monophasic versus diphasic appearance in the various leads (Figs. 1.8 and 1.13). The initial deflection of the T wave is typically longer than the terminal deflection, producing a slightly asymmetrical shape. Slight "peaking" of the T wave may occur as a normal variant, and notching of the T waves is common in children.

B. The duration of the T wave itself is not usually measured, but is instead included in the QT interval discussed below.

C. The amplitude of the T wave, like that of the QRS complex, has wide normal limits. It tends to diminish with age and is larger in males than in females. T wave amplitude tends to vary with QRS amplitude and should always be greater than that of the U wave, if present. T waves do not normally exceed 5 mm in any limb lead, or 10 mm in any precordial lead. The T wave amplitude tends to be lower at the extremes of the panoramic views (Figs. 3.5 and 3.8) of both the frontal and transverse planes: T waves do not normally exceed 3 mm in leads aVL and III, or 5 mm in leads V1 and V6.[9]

D. The direction of the T wave should be evaluated in relation to that of the QRS complex. The rationale for similar directions of these waveforms that represent the opposite myocardial events of activation and recovery has been presented in Chapter 1 ("Cardiac Electrical Activity"). The methods presented above for determining the direction of the QRS complex in the two planes should be applied for determining the direction of the T wave. The term *QRS-T angle* is used to indicate the number of degrees between the QRS complex and T wave transitional leads in the transverse plane and their axes in the frontal plane.[10]

In the normal neonate, the negative to positive transition of the T wave may be so far leftward that the T waves are negative in even the most leftward precordial leads V5 and V6. The typical positions of the transitions of the QRS complex and T wave during early childhood are presented in Figure 3.11A, *top*. During childhood, the T wave transition moves rightward until it reaches the vicinity of V1, where it tends to remain throughout life, as illustrated in Figure 3.11, *B* and *C, top*.[10]

In adults, the transverse plane T wave transition is normally more rightward than that of the QRS complex, with a QRS-T angle of less than 60° (Fig. 3.11, *B* and *C, top*). Since there is an approximately 100° arc between leads V1 and V6, the transitions of these two waveforms should not be located more than three leads apart. When the QRS transitional lead is V2 or V3, the T waves may be positive in all of the precordial leads. In this instance, there is no T wave transitional lead because the transition is outside the arc provided by the six precordial leads.

The frontal plane T wave axis tends to remain constant during adulthood, while the QRS axis moves from a vertical toward a horizontal position, as shown in Figure 3.11C, *bottom*. Therefore, during childhood the T wave axis is more horizontal than that of the QRS complex, but during adulthood the T wave axis becomes more vertical than that of the QRS. Despite these changes, the frontal plane QRS-T angle normally does not exceed 45°.[7]

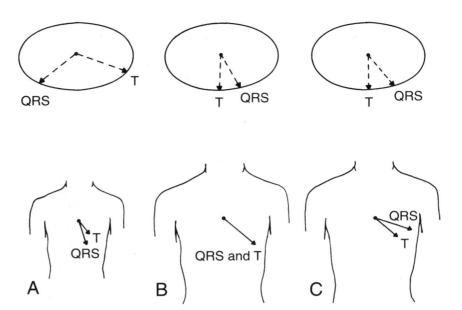

Figure 3.11. Typical locations of the QRS complex and T wave transitions in the transverse plane *(top)* and axes in the frontal plane *(bottom)*. **A.** A young child. **B.** A young adult. **C.** An elderly adult. *Dashed lines* are used to indicate locations of transitions; *solid lines*, to indicate axes.

7. U WAVE MORPHOLOGY

The U wave is normally either absent or present as a small, rounded wave following the T wave. It is normally in the same direction as the T wave, but approximately 10% of its amplitude. It is usually most prominent in leads V2 or V3. The U wave is larger at slower heart rates and both diminish in size and merge with the following P wave at faster heart rates. The U wave is usually clearly separated from the T wave with the *TU junction* along the baseline. However, there may be fusion between the T and U waves, making the measurement of the QT interval more difficult. The source of the U wave is uncertain: repolarization of endocardial structures, such as papillary muscles or the Purkinje network, or after-depolarization of ventricular myocardium have all been hypothesized.[11,12]

8. QTc INTERVAL

The QT interval measures the duration of activation and recovery of the ventricular myocardium. It varies inversely with the heart rate. To assure that there is complete recovery from one cardiac cycle before the following cycle begins, the duration of recovery must decrease as the rate of activation increases. Therefore, the "normality" of the QT interval can be determined only by correcting for the heart rate. The corrected QT interval *(QTc interval)* rather than the measured QT interval is included in routine ECG analysis. Bazett developed a formula for performing this correction,[13] which has recently been modified by Hodges and coworkers[14] and Macfarlane and Veitch Lawrie[15]:

$$QTc = QT + 1.75 \text{ (ventricular rate} - 60)$$

The normal value of QTc is approximately 0.41 sec. The QTc is slightly longer in females than in males and increases slightly with age. The accommodation of the duration of electrical recovery to the rate of electrical activation does not occur immediately, but requires several cardiac cycles. Thus, an accurate QTc can be calculated only after a series of regular, equal cardiac cycles.

The diagnostic value of the QTc interval is seriously limited by the difficulty of identifying the completion of ventricular recovery.

1. There is commonly a variation in the QT interval among the various leads. This occurs when the terminal portion of the T wave is isoelectric in some of the leads[16] (Fig. 3.12). The longest QT interval measured in multiple leads should, therefore, be considered the true QT interval.
2. The U wave may merge with the T wave, creating a TU junction, which is not on the baseline. In this instance, the onset of the U wave should be considered the approximate end of the QT interval.
3. At faster heart rates, the P wave may merge with the T wave, creating a *TP junction*, which is not on the baseline. In this instance, the onset of the P wave should be considered the approximate end of the QT interval.

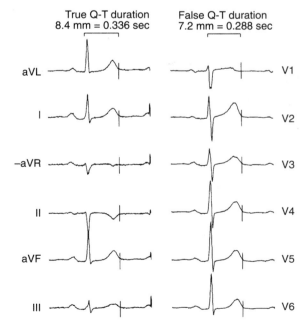

Figure 3.12. Measurement of the QT interval is confounded in lead V1 by the presence of a terminal isoelectric period of the T wave, suggesting a QT interval of 0.288 sec. *Vertical lines* on the panoramically displayed limb and precordial leads indicate the true ending of the T wave. The longest interval of 0.336 sec appearing in all leads except V1 should be considered the true QT interval. This figure has been magnified for illustrative purposes.

9. RHYTHM

The assessment of the final electrocardiographic feature, the cardiac rhythm, requires the consideration of all of the other eight features. Certain irregularities of features 1 through 3 may, in themselves, indicate rhythm abnormalities; and certain irregularities of features 3 through 8 may indicate the potential for development of rhythm abnormalities.

1) Rate and Regularity

The normal rhythm is called *sinus rhythm*, because it is produced by electrical impulses formed within the sinoatrial (SA) node. The rate of sinus rhythm is normally between 60 and 100 beats/min when the individual is awake and at rest. Below 60 beats/min the rhythm is called *sinus bradycardia*; and above 100 beats/min, *sinus tachycardia*. However, the designation of "normal" requires consideration of the level of activity of the individual: sinus bradycardia as low as 40 beats/min may be normal during sleep, and sinus tachycardia as rapid as 200 beats/min may be normal during exercise. Indeed, a rate of 90 beats/min would be "abnormal" during either sleep or vigorous exercise. Sinus rates in the bradycardia range may occur normally when awake, especially in well-trained athletes, whose heart rates may be in the 30s at rest—and often below 60 beats/min even with moderate exertion.

As indicated above, normal sinus rhythm is essentially but not absolutely regular because of continual variation of autonomic balance. Loss of this normal *heart rate variability* may be associated with significant underlying cardiac abnormalities.[17] The term *sinus arrhythmia* is used to indicate the normal variation in cardiac rate that cycles with the phases of respiration: the sinus rate accelerates with inspiration and slows with expiration (Fig. 3.13). Occasionally, sinus arrhythmia produces such marked irregularity that it can be confused with important arrhythmias.

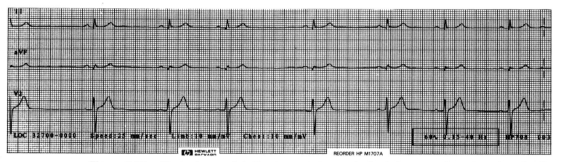

Figure 3.13. Typical normal rhythm termed sinus arrhythmia because the rate varies slightly with the inspiratory (speeding) and expiratory (slowing) phases of the respiratory cycle.

2) P Wave Morphology

Section D under "P Wave Morphology" above discusses the normal frontal plane axis of the P wave. Alteration of this axis to either less than +30° or more than +75° may indicate that the cardiac rhythm is being initiated from a site in or near the AV node in the right atrium, or in the left atrium.

3) PR Interval

An abnormal P wave axis is often accompanied by an abnormally short PR interval since the site of impulse formation has moved from the SA node to a position closer to the AV node (Fig. 3.14*B*). However, a short PR interval in the presence of a normal P wave axis suggests either an abnormally rapid conduction pathway within the AV node or the presence of an abnormal bundle of cardiac muscle connecting the atria and ventricles and bypassing the AV node (Fig. 3.14*C*). This earlier than normal activation of the ventricular myocardium is termed *ventricular preexcitation.* Preexcitation is not in itself an abnormality of the cardiac rhythm. However, the pathway either in or bypassing the AV node that is responsible for the preexcitation creates the potential for electrical *reactivation* or *reentry* into the atria, thereby producing a tachyarrhythmia.

A longer than normal PR interval in the presence of a normal P wave axis indicates delay in impulse transmission at some point along the normal pathway between the atrial and ventricular myocardium (Fig. 3.14*D*). When a prolonged PR interval is accompanied by an abnormal P wave axis, the possibility that the P wave is actually associated with the preceding rather than the following QRS complex should be considered. When such retrograde activation from ventricles to atria occurs, the PR interval is usually even longer than the preceding QRS to P (RP) interval (Fig. 3.14*E*).

When the PR interval cannot be determined, because of absence of any visible P wave, there is obvious abnormality of the cardiac rhythm.

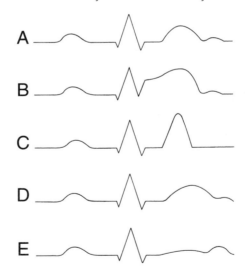

Figure 3.14. Normal P wave morphology, PR interval, and QRS complex morphology are illustrated in **A**; various abnormalities of P wave morphology and/or PR interval with persistently normal QRS morphology are shown in **B–E**. **B.** Abnormal P wave morphology and short PR interval indicate that the impulse is formed in or near the AV node. **C.** Normal P wave morphology and short PR interval indicate rapid conduction either through or bypassing the AV node into the His bundle. **D.** Normal P wave morphology and long PR interval indicate delayed conduction either through the AV node or the His bundle. **E.** Abnormal P wave morphology and long PR interval indicate that the impulse is formed beyond the AV node and then conducted retrograde to the atria.

4) QRS Complex Morphology

A normal P wave axis with an abnormally short PR interval is accompanied by a normal QRS duration when there is no AV nodal bypass directly into the ventricular myocardium (Fig. 3.14C). When such a bypass is present, there may be an additional abnormality of QRS complex morphology. Direct connection of atrial and ventricular myocardia eliminates the PR segment and creates a *fusion* between the P wave and the QRS complex (Fig. 3.15A). The initial Q or R wave begins slowly, producing prolongation of the QRS duration.

Abnormally slow impulse conduction within the normal intraventricular conduction pathways also produces abnormalities of QRS morphology, which may indicate the potential for development of cardiac rhythm abnormalities (Fig. 3.15B). The cardiac rhythm remains normal when the conduction abnormality is confined to either the right or left bundle branch. However, if the process responsible for the slow conduction spreads to the other bundle branch, the serious rhythm abnormality of partial or even total failure of AV conduction could suddenly occur.

Abnormally prolonged QRS duration in the absence of a preceding P wave suggests that the cardiac rhythm is originating from the ventricles rather than from the atria (Fig. 3.15C).

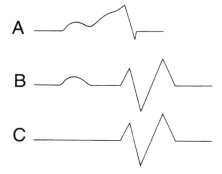

Figure 3.15. A–C illustrate various abnormalities of PR interval and/or QRS morphology. **A.** Short PR interval and abnormal initial QRS morphology indicate rapid conduction bypassing the AV node into the ventricular myocardium. **B.** Normal PR interval and abnormal overall QRS morphology indicate delayed conduction through one of the bundle branches. **C.** No P wave and abnormal overall QRS morphology indicate that the impulse is formed beyond the His bundle.

5–8) ST Segment, T Wave, U Wave, and QTc Interval

Marked elevation of the ST segment, increase or decrease in T wave amplitude, prolongation of the QTc interval, or increase in U wave amplitude may be indications of underlying cardiac conditions that may produce serious cardiac rhythm abnormalities (Fig. 3.16).

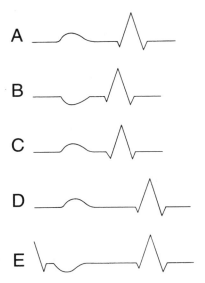

 Figure 3.16. Normal ST segment, T wave, and U wave morphologies and QTc interval are illustrated in **A**; and in various abnormalities in **B–E**. **B.** Elevation of the ST segment. **C.** Tall and peaked T wave. **D.** Long QTc interval. **E.** Flat T wave and tall U wave.

GLOSSARY

Axis: direction of an ECG waveform in the frontal plane measured in degrees.

Bradycardia: slow heart rate; less than 60 beats/min.

Extreme axis deviation: frontal plane QRS axis deviated from normal and located between −90° and +180°.

Fusion: merging of waveforms (i.e., P and T waves) together.

Intrinsicoid deflection: the time interval between the beginning of the QRS complex and the peak of the R wave; this represents the time required for the electrical impulse to travel from the endocardial to the epicardial surfaces of the ventricular myocardium.

Heart rate variability: the range of heart rates observed while an individual is in the resting state.

Left axis deviation: frontal plane QRS axis is deviated from normal and located between −30° and −90°.

QTc interval: the QT interval that measures the duration of activation and recovery of the ventricular myocardium, corrected by using a formula to consider the ventricular rate.

QRS-T angle: the number of degrees between the frontal plane axes or horizontal plane transitional leads of the QRS complex and the T wave.

Rate: measure of the frequency of occurrence of cardiac cycles expressed in beats per minute.

Regularity: the variability of cardiac rate over a period of time.

Reentry or **reactivation:** normally the electrical impulse spreads through each area of the heart only once following its initiation in specialized pacemaking cells. A partial conduction abnormality in some area of the heart may cause the impulse to spread back a second time, or even multiple times, through a structure such as the AV node or the atrial or ventricular myocardium.

Right axis deviation: frontal plane QRS axis deviated from normal and located between +90° and +180°.

Sinus arrhythmia: the normal variation in sinus rhythm that occurs during the inspiratory and expiratory phases of respiration.

Sinus rhythm: the normal cardiac rhythm originating via impulse formation in the sinoatrial or sinus node.

Transitional lead: the lead in which the positive and negative components of an ECG waveform are of almost equal amplitude, indicating that that lead is perpendicular to the direction of the waveform.

TP junction: the merging point of the T and P waves that occurs at faster heart rates.

TU junction: the point of merging of the T and U waves; sometimes on and sometimes off of the isoelectric line.

Ventricular preexcitation: normally the electrical impulse must spread through the slowly conducting AV node and rapidly conducting Purkinje system to travel from the atrial to the ventricular myocardium. Ventricular preexcitation occurs when the impulse bypasses the AV node and Purkinje system due to an abnormal bundle of muscle fibers connecting the atria and ventricles.

REFERENCES

1. Grant RP. Clinical electrocardiography: the spatial vector approach. New York: McGraw-Hill, 1957.
2. Beckwith JR. Grant's clinical electrocardiography. New York: McGraw-Hill, 1970:50.
3. Wagner GS, Freye CJ, Palmeri ST, Roark SF, Stack NC, Ideker RE, Harrell FE, Selvester RH. Evaluation of a QRS scoring system for estimating myocardial infarct size. I. Specificity and observer agreement. Circulation 1982;65:342–347.
4. Beckwith JR. Basic electrocardiography and vectorcardiography. New York: Raven Press, 1982:4–6.
5. Anderson ST, Pahlm O, Selvester RH, Bailey JJ, Berson AS, Barold SS, Clemmensen P, Dower GE, Elko PP, Galen P, Greenfield JC, Haisty WK, Kornreich F, Krucoff MW, Laks M, Marriott HJL, Macfarlane PW, Okamoto N, Page RL, Palmeri ST, Rautaharju P, Tolan G, White R, White T, Wagner GS. A panoramic display of the orderly sequenced 12 lead electrocardiogram. (submitted for publication).
6. Macfarlane PW, Veitch Lawrie TD, eds. Comprehensive electrocardiology. vol III. New York: Pergamon Press, 1989:1458.
7. Macfarlane PW, Veitch Lawrie TD, eds. Comprehensive electrocardiology. vol III. New York: Pergamon Press, 1989:1459.
8. Surawicz B. ST-T abnormalities. In: Macfarlane PW, Veitch Lawrie TD, eds. Comprehensive electrocardiology. vol I. New York: Pergamon Press, 1989:46–47.
9. Macfarlane PW, Veitch Lawrie TD, eds. Comprehensive electrocardiology. vol III. New York: Pergamon Press, 1989:1446–1457.
10. Beckwith JR. Grant's clinical electrocardiography. New York: McGraw-Hill, 1970:59–63.
11. Lepeschkin E. The U wave of the electrocardiogram. AHA Modern Concepts of Cardiovascular Disease. Aug 1969.
12. Hoffman BF, Cranefield PF. Electrophysiology of the heart. New York: McGraw-Hill, 1960:202.
13. Bazett HC. An analysis of the time relations of electrocardiograms. Heart 1920;7:353–370.
14. Hodges M, Salerno D, Erlien D. Bazett's QT correction reviewed. Evidence that a linear QT correction for heart is better [Abstract]. J Am Coll Cardiol 1983;1:694.
15. Macfarlane PW, Veitch Lawrie TD, eds. The normal electrocardiogram and vectorcardiogram. In: Comprehensive electrocardiology. vol I. New York: Pergamon Press, 1989:451–452.
16. Day CP, McComb JM, Campbell RW. QT dispersion in sinus beats and ventricular extrasystoles in normal hearts. Br Heart J 1992;67(1):39–41.
17. Kleiger RE, Miller JP, Bigger JT, Moss AJ, The Multi-Center Post-Infarction Research Group. Decreased heart rate variability and its association with increased mortality after acute myocardial infarction. Am J Cardiol 1987;59:256–262.

II

ABNORMAL WAVE MORPHOLOGY

CHAPTER 4

Chamber Enlargement

ATRIAL ENLARGEMENT

There are many cardiac problems that cause either one or both of the atrial chambers to *dilate* or *enlarge*. Atrial enlargement is usually accompanied by enlargement of one or both of the ventricles. The usual abbreviations are *RAE (right atrial enlargement)* and *LAE (left atrial enlargement)*. RAE produces ECG changes termed *P pulmonale* because it is commonly caused by pulmonary disease, and LAE produces ECG changes termed *P mitrale* because it is commonly caused by mitral valve disease.

The ECG evaluation of RAE and LAE is facilitated by the differing times of initiation of right and left atrial activation and their differing directions of spread of activation. As indicated in Section I, the optimal lead for differentiating left versus right cardiac activity is V1, with its positive electrode in the fourth intercostal space at the right sternal border. Right atrial activation begins first. It proceeds from the SA node in an inferior and anterior direction and produces an initial positive deflection of the P wave in leads II and V1 (Figs. 4.1A and 4.2A). Left atrial activation begins later. It proceeds from high in the interatrial septum in an inferior and posterior direction and produces a terminal deflection of the P wave, which is positive in lead II, but negative in lead V1 (Figs. 4.1B and 4.2B). Therefore, RAE is characterized by an increase in the initial deflection and LAE by an increase in the terminal deflection of the P wave. In most of the other standard leads, both the right and left atrial components of the P wave appear as similarly directed deflections. An increase in both the initial and terminal aspects of the P wave suggests biatrial enlargement (Figs. 4.1C and 4.2C).

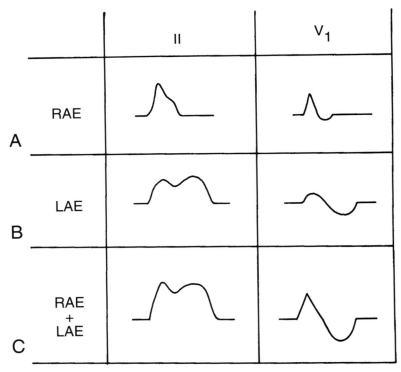

Figure 4.1. The changes in P wave morphology, typical of atrial enlargement as they appear in leads II and V1. **A.** Right atrial enlargement *(RAE)*. **B.** Left atrial enlargement *(LAE)*. **C.** Biatrial enlargement *(RAE + LAE)*.

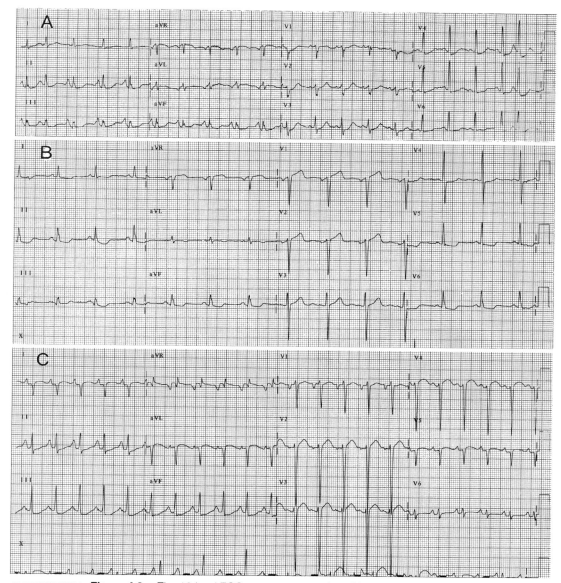

Figure 4.2. The 12-lead ECGs present examples of the typical changes in P wave morphology in patients with atrial enlargement. **A.** Right atrial enlargement. **B.** Left atrial enlargement. **C.** Biatrial enlargement.

SYSTEMATIC APPROACH TO THE EVALUATION OF ATRIAL ENLARGEMENT

The systematic approach to waveform analysis introduced in Chapter 3 ("Interpretation of the Normal Electrocardiogram") can be applied to the evaluation of atrial enlargement (Fig. 4.1):

A. Examine the Contour. The smooth contour of the P wave is disrupted by RAE, which causes a peak in the initial deflection, and by LAE, which causes an indentation in the middle. In some leads, this notch may produce an "M-like" appearance of the P wave.

B. Measure the Duration. RAE does not affect the duration. LAE prolongs the total P wave duration to >0.12 sec. It also prolongs the duration of the terminal negatively directed portion of the P wave in lead V1 to >0.04 sec.

C. Measure the Maximal Amplitude. RAE increases the maximal amplitude of the P wave to >0.25 mV. The greatest increase is usually seen in the base to apex oriented lead II. Usually, LAE does not increase the maximal amplitude of the P wave. It may, however, increase the amplitude of the terminal negatively directed portion in lead V1 to >0.10 mV.

D. Estimate the Direction in the Two Planes. RAE may cause a slight rightward shift and LAE may cause a slight leftward shift in the P wave axis in the frontal plane. However, the axis usually remains within the normal limits of 0° to +75°.

With extreme RAE, the P wave may be inverted in lead V1, creating the illusion of LAE. With extreme LAE, the P wave amplitude may increase and the terminal portion may become negative in leads II, III and aVF. Enlargement of both atria is termed *biatrial enlargement* and produces characteristics of RAE and LAE, as illustrated in Figure 4.1.

Munuswamy and colleagues,[1] using M-mode echocardiography as the standard for determining LAE, have evaluated the percentage of patients with truly positive and truly negative ECG criteria for LAE (Table 4.1). They found that the most *sensitive* is an increased duration (>0.04 sec) of the terminal negative part of the P wave in lead V1, whereas the most *specific* is a wide, notched P wave, the pattern that looks like an *intraatrial block*. Their findings are summarized in Table 4.1.

Table 4.1. The Echocardiographic Evaluation of ECG Criteria for LAE[a]

ECG Criteria	% True Positive[b]	% True Negative[c]
Duration of terminal negative P wave deflection in lead V1 > 0.04 sec	83	80
Amplitude of terminal negative P wave deflection in lead V1 > 0.10 mV	60	93
Duration between peaks of P wave notches > 0.04 sec	15	100
Maximal P wave duration > 0.11 sec	33	88
Ratio of P wave duration to PR segment duration > 1.6	31	64

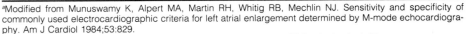

[a]Modified from Munuswamy K, Alpert MA, Martin RH, Whitig RB, Mechlin NJ. Sensitivity and specificity of commonly used electrocardiographic criteria for left atrial enlargement determined by M-mode echocardiography. Am J Cardiol 1984;53:829.
[b]Percentage of patients with LAE by echocardiogram who meet the ECG criterion for LAE.
[c]Percentage of patients without LAE by echocardiogram who do not meet the ECG criterion for LAE.

VENTRICULAR ENLARGEMENT

A cardiac chamber may be enlarged because of either an increase in the volume of blood within it or an increase in the resistance to blood flow out of it. The former is termed *volume overload* or *diastolic overload* and the latter *pressure overload* or *systolic overload.*[2] The thinner walled atrial chambers generally respond to both of these overloads by dilating. The thicker walled ventricles, however, dilate in response to receiving excess volume during diastole, but hypertrophy in response to having to exert excess pressure during systole (Fig. 4.3). Enlargement of the right or left ventricle is commonly accompanied by enlargement of its corresponding atrium. Therefore, the presence of criteria for atrial enlargement should be considered suggestive of ventricular enlargement.

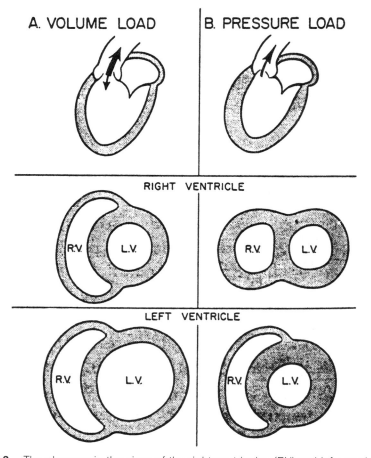

Figure 4.3. The changes in the sizes of the right ventricular *(RV)* and left ventricular *(LV)* myocardium produced by increases in volume overload (**A**) and pressure overload (**B**). (From Rushmer RF, ed. Cardiac compensation, hypertrophy, myopathy and congestive heart failure. In: Cardiovascular dynamics. 4th ed. Philadelphia: WB Saunders, 1976:538.)

RIGHT VENTRICULAR DILATION

The right ventricle dilates either during compensation for volume overload or after its hypertrophy eventually fails to compensate for a pressure overload. This dilation causes stretching of the right bundle branch, which courses from base to apex on the endocardial surface of the right side of the interventricular septum (Fig. 1.6). Conduction of impulses within these Purkinje fibers is slowed so much that the impulses reach the right ventricular myocardium only after it has already been activated by other impulses conducted via the left bundle branch. This phenomenon is referred to as *right bundle branch block (RBBB)*. Its characteristics are discussed in Chapter 5 ("Intraventricular Conduction Abnormalities"). This right ventricular conduction abnormality may appear suddenly during the early or compensatory phase of volume overload and during the advanced or failing phase of pressure overload (Fig. 4.4).[3]

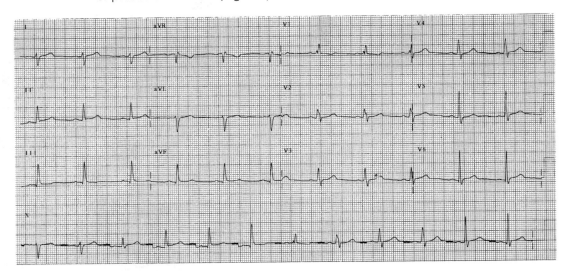

Figure 4.4. A 31-year-old woman with an ostium secundum atrial septal defect; note the RBBB and the RAD.

RIGHT VENTRICULAR HYPERTROPHY

The right ventricle hypertrophies because of compensation for pressure overload. In the neonate, the right ventricle is more hypertrophied than the left because there is greater resistance in the pulmonary circulation than in the systemic circulation during fetal development (Fig. 4.5A). Right-sided resistance is greatly diminished when the lungs fill with air, and left-sided resistance is greatly increased when the placenta is removed.[4] From this time onward, the ECG evidence of right ventricular predominance is gradually lost (Fig. 4.5B), as the left ventricle becomes hypertrophied in relation to the right. Therefore, hypertrophy, like dilation, may be a compensatory rather than a pathologic condition.[5] A pressure overload of the right ventricle may recur in later years because of increased resistance to the flow of blood through either the pulmonary valve, the pulmonary circulation, or the left side of the heart.

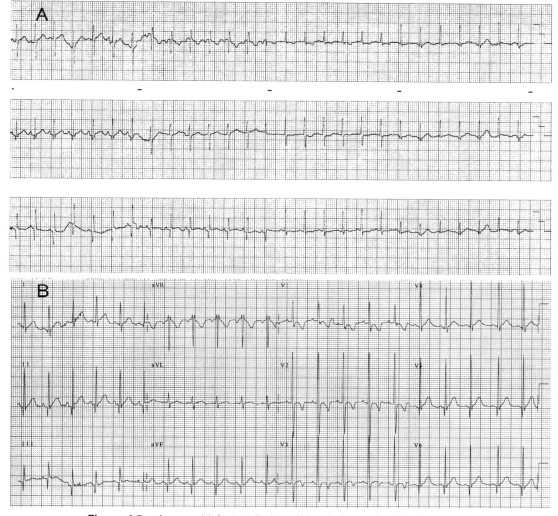

Figure 4.5. A normal infant at 7 days (**A**) and 6 months (**B**). The initial right ventricular predominance has diminished during the interim.

The thinner walled right ventricle normally completes its activation during the initial portion of the QRS complex. The remainder of the QRS complex is produced solely by activation of the thicker walled left ventricle and interventricular septum. As the right ventricle hypertrophies, it provides greater contribution than before to the early portion of the QRS complex and begins to contribute to the later portion. This hypertrophy-induced conduction delay may mimic incomplete or even complete right bundle branch block (Chapter 5). Lead V1, with its left versus right orientation, provides the optimal view of the competition between the two ventricles for electrical predominance.

Both leads V1 and V2 overlie the right ventricle (Figs. 1.1B and 1.12) and may exhibit other manifestations of a pressure overload. More time is required for electrical activation of the thickened right ventricle, thereby producing an increase in the intrinsicoid deflection (Fig. 3.7).

The normal QRS complex in the adult is predominately negative in lead V1, with a small R wave followed by a prominent S wave. When the right ventricle hypertrophies in response to a pressure overload, this negative predominance may be lost. In milder forms, a late positive R' wave appears (Fig. 4.6A). With moderate hypertrophy, the initial QRS forces move anteriorly (increased lead V1 R wave), and the terminal QRS forces move rightward (increased lead I S wave), as shown in Figure 4.6B. With marked hypertrophy, the QRS complex may even become predominately positive (Fig. 4.6C).

Severe pressure overload causes sustained delayed repolarization of the right ventricular myocardium, producing negativity of the ST segment and the T wave, which has been termed right ventricular *strain* (Fig. 4.6C).[6]

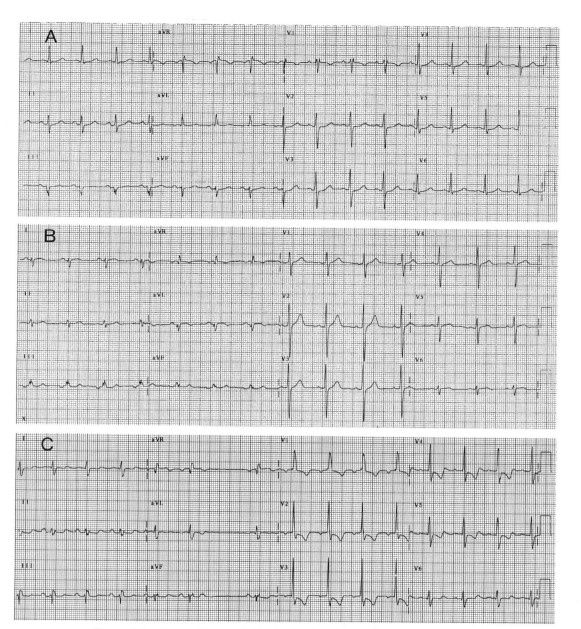

Figure 4.6. Three elderly individuals with right ventricular pressure overload due to chronic obstructive pulmonary disease exhibiting mild (**A**), moderate (**B**), and severe (**C**) right ventricular hypertrophy.

LEFT VENTRICULAR DILATION

The left ventricle dilates for the same reasons indicated previously for the right ventricle. However, the dilation does not stretch the left bundle enough to cause *left bundle branch block (LBBB)*. This is most likely due to differences between the anatomy of the right and left bundles. The right bundle continues as a single bundle along its septal surface, but the left bundle divides almost immediately into multiple fascicles (Fig. 1.6). Left ventricular dilation may produce a partial or incomplete left bundle branch block. These conduction abnormalities are discussed in Chapter 5.

Dilation enlarges the surface area of the left ventricle and moves the myocardium closer to the precordial electrodes which increases the amplitudes of leftward and posteriorly directed QRS waveforms.[7] The S wave amplitudes are increased in leads V2 and V3, and the R wave amplitudes are increased in leads V5 and V6. Figure 4.7A illustrates changes of mild to moderate dilation, while Figure 4.7B shows more severe changes with decreased R wave progression from lead V1 to V4.

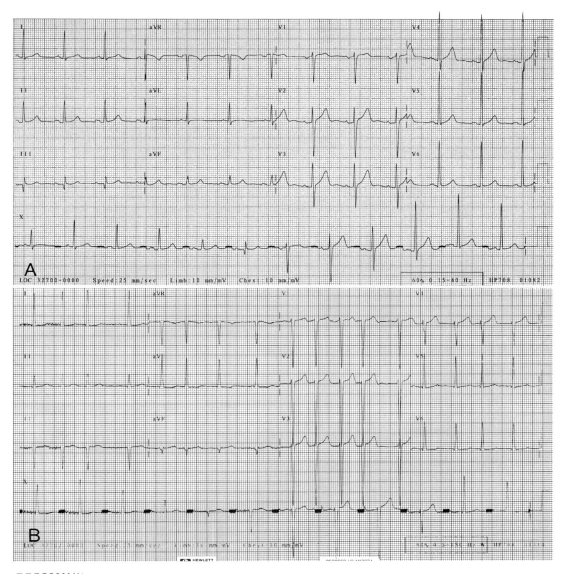

Figure 4.7. Two elderly men with left ventricular volume overload due to aortic insufficiency exhibiting mild to moderate (**A**) and severe (**B**) left ventricular dilation.

LEFT VENTRICULAR HYPERTROPHY

 As discussed above, the left ventricle normally becomes hypertrophied relative to the right ventricle following the neonatal period. Abnormal hypertrophy, which occurs in response to a pressure overload, produces exaggeration of the normal pattern of left ventricular predominance on the ECG. Like dilation, hypertrophy enlarges the surface area of the left ventricle, which increases the voltages of leftward and posteriorly directed QRS waveforms, thereby causing similar shifts in the frontal plane axis and transverse plane transitional zone.

A longer time is required for spread of electrical activation from the endocardial to epicardial surface, prolonging the intrinsicoid deflection (Fig. 3.7). Thus, a longer time is required for total left ventricular activation, thereby prolonging the QRS duration. These conduction delays, induced by hypertrophy, may mimic incomplete or even complete left bundle branch block (Fig. 4.8A).

Pressure overload leads to sustained delayed repolarization of the left ventricle, which produces negativity of both the ST segment and the T wave in leads with leftward or posterior orientation. This is referred to as left ventricular strain (Fig. 4.8B).[8] The epicardial cells no longer repolarize early, causing the spread of recovery to proceed from endocardium to epicardium. This leads to deflection of the T wave in the opposite direction of the QRS complex. The mechanism that produces the strain is uncertain, but there are several factors believed to contribute. The development of strain correlates well with increasing left ventricular mass as determined by echocardiography.[9] Myocardial ischemia and slowing of intraventricular conduction are factors that may contribute to strain.

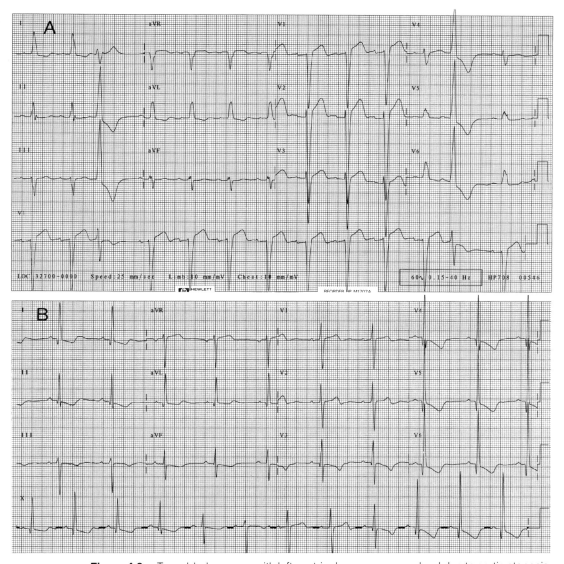

Figure 4.8. Two elderly women with left ventricular pressure overload due to aortic stenosis; note the left ventricular conduction delay and intermittent ventricular premature beats in **A** and LV strain in **B**.

COMBINED RIGHT AND LEFT VENTRICULAR HYPERTROPHY

 Enlargement of both ventricles is suggested if any of the following combinations of ECG changes are present:

1. Voltage criteria for LVH in the precordial leads combined with right axis deviation in the limb leads (Fig. 4.9A);
2. Criteria for LVH in the left precordial leads combined with prominent R waves in the right precordial leads;
3. A low amplitude S wave in lead V1 combined with a very deep S wave in lead V2;
4. Left atrial enlargement as the sole criterion for LVH combined with any criterion suggestive of RVH (Fig. 4.9B);
5. The Katz-Wachtel phenomenon consisting of equiphasic complexes in two or more limb leads and in the midprecordial leads. This is seen in many congenital lesions, but is perhaps most common in ventricular septal defect (Fig. 4.9C).

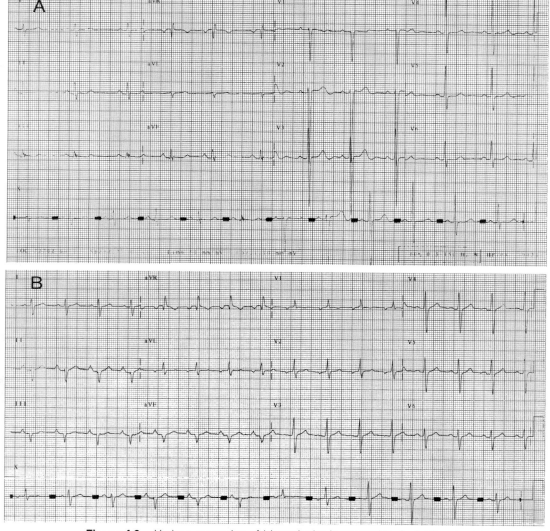

Figure 4.9. Various examples of biventricular hypertrophy. **A.** A 60-year-old woman with aortic insufficiency and LV failure. **B.** A 55-year-old woman with mitral stenosis and insufficiency. **C.** A 1-month-old child with a ventricular septal defect.

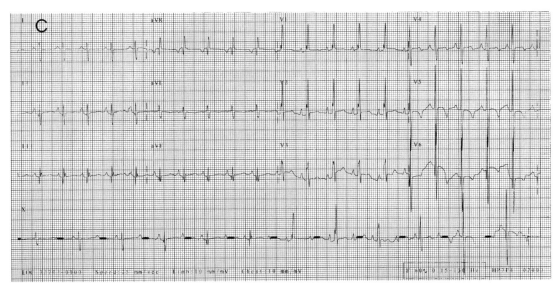

Figure 4.9C

SYSTEMATIC APPROACH TO EVALUATION OF VENTRICULAR ENLARGEMENT

Although the two varieties of ventricular enlargement have somewhat different effects on ECG waveforms, no specific sets of criteria for dilation versus hypertrophy have been developed. Indeed, the existing sets of criteria are for either right or left ventricular hypertrophy with no attempt to exclude enlargement due to dilation. Therefore, the systematic approach to waveform analysis introduced in Chapter 3 is applied to the analysis of ventricular hypertrophy.

A. Examine the Contour. Hypertrophy introduces lower frequency signals into the QRS complex. The prolongation of the intrinsicoid deflection by the hypertrophied myocardium diminishes the slope of the initial QRS waveforms. As the activation spreads, the smooth contour of the mid-QRS waveforms may be disrupted by indentations or notches (Fig. 4.9B). The terminal portions of the prolonged QRS complexes have low frequency, smooth waveforms.

The isoelectric contour of the ECG baseline may be disrupted. Ventricular hypertrophy tends to shift the J point off the baseline formed by the PR and TP segments and to cause the ST segment to slope in the direction of the T wave (Figs. 4.6C and 4.8B). When this occurs in the rightward precordial leads, it is referred to as right ventricular strain, and in the left precordial leads, as left ventricular strain.

B. Measure the Duration. Hypertrophy of either ventricle may cause prolongation of the QRS complex beyond its normal limit of 0.06–0.10 sec. Hypertrophy of the right ventricle usually does not prolong the QRS duration. The upper limit of prolongation due to right ventricular hypertrophy is 0.12–0.13 sec, resulting from complete block in the right bundle branch (Fig. 4.4). Hypertrophy of the left ventricle, even without left bundle branch block, may prolong the QRS duration to 0.13 or 0.14 sec, and with complete left bundle branch block, to 0.20 sec.

C. Measure the Maximal Amplitude. The QRS amplitude is normally maximal in the left posterior direction. This is accentuated by left ventricular hypertrophy and opposed by right ventricular hypertrophy. All criteria for left ventricular hypertrophy contain thresholds for maximal left posterior waveform amplitudes. Cornell[10] considers both frontal and transverse plane leads while Romhilt-Estes[11] and Sokolow-Lyon[12] consider both rightward and leftward transverse plane leads.

The Sokolow-Lyon criteria for right ventricular hypertrophy contain thresholds for rightward and anterior amplitudes in the transverse plane leads. The Butler-Leggett[13] criteria require that the combination of maximal anterior and maximal rightward amplitudes exceeds the maximal leftward posterior amplitude by a threshold amount.

D. Estimate the Direction in the Two Planes. Right ventricular hypertrophy shifts the frontal plane QRS axis rightward to a vertical or rightward position and the transverse plane QRS transitional zone either to or beyond lead V1 (Fig. 4.6, B and C). Left ventricular dilation and hypertrophy shift the frontal plane QRS axis only slightly leftward, but shift the transverse plane QRS transitional zone markedly leftward (Fig. 4.2C).

Right ventricular hypertrophy shifts the direction of both the ST segment and the T wave away from the right ventricle in the direction opposite to its shift of the QRS complex. Typically, in rightward oriented leads such as V1, the QRS complex would be abnormally positive, while the ST segment and T wave would be abnormally negative (Fig. 4.6C). Left ventricular hypertrophy shifts the ST segment and T wave away from the left ventricle in the direction opposite to its shift of the QRS complex. Therefore, in leftward oriented leads such as aVL and V5, the QRS complex would be abnormally positive, and the ST segment and T wave would be abnormally negative (Fig. 4.5B).

Three sets of criteria for LVH and one for RVH are presented. There is no distinction between dilation and hypertrophy.

Romhilt-Estes Scoring System for LVH[a]

1. R or S in any limb lead ≥ 0.20 mV
   or S in lead V1 or V2
   or R in lead V5 or V6 ≥ 0.30 mV   3 points[b]

2. Left ventricular strain
   ST segment and T wave in opposite direction to QRS complex
   without digitalis   3 points
   with digitalis   1 point

3. Left atrial enlargement
   Terminal negativity of the P wave in lead V1 is
   ≥ 0.10 mV in depth and ≥ 0.04 sec in duration   3 points

4. Left axis deviation of ≥ −30°   2 points

5. QRS duration ≥ 0.09 sec   1 point

6. Intrinsicoid deflection in lead V5 or V6 ≥ 0.05 sec   1 point

Total   13 points

[a]Modified from Romhilt DW, Bove KE, Norris RJ, Conyers E, Conradi S, Rowlands DT, Scott RC. A critical appraisal of the electrocardiographic criteria for the diagnosis of left ventricular hypertrophy. Circulation 1969;40:185.
[b]LVH, 5 points; probable LVH, 4 points.

Sokolow-Lyon Criteria for LVH[a]

S wave in lead V1 + R wave in lead V5 or V6 > 3.50 mV
or
R wave in lead V5 or V6 > 2.60 mV

[a]Modified from Sokolow M, Lyon TP. The ventricular complex in left ventricular hypertrophy as obtained by unipolar precordial and limb leads. Am Heart J 1949;37:161.

Cornell Voltage Criteria for LVH[a]

Females   R wave in lead aVL + S wave in lead V3 > 2.00 mV
Males   R wave in lead aVL + S wave in lead V3 > 2.80 mV

[a]Modified from Casale PN, Devereux RB, Alonso DR, Campo E, Kligfield P. Improved sex-specific criteria of left ventricular hypertrophy for clinical and computer interpretation of electrocardiograms: validation with autopsy findings. Circulation 1987;75:565.

Butler-Leggett Formula for RVH[a]

Directions	Anterior	Rightward	Posterior-leftward
Amplitude	Tallest R or R′ in lead V1 or V2	Deepest S in lead I or V6	S in lead V1
RVH formula	A + R − PL ≥ 0.70 mV		

[a]Modified from Butler PM, Leggett SI, Howe CM, Freye CJ, Hindman NB, Wagner GS. Identification of electrocardiographic criteria for diagnosis of right ventricular hypertrophy due to mitral stenosis. Am J Cardiol 1986;57:640.

Sokolow-Lyon Criteria for RVH[a]

R wave in lead V1 + S wave in lead V5 or V6 ≥ 1.10 mV

[a]Modified from Sokolow M, Lyon TP. The ventricular complex in right ventricular hypertrophy as obtained by unipolar precordial and limb leads. Am Heart J 1949;38:273–294.

TYPICAL ECG CHANGES IN SELECTED CONGENITAL HEART DISEASES

 There are certain rare congenital heart diseases that are associated with typical combinations of abnormalities on the ECG:

1. Anomalous left coronary artery originating from the pulmonary artery: Q waves, ST elevation, and T wave inversion in leads I, aVL, V4, V5, and V6.
2. Dextrocardia with situs inversus: P waves, QRS complexes, and T waves are all inverted in lead I.
3. Ostium primum atrial septal defect (common AV canal): there is marked left axis deviation of the QRS complex in the frontal plane with the typical appearance of left anterior fascicular block (Chapter 5). There is also the right bundle branch block and other changes described above for right ventricular dilation (Fig. 4.10A).
4. Ebstein's Abnormality[15]: there is the combination of extremely tall P waves indicative of right atrial enlargement without evidence of right ventricular involvement. There is also a prolonged QRS duration with the initial slowing of ventricular preexcitation (Chapter 6, "Ventricular Preexcitation") in many instances. The QRS complex is positive in lead V1, presenting an appearance of an atypical RBBB. There is also generally low QRS voltage.
5. Ventricular septal defect and patent ductus arteriosus: there is combined right and left ventricular hypertrophy. This is characterized by high voltage equiphasic QRS complexes in the midprecordial leads, as discussed above under biventricular hypertrophy. Frequently, there are also prominent Q waves in the left precordial leads or in inferiorly oriented limb leads (Figs. 4.9C and 4.10B).

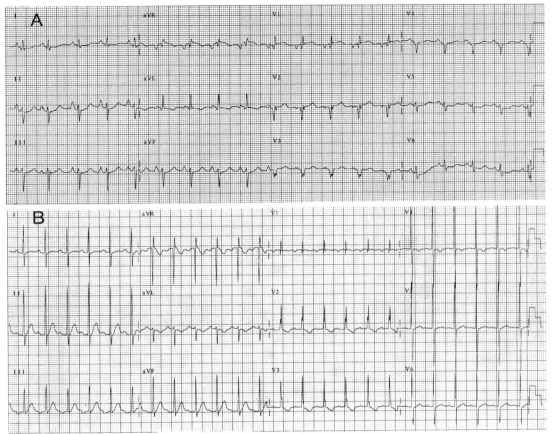

Figure 4.10. Typical ECGs of congenital cardiac abnormalities. **A.** A 67-year-old woman with an ostium primum atrial septal defect. **B.** A 4-month-old child with combined ventricular septal defect and patent ductus arteriosus.

GLOSSARY

Biatrial enlargement (BAE): enlargement of both the right and left atria.

Complete bundle branch block: total failure of conduction in the right or left bundle branch; defined by QRS duration >0.12 sec with RBBB and >0.14 with LBBB.

Dilate or enlarge: to stretch the myocardium beyond its normal dimensions.

Incomplete bundle branch block: partial failure of conduction in the right or left bundle branch; defined by QRS duration of 0.10–0.11 sec with RBBB and 0.11–0.13 sec with LBBB.

Intraatrial block: conduction delay within the atria.

Left atrial enlargement (LAE): dilation of the left atrium to accommodate an increase in volume or resistance to outflow.

Left bundle branch block (LBBB): partial or complete failure of conduction in the left bundle branch of the ventricular Purkinje system.

P mitrale: appearance of the P wave in left atrial enlargement; named for its common occurrence in mitral valve disease.

P pulmonale: appearance of the P wave in right atrial enlargement; named for its common occurrence in chronic pulmonary disease.

Pressure or systolic overload: condition in which a ventricle is forced to pump against an increased resistance during systole.

Right atrial enlargement (RAE): dilation of the right atrium to accommodate an increase in volume or resistance to outflow.

Right bundle branch block (RBBB): partial or complete failure of conduction in the right branch of the ventricular Purkinje system.

Sensitivity: expresses the ability of a test to indicate the presence of a condition (i.e., if the test is positive in every subject with the disease, it attains 100% sensitivity).

Specificity: expresses the ability of a test to indicate the absence of a condition (i.e., if the test is negative in every control subject, it attains 100% specificity).

Strain: a condition resulting from excessive tension; it is an ECG characteristic of marked hypertrophy indicated by ST segment and T wave changes.

Volume or diastolic overload: condition in which a ventricle has been filled with an increased amount of blood during diastole.

REFERENCES

1. Munuswamy K, Alpert MA, Martin RH, Whitig RB, Mechlin NJ. Sensitivity and specificity of commonly used electrocardiographic criteria for left atrial enlargement determined by M-mode echocardiography. Am J Cardiol 1984;53:829.
2. Rushmer RF, ed. Cardiac compensation, hypertrophy, myopathy and congestive heart failure. In: Cardiovascular dynamics. Philadelphia: WB Saunders, 1976;532–565.
3. Walker IC, Scott RC, Helm RA. Right ventricular hypertrophy; II. Correlation of electrocardiographic right ventricular hypertrophy with the anatomic findings. Circulation 1955;11:215.
4. Rushmer RF, ed. Cardiovascular dynamics. Philadelphia: WB Saunders, 1991;452–456.
5. Rushmer RF, ed. Cardiac compensation, hypertrophy, myopathy and congestive heart failure. In: Cardiovascular dynamics. Philadelphia: WB Saunders, 1976;532–565.
6. Cabrera E, Monroy JR. Systolic and diastolic loading of the heart. II. Electrocardiographic data. Am Heart J 1952;43:669.
7. Cabrera E, Monroy JR. Systolic and diastolic loading of the heart. II. Electrocardiographic data. Am Heart J 1952;43:661.
8. Devereux RB, Reichek N. Repolarization abnormalities of left ventricular hypertrophy. J Electrocardiol 1982;15:47.
9. Casale PN, Devereux RB, Kligfield P, Eisenberg RR, Miller DH, Chaudhary BS, Phillips MC. Electrocardiographic detection of left ventricular hypertrophy: development and prospective validation of improved criteria. J Am Coll Cardiol 1985;6:572.
10. Casale PN, Devereux RB, Alonso DR, Campo E, Kligfield P. Improved sex-specific criteria of left ventricular hypertrophy for clinical and computer interpretation of electrocardiograms: validation with autopsy findings. Circulation 1987;75:565.
11. Romhilt DW, Bove KE, Norris RJ, Conyers E, Conradi S, Rowlands DT, Scott RC. A critical appraisal of the electrocardiographic criteria for the diagnosis of left ventricular hypertrophy. Circulation 1969;40:185.
12. Sokolow M, Lyon TP. The ventricular complex in left ventricular hypertrophy as obtained by unipolar precordial and limb leads. Am Heart J 1949;37:161.
13. Butler PM, Leggett SI, Howe CM, Freye CJ, Hindman NB, Wagner GS. Identification of electrocardiographic criteria for diagnosis of right ventricular hypertrophy due to mitral stenosis. Am J Cardiol 1986;57:639–643.
14. Sokolow M, Lyon TP. The ventricular complex in right ventricular hypertrophy as obtained by unipolar precordial and limb leads. Am Heart J 1949;38:273–294.
15. Schiebler GL, Adams P Jr, Anderson RC. The Wolff-Parkinson-White syndrome in infants and children. Pediatrics 1959;24:585.

CHAPTER 5

Intraventricular Conduction Abnormalities

NORMAL CONDUCTION

 Many cardiac conditions cause electrical impulses to be conducted abnormally through the ventricular myocardium, producing changes of QRS complexes and T waves. Therefore, normal QRS complex and T wave appearance requires that several factors be present:

1. The left and right ventricles are not in an enlarged state, prolonging the time required for their activation and recovery (Chapter 4, "Chamber Enlargement").

2. Myocardial ischemia or infarction is not present or is of insufficient magnitude to disrupt the spread of the activation and recovery waves (Chapter 7, "Myocardial Ischemia and Infarction").

3. There is rapid impulse conduction through the right and left ventricular Purkinje networks so that the endocardial surfaces are activated almost simultaneously (Chapter 5, "Intraventricular Conduction Abnormalities").

 4. There are no accessory pathways for conduction from the atria to the ventricles (Chapter 6, "Ventricular Preexcitation").

CLINICAL PERSPECTIVE OF INTRAVENTRICULAR CONDUCTION DISTURBANCES

Both right bundle branch block (RBBB) and left bundle branch block (LBBB) are occasionally seen in apparently normal individuals.[1] The cause is fibrosis of the Purkinje fibers, which has been described as *Lenègre's disease*[2] or *Lev's disease*.[3] The process of Purkinje fibrosis progresses slowly: a 10-year follow-up study of healthy aviators with BBB revealed no incidence of complete AV block, syncope, or sudden death.[4] The pathologic process may be accelerated by systemic hypertension. Indeed, hypertension preceded the appearance of BBB in 60% of the individuals in the Framingham study. The mean age of onset was 61 years.[5]

Insight into the long-term prognosis of individuals with chronic BBB but no other evidence of cardiac disease comes from studies of the ECG changes preceding the development of transient or permanent complete AV block. Friedberg and associates have documented the common presence of some combination of bundle branch or fascicular block immediately prior to the onset of the AV block. The most common combination was RBBB with left anterior-superior fascicular block (LAFB).[6]

The combined results of these studies suggest that Lenègre's or Lev's disease is a slowly developing process of fibrosis of the Purkinje fibers that has the ultimate potential of such complete bilateral involvement that complete AV block occurs. Since the Purkinje cells lack the physiologic capability of the AV nodal cells to conduct at varying speeds, a sudden progression from no AV block to complete (third degree) AV block may occur.[7] When this does occur, ventricular activation can result only from impulse formation within a Purkinje cell beyond the site of the block. Several clinical conditions may arise, including syncope and sudden death.

Bundle branch or fascicular block may also be the result of other serious cardiac diseases. In Central and South America, *Chagas disease* produced by infection with *Trypanosoma cruzi* is almost endemic and is a common cause of RBBB with LAFB.[8] As indicated in Chapter 4, RBBB is commonly produced by the distention of the right ventricle that occurs with volume overloading. Transient RBBB is often produced during right heart catheterization and may complicate monitoring with a *Swan-Ganz catheter* (Fig. 5.1, *A* and *B*).

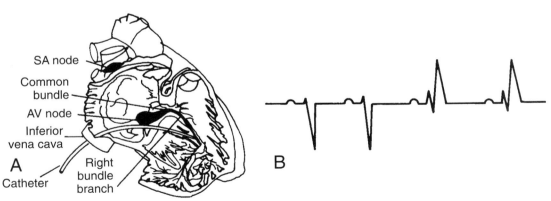

Figure 5.1. RBBB is induced by trauma to the right bundle branch. In **A**, a catheter has been advanced from the leg via the inferior vena cava, and its tip lies against the right ventricular endocardium in the vicinity of the right bundle branch. The resultant RBBB is illustrated in the third and fourth beats of **B**. (Modified from Netter FH. The Ciba collection of medical illustrations. vol 5. Heart. Summit: Ciba-Geigy, 1978:13.)

Any combination of the bundle branches or proximal fascicles may be blocked during an acute myocardial infarction in a patient with coronary atherosclerosis. These structures receive their blood supply via the very proximal septal perforating branch of the left anterior descending coronary artery (Fig. 5.2). Therefore, the bundle branches and their proximal fascicles become ischemic only when there is an occlusion in either the left main coronary artery or the origin of its anterior descending branch. Individuals who survive to reach the hospital after occlusion of such a major coronary artery may have any combination of bundle branch or fascicular blocks complicating extensive myocardial infarction. Since the acute and long-term mortality rates in these patients are very high, they do not represent a significant portion of the overall population of individuals with chronic bundle branch and fascicular block.[9]

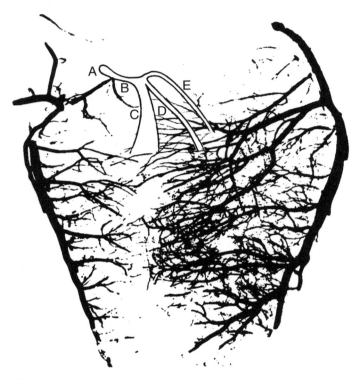

Figure 5.2. The specialized conduction system is shown in relation to its blood supply from a right anterior oblique view. **A.** AV node. **B.** Common bundle. **C.** Left inferior-posterior fascicle. **D.** Left anterior-superior fascicle. **E.** Right bundle branch. Note the length of the septal perforating branches of the left anterior descending artery in contrast to those of the posterior descending artery. (Reproduced with permission from Rotman M, Wagner GS, Wallace AG. Bradyarrhythmias in acute myocardial infarction. Circulation 1972;45:705. Copyright 1972 American Heart Association.)

Intermittent bundle branch block (prolonged QRS complexes present at some times but not at others) usually represents a transition stage before permanent block is established (Fig. 5.3, *A* and *B*).

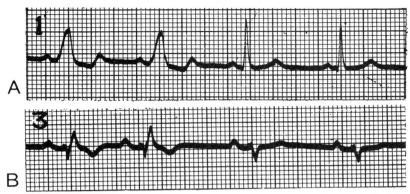

Figure 5.3. Intermittent left (**A**) and right (**B**) bundle branch block. The typical wide monophasic (LBBB) and triphasic (RBBB) appearances of these intraventricular conduction abnormalities disappear in the third and fourth beats in both examples.

At times, intermittent BBB is determined by the heart rate. As the rate accelerates, the *RR interval* shortens and the descending impulse finds one of the bundle branches still in its *refractory period* (Fig. 5.4). With this *tachycardia-dependent BBB*, slowing of the heart rate allows descending impulses to arrive following the refractory period of the entire conduction system, and normal conduction is resumed. A rarer form of intermittent BBB, which develops only when the cycle lengthens rather than shortens (Fig. 5.5), is termed *bradycardia-dependent BBB*. Intermittent BBB is a form of intermittent aberrant conduction of the electrical impulses through the ventricular myocardium.

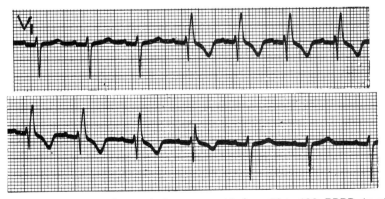

Figure 5.4. As the rate accelerates in the *upper strip* from 98 to 102, RBBB develops. In the *lower strip*, the complete RBBB persists until the rate slows to about 90, when incomplete RBBB and then normal conduction appear.

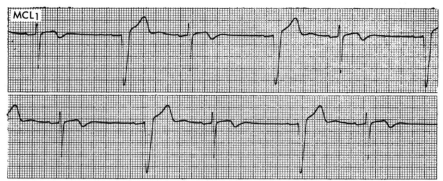

Figure 5.5. All beats are conducted sinus beats grouped in pairs. Those ending the shorter cycles are conducted normally, while those ending the longer cycles are conducted with LBBB.

BUNDLE BRANCH AND FASCICULAR BLOCK

Since the activation of the ventricular Purkinje system is not represented on the surface ECG (Fig. 1.8), abnormalities of its conduction must be detected indirectly by their effects on myocardial activation and recovery. The most specific changes occur within the QRS complex. A conduction disturbance within the right bundle branch, left bundle branch, left bundle fascicles, or between the Purkinje fibers and the adjacent myocardium may alter the QRS complex and T wave. A conduction disturbance in the common or His bundle has similar effects on the entire distal Purkinje system and, therefore, does not alter the appearance of the QRS complex or T wave (Fig. 5.6).

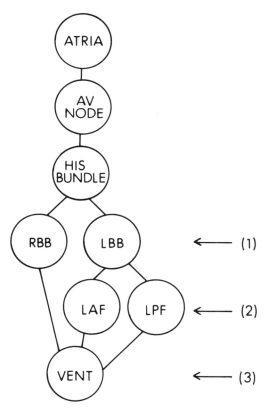

Figure 5.6. The structures responsible for conducting the electrical impulses between the atrial and ventricular myocardium are illustrated schematically. LAF and LPF indicate left anterior-superior and left posterior-inferior fascicles respectively. *(1)*, *(2)*, and *(3)* indicate the locations where conduction abnormalities can produce alterations of the QRS complexes and T waves. (Modified from Wagner GS, Waugh RA, Ramo BW. Cardiac arrhythmias. New York: Churchill Livingstone, 1983;18.)

Block of an entire bundle branch requires that its ventricle must be activated by myocardial spread from the other ventricle, and the overall QRS duration is prolonged. Block of the entire right bundle branch is termed complete right bundle branch block while block of the entire left bundle branch is termed complete left bundle branch block. The ventricles are activated successively instead of simultaneously. The other situations in which the ventricles are activated successively occur when one ventricle is preexcited via an accessory AV pathway (Chapter 6) and when there are independent ventricular rhythms (Chapters 13 and 17). Under these conditions, there is a fundamental similarity in the distortions of the ECG waveforms: the duration of the QRS complex is prolonged and the ST segment slopes into the T wave in the direction away from the ventricle in which the abnormality is located (Fig. 5.7).

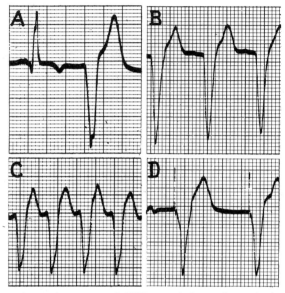

Figure 5.7. Comparison of patterns of QRS morphology of ventricular premature beats (**A**), bundle branch block (**B**), ventricular tachycardia (**C**), and artificially paced ventricular rhythm (**D**).

A ventricular conduction delay with only slight QRS prolongation could be termed incomplete BBB. However, it is important to remember from Chapter 4 that enlargement of the right ventricle may produce a distortion of the QRS complex that would mimic incomplete RBBB, whereas enlargement of the left ventricle may produce a prolongation of the QRS complex that would mimic incomplete LBBB (Fig. 4.6C). Since the LBB has multiple fascicles, another form of incomplete LBBB could be produced by a disturbance in one of its major groups of fascicles.

The ventricular Purkinje system has been considered trifascicular. It consists of the RBB and the anterior-superior and posterior-inferior portions of the left bundle branch. The proximal RBB is small and compact, so it may be considered either a bundle branch or a fascicle. The proximal LBB is also compact, but too large to be considered a fascicle. It remains compact for 1–2 cm and then fans into three rather than two groups of individual fascicles.[10] As Demoulin and Kulbertus have demonstrated in humans,[11] there are multiple anatomic variations among individuals. Based on their anatomic locations, the three groups of fascicles are probably best termed left septal (LS), left anterior-superior (LA) and left posterior-inferior (LP) as seen in Figure 5.8. The LA division of the LBB courses toward the anterior-superior papillary muscle, the LP division toward the posterior-inferior papillary muscle, and the LS division into the midseptum. The LS fascicles proceed along the surface of the interventricular septum and initiate left to right spread of activation through the septum.

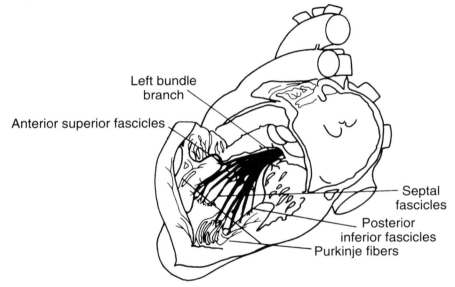

Figure 5.8.   The left ventricle has been opened to reveal the LBB and its fascicles as originally presented in Figure 1.6C. (From Netter FH. The Ciba collection of medical illustrations. vol 5. Heart. Summit: Ciba-Geigy, 1978:13.)

Rosenbaum et al. described the concept of blocks in the major fascicles of the left bundle branch, which they termed *left anterior and posterior hemiblock.*[12] However, they are more appropriately termed left anterior-superior fascicular block (LAFB) and left posterior-inferior fascicular block (LPFB). Isolated LAFB, LPFB, or RBBB is considered *unifascicular block.* Complete LBBB or combinations of either RBBB with LAFB or RBBB with LPFB are *bifascicular blocks,* and the combination of RBBB with both LAFB and LPFB is considered *trifascicular block.*

UNIFASCICULAR BLOCKS

 This term is used when there is ECG evidence of blockage of only one of the fascicles. Isolated RBBB or LAFB commonly occur while both left septal and left posterior-inferior fascicular blocks are rare. Rosenbaum et al. identified only 30 patients with LPFB as compared with 900 patients with LAFB.[12]

1. Right Bundle Branch Block

Since the right ventricle contributes minimally to the normal QRS complex, RBBB produces little distortion during the time required for left ventricular activation. Figure 5.6 illustrates the minimal distortion of the early portion and marked distortion of the late portion of the QRS complex that typically occurs with RBBB. The minimal contribution of the normal right ventricular myocardium is completely subtracted from the early portion of the QRS complex and then added later when the right ventricle is activated via the spread of impulses from the left ventricle. This produces a late prominent positive wave in lead V1 termed R′ because it follows the earlier positive R wave produced by normal left to right spread of activation through the interventricular septum (Fig. 5.9 and Table 5.1)

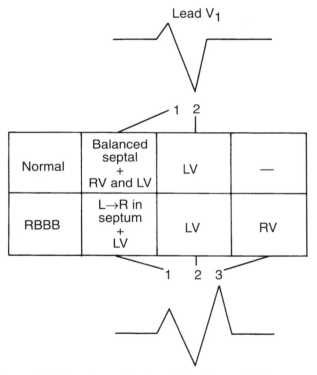

Figure 5.9. The contributions from activation of the interventricular septum and the right and left ventricular free walls to the appearances of the QRS complex in lead V1 are presented during normal conduction (*top*) and RBBB (*bottom*). The *numbers* refer to the first, second, and third sequential 0.04-sec portions of the QRS complex.

Table 5.1. Criteria for Right Bundle Branch Block

Lead V1	Late intrinsicoid, M-shaped QRS (RSR′ variant); sometimes wide R or qR
Lead V6	Early intrinsicoid, wide S wave
Lead 1	Wide S wave

There are many variations in the appearance of RBBB as illustrated by the examples in Figure 5.10, A–C.

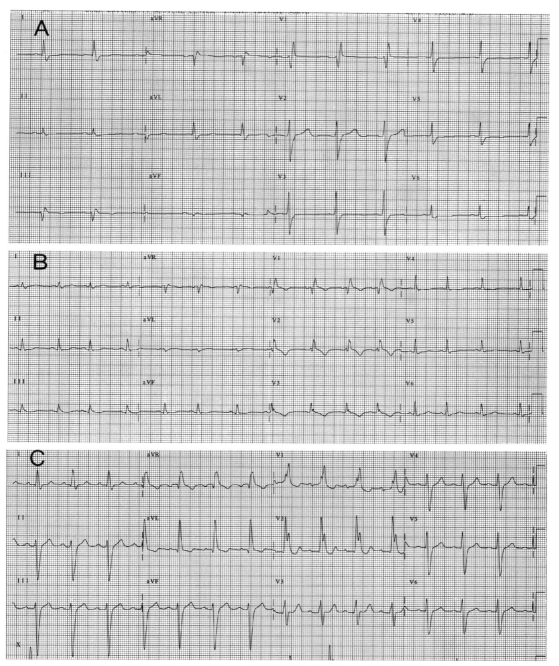

Figure 5.10. Three variations of RBBB. **A.** A 17-year-old girl with ostium secundum atrial septal defect. **B.** An 81-year-old woman with fibrosis of the right bundle branch. **C.** An 82-year-old man with fibrosis of the right bundle branch and the anterior-superior fascicle of the left bundle branch.

2. Left Fascicular Blocks

Normal activation of the left ventricular free wall spreads simultaneously from two sites (near the insertions of the papillary muscles of the mitral valve). Wave fronts of activation spread from these endocardial sites to the overlying epicardium. Since the wave fronts travel in opposite directions, they neutralize each other's influence in a phenomenon called *cancellation*. When block in either the LA or LP fascicle is present, activation of the free wall proceeds from one site instead of two. The cancellation is removed and the waveforms of the QRS complex change, as described below (Fig. 5.11 and Tables 5.2 and 5.3).

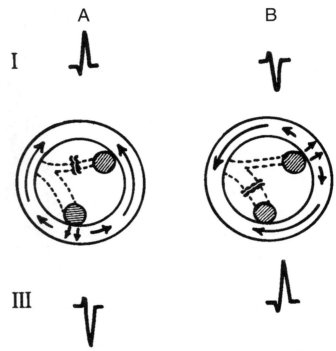

Figure 5.11. The typical appearances of the QRS complexes in leads *I* (*top*) and *III* (*bottom*) are presented for left anterior-superior (**A**) and left posterior-inferior (**B**) fascicular blocks. *Dashed lines* within the inner circles represent the fascicles; *wavy lines* indicate the sites of block. *Small cross-hatched circles* represent the papillary muscles; *outer rings* represent the left ventricular myocardium. *Arrows* within these rings indicate the directions of the wavefronts of activation as they spread from the unblocked fascicles.

Table 5.2.   Criteria for Left Anterior-Superior Fascicular Block

1. Left axis deviation (usually −60°)
2. Small Q in lead 1 and aVL, small R in 2, 3 and aVF
3. Normal QRS duration
4. Late intrinsicoid deflection aVL (>0.045)
5. Increased QRS voltage in limb leads

Table 5.3.   Criteria for Left Posterior-Inferior Fascicular Block

1. Right axis deviation (usually +120°)
2. Small R in lead 1 and aVL, small Q in 2, 3 and aVF
3. Normal QRS duration
4. Late intrinsicoid deflection aVF (>0.045)
5. Increased QRS voltage in limb leads
6. No evidence for right ventricular hypertrophy

A. Left Anterior-Superior Fascicular Block. If the LA fascicles of the LBB are blocked (Fig. 5.12A), the initial activation of the left ventricular free wall occurs via the LP fascicles. Activation spreading from endocardium to epicardium in this region is directed inferiorly and rightward. Since the block in the LA fascicles has removed the competition from activation directed superiorly and leftward, Q waves appear in leads with their positive electrode on the left arm (leads I and aVL). Following this initial period, the activation wave spreads over the remainder of the left ventricular free wall in a superior and leftward direction. This produces prominent R waves in leads I and aVL and prominent S waves in leads II, III, and aVF. Furthermore, it produces a consequent leftward shift of the QRS axis to at least −45°. The overall QRS duration is prolonged by 0.10–0.20 sec (Fig. 5.12B).[14]

LAFB is by far the most commonly occurring conduction abnormality involving the LBB. Its presence was detected in 1.5% of a population of 8000 men, ages 45–69 years.[15]

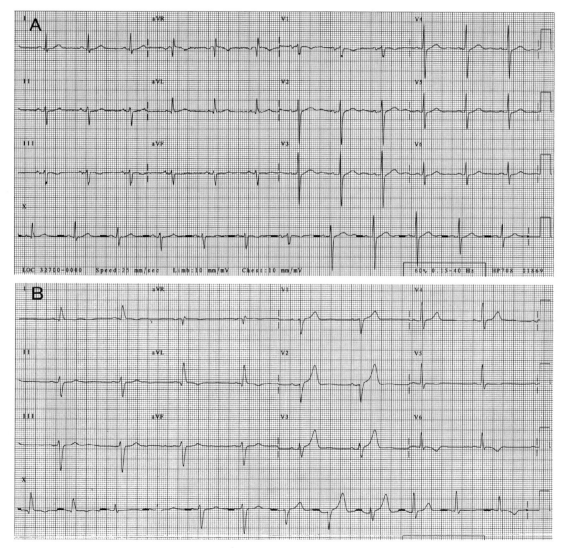

Figure 5.12. Examples of left anterior-superior fascicular block from two elderly individuals. In **A**, there is normal QRS duration and normal T wave appearance; in **B**, the QRS is prolonged to 0.12 sec and the QRS-T angle is increased.

B. Left Posterior-Inferior Fascicular Block.   If the LP fascicles of the LBB are blocked, the situation is reversed. The initial left ventricular free wall activation occurs via the LA fascicles. Activation spreading from endocardium to epicardium in this region is directed superiorly and leftward. Since the block in the LP fascicles has removed the competition provided by activation directed inferiorly and right-ward, Q waves appear in leads with their positive electrode on the left leg (leads II, III, and aVF). Following this initial period, the activation wave spreads over the remainder of the left ventricular free wall in an inferior and rightward direction. This produces prominent R waves in leads II, III, and aVF and prominent S waves in leads I and aVL as well as a consequent rightward shift of the QRS axis to at least +90°.[16] The QRS duration is slightly prolonged as in LAFB (Fig. 5.13).

The diagnosis of LPFB requires that there be no evidence of RVH from either the precordial leads or from other clinical data. This additional criterion is necessary because RVH itself can produce the same pattern in the limb leads as LPFB (Fig. 4.6B).

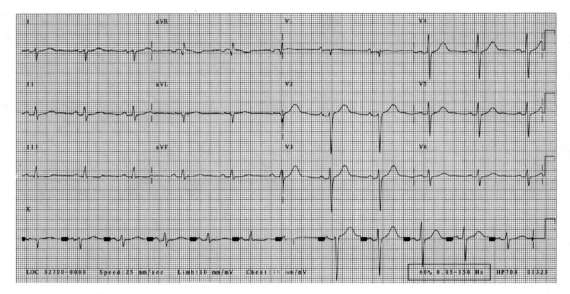

Figure 5.13.   A 73-year-old woman with extreme right axis deviation (RAD), suggesting left posterior-inferior fascicular block.

C. Left Septal Fascicular Block. The LS fascicles of the LBB have the unique responsibility of providing the earliest activation of the ventricles and, therefore, of producing the initial waveform of the QRS complex. This occurs before the left ventricular free wall is activated via the other fascicles. After a short course along the endocardial surface, the LS fascicles activate the myocardium in the middle third of the ventricular septum. The wave front of activation spreads from left to right, producing initial R waves in leads V1 and V2 and Q waves (commonly termed *septal Q waves*) in leads I, aVL, V5, and V6. If the LS fascicles are blocked, the initial activation of the septum occurs via the RBB. This results in right to left spread of the septal activation sequence, producing Q waves in leads V1 and V2 and initial R waves in those leads that normally have septal Q waves.[17] Since the remainder of the left ventricle is activated normally, there is no overall QRS prolongation. Figure 5.14 illustrates the combination of blocks in both the left septal and left anterior-superior fascicles.

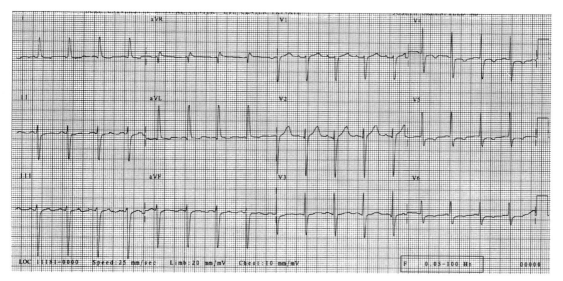

Figure 5.14. An 85-year-old woman with extreme left axis deviation (LAD), suggesting left anterior-superior fascicular block and also a narrow R wave in V1 and Q waves in leads V2 and V3, suggesting left septal fascicular block.

BIFASCICULAR BLOCKS

This term is used when there is ECG evidence of involvement of two of the fascicles discussed above. Such evidence may appear at different times or may coexist on the same ECG. The combination of LS and LA fascicular blocks has occasionally been described,[18] but this combination is not typically considered to be a bifascicular block. That term is sometimes applied to complete LBBB and is commonly applied to the combination of RBBB with either LAFB or LPFB. The term bilateral bundle branch block is also appropriate when RBBB and either LAFB or LPFB are present.[19] When there is bifascicular block, the QRS duration is prolonged to at least 0.12 sec.

1. Left Bundle Branch Block

Figure 5.15 illustrates the marked distortion of the entire QRS complex produced by LBBB. Complete LBBB may be caused by disease either in the main LBB (*predivisional*) or in all of its fascicles (*postdivisional*). When the impulse cannot progress along the LBB, it must first enter the right ventricle and then travel through the interventricular septum to the left ventricle.

Normally, the interventricular septum is activated from left to right, producing an initial R wave in the right precordial leads and a Q wave in leads I, aVL, and the left precordial leads. When complete LBBB is present, the septum is activated from right to left. This produces initial Q waves in the right precordial leads and eliminates the normal Q waves in the leftward oriented leads. The activation of the left ventricle then proceeds sequentially from the interventricular septum to the adjacent anterior-superior and inferior walls to the posterior-lateral free wall. This sequence of ventricular activation in complete LBBB tends to produce monophasic QRS complexes: QS in lead V1, and R in leads I, aVL, and V6 (Table 5.4).

Figure 5.15. The format of Figure 5.9 is repeated to illustrate the contributions from activation of the various aspects of the ventricular myocardium to the appearances of the QRS complex in lead V1 during LBBB.

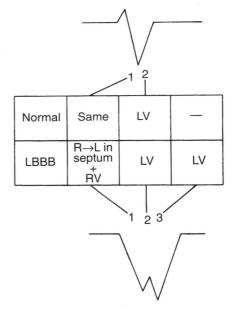

Table 5.4. Criteria for Left Bundle Branch Block

Lead V1	QS or rS
Lead V6	Late intrinsicoid, no Q waves, monophasic R
Lead 1	Monophasic R wave, no Q

There are many variations in the appearance of LBBB as illustrated by the examples in Figure 5.16, *A–C*.

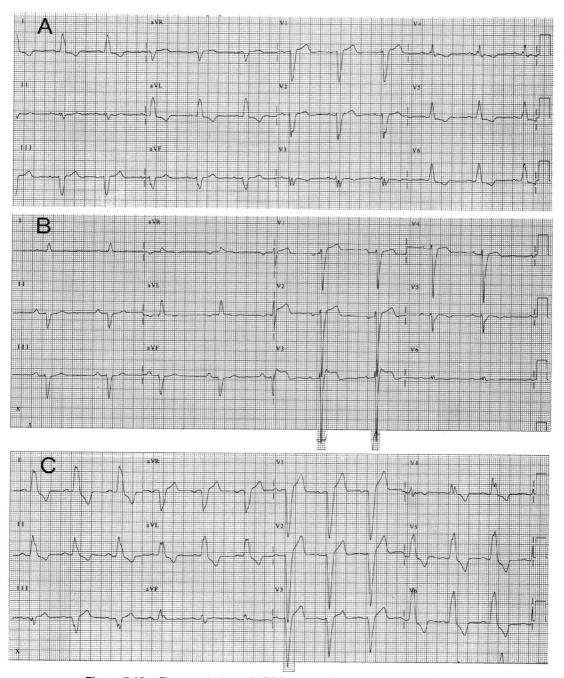

Figure 5.16. Three variations of LBBB. **A.** An 82-year-old woman with typical appearance of LBBB. **B.** A 71-year-old man in whom LAD suggests more delay in the anterior-superior than in the posterior-inferior fascicle. **C.** A 74-year-old man in whom the extremely long QRS duration (0.17 sec) suggests underlying LVH.

2. Right Bundle Branch Block with Left Anterior-Superior Fascicular Block (RBBB + LAFB)

Just as LAFB appears as a unifascicular block much more commonly than LPFB, it more commonly accompanies RBBB as a bifascicular block. The diagnosis is made by observing the late prominent R or R′ wave in precordial lead V1 of RBBB and the initial R waves and the prominent S waves in limb leads II, III, and aVF of LAFB. The QRS duration should be at least 0.12 sec and the frontal plane axis should be between −45 and −120° (Fig. 5.17).[16]

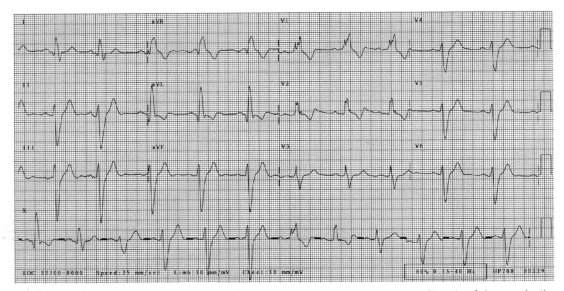

Figure 5.17. A 66-year-old man with RBBB and LAFB due to fibrosis of the conduction system. The markedly prolonged QRS duration (0.20 sec) suggests underlying LVH.

3. Right Bundle Branch Block with Left Posterior-Inferior Fascicular Block (RBBB + LPFB)

This example of bifascicular block rarely occurs. Even when the ECG changes are entirely typical, the diagnosis should be made only if there is no clinical evidence of RVH. The diagnosis of RBBB with LPFB should be considered when there are typical changes in precordial lead V1 of RBBB and the initial R waves and prominent S waves in limb leads I and aVL of LPFB. The QRS duration should be at least 0.12 sec and the frontal plane axis at least +90° (Fig. 5.18).[20]

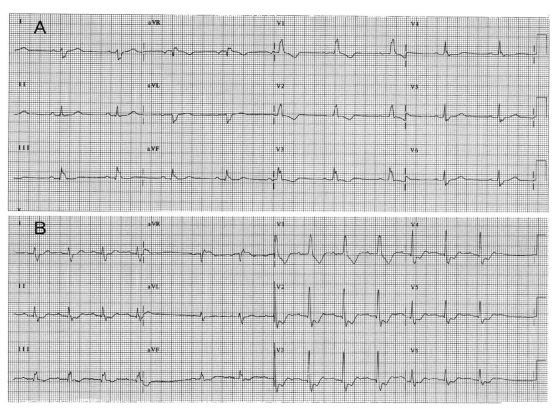

Figure 5.18. A 71-year-old woman (**A**) and a 77-year-old man (**B**) with the combination of RBBB and LPFB presumably due to fibrosis of the conduction system. Note the prolonged PR interval in **B**, suggesting involvement of the left anterior-superior fascicle in addition.

SYSTEMATIC APPROACH TO THE ANALYSIS OF BUNDLE BRANCH AND FASCICULAR BLOCKS

 A. Examine the Contour. RBBB and LBBB have opposite effects on the contour of the QRS complex. RBBB adds a new waveform directed toward the right ventricle following the completion of slightly altered waveforms directed toward the left ventricle. Therefore, the QRS complex in RBBB tends to have a triphasic appearance. In lead V1, which is optimal for visualizing right- versus left-sided conduction delay, this triphasic QRS has the appearance of "rabbit ears" (Figs. 5.1, 5.4, 5.9, and 5.10, A and B). Typically, the "left ear" or R wave is shorter than the "right ear" or R' wave. When the RBBB is accompanied by block in one of the LBB fascicles, the positive deflection in V1 is often monophasic as in Figures 5.10C, 5.17, and 5.18.

LBBB replaces the competing simultaneous spreads of activation through the interventricular septum and LV free wall with a sequential spread of activation through these areas. Therefore, the QRS complex tends to have a monophasic appearance that is notched rather than smooth.

Though there are many similarities between LBB and LVH, there are also marked differences. Whereas the normal Q waves over the left ventricle may be present or even exaggerated in LVH, they are absent in LBBB. When the LBB is completely blocked, the septum is entirely activated from its right side. Figure 5.19 illustrates the appearance of incomplete (B) and complete (C) LBBB in a patient with LVH (A).

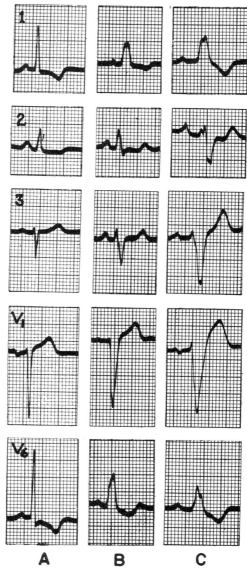

Figure 5.19. **A–C** illustrate the evolving ECG changes in a patient with severe hypertension as the LVH is complicated by LBBB.

B. Measure the Duration. The QRS duration is increased by 0.03–0.04 sec by complete RBBB and by 0.04–0.05 sec by complete LBBB. Block within the LA or LP fascicles of the LBB usually prolongs the duration of the QRS complex by only 0.01–0.02 sec (Figs. 5.13 and 5.14).[14]

C. Measure the Maximal Amplitude. BBB produces QRS waveforms with lower voltage and more definite notching than those that occur with ventricular hypertrophy. However, the amplitude of the QRS complex does increase in LBBB because of the relatively unopposed spread of activation over the left ventricle.

One general rule for differentiating between LBBB and LVH is that the greater the QRS amplitude, the more likely the cause is LVH. Similarly, the greater the QRS prolongation, the more likely the cause is LBBB. Klein et al.[21] have suggested that in the presence of LBBB either of the following criteria are associated with LVH:

1. SV2 + RV6 > 45 mm
2. Evidence of LAE with QRS duration > 0.16 sec

D. Estimate the Direction in the Two Planes. Since complete RBBB and complete LBBB alter conduction to entire ventricles, they might not be expected to produce much net alteration of the frontal plane QRS axis. However, Rosenbaum studied patients with intermittent LBBB in which blocked and unblocked complexes could be examined side by side.[14] LBBB was often observed to produce significant left axis shift and sometimes even right axis shift. The axis was unchanged in only a minority.

However, block in either the anterior-superior or posterior-inferior fascicles of the LBB alone produces marked axis deviation. The initial 0.20 sec of the QRS complex is directed away, and the middle and late portions are directed toward, the blocked fascicles, causing the overall QRS direction to be directed toward the site of the block (Figs. 5.13 and 5.14).[16] When block in either of these LBB fascicles is accompanied by RBBB, an even later waveform is added to the QRS complex, thereby further prolonging its duration. The direction of this final waveform in the frontal plane is in the vicinity of +180° caused by the RBBB (Fig. 5.10).[16]

In BBB, the T wave is usually directed opposite to the later portion of the QRS complex (e.g., in Figure 5.20A, the T wave in lead I is inverted and the later part of the QRS is upright; in Figure 5.20B, the T wave is upright and the later part of the QRS is negative). This opposite polarity is the natural result of the depolarization-repolarization disturbance produced by LBBB and the T wave changes. Therefore, it is termed *secondary*. Indeed, if the direction of the T wave is similar to that of the terminal part of the QRS (Fig. 5.20C), it should be considered abnormal. Such T wave changes are *primary* and they imply myocardial disease. The diagnosis of myocardial infarction in the presence of BBB is considered in Chapter 6.

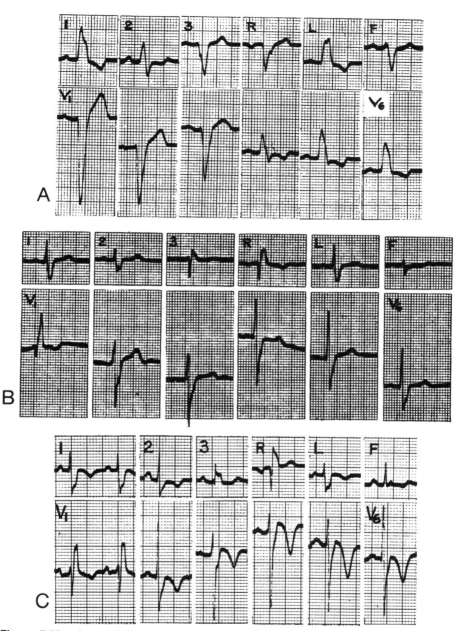

Figure 5.20. **A** and **B** illustrate the opposite directions of the latter portion of the QRS complexes and the T waves of the typical "secondary T wave changes" that occur with both LBBB (**A**) and RBBB (**B**). In contrast, **C** illustrates the similar directions of the latter portion of the QRS complexes and the T waves of the "primary T wave changes" that occur with RBBB.

One method of gauging the prognostic severity of T wave changes in BBB is to measure the angle between the axis of the T wave and that of the terminal part of the QRS complex. Obviously, if the two are oppositely directed (as they are with secondary T wave changes), the angle between them will be wide and may approach 180°. It is proposed that, if this angle is more than 110°, serious organic heart disease is indicated. In Figure 5.20B, the angle is about 165°, whereas in Figure 5.20C, it is only a few degrees, with each axis being close to 180°.

GLOSSARY

Bifascicular block: an intraventricular conduction abnormality involving two of the three of: the right bundle branch, the anterior-superior division of the left bundle branch, the posterior-inferior division of the left bundle branch

Bilateral bundle branch block: an intraventricular conduction abnormality involving both the right and left bundle branch, as indicated either by presence of some conducted beats with RBBB and others with LBBB, or by AV block located distal to the common bundle.

Bradycardia-dependent BBB: right or left BBB that is intermittent, appearing only with a slowing of the atrial rate.

Cancellation: since the ECG waveforms represent the summation of the wavefronts of activation and recovery within the heart, an abnormality produced by a particular cardiac problem may be removed or "cancelled" by a similar abnormality in a distant part of the heart or a different abnormality in the same part of the heart.

Chagas disease: a tropical disease that is caused by a flagellate of the genus *Trypanosoma (T. cruzi)* and is marked by prolonged high fever, edema, and enlargement of the spleen, liver, and lymph nodes, and complicated by cardiac involvement.

Left anterior fascicular block: term applied by Rosenbaum and coworkers to a conduction abnormality in the anterior-superior fascicle of the left bundle branch.

Left posterior fascicular block: term applied by Rosenbaum and coworkers to a conduction abnormality in the posterior-inferior fascicle of the left bundle branch.

Lenègre's (Lev's) disease: both Lenègre and Lev described variations of fibrosis of the intraventricular Purkinje fibers in the absence of other significant cardiac disease.

Predivisional and postdivisional: block within the LBB either "pre" proximal to its division into fascicles, or "post" involving both the anterior-superior and posterior-inferior fascicles.

Primary and secondary T wave changes: in the presence of RBBB or LBBB, "primary T wave changes" refers to abnormal T waves that are directed similarly to the latter portion of the QRS complex, and "secondary T wave changes" refers to normal T waves that are directed opposite to the latter portion of the QRS complex.

Refractory period: time following electrical activation during which a cardiac cell cannot be reactivated.

RR interval: the time between successive QRS complexes.

Septal Q wave: normal initial negative QRS waveform that appears in leftward oriented ECG leads because of earliest activation of the interventricular septum via the septal fascicles of the LBB.

Swan-Ganz catheter: a flexible catheter with a balloon tip that is used for measuring pressure and oxygen saturation in the pulmonary circulation.

Tachycardia-dependent BBB: right or left BBB that is intermittent, appearing only with an acceleration of the atrial rate.

Trifascicular block: an intraventricular conduction abnormality involving the right bundle branch and both the anterior-superior and posterior-inferior fascicles of the left bundle branch.

Unifascicular block: an intraventricular conduction abnormality involving only one of the three principal fascicles of the intraventricular Purkinje system.

REFERENCES

1. Hiss RG, Lamb LE. Electrocardiographic findings in 122,043 individuals. Circulation 1962;25:947.
2. Lenègre J. Etiology and pathology of bilateral bundle branch block in relation to complete heart block. Progr Cardiovasc Dis 1964;6:409.
3. Lev M. Anatomic basis for atrioventricular block. Am J Med 1964;37:742.
4. Rotman M, Triebwasser JH. A clinical and follow-up study of right and left bundle branch block. Circulation 1975;51:477.
5. Schneider JF, Thomas HE, McNamara PM, Kannel WB. Clinical-electrocardiographic correlates of newly acquired left bundle branch block: the Framingham study. Am J Cardiol 1985;55:1332.
6. Lasser RP, Haft JI, Friedberg CK. Relationship of right bundle-branch block and marked left axis deviation (with left parietal of peri-infarction block) to complete heart block and syncope. Circulation 1968; 47:429–437.
7. Pick A, Langendorf R. Interpretation of complex arrhythmias. Philadelphia: Lea & Febiger, 1979: 314–317.
8. Acquatella H, Catalioti F, Comez-Mancebo JR, Davalos V, Villalobos L. Long term control of Chagas disease in Venezuela: effects on serologic findings, electrocardiographic abnormalities and clinical outcome. Circulation 1987;76:556–562.
9. Hindman MC, Wagner GS, JaRo M, Atkins JM, Scheinman MM, DeSanctis RW, Hutter AH, Yeatman L, Rubenfire M, Pujura C, Rubin M, Morris JJ. The clinical side of bundle branch block complicating acute myocardial infarction. I. Clinical characteristics, hospital mortality, and one year follow-up. Circulation 1978;58:679.
10. Wellens HJJ, Lie KI, Janse MJ, eds. The conduction system of the heart: structure, function and clinical implications. The Hague: Martinus Nijhoff, 1978:287–295.
11. Demoulin JC, Kulbertus HE. Histopathological examination of concept of left hemiblock. Br Heart J 1972;34:807.
12. Rosenbaum MB, Elizari MV, Lazzari JO. The hemiblocks. Oldsmar, FL: Tampa Tracings, 1970.
13. Papa LA, Scariato A, Gottlieb R, Duca P, Kasparian H. Coronary angiographic assessment of left posterior hemiblock. J Electrocardiol 1983;16:297.
14. Rosenbaum MB. Types of left bundle branch block and their clinical significance. J Electrocardiol 1969;2:197.
15. Yano K, Peskoe SM, Rhoads GG, Moore JO, Kagan A. Left axis deviation and left anterior hemiblock among 8,000 Japanese-American men. Am J Cardiol 1975;35:809.
16. Rosenbaum MB. The hemiblocks: diagnostic criteria and clinical significance. Mod Concepts Cardiovasc Dis 1970;39:141–146.
17. Gambetta M, Childers RW. Rate-dependent right precordial Q waves: "septal fascical block." Am J Cardiol 1973;32:196.
18. Hassett MA, Williams RR, Wagner GS. Transient QRS changes simulating myocardial infarction. Circulation 1980;62:975–979.
19. Hindman MC, Wagner GS, JaRo M, Atkins JM, Scheinman MM, De Sanctis RW, Hutter AH, Yeatman L, Rubenfire M, Pujura C, Rubin M, Morris JJ. The clinical side of bundle branch block complicating acute myocardial infarction. II. Indications for temporary and permanent insertion. Circulation 1978;58:689–699.
20. Willems JL, Robles De Medina EO, Bernard R, Coumel P, Fisch C, Krikler D, Mazur NA, Meijler FL, Mogensen L, Moret P, Pisa Z, Rautaharju PM, Surawicz B, Watanabe Y, Wellens HJJ. Criteria for intraventricular-conduction disturbances and pre-excitation. J Am Coll Cardiol 1985;5:1261–1275.
21. Klein RC, Vera Z, DeMaria AN, Mason DT. Electrocardiographic diagnosis of left ventricular hypertrophy in the presence of left bundle branch block. Am Heart J 1984;108:502.

CHAPTER 6

Ventricular Preexcitation

HISTORICAL PERSPECTIVE

In 1930, Wolff and White in Boston and Parkinson in London published their research of a combined series of 11 patients with bizarre ventricular complexes and short PR intervals titled "Bundle Branch Block with Short PR Interval".[1] In 1893, Kent had described muscular connections between the atria and ventricles but wrongly assumed that they represented pathways of normal conduction from the atria to the ventricles (Fig. 6.1).[2] Mines suggested that this *bundle of Kent* might mediate reentering tachycardias in 1914. Finally, in 1914 Segers connected the short PR interval, widened QRS complex with a prolonged upstroke, and tachyarrhythmia into the Wolff-Parkinson-White syndrome (*WPW syndrome*). This syndrome was caused by *ventricular preexcitation* via a bundle of Kent. He termed the prolonged upstroke of the QRS complex a *delta wave*.

In 1952, Lown and coworkers published a study of the relationship between a short PR interval but normal QRS complex on the ECG and the presence of tachyarrhythmias.[3] This combination has since been termed the *LGL syndrome*. The possible existence of a preexcitation pathway directly entering the common bundle rather than the ventricular myocardium was considered. However, electrophysiologic studies have revealed that there is typically a less-than-normal delay in the AV node rather than an AV nodal bypass tract.

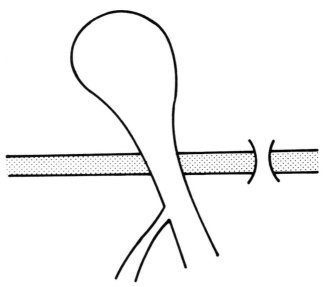

Figure 6.1. The anatomic relationship between the normal AV conduction system and the accessory AV conduction pathway provided by the "bundle of Kent" is illustrated schematically. The *solid bar* represents the nonconducting structures that prevent conduction of the electrical impulses from the atrial myocardium to the ventricular myocardium.

CLINICAL PERSPECTIVE

 Ventricular preexcitation refers to a congenital cardiac abnormality in which a part of the ventricular myocardium receives electrical activation from the atria prior to the time of arrival of an impulse via the normal AV conduction system. Atrioventricular myocardial bundles commonly exist during fetal life, but then disappear by the time of birth.[4] When even a single myocardial connection persists, there is the potential for ventricular preexcitation. In some individuals, evidence of preexcitation may not appear until late in life. In other individuals with lifelong ECG evidence of ventricular preexcitation, the WPW syndrome may not occur until late in life. Conversely, infants with the WPW syndrome may outgrow any or all evidence of this abnormality within a few years.[5] Figure 6.2 illustrates the contrast between the alteration of the PR and QRS intervals that results from BBB and from ventricular preexcitation.

Figure 6.2. The two types of altered or "aberrant" conduction from the atria to the ventricles are presented. Right or left bundle branch block (**A**) does not alter the PR interval but prolongs the QRS complex by delaying the activation of one of the ventricles. Ventricular preexcitation (**B**) shortens the PR interval and produces a "delta wave" in the initial part of the QRS complex.

The total time from the beginning of the P wave to the end of the QRS complex remains the same because conduction via the abnormal pathway does not interfere with conduction via the normal AV conduction system. Therefore, before the entire ventricular myocardium can be activated by the progression of the preexcitation wave front, electrical impulses from the normal conducting system arrive to activate the remainder of the ventricular myocardium. The mass of right and left ventricular myocardium is activated from two sources as indicated in Figure 6.3: (*a*) via the preexcitation pathway; and (*b*) via the normal AV conduction pathway. The resultant abnormal QRS complex is termed a *fusion beat*.

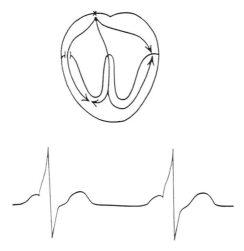

Figure 6.3. The relationship between the anatomic presence of a Kent bundle and the physiologic preexcitation of the ventricular myocardium is illustrated at the *top*. The typical ECG changes of ventricular preexcitation are presented at the *bottom*. (From Wagner GS, Waugh RA, Ramo BW. Cardiac arrhythmias. New York: Churchill Livingstone, 1983:13.)

The ECG of an individual with ventricular preexcitation is abnormal in several ways:

1. In the presence of a normal sinus rhythm, the PR interval is abnormally short and the QRS duration abnormally prolonged. There is a prolonged upstroke of the QRS complex, which has been termed a delta wave (Fig. 6.4).

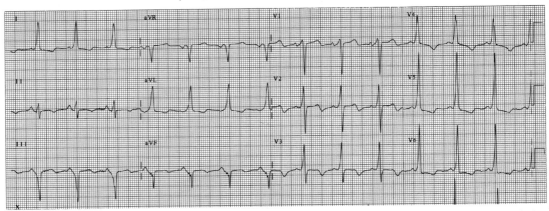

Figure 6.4. ECG recording of a 67-year-old woman with ventricular preexcitation during sinus rhythm.

2. In the presence of an atrial tachyarrhythmia, such as atrial flutter/fibrillation (Chapter 15, "Atrial Flutter/Fibrillation Spectrum"), the ventricular rate also becomes rapid. The ventricles are no longer "protected" by the slowly conducting AV node (Fig. 6.5).

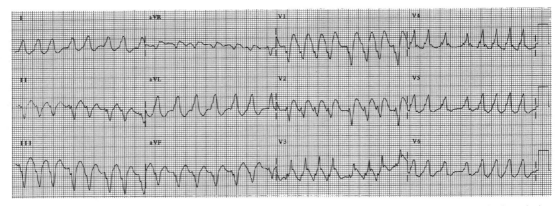

Figure 6.5. ECG recording of a 24-year-old woman with ventricular preexcitation during atrial fibrillation. On the lead V1 rhythm strip (*bottom*), the irregularities of both the ventricular rate and QRS morphology are apparent.

3. The abnormal AV muscular connection completes a circuit by providing a pathway for electrical reactivation of the atria from the ventricles. This circuit provides a continuous loop for the electrical current, which may result in a single premature beat or a prolonged, regular, rapid atrial and ventricular rate called a *tachyarrhythmia* (Fig. 6.6).

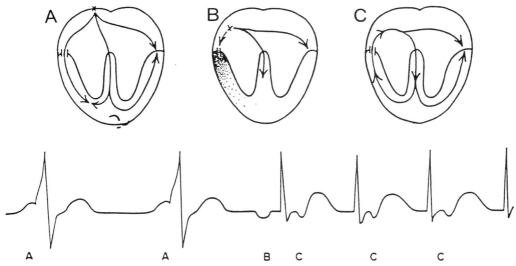

Figure 6.6. The schematic illustration from Figure 6.3 is repeated on the *left* (**A**). In **B**, an atrial premature beat occurs before the Kent bundle has completed its period of refractoriness following the previous sinus beat, preventing antegrade ventricular preexcitation. Normal ventricular activation is then followed by retrograde atrial excitation (**C**). The resultant macroreentrant circuit forms the basis for the tachyarrhythmia. (From Wagner GS, Waugh RA, Ramo BW. Cardiac arrhythmias. New York: Churchill Livingstone, 1983:13.)

The influence of the presence of ventricular preexcitation on the ventricular rate during atrial flutter/fibrillation and on accessory pathway-induced tachyarrhythmias is discussed in Chapters 15 and 16 ("Reentrant Junctional Tachycardias"), respectively. The combination of PR interval <0.12 sec, a delta wave at the beginning of the QRS complex, and a rapid, regular tachyarrhythmia has been termed the Wolff-Parkinson-White (WPW) syndrome.

The PR interval is short because the descending electrical impulse bypasses the normal AV nodal conduction delay. The delta wave is produced by slow intramyocardial conduction that results when the impulse, instead of being delivered to the ventricular myocardium via the normal conduction system, is delivered directly into the ventricular myocardium via an abnormal or "anomalous" bundle. The QRS duration is prolonged because it begins too early in contrast to the situations presented in Chapters 4 ("Chamber Enlargement") and 5 ("Intraventricular Conduction Abnormalities"), where the QRS duration is prolonged because it ends too late. The ventricles are activated successively rather than simultaneously: the preexcited ventricle via the bundle of Kent and then the other ventricle via the normal AV node and His-Purkinje system (Fig. 6.3).

Various terms have been applied to the abnormal anatomic structure and resulting abnormal electrophysiologic function responsible for the WPW syndrome:

Anatomic Structure	Electrophysiologic Function
Myocardial bundle	Ventricular preexcitation
Bundle of Kent	Accessory conduction pathway
Bypass tract	AV nodal bypass pathway

ECG DIAGNOSIS OF VENTRICULAR PREEXCITATION

 Typically, the PR interval is less than 0.12 sec and the QRS complex is greater than 0.10 sec. However, when ventricular preexcitation is present, the PR interval is not always abnormally short and the QRS duration is not always abnormally prolonged (Fig. 6.7A). Of almost 600 patients with documented ventricular preexcitation, 25% had PR intervals of 0.12 sec or longer and 25% had QRS duration of 0.10 sec or shorter (Fig. 6.7B).[6]

When the presence of ventricular preexcitation is suspected in a patient with tachyarrhythmias but no ECG evidence, various diagnostic procedures may be helpful:

1. Pace the atria electronically at increasingly rapid rates to induce conduction via any existing accessory pathway.
2. Produce vagal nerve stimulation to impair normal conduction through the AV node to induce conduction via any existing accessory pathway.
3. Infuse digoxin intravenously for the same purpose as in procedure 2.

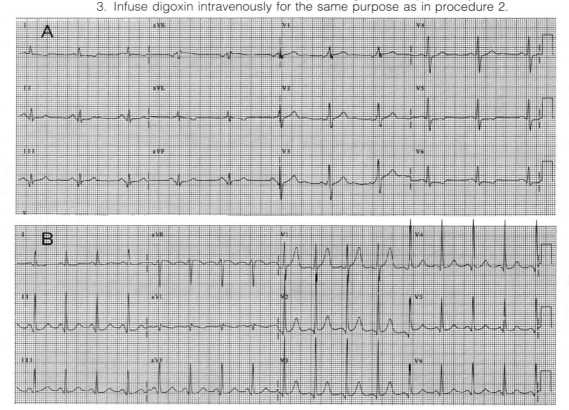

Figure 6.7. Two examples of atypical appearances of ventricular preexcitation in elderly individuals. In **A**, note the normal PR interval of 0.14 sec preceding the prolonged QRS complex; in **B**, note the normal QRS duration of 0.09 sec following the shortened PR interval.

Ventricular preexcitation may mimic a number of other cardiac abnormalities. When there is a wide, positive QRS complex in leads V1 and V2, it may simulate right bundle branch block, right ventricular hypertrophy, or a posterior myocardial infarction. When there is a wide, negative QRS complex in lead V1 or V2, preexcitation may be mistaken for left bundle branch block (Fig. 6.8A) or even left ventricular hypertrophy (Fig. 6.8B). A negative delta wave, producing Q waves in the appropriate leads, may imitate anterior, lateral, or inferior infarction. The QS complex in lead V1 in Figure 6.8B could be mistaken for anterior infarction. The deep, wide Q waves in leads II, III, and aVF in Fig. 6.8C are suggestive of inferior infarction.

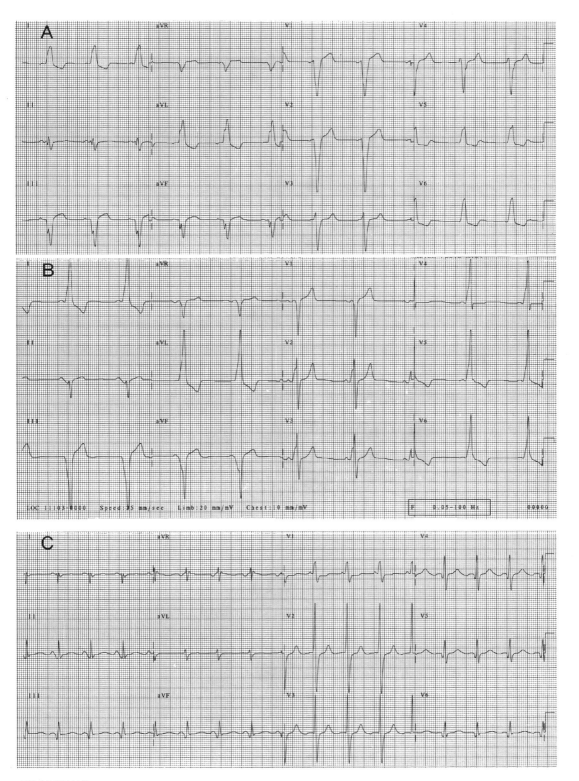

Figure 6.8. Examples from young adults with ventricular preexcitation producing QRS complexes that mimic bundle branch block (**A**), and myocardial infarcts (**B** and **C**).

ECG LOCALIZATION OF THE PREEXCITATION PATHWAY

 There have been many attempts to determine the myocardial location of ventricular preexcitation according to the direction of the delta waves on the various ECG leads. Rosenbaum and colleagues[7] divided patients into groups A and B on the basis of the direction of the "main deflection of the QRS complex" in the transverse plane leads V1 and V2.

ECG Appearance	Location of Abnormal Pathway
Group A: QRS mainly positive leads V1 and V2	LA-LV
Group B: QRS mainly negative leads V1 and V2	RA-RV

Other classification systems considered the direction of only the abnormal delta wave in attempting to better localize the preexcitation pathway. Since curative surgical and ablative techniques have become available, more precise localization of the accessory pathway is clinically important.[8] Many additional ECG criteria have been proposed. However, precise localization is made difficult by several factors: minor degrees of preexcitation, the presence of more than one accessory pathway, QRS distortions caused by superimposed myocardial infarction, or ventricular hypertrophy. Nevertheless, Milstein and his associates[9] devised the algorithm presented in Figure 6.9 that enabled them to correctly identify the location of 90% of over 140 accessory pathways.

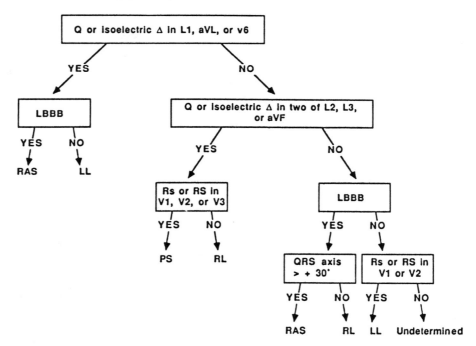

Figure 6.9. Milstein's algorithm for localization of accessory pathways. Note: For purposes of this schema, *LBBB* indicates a positive QRS in lead 1 with duration of at least 0.09 sec with rS complexes in leads V1 and V2. *RAS*, right anteroseptal; *LL*, left lateral; *PS*, posteroseptal; *RL*, right lateral. (From Milstein S, Sharma AD, Guiraudon GM, Klein GJ. An algorithm for the electrocardiographic localization of accessory pathways in the Wolff-Parkinson-White syndrome. Pace 1987;10:555.)

Although accessory pathways may be found anywhere in the connective tissue between the atria and ventricles, nearly all are found in three general locations:

1. Laterally between the left atrial and left ventricular free walls (50%);
2. Posteriorly between the atrial and ventricular septa (30%);
3. Laterally between the right atrial and right ventricular free walls or anteriorly near the pulmonary artery (20%).

Tonkin et al. presented a simple method for localizing accessory pathways in one of these areas based on the direction of the delta wave (Fig. 6.10).[10] They used a point 0.02 sec after the onset of the delta wave in the QRS complex as their reference.

Postion of the Delta Wave at QRS Onset + 0.02 sec	Location of the Preexcitation Pathway	Incidence Correct
Rightward	LA-LV free wall	10 of 10
Leftward and superior	Posterior septal	9 of 10
Leftward and inferior	RA-RV free wall[a]	6 of 7

[a]In two of the patients with leftward and inferior delta waves, the accessory pathway was located markedly anterior in the vicinity of the pulmonary artery.

Approximately 10% of the patients with preexcitation have multiple accessory pathways. The most common combination of locations is the posterior septum and RA-RV free wall.

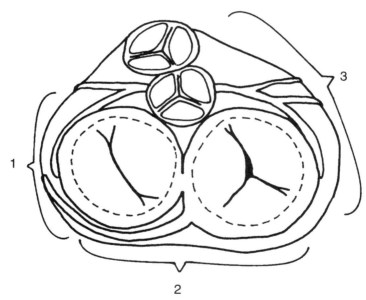

2

Figure 6.10. A schematic view (from above) of a cross-section of the heart at the junction between the atria and the ventricles. The ventricular outflow aortic and pulmonary valves are located anteriorly, and the ventricular inflow mitral (bicuspid) and tricuspid valves posteriorly. The three general locations of Kent bundles are: *1*, LA-LV free wall; *2*, posterior septal; and *3*, the right anteroseptal and right lateral locations of Milstein et al. combined as "RA-RV free wall." (Modified from Tonkin AM, Wagner GS, Gallagher JJ, Cope GD, Kasell J, Wallace AG. Initial forces of ventricular depolarization in the Wolff-Parkinson-White syndrome. Analysis based upon localization of the accessory pathway by epicardial mapping. Circulation 1975;52:1031.)

ABLATION OF ACCESSORY PATHWAYS

Figures 6.11A and 6.12A illustrate the typical appearances of preexcitation of the right ventricular free wall and the interventricular septum, respectively. Successful ablation of the accessory pathways revealed the presence of LVH (Fig. 6.11B) and the absence of an inferior infarction (Fig. 6.12B).

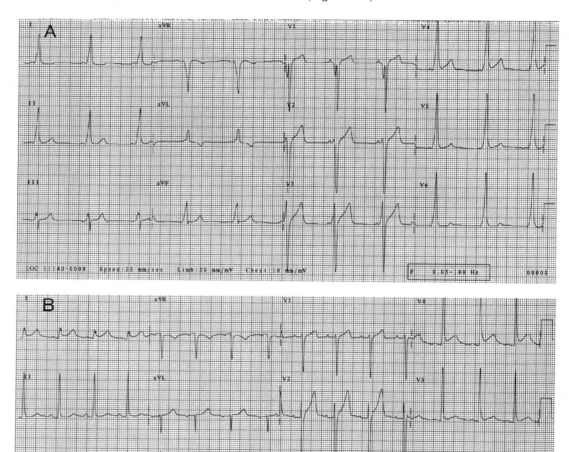

Figure 6.11. ECG recordings of a 17-year-old boy from before (**A**) and after (**B**) ablation of a preexcitation pathway connecting his right atrium and ventricle.

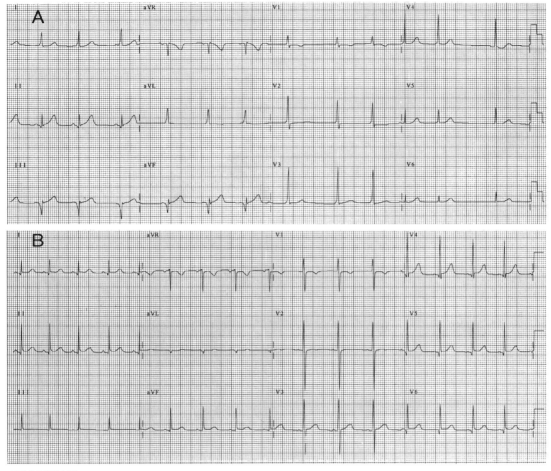

Figure 6.12. ECG recordings from a 35-year-old man from before (**A**) and after (**B**) ablation of a posterior septal preexcitation pathway.

GLOSSARY

Bundle of Kent: a congenital abnormality in which a bundle of myocardial fibers connects the atria and the ventricles.

Delta wave: a slowing of the initial aspect of the QRS complex caused by premature excitation (preexcitation) of the ventricles via a bundle of Kent.

Fusion beat: the ventricles are activated by two different wave fronts, resulting in abnormal appearance of the QRS complexes.

LGL syndrome: the clinical combination of a short PR interval, normal QRS appearance, and supraventricular tachyarrhythmias.

Tachyarrhythmia: an abnormal cardiac rhythm with a ventricular rate $\geq$ 100 beats/min.

Ventricular preexcitation: premature activation of the ventricular myocardium via an abnormal AV pathway called a bundle of Kent.

WPW syndrome: the clinical combination of a short PR interval, an increased QRS duration caused by an initial slow deflection (delta wave), and supraventricular tachyarrhythmias.

REFERENCES

1. Wolff L. Syndrome of short P-R interval with abnormal QRS complexes and paroxysmal tachycardia (Wolff-Parkinson-White syndrome). Circulation 1954;10:282.
2. Kent AFS. Researches on the structure and function of the mammalian heart. J Physiol 1893;14:233.
3. Lown B, Ganong WF, Levine SA. The syndrome of the short P-R interval, normal QRS complex and paroxysmal rapid heart action. Circulation 1952;5:693.
4. Becker AE, Anderson RH, Durrer D, Wellens HJJ. The anatomical substrates of Wolff-Parkinson-White syndrome. Circulation 1978;57:870.
5. Giardina ACV, Ehlers KH, Engle MA. Wolff-Parkinson-White syndrome in infarcts and children: a long term follow up study. Br Heart J 1972;34:839.
6. Sherf L, Neufeld NH. The preexcitation syndrome: fact and theories. New York: Yorke Medical Books, 1978.
7. Rosenbaum FF, Hecht HH, Wilson FN, Johnston FD. Potential variations of thorax and esophagus in anomalous atrioventricular excitation (Wolff-Parkinson-White syndrome). Am Heart J 1945;29:281–326.
8. Gallagher JJ, Gilbert M, Svenson RH, Sealy WC, Kasell J, Wallace AG. Wolff-Parkinson-White syndrome: the problem, evaluation, and surgical correction. Circulation 1975;51:767.
9. Milstein S, Sharma AD, Guiraudon GM, Klein GJ. An algorithm for the electrocardiographic localization of accessory pathways in the Wolff-Parkinson-White syndrome. Pace 1987;10:555.
10. Tonkin AM, Wagner GS, Gallagher JJ, Cope GD, Kasell J, Wallace AG. Initial forces of ventricular depolarization in the Wolff-Parkinson-White syndrome: analysis based upon localization of the accessory pathway by epicardial mapping. Circulation 1975;52:1030–1036.

CHAPTER 7

Myocardial Ischemia and Infarction

INTRODUCTION TO ISCHEMIA AND INFARCTION

 The energy required to maintain the cardiac cycle is obtained via a process, known as *aerobic metabolism*, in which oxygen and glucose are used. These nutrients are retrieved by the myocardial cells from the blood, primarily supplied by the coronary arteries. If the blood supply becomes insufficient, causing an inadequate oxygen supply, an energy deficiency occurs. To compensate for diminished aerobic metabolism, the myocardial cells must use a different metabolic process, *anaerobic metabolism*, in which oxygen is not required. In this process, the cells use their reserve supplies of glucose stored in glycogen molecules to generate energy in a process in which oxygen is not needed. This process, however, is less efficient and can be sustained only for a limited time.

During the period of time that the availability of oxygen is not sufficient to meet the myocardial demand, the myocardial cells become ischemic. In order to sustain themselves, myocardial cells with an energy deficiency must uncouple their electrical activation from mechanical contraction and remain in their resting state. Thus, the area of the myocardium that is ischemic is unable to participate in the pumping process.[1,2]

Various areas of the myocardium are more or less susceptible to ischemia. There are several determining factors:

1. Proximity to the Intracavitary Blood Supply

The internal layers of myocardial cells, or endocardium, have a secondary source of nutrients, the intracavitary blood, which provides protection from ischemia.[3,4] The entire myocardium of the right and left atria has so few cell layers that it is essentially endocardium (Fig. 7.1). In the ventricles, only the innermost cell layers are similarly protected. The Purkinje system is located in these layers and, therefore, is relatively well protected against ischemia.[5]

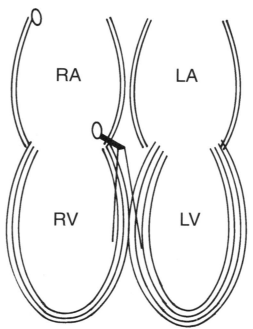

Figure 7.1. The relative thicknesses of the myocardium in the four cardiac chambers are compared schematically. The ovals indicate the locations of the SA and AV nodes; the common bundle and right and left bundle branches descend from the AV node into the interventricular septum. (Modified from Wagner GS, Waugh RA, Ramo BW. Cardiac arrhythmias. New York: Churchill Livingstone, 1983:2.)

2. Distance from the Major Coronary Arteries

The ventricles consist of multiple myocardial layers that depend on the coronary arteries for their blood supply. These arteries arise from the aorta and course along the epicardial surfaces before penetrating the thickness of the myocardium where they pass sequentially through the epicardial, middle, and subendocardial layers. Since the subendocardial layer is the most distant, it is the most susceptible to ischemia.[6]

3. Workload as Indicated by the Pressure Required to Pump Blood

The greater the pressure required by a cardiac chamber to pump blood, the greater its workload and the greater its metabolic demand for oxygen. The myocardial workload is smallest in the atria, intermediate in the right ventricle, and greatest in the left ventricle. Therefore, the susceptibility to ischemia is also lowest in the atria, intermediate in the right ventricle, and greatest in the left ventricle.

Ischemia is a *relative* condition that depends on the balance among the coronary blood supply, the level of oxygenation of the blood, and the myocardial workload. Theoretically, an individual with normal coronary arteries and fully oxygenated blood could develop *myocardial ischemia* if the workload were increased either by an extremely elevated arterial blood pressure or an extremely high heart rate. Alternatively, an individual with normal coronary arteries and a normal myocardial workload could develop ischemia if the blood oxygenation became extremely diminished. Conversely, someone with severe narrowings (stenoses) in all coronary arteries might never become ischemic if the workload remained low and the blood was well oxygenated.

When myocardial ischemia is produced by an increased workload, it is normally reversed by returning to the resting state before the reserve supply of glycogen is entirely depleted. However, a condition that produces myocardial ischemia by decreasing the coronary blood supply may not be reversed so easily.

Coronary arteries may gradually become partially obstructed by plaques in the chronic process of *atherosclerosis*. When this occurs, myocardial blood supply is sufficient at a resting workload, but may become insufficient, resulting in ischemia, when the workload is increased by either emotional or physical stress. The gradual progression of the atherosclerotic process is accompanied by growth of collateral arteries, which supply blood to the myocardium beyond the level of the obstruction. Indeed, these collaterals may be sufficient to entirely replace the native artery if it becomes completely obstructed by the atherosclerotic plaque.[7]

Partially obstructed atherosclerotic coronary arteries may suddenly become completely obstructed by the acute processes of either spasm of their smooth muscle layer or thrombosis within the remaining lumen.[8,9] Ischemia develops immediately unless the resting metabolic demands can be satisfied by the collateral blood flow. If the spasm is relaxed or the thrombus is resolved (lysis) before the glycogen reserve is severely depleted, the cells promptly resume their contraction. However, if the acute, complete obstruction continues until the glycogen is severely depleted, the myocardial cells become *stunned*.[10] Even after blood flow is restored, the cells are unable to resume contraction until they have repleted their glycogen reserves. Stunned myocardial cells remain in their resting state even when they are no longer ischemic until they have repleted their glycogen reserve. If the complete obstruction continues until the glycogen is entirely depleted, the myocardial cells are unable to sustain themselves, are irreversibly damaged, and become necrotic or infarcted. This clinical process is termed a heart attack or *myocardial infarction* (MI).

ECG CHANGES DURING MYOCARDIAL ISCHEMIA

 The process of electrical recovery is more susceptible to ischemia than that of electrical activation. Since ischemia caused by an increase in myocardial demand is not as profound as that caused by a complete cessation of coronary blood supply, it is manifested on the ECG only by primary changes in the waveforms representing the recovery process—the ST segments and T waves. The more profound ischemia that occurs when there is complete cessation of coronary blood supply is also manifested by primary changes in the QRS complexes and by unique changes in the ST segments and T waves (Table 7.1).[11,12]

Table 7.1

Cause of Ischemia	Electrical Process Primarily Affected	ECG Waveforms Altered
Increased demand	Recovery	ST segment, T wave
Decreased supply	Recovery, activation	QRS complex, ST, T

The myocardial cell layers most likely to become ischemic are those located "at the end of the supply line," as discussed above and illustrated in Figure 7.2. The subendocardial layer is most susceptible to ischemia when there is chronic coronary atherosclerosis and either an increase in myocardial demand or a decrease in blood supply.[3,4] The thicker walled left ventricle is much more susceptible to ischemia than the thinner walled right ventricle because of both the thickness itself and also the more common occurrence of increased workload in the systemic when compared to the pulmonary circulation.

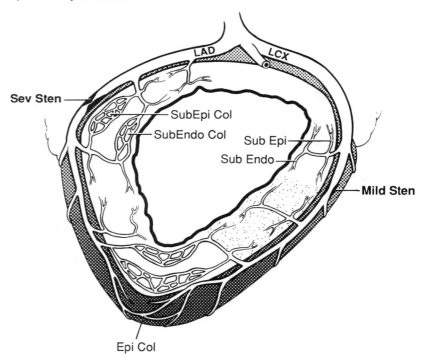

Figure 7.2. A cross-section of the left ventricle from the left anterior oblique view. The epicardial courses of the main branches of the left coronary artery (*LAD* and *LCX*) and their intramyocardial branches are shown. Subepicardial (*Sub Epi*) and subendocardial (*Sub Endo*) branches are present throughout; epicardial (*Epi Col*), subepicardial (*SubEpi Col*), and subendocardial (*SubEndo Col*) collaterals are present distal to the severe stenosis (*Sev Sten*) in the LAD. (From Califf RM, Mark DB, Wagner GS, eds. Acute coronary care in the thrombolytic era. 2nd ed. St. Louis: Mosby-Year Book, 1994. In press.)

The typical ECG manifestation of ischemia caused by an increase in myocardial demand is deviation of the ST segments and T waves away from the involved ventricle. The typical ECG manifestation of ischemia caused by decreased myocardial blood supply is deviation of the QRS complexes, ST segments, and T waves toward the specifically involved area of the ventricles. The typical manifestation of infarction is deviation of the QRS complexes and T waves away from the involved area (Table 7.2).[13]

Table 7.2

Pathologic Process	Waveforms Involved	Direction Deviated
Ischemia of increased demand	ST, T	Away from ventricular area
Ischemia of decreased supply	ST, T, QRS	Toward ventricular area
Infarction	QRS, T	Away from ventricular area

The ECG changes associated with each of these three pathologic processes are presented in Chapters 8, ("Ischemia Due to Increased Myocardial Demand"), 9 ("Ischemia Due to Insufficient Blood Supply"), and 10 ("Myocardial Infarction"). In each chapter, the involved ECG waveforms are discussed in the order of their importance for that particular pathologic process.

GLOSSARY

Aerobic metabolism: the intracellular method for converting glucose into energy which requires the presence of oxygen and produces enough energy to nourish the cell and also to cause it to contract.

Anaerobic metabolism: the intracellular method for converting glucose into energy which does not require oxygen, but produces only enough energy to nourish the cell.

Atherosclerosis: a process in which the arterial walls "harden" as they develop plaques that extend out into, and narrow, the lumen.

Myocardial ischemia: reduction in the supply of oxygen below the amount required by the myocardial cells to maintain aerobic metabolism.

Myocardial infarction: death of myocardial cells as a result of failure of the circulation to provide oxygen to restore metabolism after the intracellular stores of glycogen have been depleted.

Stunned myocardium: cardiac cells that are using anaerobic metabolism and are, therefore, ischemic but neither infarcted nor capable of contraction.

REFERENCES

1. Rushmer RF. Cardiovascular dynamics. Philadelphia: WB Saunders, 1976:367–369.
2. Reimer KA, Jennings RB, Tatum AH. Pathobiology of acute myocardial ischemia: metabolic, functional and intrastructural studies. Am J Cardiol 1983; 52:72A–81A.
3. Reimer KA, Lowe JE, Rasmussen MM, Jennings RB. The wavefront phenomenon of ischemic cell death: I. Myocardial infarct size vs. duration of coronary occlusion in dogs. Circulation 1977;56:786–794.
4. Reimer KA, Jennings RB. The "wavefront phenomenon" of myocardial ischemic cell death: II. Transmural progression of necrosis within the framework of ischemic bed size (myocardium at risk) and collateral flow. Lab Invest 1979;40:633–644.
5. Hackel DB, Wagner G, Ratliff NB, Cies A, Estes EH Jr. Anatomic studies of the cardiac conducting system in acute myocardial infarction. Am Heart J 1972;83:77–81.
6. Bauman RP, Rembert JC, Greenfield JC. The role of the collateral circulation in maintaining cellular viability during coronary occlusion. In: Califf RM, Mark DB, Wagner GS, eds. Acute coronary care in the thrombolytic era. 2nd ed. St. Louis: Mosby-Year Book, 1994. In press.
7. Cohen M, Reutzop KP. Limitation of myocardial ischemia by collateral circulation during sudden con-
trolled coronary artery occlusion in tumor subjects: a prospective study. Circulation 1906;74:469–476.
8. Davies MJ, Woolf N, Robertson WB. Pathology of acute myocardial infarction with particular reference to occlusive coronary thrombi. Br Heart J 1976; 38:659–664.
9. Davies MJ, Fulton WFM, Robertson WB. The relation of coronary thrombosis to ischemic myocardial necrosis. J Pathol 1979;127:99–110.
10. Braunwald E, Kloner RA. The stunned myocardium: prolonged post-ischemic ventricular dysfunction. Circulation 1982;66:1146–1149.
11. Ekmekci A, Toyoshima HJ, Kwoczynski JK, Nagaya T, Prinzmetal M. Angina pectoris: giant R and receding S wave in myocardial ischemia and certain nonischemic conditions. Am J Cardiol 1961;7:521–532.
12. Wagner NB, Sevilla DC, Krucoff MW, Lee KL, Peiper KS, Kent KK, Bottner RK, Selvester RH, Wagner GS. Transient alterations of the QRS complex and the ST segment during percutaneous transluminal balloon angioplasty of the left anterior descending artery. Am J Cardiol 1988;62:1038–1042.
13. Wagner NB, Wagner GS, White RD. The twelve lead ECG and the extent of myocardium at risk of acute infarction: cardiac anatomy and lead locations, and the phases of serial changes during acute occlusion. In: Califf RM, Mark DB, Wagner GS, eds. Acute coronary care in the thrombolytic era. Chicago: Year Book, 1988:31–45.

CHAPTER 8

Ischemia Due to Increased Myocardial Demand

ST SEGMENT CHANGES

Normally, the ST segment is part of the baseline of the ECG because it is isoelectric with the PR and TP segments (Fig. 1.11). Observation of the stability of the position of the ST segment on the ECG of a patient receiving a graded exercise stress test provides clinical information regarding the presence or absence of myocardial ischemia.[1] If coronary blood flow is capable of increasing to satisfy the metabolic demands of even those cells in the left ventricular subendocardium, there is minimal alteration in ST segment appearance. The typical normal appearance of the ST segments during exercise stress testing is illustrated in Figure 8.1.[2] Note the minor depression of the J point with the ST segment upsloping toward the upright T wave.

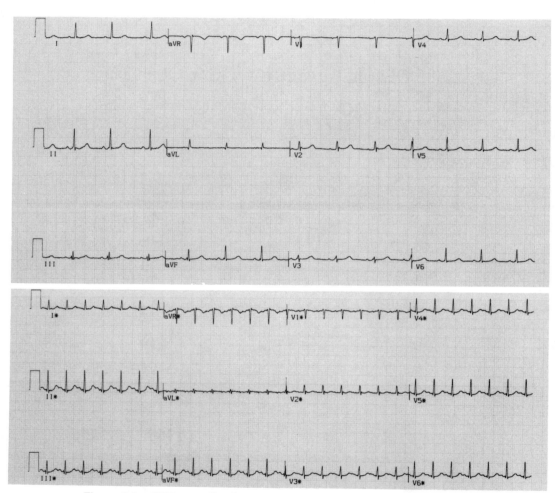

Figure 8.1. ECG recording from a 54-year-old woman with a normal resting 12-lead ECG (*top*) remains normal during an exercise stress test (*bottom*).

When a partial obstruction within the coronary arteries prevents the blood flow from increasing sufficiently during a graded exercise stress test, the resulting *subendocardial ischemia* (*SEI*) is manifested by specific ST segment changes (Fig. 8.2, *A–C*).[3] Another term applied to these changes is *subendocardial injury* because experimental studies have described a current of injury produced by the imbalance between the ischemic subendocardial layer and the nonischemic middle and epicardial layers of the left ventricular myocardium.[4] However, the ST segment changes typically disappear when the myocardial demands are returned to baseline by stopping the exercise. This suggests that the myocardial cells have been reversibly ischemic and have not actually sustained injury. Since the ECG changes occur only during the period of stress, the term ischemia seems more appropriate than injury.

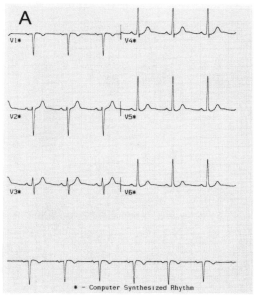

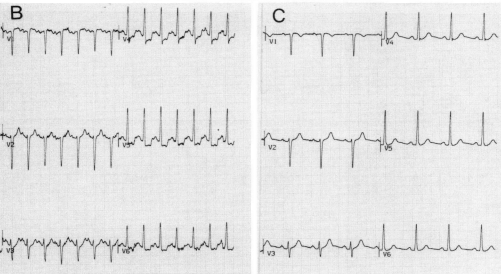

Figure 8.2. ECG recording from a 60-year-old man with a normal resting ECG in the standard precordial leads V1 to V6 (**A**) who develops ST segment changes indicating SEI during an exercise stress test (**B**) which return to normal as soon as the exercise is stopped (**C**).

A combination of two diagnostic criteria, on either a resting or exercise recording, have been typically required in at least one ECG lead for the diagnosis of left ventricular SEI:

1. At least 1.0 mm (0.10 mV) depression at the J point;
2. Either a horizontal or downward slope toward the end of the ST segment at its junction with the T wave.

Lesser deviations of the ST segments, as illustrated in Figure 8.3, could be caused by SEI or could be variations of normal. Even the "diagnostic" ST segment changes could be due to an extreme variation of normal. When these ECG changes appear, on either resting or exercise recordings, they should be considered in the context of other manifestations of ischemia such as typical or atypical precordial pain, decreased blood pressure, or cardiac arrhythmias.[3,5]

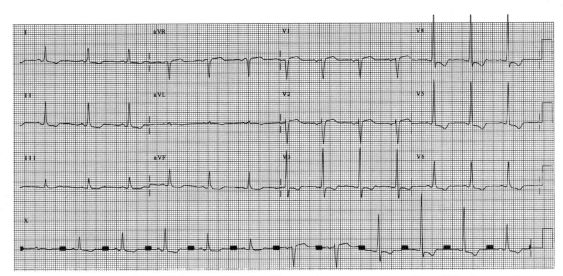

Figure 8.3. ECG recording of a 69-year-old woman with resting ECG changes that are suggestive, but not diagnostic for, SEI. Note the <0.10-mV depression of the J point with the ST segments downsloping toward a biphasic (negative and then positive) T wave.

Horizontal or downsloping depression of ST segments has been considered most significant, and upsloping segments, relatively benign. However, more recent investigation suggests that significant depression associated with upsloping ST segments may also be abnormal.[2] An upsloping ST that still remains 1.0 mm or more below the baseline 0.08 sec after the J point[6] or a depression of the J point of more than 2.0 mm with upsloping ST still 2.0 mm below the isoelectric line 0.08 sec later[7] are sometimes considered "diagnostic" of SEI (Fig. 8.4).

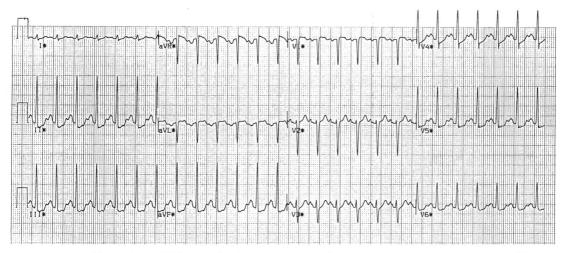

Figure 8.4. ECG recording from a 47-year-old man with a normal resting 12-lead ECG who develops 0.20-mV J point depression in multiple leads during exercise stress testing.

Another clinical test used in the diagnosis of SEI is continuous ECG monitoring. This method has been termed *Holter monitoring* after its developer and is discussed in Chapter 2 ("Recording the Electrocardiogram"). Originally, only a single ECG lead was monitored, but current methods provide three leads during ambulatory activity and all 12 standard leads at the bedside. Figure 8.5 illustrates an episode of ST segment depression during walking, accompanied by nonsustained ventricular tachycardia. The diary entry relates the cardiac event to the precipitating activity and the symptoms perceived. Since the episode was not accompanied by any chest pain, it could be considered an example of *silent ischemia*.[8-10]

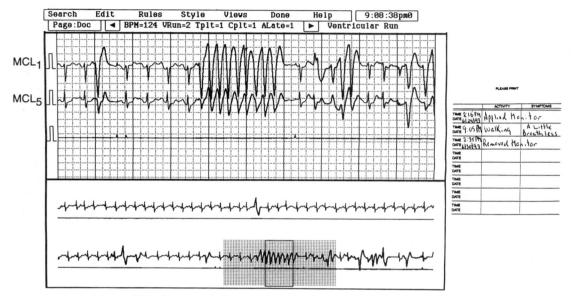

Figure 8.5. During a 24-hour period of Holter monitoring, this 57-year-old man developed an episode of ECG changes suggesting SEI, accompanied by symptoms of breathlessness sufficient to prompt a diary entry. Leads MCL₁ and MCL₅ reveal a short burst of nonsustained ventricular tachycardia during the period that ST segment depression is present in lead MCL₅.

As indicated in Chapter 2, the positive poles of most of the standard limb and precordial ECG leads are directed toward the left ventricle. In deviating away from the left ventricle, the ST segment changes of SEI appear negative or depressed in a group of either leftward (I, aVL, or V4–V6) or inferiorly (II, III, aVF) oriented leads (Fig. 8.6, A and B). The location of the ECG leads showing the ST segment depression is not indicative of the area of the left ventricular subendocardium, which is ischemic.

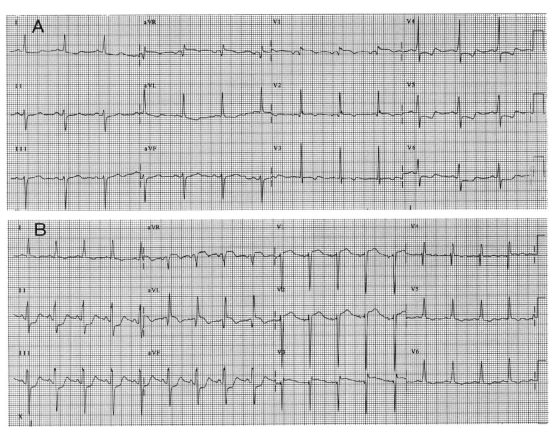

Figure 8.6. Elderly men with abnormal resting 12-lead ECG developed evidence of SEI in the first minute of exercise stress testing. In **A**, the SEI appears in leads V4–V6, with lesser reciprocal ST segment elevation in lead V1. In **B**, the SEI appears in leads II, III, and aVF, with lesser reciprocal ST segment elevation in leads aVL and V1–V3.

Since the ST segments are deviated from the PR and *TP segment* baselines in space, they appear as elevated in leads with their positive poles directed away from the left ventricle such as limb lead aVR and precordial leads V1 and V2, as indicated in Figure 8.6. This concept can be appreciated by observing the vectorcardiogram, which presents a single view of the electrical activity in a plane of the body. Figure 8.7 illustrates the ST segment deviation typical of left ventricular SEI. The maximal deviation appears as ST depression in leftward and inferiorly oriented leads. When the PR and ST segments are isoelectric, the QRS begins and ends at the same place. The ST segment depression of SEI may be accompanied by ST segment elevation in rightward or superiorly oriented leads such as aVR, aVL, V_1, or V_2.

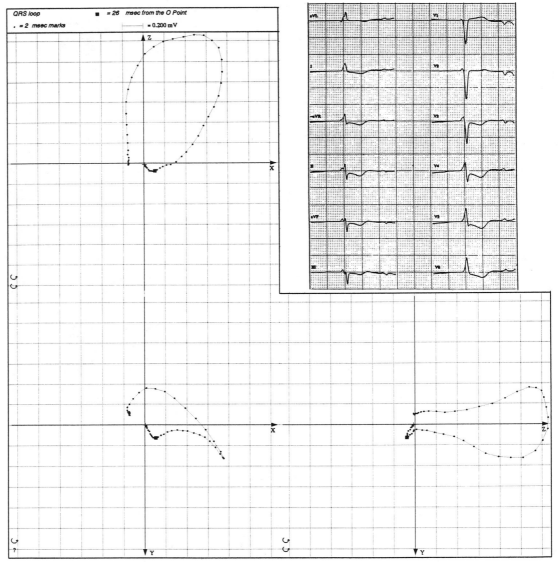

Figure 8.7. A vectorcardiogram provides a view of the ST segment deviation of SEI in three-dimensional space. Recordings of the standard leads indicate the typical appearance of SEI. The vectorcardiogram reveals that the end of the QRS complex (J point) is deviated to the right and superior to the beginning of the QRS complex.

The appearance of the ST segments with left ventricular SEI is similar to that described in Chapter 4 ("Chamber Enlargement") with left *ventricular strain*, which is a typical change associated with a left ventricular pressure or systolic overload (Fig. 4.8). The ST segment depression of left ventricular strain appears chronically as one of the manifestations of left ventricular hypertrophy.

The maximal ST depression during stress tests is almost never seen in leads V1–V3. When these leads do exhibit the maximal ST depression, the cause is either right ventricular strain (Chapter 4) or posterior transmural ischemia (Chapter 9, "Ischemia Due to Insufficient Blood Supply"). The ST segment depression of left ventricular SEI usually resolves when the workload is reduced by returning to the resting condition. Occasionally, ST segment depression continues in the absence of a persistent increase in the left ventricular workload. In this case, the presence of subendocardial infarction should be investigated.[11]

The abnormality of electrical recovery, manifested on the ECG by ST segment deviation, occurs for each of the individual subendocardial cells at the time they complete their own activation process (Fig. 1.10). Therefore, the subendocardial ischemia, which appears as depression of the ST segments, actually begins during the QRS complex. This may result in secondary deviation of the QRS waveforms in the same direction as that of the ST segments illustrated in Figure 8.8, *A* and *B*. This distortion affects the amplitudes but not the durations of the QRS waveforms and affects the later more than the earlier waveforms.[12]

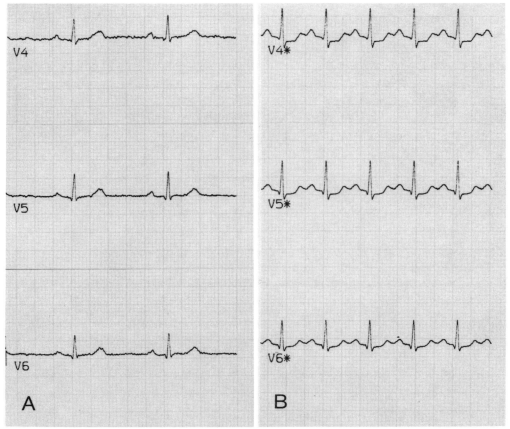

Figure 8.8. The ECG recording of a 67-year-old woman has a normal resting appearance of leads V4–V6 (**A**), but 0.1-mV ST segment depression in lead V4 during exercise (**B**). The small terminal S waves in all three leads move downward with the ST segments.

T WAVE CHANGES

 Normally, the directions of the QRS complexes and T waves are similar rather than opposite because of prolonged maintenance of the activated condition in the endocardial layer of myocardium, as illustrated in Figure 1.10. The ischemic subendocardial cells are unable to maintain prolonged activation, thereby causing the T wave on the ECG to assume the opposite direction. These ischemic T waves are inverted in relation to the QRS complexes (Fig. 8.9). As indicated in Chapter 3 ("Interpretation of the Normal Electrocardiogram"), there is normally an angle of <45° between the directions of the QRS complexes and the T waves in the frontal plane and <60° in the transverse plane. When the angles exceed these limits in the absence of other abnormal conditions such as ventricular hypertrophy or bundle branch block, the presence of ischemic T waves should be considered.

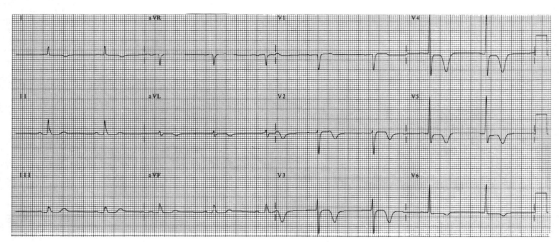

Figure 8.9. A 59-year-old man has a normal resting ECG except for widespread inversion of the T waves, increasing the QRS-T angle beyond its normal limits.

The location of the ECG leads demonstrating ischemic T waves is sometimes indicative of the specific location of the ischemic area within the left ventricular myocardium. Ischemic ST segments generally deviate away from the left ventricle. However, ischemic T waves may deviate away from the involved area of myocardium within the left ventricle. Figure 8.10, *A–C*, illustrates the typical lead groups that localize the ischemia in the distributions of the three major coronary arteries.

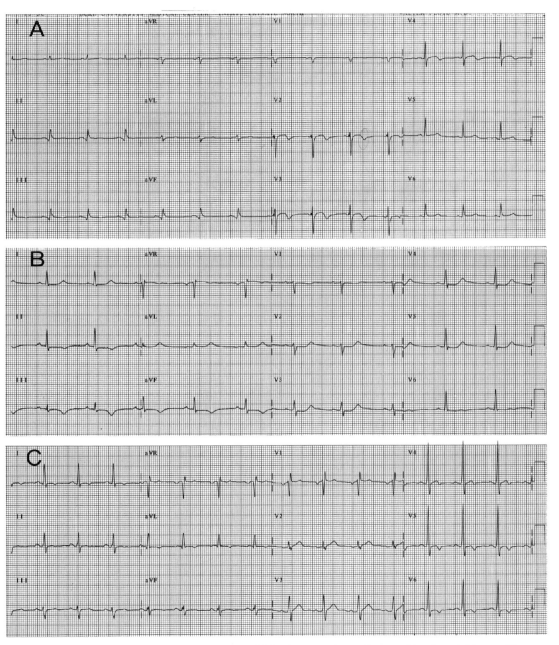

Figure 8.10. The three resting ECGs have various abnormalities in addition to T wave inversion, suggesting ischemia in various areas of the left ventricle. **A.** Anteriorly in the distribution of the anterior descending artery. **B.** Inferiorly in the distribution of the posterior descending artery. **C.** Laterally and apically in the distribution of a diagonal branch of either the anterior descending or the circumflex artery.

T wave changes are not as reliable as ST segment changes for establishing the diagnosis of myocardial ischemia due to increased demand. T wave inversion is not a specific sign of left ventricular SEI. Many noncardiac conditions have been observed to cause T wave inversion.[13] T wave inversion is also not a sensitive sign of left ventricular SEI. Figure 8.11, A and B, presents the typical ST segment changes of SEI in both the presence and absence of T wave inversion during exercise stress testing.

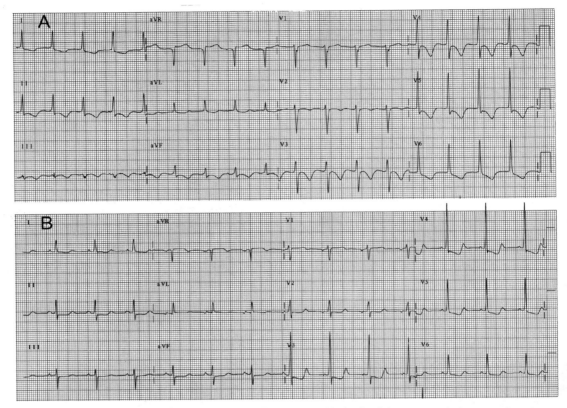

Figure 8.11. ST segment deviation occurred in both of these men during exercise stress testing. In **A**, it is accompanied by T wave inversion, but in **B**, the T wave retains its normal relationship to the QRS complex.

Like ST segment depression, T wave inversion usually resolves when the increased left ventricular workload is removed. Unlike ST depression, however, T wave inversion is typically present for a prolonged period following the acute phase of myocardial infarction. This chronic T wave inversion should not be considered evidence for persistent ischemia. It represents an alteration in electrical recovery secondary to the infarction-induced changes in electrical activation in the same manner that T wave inversion is an expected secondary occurrence with left bundle branch block (Fig. 8.12, A and B).

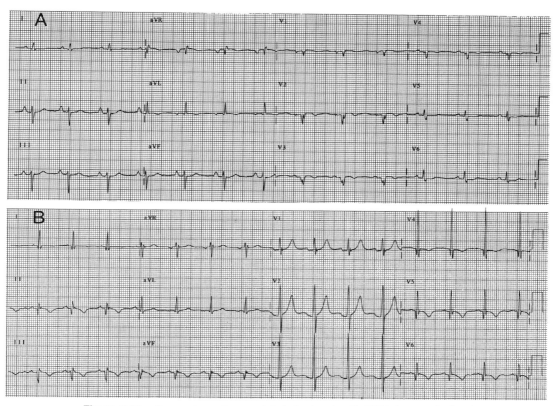

Figure 8.12. T wave inversion persists in the leads with QRS changes indicating an anterior-apical infarction (**A**), and an inferior-posterior-apical infarction (**B**). Note that the inversion indicating the posterior involvement in **B** produces a positive, rather than a negative, deviation of the T waves.

Pardee has described T wave inversion accompanied by ST segment elevation[14], as illustrated in Figure 8.13. This particular variety of repolarization abnormality has been associated with a high risk of development of acute transmural ischemia, as discussed in Chapter 9.

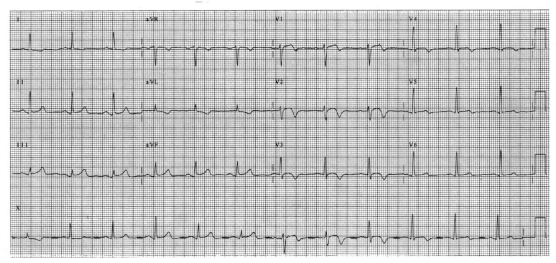

Figure 8.13. A 65-year-old woman with an otherwise normal resting 12-lead ECG has the combination of elevation of the ST segments and inversion of the T waves in leads V1–V5 described by Pardee.

GLOSSARY

Holter monitoring: continuous ECG recording of one or more leads, either for the detection of abnormalities of morphology suggestive of ischemia or abnormalities of rhythm.

Silent ischemia: evidence of myocardial ischemia appearing on an ECG recording in the absence of any awareness of symptoms of ischemia.

Subendocardial injury: a term used for the deviation of the ST segments that occurs with subendocardial ischemia.

Subendocardial ischemia (SEI): deviation of the ST segments away from the ventricle (always the left ventricle) in which only the inner part of the myocardium is ischemic.

TP segment: time from the end of the T wave to the onset of the P wave.

Ventricular strain: deviation of the ST segments and T waves away from the ventricle in which there is either a severe systolic overload or marked hypertrophy.

REFERENCES

1. Sheffield LT, Holt JH, Reeves TJ. Exercise graded by heart rate in electrocardiographic testing for angina pectoris. Circulation 1965;32:622.
2. Stuart RJ, Ellestad MH. Upsloping ST segments in exercise stress testing. Am J Cardiol 1976;37:19.
3. Ellestad MH, Cooke BM, Greenberg PS. Stress testing; clinical application and predictive capacity. Prog Cardiovasc Dis 1979;21:431–460.
4. Lepeschkin E. Modern electrocardiography. vol I. Baltimore: Williams & Wilkins, 1951;798.
5. Ellestad MH, Savitz S, Bergdall D, Teske JE. The false positive stress test: multivariate analysis of 215 subjects with hemodynamic, angiographic and clinical data. Am J Cardiol 1977;40:681.
6. Rijneki RD, Ascoop CA, Talmon JL. Clinical significance of upsloping ST segments in exercise electrocardiography. Circulation 1980;61:671.
7. Kurita A, Chaitman BR, Bourassa MG. Significance of exercise-induced junctional ST depression in evaluation of coronary artery disease. Am J Cardiol 1977;40:492–497.
8. Wolf F, Tzivoni D, Stern S. Comparison of exercise tests and 24-hour ambulatory electrocardiographic monitoring in detection of ST-T changes. Br Heart J 1974:36:90–95.
9. Selwyn A, Fox K, Eves M, Oakley D, Dargie H, Shillingford J. Myocardial ischemia in patients with frequent angina pectoris. Br Med J 1978;2:1594–1596.
10. Krucoff MW, Pope JE, Bottner RK, Adams IM, Wagner GS, Kent KM. Dedicated ST segment monitoring in the CCU after successful coronary angioplasty: incidence and prognosis of silent and symptomatic ischemia. In: van Armin T, Maseri A, eds. Silent ischemia: current concepts and management. Darmstadt: Steinkopff Verlag, 1987:140–146.
11. Hurst JW, Logue RB. The heart: arteries and veins. New York: McGraw-Hill, 1966:147.
12. Glazier JJ, Chierchia S, Margonato A, Maseri A. Increase in S-wave amplitude during ischemic ST-segment depression in stable angina pectoris. Am J Cardiol 1987;59:1295–1299.
13. Taggart P, Carruthers M, Joseph S, Kelly HB, Marcomichelakis J, Noble D, O'Neill G, Somerville W. Electrocardiographic changes resembling myocardial ischaemia in asymptomatic men with normal coronary arteriograms. Br Heart J 1979;41:214–225.
14. Pardee HEB. Heart disease and abnormal electrocardiograms with special reference to the coronary T wave. Am J Med Sci 1925;169:270.

CHAPTER 9

Ischemia Due to Insufficient Blood Supply

ST SEGMENT CHANGES

Just as ST segment changes are reliable indicators of ischemia due to increased myocardial demand, they are also reliable indicators of ischemia due to insufficient coronary blood supply. Observation of the position of the ST segments (relative to the PR and TP segments) on the ECG of a patient experiencing acute precordial pain provides clinical evidence regarding the presence or absence of myocardial ischemia or infarction. However, there are many normal variations in the appearance of ST segments, as illustrated in Figure 9.1, A and B.[1-3]

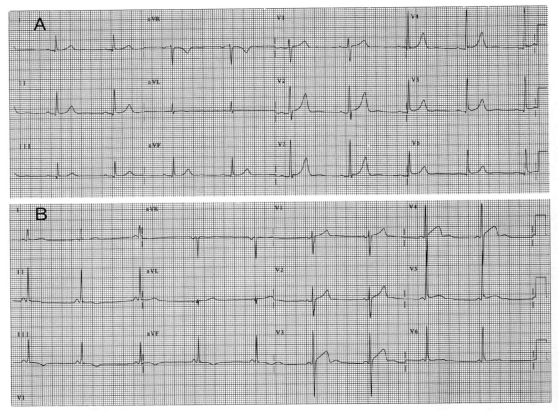

Figure 9.1. **A** and **B** present the stable appearances of the resting ECGs of two healthy young men. The ST segment elevations in the precordial leads, which represent variations of normal in these men, are identical to the changes that would be considered abnormal in a patient with acute symptoms.

When a sudden, complete obstruction of a coronary artery prevents any blood flow from reaching an area of myocardium, the resulting transmural ischemia (TMI)[4] is manifested by ST segment deviation toward the ischemic area. Another term applied to these changes is *epicardial injury* because experimental studies have described a current of injury produced by the epicardial layer of myocardium.[5,6] However, as shown in the patient receiving percutaneous transluminal coronary angioplasty (PTCA) in Figure 9.2, A–C, the ST segment changes typically disappear abruptly when the coronary blood flow is returned to baseline by removing the obstruction after a brief period of time. This suggests that the myocardial cells have been reversibly ischemic and have not actually sustained injury. Since all of the layers of the ventricular wall are involved and the ECG changes occur only during the period of complete obstruction, the term transmural ischemia seems more appropriate than epicardial injury.

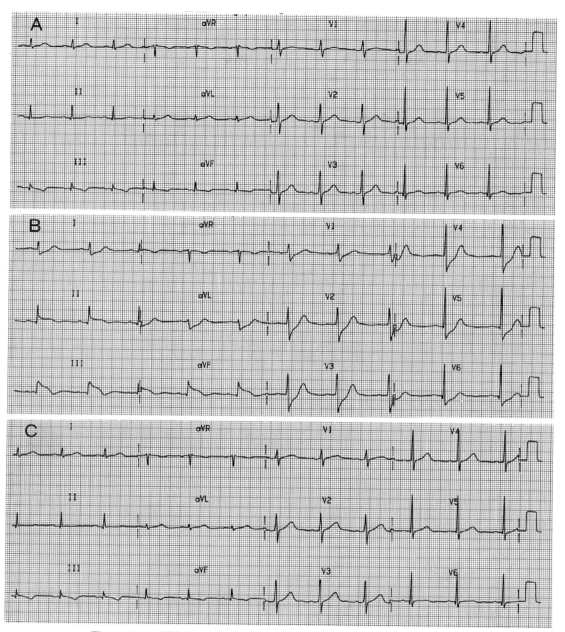

Figure 9.2. ECG recordings of a 58-year-old man with chest pain on exertion caused by a 90% obstruction of the right coronary artery. Note the T wave inversions in inferior leads in the baseline (**A**) and 2 minute post deflation (**B**) ECGs. The ST elevation in the inferiorly oriented leads, after 2 minutes of balloon occlusion of the involved artery, is accompanied by a similar amount of ST depression in the precordial leads (**C**).

It may be difficult to differentiate the abnormal ST segment changes of TMI from variations of normal when the ST segment deviation is minimal. Presence of one of the following criteria is typically required for diagnosis of TMI:

1. Elevation of the origin of the ST segment at its junction (J point) with the QRS of:
   a. ≥1.0 mm (0.10 mV) in two or more limb leads
   or
   b. ≥2.0 mm (0.20 mV) in two or more precordial leads
   or
2. Depression of the origin of the ST segment at the J point of ≥2.0 mm (0.20 mV) in at least two of the three leads V1 to V3

The deviated ST segments typically are either horizontal or slope toward the direction of the T waves, as illustrated in Figure 9.3, A and B. Sloping produces greater deviation of the ST segment as it moves further from the J point toward the T wave. Various positions along the ST segment are sometimes selected for measurement of ST segment deviation either for establishing the diagnosis of TMI or for estimating its extent. "J + 0.02 sec" and "J + 0.06 sec" have been used in some clinical situations and are illustrated in Figure 9.3, A and B. The ECG criteria for TMI may be accompanied by other manifestations of ischemia such as typical or atypical precordial pain, decreased blood pressure, or cardiac arrhythmias.

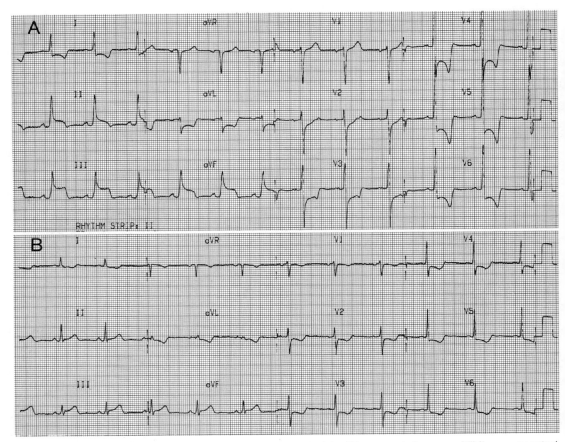

Figure 9.3. Variations in the appearances of the ST segment changes of TMI are presented in two patients after 2 minutes of balloon occlusion of the right coronary artery. In **A**, there is horizontal ST elevation, and in **B**, the ST segments slope toward the peak of the T wave. In **A**, the ST depression in the precordial leads exceeds the elevation in the limb leads, which sometimes occurs with inferior wall TMI.

The ST segment changes of TMI deviate toward the involved area of the ventricular myocardium and, therefore, appear positive or elevated in some combination of leftward, inferiorly, or anteriorly oriented leads (Fig. 9.4, A–C). The ST segments appear reciprocally negative in the ECG leads with their positive poles oriented away from the involved area of myocardium. When both ST segment elevation and depression appear on different leads of an ECG, the direction of the maximal deviation should usually be considered primary and the direction of the lesser deviation considered secondary or *reciprocal*. When, as in *B* and *C*, the ST depression in leads V1 to V3 equals or exceeds the elevation in II, III, and aVF, the designation should be "inferior and posterior TMI."

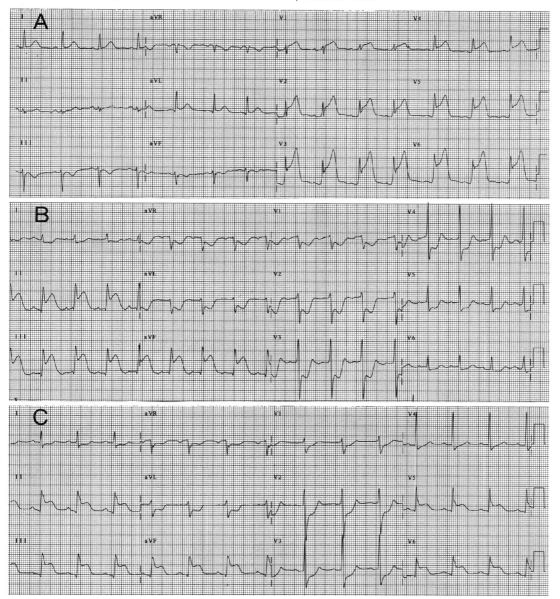

Figure 9.4. Examples of TMI due to balloon occlusions of the three major coronary arteries. **A.** Left anterior descending. **B.** Dominant right coronary. **C.** Dominant left circumflex. Note that the TMI can involve the inferior apical sector when either the anterior descending (**A**) or posterior descending (**C**) artery is occluded, as indicated by the ST elevation in leads V5 and V6.

TMI most commonly occurs in the distal aspect of the area of the left ventricular myocardium supplied by one of the three major coronary arteries, as indicated in Figure 9.5.[7] The relationships among the coronary artery, left ventricular (LV) quadrant, sectors of that quadrant, and diagnostic ECG leads are indicated in Table 9.1.

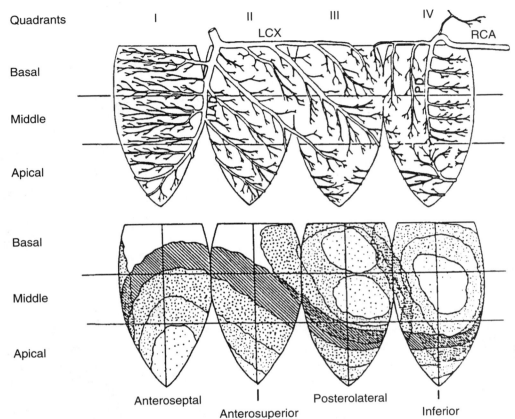

Figure 9.5. The 12 sectors of the left ventricular myocardium are defined by the four quadrants and the three levels. The distributions of the coronary arteries (*top*) are related to the distributions of infarctions that result from their occlusions (*bottom*). The four grades of *shading from light to dark* indicate infarct size as small, medium, large, and very large, respectively. (From Califf RM, Mark DB, Wagner GS. Acute coronary care in the thrombolytic era. 1st ed. Chicago: Year Book, 1988:20–21.)

Table 9.1

Coronary Artery	LV Quadrant	Sectors	Diagnostic Leads
Left anterior descending	Anteroseptal	All	V1–V3 (elevation)
	Anterosuperior	All	I, aVL (elevation)
	Inferior	Apical	V4–V6 (elevation)
	Posterolateral	Apical	V4–V6 (elevation)
Posterior descending	Inferior	Basal, middle	II, III, aVF (elevation)
Left circumflex	Posterolateral	Basal, middle	V1–V3 (depression)

In about 90% of individuals, the posterior descending artery originates from the right coronary artery and the left circumflex artery supplies only the area indicated in Table 9.1. This has been termed *right coronary dominance*. In the other 10% with *left coronary dominance*, the posterior descending artery originates from the left circumflex artery, and the right coronary artery supplies only the right ventricle.

The basal and middle sectors of the posterior-lateral quadrant of the left ventricle are located distant from the positive poles of all 12 of the standard ECG leads. Therefore, posterior-lateral TMI is indicated by depression rather than elevation of the ST segment (Fig. 9.6). Additional leads on the posterior-lateral thorax would be required to record ST segment elevation due to TMI in this area.[8]

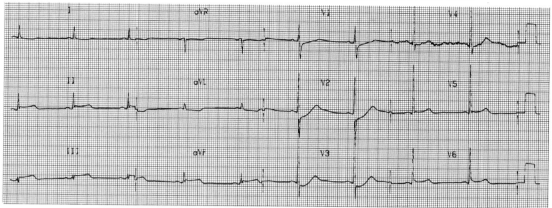

Figure 9.6. Recording after 2 minutes of balloon occlusion of a nondominant left circumflex coronary artery.

TMI may also involve the thinner walled right ventricular myocardium when its blood supply via the right coronary artery becomes insufficient. Right ventricular TMI is represented on the standard ECG as ST segment elevation in leads V1 and V2, with greater elevation in lead V1 than in V2 and with even greater elevation in the more rightward additional leads V3R and V4R (Fig. 9.7).

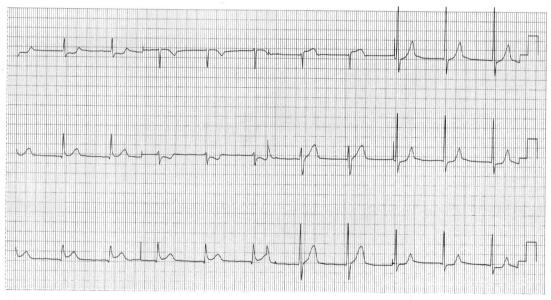

Figure 9.7. A 65-year-old woman presenting with acute symptoms; coronary angiography revealed complete obstruction at the beginning of the right coronary artery proximal to the first right ventricular branch.

As illustrated in Figure 9.2, the entire ST segment elevation disappears abruptly when TMI persists for only the 1–2 minutes required for PTCA. However, TMI produced by coronary thrombosis typically persists throughout the minutes to hours required for clinical administration of some form of thrombolytic therapy. Figure 9.8A illustrates the resolution of ST segment elevation following angiographically documented thrombolysis 2 hours after the onset of acute precordial pain. The disappearance of the ST segment elevation may reveal already developed QRS changes of infarction that have previously been obscured. In some patients, multiple episodes of ST segment elevation and resolution have been documented by continuous monitoring following the initiation of intravenous thrombolytic therapy (Fig. 9.8B). In the absence of successful thrombolytic therapy, there is eventual gradual resolution of the ST segment elevation as the area with TMI becomes infarcted (Fig. 9.8C).[9,10]

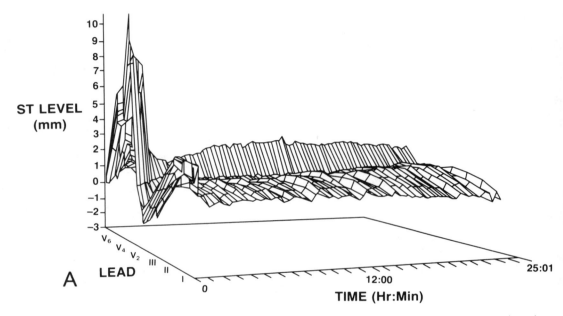

Figure 9.8. Continuous ECG monitoring of three patients who received intravenous thrombolytic therapy during the early hours of acute myocardial infarction. **A** and **B.** Anterior. **C.** Inferior. The magnitude of ST segment deviation (millimeters) is indicated on the y axis, in each of the six ECG leads indicated on the x axis, over the periods or time following initiation of the therapy indicated on the z axis. (**A** from Krucoff MW, Wagner NB, Pope JE, Wagner GS, et al. The portable programmable microprocessor-driven real-time 12-lead electrocardiographic monitor: a preliminary report of a new device for the noninvasive detection of successful reperfusion or silent coronary reocclusion. Am J Cardiol 1990;65:145. **B** reproduced with permission from Krucoff MW, Croll MA, Pope JE, et al. Continuous 12-lead ST-segment recovery analysis in the TAMI 7 study. Circulation 1993:88;439. Copyright 1993 American Heart Association.)

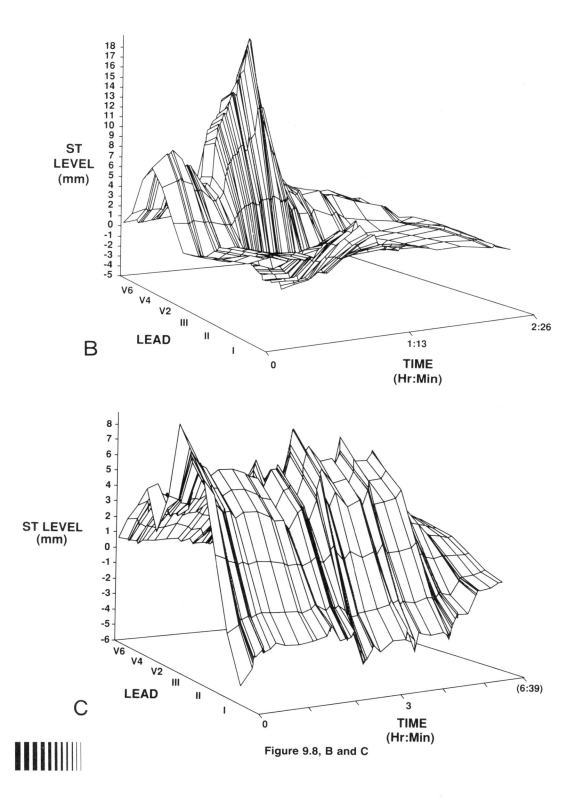

Figure 9.8, B and C

T WAVE CHANGES

Just as T wave changes are unreliable indicators of ischemia due to increased myocardial demand, they are also unreliable indicators of ischemia due to insufficient coronary blood supply. Figure 9.9, *A–C*, presents the changes in ST segments and T waves immediately following acute balloon inflation in the left anterior descending coronary arteries of several patients. Both of these ECG waveforms deviate toward the anterior aspect of the left ventricle in all patients. In some, the amount of T wave deviation is similar to that of the ST segment and, therefore, should be considered secondary. In others, there is a markedly greater deviation of the T waves. These primary T wave elevations have been termed *hyperacute T waves* and are present for only a brief period of time in patients with acute coronary thrombosis.[11] Hyperacute T waves may, therefore, be useful in timing the duration of the TMI when a patient presents with acute precordial pain.

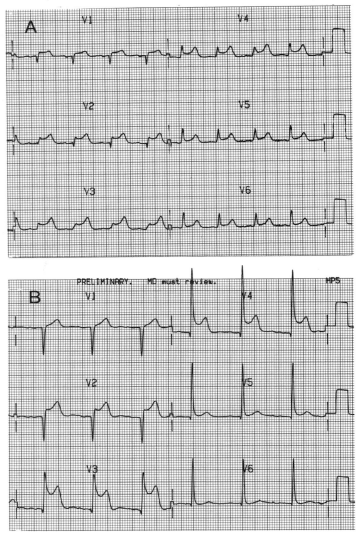

Figure 9.9. ST segment elevation is apparent in the precordial leads of three patients after 2 minutes of balloon occlusion of the left anterior descending coronary artery. In **A** and **B**, the relative heights of the ST segments and T waves are similar, but in **C**, "hyperacute T waves" are present.

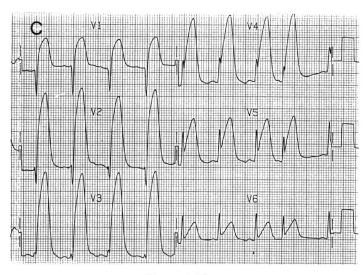

Figure 9.9C

Definition of the amplitude of the T wave required to identify primary changes during TMI requires reference to the upper limits of T wave amplitudes in the various ECG leads of normal subjects. Table 9.2 presents the upper limit T wave amplitudes (in millivolts) in each of the 12 standard leads for females and males in the 40–49- and ≥50-year-old age groups in the Glasgow, Scotland, normal data base.[12] A rough estimate of the normal upper limits of T wave amplitude would be: at least 5.0 mm (0.50 mV) in the limb leads, and at least 10.0 mm (1.00 mV) in the precordial leads. Amplitudes exceeding these limits are required to identify the hyperacute T waves that may appear during the earliest phase of TMI.

Table 9.2[a,b]

Lead	Males 40–49	Females 40–49	Males 50 +	Females 50 +
aVL	0.35	0.30	0.30	0.30
I	0.55	0.45	0.45	0.45
− aVR	0.55	0.45	0.45	0.45
II	0.65	0.55	0.55	0.45
aVF	0.50	0.40	0.45	0.35
III	0.35	0.30	0.35	0.30
V1	0.65	0.20	0.50	0.35
V2	1.45	0.85	1.40	0.70
V3	1.35	0.85	1.35	0.85
V4	1.15	0.85	1.10	0.75
V5	0.90	0.70	0.95	0.70
V6	0.65	0.55	0.65	0.50

[a]Modified from Macfarlane PW, Veitch Lawrie TD. In: Comprehensive electrocardiology. vol 3. New York: Pergamon Press, 1989:1446–1457.
[b]Presentation of upper limit T wave amplitudes (in millivolts rounded to the nearest 0.05) in each lead by gender and age for the normal subjects from Glasgow, Scotland. The leads are arranged in the panoramic format.

QRS COMPLEX CHANGES

The epicardial injury current, which appears as elevation of the ST segments, actually begins during the QRS complex. This may result in secondary deviation of the QRS waveforms in the same direction as that of the ST segments, as illustrated in Figure 9.10. This distortion affects the amplitudes but not the durations of the QRS waveforms. In addition, it affects the later more than the earlier waveforms.[13]

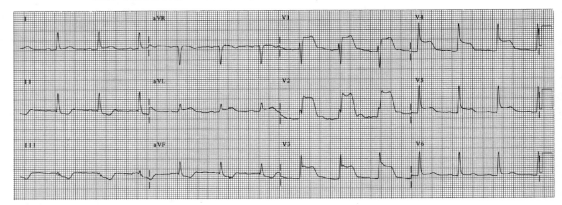

Figure 9.10. A 63-year-old man with acute substernal chest pain. The marked ST segment elevation of anterior TMI has also produced elevation of the QRS waveforms in leads V1–V4; even the nadir of the S wave in lead V2 has been elevated above the TP and PR segment baseline.

The deviation of the ST segments confounds the capability of measuring the amplitudes of the QRS waveforms. As illustrated in Figure 9.11, the PR segment baseline remains as the reference for the initial waveform, but the terminal waveform maintains its relationship with the ST segment baseline.

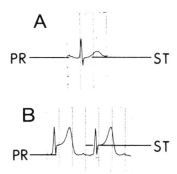

Figure 9.11. The secondary changes in QRS waveforms during TMI is illustrated by comparison of the appearances of initial R and terminal S waves at baseline (**A**) and after 2 minutes of balloon occlusion (**B**). Note that the S wave amplitude during TMI would be zero, if measured from the PR segment baseline. (Reproduced with permission from Wagner NB, Sevilla DC, Krucoff MW, Wagner GS, et al. Transient alterations of the QRS complex and the ST segment during percutaneous transluminal balloon angioplasty of the left anterior descending coronary artery. Am J Cardiol 1988;62:1039.)

Figure 9.12, *A* and *B*, presents examples of primary changes in the QRS complexes immediately following the onset of TMI produced by balloon inflation during coronary PTCA. The deviation of the QRS waveforms toward the area of the TMI is considered primary because its increase in amplitude is greater than that of the ST segment and its duration is also prolonged. The most likely cause of the primary QRS deviation is ischemic-induced delay in transmyocardial electrical activation. The epicardial layer of the area with TMI is activated late, thereby producing an unopposed positive QRS waveform. This deviation would appear in the negative direction in leads V1–V3 with TMI in the posterior-lateral left ventricle.[14]

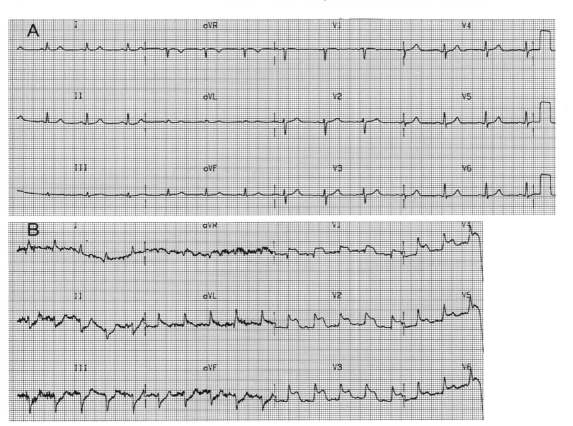

Figure 9.12.   A 53-year-old man with exertional chest pain caused by a subtotal obstruction of the left anterior descending coronary artery has a normal resting 12-lead ECG (**A**). After 2 minutes of complete balloon occlusion (**B**), anterior TMI has produced primary changes in QRS morphology resembling left anterior-superior fascicular block.

Figure 9.13 illustrates the difference in QRS appearance when TMI produces primary versus only secondary changes. In the same patient, some balloon occlusions of the left anterior descending artery caused only secondary QRS changes, but others caused primary changes.

Control

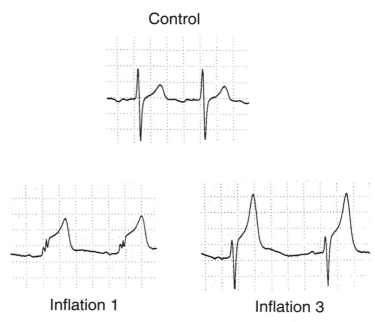

Inflation 1   Inflation 3

Figure 9.13. Recordings of two cardiac cycles of lead V2 from baseline (*control*) and after 2 minutes of two different periods of balloon occlusion of the LAD. Comparison of the appearances of the R and S waves illustrates both primary (*inflation 1*) and secondary (*inflation 2*) QRS morphologic changes. (Reproduced with permission from Wagner NB, Sevilla DC, Krucoff MW, Wagner GS, et al. Transient alterations of the QRS complex and the ST segment during percutaneous transluminal balloon angioplasty of the left anterior descending coronary artery. Am J Cardiol 1988;62:1041.)

GLOSSARY

Epicardial injury: the deviation of the ST segments that occurs with transmural ischemia or with pericardial irritation.

Hyperacute T waves: the tall peaked T waves that occur during the early phase of transmural ischemia.

Left coronary dominance: unusual coronary artery anatomy in which the posterior descending artery is a branch of the left circumflex coronary.

Reciprocal: deviation of the ST segments in the opposite direction from the maximal deviation.

Right coronary dominance: the usual coronary artery anatomy in which the posterior descending artery is a branch of the right coronary.

REFERENCES

1. Prinzmetal M, Goldman A, Massumi RA, Rakita L, Schwartz L, Kennamer R, Kuramoto K, Pipberger H. Clinical implications of errors in electrocardiographic interpretations: heart disease of electrocardiographic origin. JAMA 1956;161:138.
2. Levine HD. Non-specificity of the electrocardiogram associated with coronary artery disease. Am J Med 1953;15:344.
3. Marriott HJL. Coronary mimicry: normal variants, and physiologic, pharmacologic and pathologic influences that simulate coronary patterns in the electrocardiogram. Ann Intern Med 1960;52:411.
4. Vincent GM, Abildskov JA, Burgess MJ. Mechanisms of ischemic ST-segment displacement: evaluation by direct current recordings. Circulation 1977; 56:559–566.
5. Kleber AG, Janse MF, van Capelle FJL, Durrer D. Mechanism and time course of S-T and T-Q segment changes during acute regional myocardial ischemia in the pig heart determined by extracellular and intracellular recordings. Circ Res 1978;48:603–613.
6. Janse MJ, Cinca J, Morena H, Fiolet JW, Kleber AG, deVries GP, Becker AE, Durrer D. The "border zone" in myocardial ischemia: an electrophysiological, metabolic and histochemical correlation in the pig heart. Circ Res 1979;44:576–588.
7. Wagner GS, Wagner NB. The 12-lead ECG and the extent of myocardium at risk of acute infarction: anatomic relationships among coronary, Purkinje, and myocardial anatomy. In: Califf RM, Mark DB, Wagner GS, eds. Acute coronary care in the thrombolytic era. Chicago: Year Book, 1988:20–21.
8. Seatre HA, Startt/Selvester RH, Solomon JC, Baron KA, Ahmad J, Ellestad ME. 16-lead ECG changes with coronary angioplasty: location of ST-T changes with balloon occlusion of five arterial perfusion beds. J Electrocardiol 1991;24 suppl:153–162.
9. Krucoff MW, Croll MA, Pope JE, Pieper KS, Kanani PM, Granger CB, Veldkamp RF, Wagner BL, Sawchak ST, Califf RM. Continuously updated 12-lead ST-segment recovery analysis for myocardial infarct artery patency assessment and its correlation with multiple simultaneous early angiographic observations. Am J Cardiol 1993;71:145–151.
10. Kondo M, Tamura K, Tanio H, Shimono Y. Is ST segment re-elevation associated with reperfusion an indicator of marked myocardial damage after thrombolysis? J Am Coll Cardiol 1993;21:62–67.
11. Dressler W, Roesler H. High T waves in the earliest stage of myocardial infarction. Am Heart J 1947; 34:627–645.
12. Macfarlane PW, Lawrie TDV, eds. Comprehensive electrocardiography. New York: Pergamon Press, 1989:1446–1457.
13. Wagner NB, Sevilla DC, Krucoff MW, Lee KL, Pieper KS, Kent KK, Bottner RK, Selvester RH, Wagner GS. Transient alterations of the QRS complex and ST segment during percutaneous transluminal balloon angioplasty of the left anterior descending artery. Am J Cardiol 1988;62:1038–1042.
14. Selvester RH, Wagner NB, Wagner GS. Ventricular excitation during percutaneous transluminal angioplasty of the left anterior descending coronary artery. Am J Cardiol 1988;62:1116–1121.

CHAPTER 10

Myocardial Infarction

QRS CHANGES

When insufficient coronary blood supply persists after the myocardial glycogen reserves have been depleted, the cells become irreversibly ischemic and the process of *necrosis* or myocardial infarction begins.[1,2] The QRS complex is the most useful aspect of the ECG for the evaluation of the presence, location, and extent of myocardial infarction. As indicated in Chapter 9 ("Ischemia Due to Insufficient Blood Supply"), the QRS waveforms deviate toward the area of potentially reversible transmural ischemia, secondarily due to the current of injury and primarily due to myocardial activation delay. The process of infarction begins in the most severely ischemic subendocardial layer. QRS deviation toward the ischemic area is replaced by QRS deviation away from the infarcted area.[3] Since there is no electrical activation of the infarcted myocardium, the summation of activation spread is away from the involved area, as illustrated in Figure 10.1, *A* and *B*.

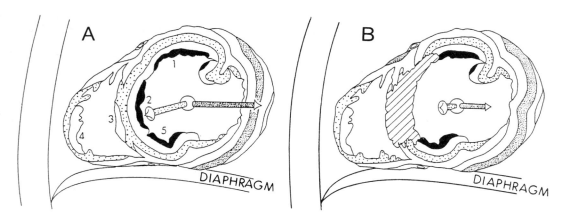

Figure 10.1. Schematic cross-sections of the right and left ventricular myocardia with isochronic lines at 10-msec intervals viewed from an apical perspective. The normal sequence of activation (**A**) is contrasted with the abnormal sequence resulting from an anterior infarction (*hatched area* in **B**). The *numbers* in **A** indicate the sites of the endocardial insertions of the anterior-superior (*1*), posterior-inferior (*2*), and septal (*5*) fascicles of the LBB, and the septal (*3*) and right ventricular (*4*) fascicles of the RBB. The 0–10-msec isochrones are in *black*, the 20–30 msec in *light stippling*, and the 50–60 msec in *dark stippling*. The *arrows* indicate the summated directions of the 20–30- and 50–60-msec isochrones pre- and post anterior infarction. (From Selvester RH, Wagner NB, Wagner GS. Ventricular excitation during percutaneous transluminal angioplasty of the left anterior descending coronary artery. Am J Cardiol 1988;62:1117,1120.)

The rapid appearance of the abnormalities of the QRS complex produced by an *anterior infarction* during continuous ischemia monitoring is illustrated in Figure 10.2. Secondary changes in QRS morphology during TMI have shifted the waveforms toward the anterior LV wall. Thrombolysis is accompanied by rapid resolution of the TMI and a shift of the QRS waveforms away from the anterior LV wall. Though it may appear that the therapy has caused the infarction, it is much more likely that the infarction had already occurred prior to the initiation of the therapy, but its detection on the ECG was obscured by the secondary QRS changes of the TMI.

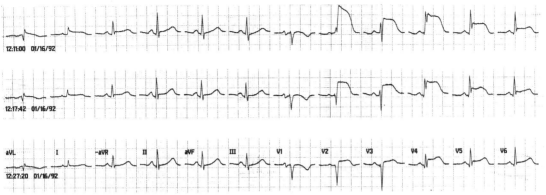

Figure 10.2. Continuous ischemia monitoring is illustrated during the first 27 minutes of intravenous thrombolytic therapy (begun at 12:00:00) in a patient with acute thrombotic occlusion of the LAD. The 12 standard leads are presented in the panoramic format after 11, 17, and 27 minutes of therapy.

TMI involving the thin right ventricular free wall may be manifested on the ECG by ST segment deviation (Chapter 9), but right ventricular infarction is not manifested by significant alteration of the QRS complex. Right ventricular free wall activation is insignificant in comparison with activation of the thicker interventricular septum and left ventricular free wall.

Myocardial infarction evolves from TMI in the distal aspects of the areas of left ventricular myocardium supplied by one of the three major coronary arteries, as previously illustrated in Figure 9.5 and Table 9.1.[4]

The basal and middle sectors of the posterior-lateral quadrant of the left ventricle are located away from the positive poles of all 12 of the standard ECG leads. Therefore, *posterior infarction* is indicated by a positive rather than negative deviation of the QRS complex (Fig. 10.3). Additional leads on the posterior-lateral thorax would be required to record ST segment elevation due to TMI and negative QRS deviation due to myocardial infarction in this area.[5]

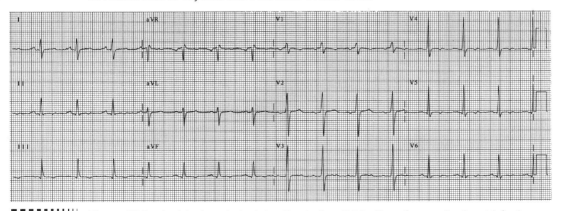

Figure 10.3. Isolated posterior infarction in the distribution of a nondominant left circumflex coronary.

QRS CRITERIA FOR DIAGNOSIS OF INFARCTION

 ## *Abnormal Q Waves*

The initial portion of the QRS complex deviates most prominently away from the area of infarction. This deviation away from the area of infarction may be represented on the ECG by prolonged Q wave duration. As presented in Figure 3.4, the initial QRS waveform may normally be negative. The presence of any Q wave is considered abnormal in only three of the 12 standard leads. Table 10.1 indicates the upper limits of normal of the Q wave duration in the various ECG leads.[6] Instead of amplitude, duration of the Q wave should be used in the definition of abnormal because the amplitudes of the individual QRS waveforms vary with the overall QRS amplitude. As discussed in the next section, Q wave amplitudes may be considered abnormal only in relation to R wave amplitudes.

Table 10.1[a]

Limb Leads		Precordial Leads	
Lead	Upper Limit	Lead	Upper Limit
I	<0.03 sec	V1	Any
II	<0.03 sec	V2	Any
III		V3	Any
aVR		V4	<0.02 sec
aVL	<0.03 sec	V5	<0.03 sec
aVF	<0.03 sec	V6	<0.03 sec

[a]Modified from Wagner GS, Freye CJ, Palmeri ST, Roark SF, Stack NC, Ideker RE, Harrell FE Jr, Selvester RH. Evaluation of a QRS scoring system for estimating myocardial infarct size. I . Specificity and observer agreement. Circulation 1982;65:345.

Many cardiac conditions other than myocardial infarction are capable of producing Q waves beyond the normal range. As indicated in Chapters 4–6 ("Chamber Enlargement," "Intraventricular Conduction Abnormalities," and "Ventricular Preexcitation," respectively), ventricular hypertrophy, intraventricular conduction abnormalities, and ventricular preexcitation commonly cause prolongation of Q wave duration. Therefore, the following steps should be considered in the evaluation of Q waves regarding the presence of myocardial infarction:

1. Are abnormal Q waves present in any lead?
2. Are criteria for other cardiac conditions that are capable of producing abnormal Q waves present?
3. Does the extent of Q wave abnormality exceed that which could have been produced by that other cardiac condition?

Abnormal R Waves

The deviation of the QRS complex away from the area of the myocardial infarction may, in the absence of abnormal Q waves, be represented by diminished R waves. Table 10.2 indicates the leads in which R waves of less than a certain amplitude or duration may be indicative of myocardial infarction.[7]

Table 10.2

Limb Leads		Precordial Leads	
Lead	Criteria for Abnormal	Lead	Criteria for Abnormal
I	R amp ≤ 0.20 mV[a]	V1	
II		V2	R dur ≤ 0.01 sec or amp ≤ 0.10 mV
III		V3	R dur ≤ 0.02 sec or amp ≤ 0.20 mV
aVR		V4	R amp ≤ 0.70 mV or ≤ Q amp
aVL	R amp ≤ Q amp	V5	R amp ≤ 0.70 mV or ≤ 2 × Q amp
aVF	R amp ≤ 2 × Q amp	V6	R amp ≤ 0.60 mV or ≤ 3 × Q amp

[a]amp, amplitude; dur, duration.

As indicated earlier, infarction in the posterior-lateral area of the left ventricle is represented by a positive rather than negative deviation of the QRS complex. This results in increased rather than decreased R wave duration and amplitude in precordial leads V1 and V2[7] (Table 10.3):

Table 10.3

Lead	Criteria for Abnormal
V1	R dur ≥ 0.04 sec, R amp ≥ 0.60 mV, R amp ≥ S amp
V2	R dur ≥ 0.05 sec, R amp ≥ 1.50 mV, R amp ≥ 1.5 × S amp

QRS CRITERIA FOR LOCALIZING INFARCTION

Table 10.4 indicates the relationships among the coronary arteries, left ventricular quadrants, and ECG leads which provide a basis for localizing myocardial infarcts.[4]

Table 10.4

Coronary Artery	LV Quadrant	Sectors	Diagnostic Leads
Left anterior descending	Anteroseptal	All	V1–V3 (away from)
	Anterosuperior	All	I, aVL (away from)
	Inferior	Apical	V4–V6 (away from)
	Posterolateral	Apical	V4–V6 (away from)
Posterior descending	Inferior	Basal, middle	II, III, aVF (away from)
Left circumflex	Posterolateral	Basal, middle	V1–V3 (toward)

An infarct produced by insufficient blood supply via the left anterior descending artery might be limited to the anterior-septal quadrant, as illustrated in Figure 10.4, *A* and *B*. It might also extend into the anterior-superior quadrant (Fig. 10.4*C*) or into the apical sectors of other quadrants (Fig. 10.4*D*) commonly referred to as anterior, anterior-*lateral*, or anterior-*apical infarction*, respectively.

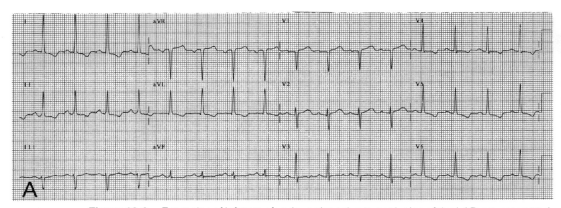

Figure 10.4. Examples of infarcts of various sizes due to occlusion of the LAD are presented in **A–D**.

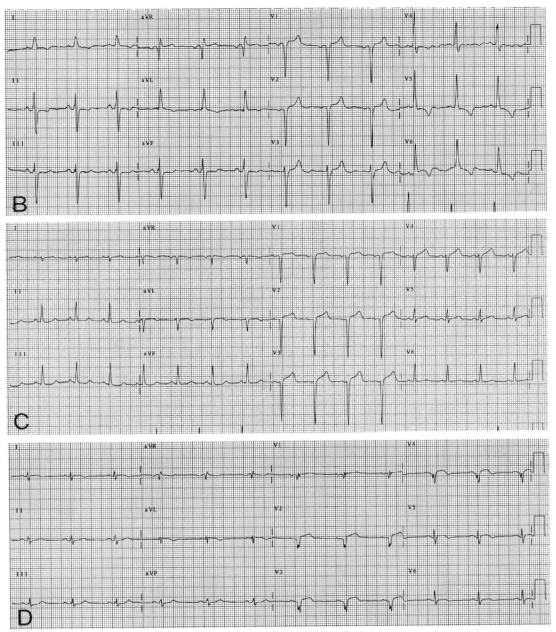

Figure 10.4.   B–D

When the right coronary is dominant (Chapter 9), its sudden complete obstruction typically produces an *inferior infarction* in the basal and middle sectors of the inferior quadrant (Fig. 10.5*A*). The patient progresses sequentially through the acute (Fig. 10.5*A*), subacute (Fig. 10.5*B*), and chronic (Fig. 1.5*C*) phases of the infarction process during the days following the complete coronary obstruction.

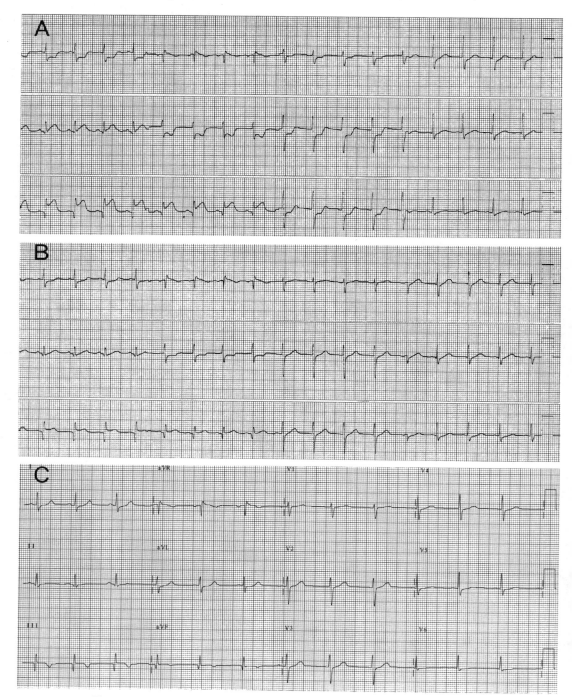

Figure 10.5. **A–C** present three patients with inferior infarcts in the various places.

When the right coronary artery is dominant, the typical distribution of the left circumflex is limited to the left ventricular free wall between the distributions of the anterior and posterior descending arteries. Sudden complete occlusion produces only a posterior infarction, as illustrated by QRS deviation away from that region in Figure 10.3. Figure 10.6 presents an example of the almost complete QRS deviation away from the left ventricular free wall which would be expected from more extensive *posterior infarction*.

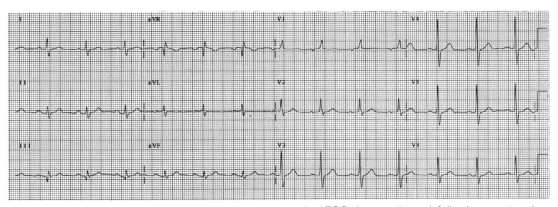

Figure 10.6. A 77-year-old man with the typical ECG changes 1 month following an extensive posterior infarction.

When the left coronary artery is dominant, a sudden complete obstruction of the right coronary artery can only produce infarction in the right ventricle, which is not represented by changes in the QRS complex. The left circumflex artery then supplies the middle and basal sectors of both the posterior-lateral and inferior quadrants, and its obstruction can produce an inferior-posterior infarction (Fig. 10.7, A and B). This same combination of left ventricular locations can be involved when there is right coronary dominance and the extension of one of its branches into the typical circumflex distribution.

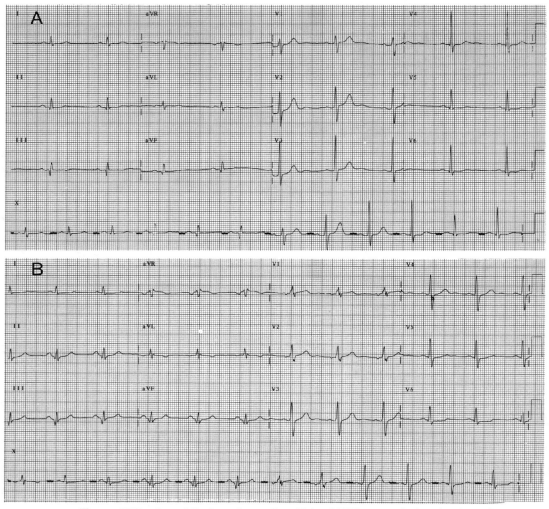

Figure 10.7. **A** and **B** show the resting 12-lead ECGs recorded at the time of coronary angiography 3 months following uncomplicated inferior-posterior infarcts. In both, the angiography revealed the occlusion to be in a dominant left circumflex coronary artery.

There are variations among individuals regarding the areas of left ventricular myocardium supplied by the three major coronary arteries. These variations may occur either congenitally or because atherosclerotic obstruction in one artery results in *collateral blood supply* from another artery. For example, the posterior descending artery may extend its supply to include the apical sector of the inferior quadrant. In this instance, its sudden complete obstruction could result in QRS deviation away from leads V4–V6 in addition to leads II, III, and aVF, causing an *inferior-apical infarction* (Fig. 10.8A). Similarly, the left circumflex artery could supply the apical sector of the posterior-lateral quadrant, causing a *posterior-apical infarction* (Fig. 10.8B). A marginal branch of the left circumflex may supply a portion of the anterior-superior quadrant and be responsible for a posterior-lateral infarction (Fig. 10.8C).

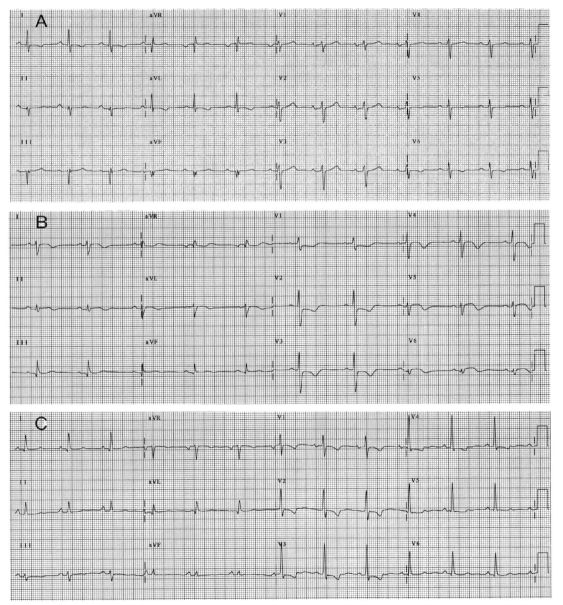

Figure 10.8. ECGs obtained from three patients (**A–C**) during the first week following initial myocardial infarcts involving multiple areas of the left ventricle.

The posterior aspect of the apex may be involved when either a dominant right or left circumflex artery is acutely obstructed. Inferior, posterior, and apical locations are apparent on the ECG, as illustrated in Figure 10.9A. The posterior aspect of the apex may also be involved by a very proximal obstruction of a nondominant circumflex artery, as seen in Figure 10.9B.

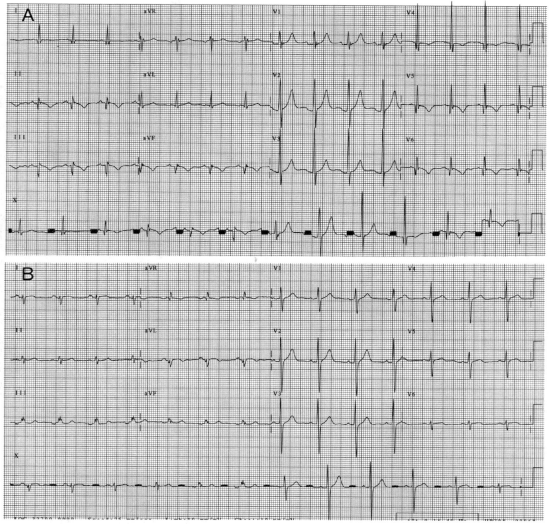

Figure 10.9. ECGs obtained from two patients during the first week following initial myocardial infarcts involving multiple areas of the left ventricle. In **A**, occlusion of a dominant RCA has produced an inferior-posterior-apical infarction; in **B**, occlusion of a nondominant LCX has produced a lateral-posterior-apical infarction.

QRS CRITERIA FOR ESTIMATING INFARCT SIZE

An individual patient may have single infarcts varying in size in the distributions of any of the three major coronary arteries or may even have multiple infarcts. Selvester and his coworkers developed a method for estimating the total percentage of the left ventricle infarcted using a weighted scoring system.[8] Computerized simulation of the sequence of electrical activation of the normal human left ventricle formed the basis for the 32-point scoring system, with each point accounting for 3% of the left ventricle.[9] The Selvester QRS scoring system includes 54 criteria from 10 of the 12 standard leads with weights ranging from one to three points per criteria (Fig. 10.10) There are criteria in precordial leads V1 and V2 for both anterior and posterior infarct locations. In addition to the Q wave and decreased R wave criteria typically used for diagnosis and localization of infarcts, this system for size estimation also contains criteria relating to the S wave.[7]

	Complete 54-Criteria, 32-Point QRS Scoring System*									

Left section:

Lead	Maximum Lead Points	Criteria	Points
I	(2)	Q≥30 ms	(1)
		{ R/Q ≤1	(1)
		{ R≤0.2 mV	(1)
II	(2)	{ Q≥40 ms	(2)
		{ Q≥30 ms	(1)
aVL	(2)	Q≥30 ms	(1)
		R/Q ≤1	(1)
aVF	(5)	{ Q≥50 ms	(3)
		{ Q≥40 ms	(2)
		{ Q≥30 ms	(1)
		{ R/Q ≤1	(2)
		{ R/Q ≤2	(1)

Middle section:

V₁				
Anterior	(2)	Any Q	(1)	
		Q or S≥1.8 mV	(1)	
Posterior	(4)	R/S ≥1	(1)	
		{ R≥50 ms	(2)
		{ R≥1.0 mV	(2)
		{ R≥40 ms	(1)
		{ R≥0.6 mV	(1)
		Q and S≤0.3 mV	(1)	

V₂				
Anterior	(1)	{ Any Q	(1)
		{ R≤10 ms	(1)
		{ R≤0.1 mV	(1)
		{ R≤R V₁ mV	(1)
Posterior	(4)	R/S ≥1.5	(1)	
		{ R≥60 ms	(2)
		{ R≥2.0 mV	(2)
		{ R≥50 ms	(1)
		{ R≥1.5 mV	(1)
		Q and S≤0.4 mV	(1)	

Right section:

V₃	(1)	{ Any Q	(1)
		{ R≤20 ms	(1)
		{ R≤0.2 mV	(1)
V₄	(3)	Q≥20 ms	(1)
		{ R/S ≤0.5	(2)
		{ R/Q ≤0.5	(2)
		{ R/S ≤1	(1)
		{ R/Q ≤1	(1)
		{ R≤0.7 mV	(1)
		{ Notched R	(1)
V₅	(3)	Q≥30 ms	(1)
		{ R/S ≤1	(2)
		{ R/Q ≤1	(2)
		{ R/S ≤2	(1)
		{ R/Q ≤2	(1)
		{ R≤0.7 mV	(1)
		{ Notched R	(1)
V₆	(3)	Q≥30 ms	(1)
		{ R/S ≤1	(2)
		{ R/Q ≤1	(2)
		{ R/S ≤3	(1)
		{ R/Q ≤3	(1)
		{ R≤0.6 mV	(1)
		{ Notched R	(1)

*When more than one criterion in the brace is met, select the one with the most points. Notched R indicates a notch that begins within the first 40 ms.

Figure 10.10. The QRS criteria from 10 of the 12 standard leads are indicated. Only one criterion can be selected from each group of criteria within a *bracket*. All criteria involving R/Q or R/S ratios consider the relative amplitudes. (From Selvester RH, Wagner GS, Hindman NB. The development and application of the Selvester QRS scoring system for estimating myocardial infarct size. Arch Intern Med 1985;145:1878. Copyright 1985 American Medical Association.)

In this scoring system, a very important criterion is the Q wave duration. This measurement is easy when the QRS complex has discrete Q, R, and S waves, as illustrated in Figure 10.11A.[7] The subsequent panels (Fig. 10.11, *B–E*) present sequentially smaller positive deflections between the initial negative deflection (Q wave) caused by the infarction and the terminal negative deflection (S wave), which was a component of the preinfarction QRS complex. The Q wave duration should be measured along the baseline from the onset of the initial negative deflection to either the onset of the positive deflection or a point directly above the peak of the notch in the negative deflection. Figure 10.11 illustrates a smooth Q wave that is clearly >0.05 sec in duration.

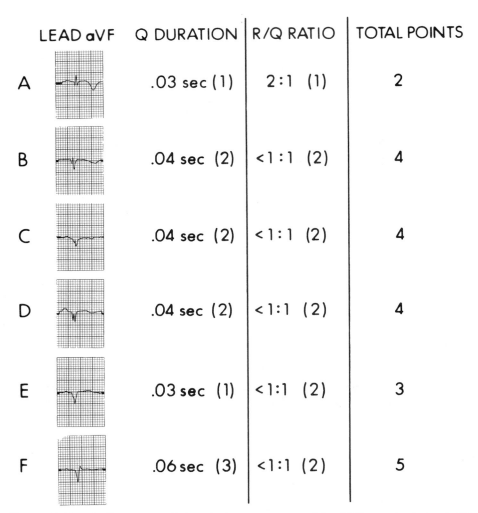

	LEAD aVF	Q DURATION	R/Q RATIO	TOTAL POINTS
A		.03 sec (1)	2:1 (1)	2
B		.04 sec (2)	<1:1 (2)	4
C		.04 sec (2)	<1:1 (2)	4
D		.04 sec (2)	<1:1 (2)	4
E		.03 sec (1)	<1:1 (2)	3
F		.06 sec (3)	<1:1 (2)	5

Figure 10.11. **A–F** present variations in the appearance of the QRS complex in lead aVF representing the changes of inferior infarction. The number of QRS points awarded for the Q wave duration and the R/Q amplitude ratios are indicated in *parentheses*. The total number of QRS points awarded for lead aVF is indicated for each example in the *final column*. (Modified from Wagner GS, Freye CJ, Palmeri ST, Roark SF, Stack NC, Ideker RE, Harrell FE Jr, Selvester RH. Evaluation of a QRS scoring system for estimating myocardial infarct size. I. Specificity and observer agreement. Circulation 1982;65:345.)

Satisfaction of only a single criterion may represent either a normal variant or an extremely small infarct. This system may be confounded by two infarcts located in opposite sectors of the left ventricle. The opposing effects on the summation of the electrical forces may cancel each other, producing falsely negative ECG changes. Figure 10.12, *A* and *B*, illustrates the coexistence of both anterior and posterior infarcts and the potential for underestimation of the total percentage of left ventricle infarcted.

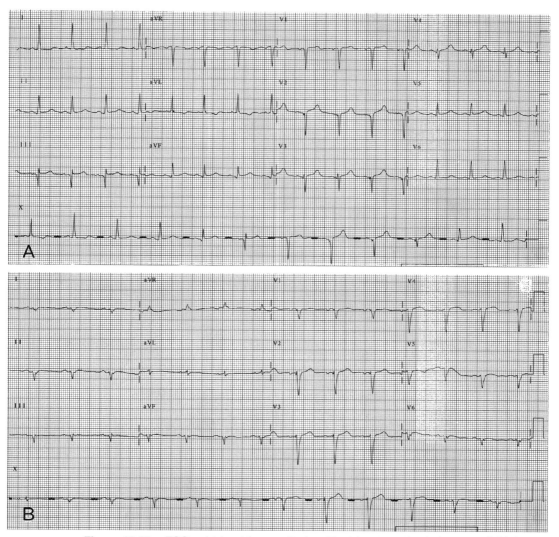

Figure 10.12. ECGs obtained from patients with at least two healed myocardial infarcts. Note the QR patterns in leads V2–V4 in **A** and in leads V1–V3 in **B**, suggesting that "canceling" infarction may be present in the anterior-septal and posterior-lateral quadrants of the left ventricle.

ST SEGMENT CHANGES

 The ST segment changes that are prominent during TMI typically disappear when the ischemic myocardium either infarcts or regains sufficient blood supply. Their time course of resolution is accelerated by reperfusion via the infarct-related artery, as discussed in Chapter 9. When reelevation of the ST segments is observed, further TMI or a disturbance in the pericardium is suggested. TMI is typically limited to a particular area of the left ventricle. When the ST elevation occurs in leads representing multiple left ventricular areas, acute bleeding into the pericardium should be considered (Fig. 10.13).[10] This may be the first indication that the infarct has caused a *myocardial rupture* with leakage of blood into the pericardial sac. If this process remains undetected, cardiac arrest may result from *pericardial tamponade*, in which myocardial relaxation is restricted by the blood in the enclosed pericardial space. The ECG changes are similar to those of acute pericarditis, discussed in Chapter 11 ("Miscellaneous Conditions").

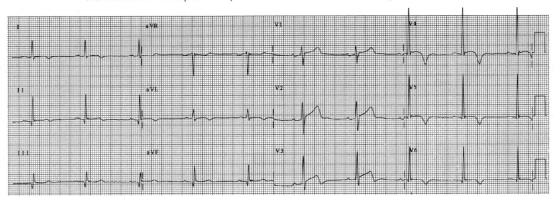

Figure 10.13. ECG obtained during the first week following an acute inferior infarction. Reelevation of the ST segment appeared in leads II, III, and aVF, along with elevation in additional leads V1–V4.

In some patients, the ST segment elevation does not completely resolve during the acute phase of the myocardial infarction (Fig. 10.14). This more commonly occurs with anterior infarcts than with those in the other locations.[7] This lack of ST segment resolution has been associated with the thinning of the left ventricular wall caused by *infarct expansion*.[11,12] The extreme manifestation of infarct expansion is the formation of a *ventricular aneurysm*. The incidence of such extreme infarct expansion may be reduced by successful thrombolytic therapy.

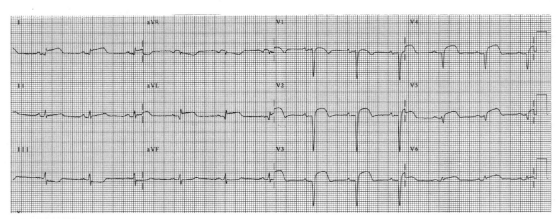

Figure 10.14. An ECG obtained 2 weeks following an acute anterior-lateral-apical infarction reveals persistent ST segment elevation without evolution of T wave inversion.

T WAVE CHANGES

The movement of the T waves toward the area of the TMI, like that of the ST segments, resolves as the ischemic myocardium either recovers or infarcts. Unlike the ST segment, however, the T waves do not typically return to their normal positions as the process of infarction evolves. The T waves move past the isoelectric position until they are directed away from the area of infarction.[13] They assume an appearance identical to that described in Chapter 7 ("Myocardial Ischemia and Infarction") as "ischemic T waves", even though there is no ongoing myocardial ischemia. This evolution of the T wave direction, from toward the area of TMI to away from the area of infarction, is illustrated in Figure 10.15, *A* and *B*. Typically, the terminal portion of the T wave is the first to become inverted, followed by the middle and initial portions.

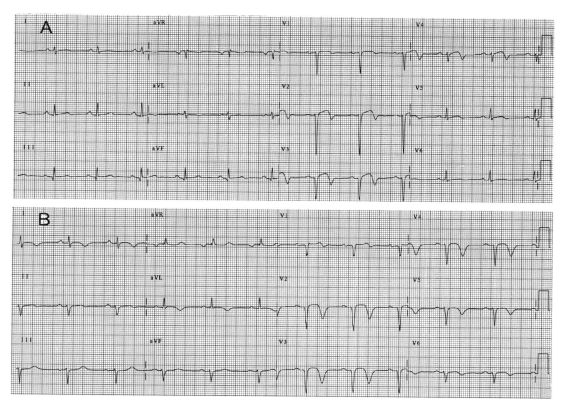

Figure 10.15. ECGs from two patients during the week following initial acute anterior-apical infarcts. In **A**, by the second day, the resolving ST segment elevation is accompanied by inversion of the terminal and middle portions of the T waves. In **B**, by the fourth day, the ST segment elevation has almost completely resolved and the T waves are completely inverted.

When the posterior-lateral quadrant of the LV is involved, the T waves eventually become markedly positive. Figure 10.16 illustrates the tall positive T waves in leads V1 and V2 which accompany the negative T waves in other leads during the chronic phase of an inferior-posterior-apical infarction.

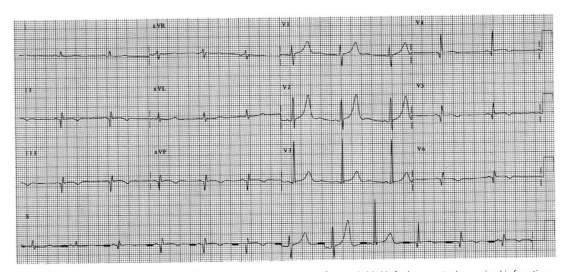

Figure 10.16. An ECG from a patient 5 days after an initial inferior-posterior-apical infarction. Note that the "T wave inversion" includes both negative inversion in leads II, III, aVF, and V4–V6, and positive inversion in leads V1–V3.

GLOSSARY

Anterior infarction: infarction in the distribution of the left anterior descending coronary artery, involving primarily the middle and apical sectors of the anterior-septal quadrant of the left ventricle.

Apical infarction: infarction in the distribution of any of the major coronary arteries, involving primarily the apical sectors of the posterior-lateral and inferior quadrants of the left ventricle.

Collateral blood supply: the perfusion of an area of myocardium via arteries that have developed to compensate for an obstruction of one of the principal coronary arteries.

Infarct expansion: partial disruption of the myocardial wall in the area of a recent infarction which results in thinning of wall and dilation of the chamber.

Inferior infarction: infarction in the distribution of the posterior descending coronary artery, involving primarily the basal and middle sectors of the inferior quadrant of the left ventricle, but often extending into the posterior aspect of the right ventricle.

Lateral infarction: infarction in the distribution of a "diagonal" or "marginal" coronary artery, involving primarily the basal and middle sectors of the anterior-superior quadrant of the left ventricle.

Necrosis: death of a living tissue; termed an infarction when it is caused by insufficient supply of oxygen via the circulation.

Myocardial rupture: complete disruption of the myocardial wall in the area of a recent infarction which results in leakage of blood out of the chamber.

Pericardial tamponade: filling the pericardial sac with fluid which restricts the relaxation of the cardiac chambers.

Posterior infarction: infarction in the distribution of the left circumflex coronary artery, involving primarily the basal and middle sectors of the posterior-lateral quadrant of the left ventricle.

Ventricular aneurysm: the extreme of infarct expansion, in which the wall becomes so thin that it bulges outward (dyskinesia) during systole.

REFERENCES

1. Reimer KA, Lowe JE, Rasmussen MM, Jennings RB. The wavefront phenomenon of ischemic cell death: I. Myocardial infarct size vs. duration of coronary occlusion in dogs. Circulation 1977;56:786–794.
2. Reimer KA, Jennings RB. The "wavefront phenomenon" of myocardial ischemic cell death: II. Transmural progression of necrosis within the framework of ischemic bed size (myocardium at risk) and collateral flow. Lab Invest 1979;40:633–644.
3. Wagner NB, White RD, Wagner GS. The 12-lead ECG and the extent of myocardium at risk of acute infarction: cardiac anatomy and lead locations, and the phases of serial changes during acute occlusion. In: Califf RM, Mark DB, Wagner GS, eds. Acute coronary care in the thrombolytic era. Chicago: Year Book, 1988:36–41.
4. Wagner GS, Wagner NB. The 12-lead ECG and the extent of myocardium at risk of acute infarction: anatomic relationships among coronary, Purkinje, and myocardial anatomy. In: Califf RM, Mark DB, Wagner GS, eds. Acute coronary care in the thrombolytic era. Chicago: Year Book, 1988:16–30.
5. Flowers NC, Horan LG, Sohi GS, Hand RC, Johnson JC. New evidence for inferior-posterior myocardial infarction on surface potential maps. Am J Cardiol 1976;38:576.
6. Wagner GS, Freye CJ, Palmeri ST, Roark SF, Stack NC, Ideker RE, Harrell FE, Selvester RH. Evaluation of a QRS scoring system for estimating myocardial infarct size. I. Specificity and observer agreement. Circulation 1982;65:342–347.
7. Hindman NB, Schocken DD, Widmann M, Anderson WD, White RD, Leggett S, Ideker RE, Hinohara T, Selvester RH, Wagner GS. Evaluation of a QRS scoring system for estimating myocardial infarct size. V. Specificity and method of application of the complete system. Am J Cardiol 1985;55:1485–1490.
8. Selvester RH, Wagner JO, Rubin HB. Quantitation of myocardial infarct size and location by electrocardiogram and vectorcardiogram. In: Boerhave course in quantitation in cardiology. The Netherlands: Leyden University Press, 1972:31.
9. Selvester RH, Soloman J, Sapoznikov D. Computer simulation of the electrocardiogram. In: Computer techniques in cardiology. New York: Marcel Dekker, 1979:417.
10. Oliva PB, Hammill SC, Edwards WD. Electrocardiographic diagnosis of post infarction regional pericarditis: ancillary observations regarding the effect of reperfusion on the rapidity and amplitude of T wave inversion after acute myocardial infarction. Circulation 1993;88:896–904.
11. Lindsay J Jr, Dewey RC, Talesnick BS, Nolan NG. Relation of ST segment elevation after healing of acute myocardial infarction to the presence of left ventricular aneurysm. Am J Cardiol 1984;54:84–86.
12. Arvan S, Varat MA. Persistent ST-segment elevation and left ventricular wall abnormalities: 2-dimensional echocardiographic study. Am J Cardiol 1984;53:1542–1546.
13. Mandel WJ, Burgess MJ, Neville J Jr, Abildskov JA. Analysis of T wave abnormalities associated with myocardial infarction using a theoretic model. Circulation 1968;38:178–188.

CHAPTER 11

Miscellaneous Conditions

PERICARDIAL ABNORMALITIES

 There is a small fluid-filled space called the *pericardial sac* that separates the heart from the other structures in the thorax. The sac is lined by two layers of connective tissue referred to as the pericardium. The inner layer, or visceral pericardium, adheres to the myocardium, while the outer layer, or parietal pericardium, encloses the pericardial fluid. These tissues can become inflamed for many reasons, thereby resulting in *pericarditis*, which usually resolves following an acute phase, but may progress to a chronic phase. The acute phase may be complicated by excess pericardial fluid called *pericardial effusion*. Chronic persistence of the inflammatory process may result in thickening of the tissues and is called constrictive pericarditis.

1. AcutePericarditis

Typically, acute pericarditis persists for 3 or 4 weeks, and ECG changes evolve through two stages. The characteristic ECG abnormality during the earliest stage of acute pericarditis is elevation of the ST segments in many leads, accompanied by upright T waves (Fig. 11.1).[1] In 28 of a series of 44 consecutive patients with acute pericarditis, PR segment depression was also present.[2] However, these changes were present in only 25 of these patients, while the others were atypical in some way.

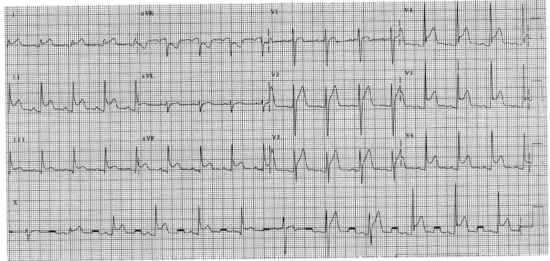

Figure 11.1. ECG recording of a 22-year-old man presenting to an emergency facility with acute chest pain.

The ST segment elevation occurs because the inflammation also involves the immediately adjacent epicardial layer of myocardium, which produces the epicardial injury discussed in Chapter 9 ("Ischemia Due to Insufficient Blood Supply"). When the epicardial injury is produced by transmural ischemia, the changes are restricted to the ECG leads that overlie the myocardium supplied by the obstructed coronary artery. In pericarditis, the entire epicardium is usually involved, resulting in more widespread ST segment elevation. However, differentiation between acute pericarditis and acute transmural ischemia becomes difficult when the epicardial inflammation is localized rather than diffuse and the ST segment elevation is restricted to only a few leads (Fig. 11.2). In both conditions, the patient may present with precordial pain and an additional clinical evaluation is required to reach the correct diagnosis.

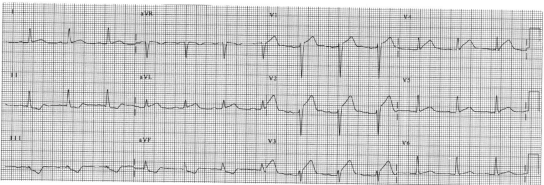

Figure 11.2. ECG recording of a 57-year-old woman with carcinoma of the breast and acute chest pain.

Acute pericarditis must also be differentiated from the normal variant early repolarization discussed in Chapter 3 ("Interpretation of the Normal Electrocardiogram"). As Spodick has suggested[1], pericarditis is more likely to present with:

a. ST elevation in both the limb and precordial leads;
b. A frontal plane ST axis to the left of the T wave axis;
c. ST segment depression in lead V1.

Figure 11.3 presents a typical example that could represent either a normal variant or the first stage of acute pericarditis.

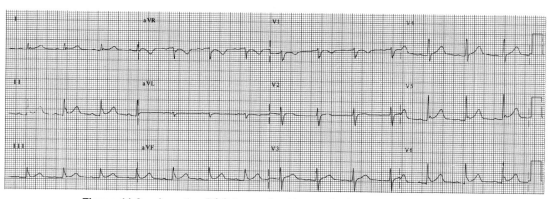

Figure 11.3. A routine ECG from a healthy medical student.

Occasionally, the ST segment elevation resolves and there is no progression to the second stage.[3] More often, when the ST segments return to the isoelectric level, there is widespread T wave inversion typical of the second stage of acute pericarditis (Fig. 11.4).

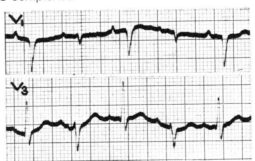

Figure 11.4. ECG recording of a 19-year-old woman after 1 week in the hospital with acute pericarditis.

2. Pericardial Effusion

A generalized decrease in all of the ECG waveform amplitudes, termed *low voltage*, occurs if significant pericardial effusion or thickening develops. This probably occurs because the cardiac impulses are "short circuited" by the pericardial fluid or thickened pericardium. A triad of ECG changes that is virtually diagnostic of pericardial effusion is presented in Figure 11.5:

a. Low voltage;
b. ST segment elevation;
c. Total electrical alternans.

Total electrical alternans refers to the alternation of all ECG waveforms, P waves as well as the QRS complexes.[4,5]

Figure 11.5. ECG recording of a 64-year-old man with carcinoma of the lung and malignant pericardial effusion.

3. Chronic Constrictive Pericarditis

In chronic constrictive pericarditis, the second stage ECG changes of acute pericarditis persist and are accompanied by a decrease in voltage.[6] The depth of inversion of the T waves has been reported to correlate with the degree of pericardial adherence to the myocardium.[7] This may be clinically important because surgical "stripping" of the thickened pericardium is more difficult when it is adhered tightly to the myocardium.

ENDOCRINE AND METABOLIC ABNORMALITIES

 ## 1. Thyroid Abnormalities

The hypothyroid condition is termed *myxedema* and the hyperthyroid condition is termed *thyrotoxicosis*. Both are often accompanied by typical changes in ECG waveform morphology. Since the thyroid hormone, thyroxin, mediates sympathetic nervous activity, a hypothyroid state is accompanied by a slowing down of the sinus rate (sinus bradycardia). On the other hand, a hyperthyroid state is accompanied by a speeding up of the sinus rate (sinus tachycardia).[8] Similarly, AV conduction may be impaired in hypothyroidism and accelerated in hyperthyroidism.[9]

a. Myxedema. The diagnosis of myxedema should be suspected when the following combination of ECG changes is present (Fig. 11.6):

1. Low voltage of all waveforms;
2. Inverted T waves without ST segment deviation in many or all leads;
3. Sinus bradycardia.

These changes may be related to cardiac deposits of myxomatosis material, pericarditis, diminished sympathetic nervous activity, and/or the effect on the myocardium of lowered levels of thyroxin.[10]

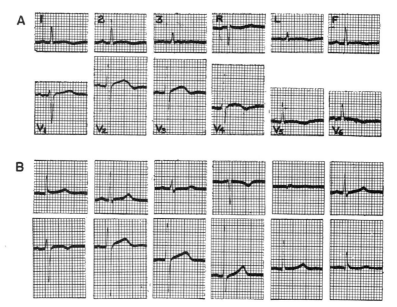

Figure 11.6. ECG recordings of a 43-year-old woman with myxedema at the time of initial presentation with typical symptoms of hypothyroidism (**A**) and after 10 weeks of treatment with thyroid extract (**B**).

b. Thyrotoxicosis. The diagnosis of thyrotoxicosis should be suspected when there is an increase in the amplitudes of all of the ECG waveforms.[11] This simulates right atrial and left ventricular enlargement as discussed in Chapter 4 ("Abnormal Wave Morphology"). Though the QT interval decreases as the sinus rate increases, the corrected QT interval (QTc) may be prolonged.[12]

2. Obesity

Obesity has the potential for affecting the ECG in several ways:

a. Displacement of the heart by elevating the diaphragm;
b. Increasing the cardiac workload;
c. Increasing the distance between the heart and the recording electrodes.

In a study of over 1000 obese individuals, the heart rate, PR interval, QRS interval, QRS voltage, and QTc interval all showed an increase with increasing obesity.[13] The QRS axis also tended to shift leftward. Interestingly, only 4% of this population had low QRS voltage. One study has reported increased incidence of false-positive criteria for inferior myocardial infarction in both obese individuals and in women in the final trimester of pregnancy, presumably because of diaphragmatic elevation.[14]

3. Hypothermia

Hypothermia may be defined as a rectal temperature below 36.6 °C or 97.9 °F. At these lower temperatures, characteristic ECG changes develop, as illustrated in Figure 11.7. All intervals, including RR, PR, QRS, and QT, may lengthen. Characteristic *Osborn waves* appear as deflections at the J point in the same direction as the QRS complex.[15] The height of the Osborn waves is roughly proportional to the degree of hypothermia.

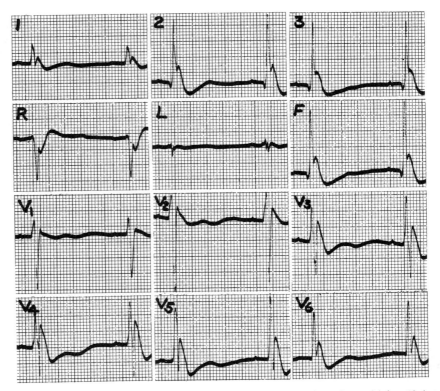

Figure 11.7. ECG recording of an 82-year-old man exposed to the cold for 48 hours presenting with a body temperature of 91 °F.

4. Amyloidosis

An abnormal protein called amyloid is deposited in the heart during various disease states. Its accumulation causes cardiac amyloidosis, which eventually produces heart failure. Amyloidosis may be suspected when the following combination of ECG changes appear (Fig. 11.8)[16]:

a. Low voltage of all waveforms in the limb leads;
b. Marked left axis deviation typical of LAFB;
c. QS or minimal R waves in leads V1–V3 or in lead V4;
d. Prolonged AV conduction time.

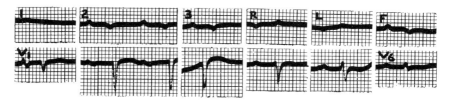

Figure 11.8.   ECG recording of an elderly man with severe heart failure. (From Marriott HJL. Correlations of electrocardiographic and pathologic changes. In: Pathology of the heart and blood vessels. Springfield, IL: Charles C Thomas, 1968.)

ELECTROLYTE ABNORMALITIES

 Either abnormally low (hypo-) or high (hyper-) serum levels of the electrolytes potassium or calcium may produce marked abnormalities of the ECG waveforms. Indeed, typical ECG changes may provide the first clinical evidence of the presence of these conditions.

1. Potassium

The terms *hypo-* and *hyperkalemia* rather than "potassemia" are commonly used for alterations in serum levels of this important electrolyte. Since abnormalities at either extreme may be life threatening, understanding of the ECG changes is important.

a. Hypokalemia. A significant potassium deficit may be encountered in many metabolic disorders including:

1. Cirrhosis of the liver;
2. Diabetic coma after vigorous treatment;
3. Hypochloremic alkalosis from any one of various causes (vomiting, diuresis, etc.);
4. Excessive secretion or administration of corticosteroids (Cushing's syndrome or primary aldosteronism);
5. Following vigorous resuscitation from cardiac arrest.[17]

The typical ECG signs of hypokalemia may appear when the serum potassium is within normal limits or, conversely, the ECG may be normal when serum levels are elevated. The ECG changes, as illustrated in Figures 11.9 and 11.10, are[18]:

1. Flattening or inversion of the T wave;
2. Increased prominence of the U wave;
3. Slight depression of the ST segment;
4. Increased amplitude and width of the P wave;
5. PR interval prolongation;
6. Premature beats and sustained tachyarrhythmias.

The characteristic reversal in the relative amplitudes of the T and U waves, discussed in Chapter 3, is the most characteristic change in waveform morphology. The U wave prominence is caused by prolongation of the recovery phase of the cardiac action potential. This can lead to the life-threatening *torsades de pointes* type of ventricular tachyarrhythmia, as discussed in Chapter 17 ("Ventricular Tachyarrhythmias").[19] Hypokalemia also potentiates the tachyarrhythmias produced by digitalis toxicity, discussed in Chapter 22 ("Drug Toxicity").

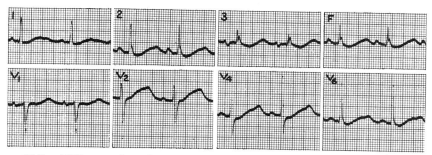

Figure 11.9. ECG recording of a 53-year-old man receiving diuretic therapy for chronic heart failure. The serum potassium level was 1.7 mEq/L. The normal range is from 4.0 to 5.0 mEq/L.

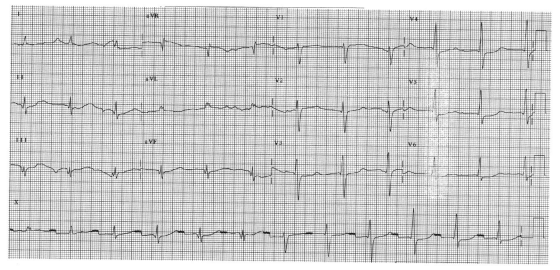

Figure 11.10. ECG recording of a 23-year-old woman on the morning after treatment for diabetic ketoacidosis. Serum potassium level was 3.2 mEq/L.

b. Hyperkalemia.   Hyperkalemia may have a variety of causes:

1. Renal failure;
2. Excess potassium replacement therapy;
3. Acidosis from any one of various causes (diabetic ketoacidosis, lactic acidosis, etc.);
4. Presence of insufficient corticosteroids (Addison's disease).

As in hypokalemia, there may be a poor correlation between serum potassium levels and the typical ECG changes.[20] The earliest ECG evidence of hyperkalemia usually appears in the T waves, as illustrated in Figure 11.11. The variety of changes include:

1. Increased amplitude and peaking of the T wave;
2. PR interval prolongation;
3. QRS interval prolongation.
4. Flattening of the P wave.

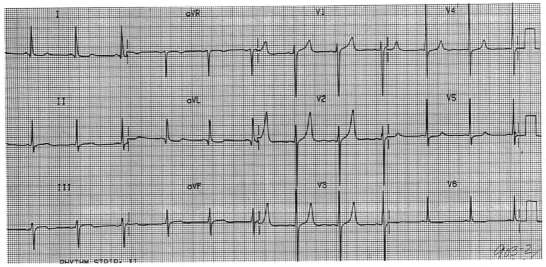

Figure 11.11.   ECG recording of a 42-year-old man with acute renal failure. The serum potassium level was 7.1 mEq/L.

The AV conduction may become so delayed that advanced AV block appears, as discussed in Chapter 22.[21] Prolongation of the QRS complex and flattening of the P waves occur because the high potassium levels delay the spread of impulse through the myocardium. This abnormally slow conduction can lead to cardiac arrest due to ventricular fibrillation, as discussed in Chapter 19 ("Decreased Automaticity").[22] The P waves may totally disappear, as illustrated in Figure 11.12. Hyperkalemia may also reduce the myocardial response to artificial pacemaker stimulation.[23]

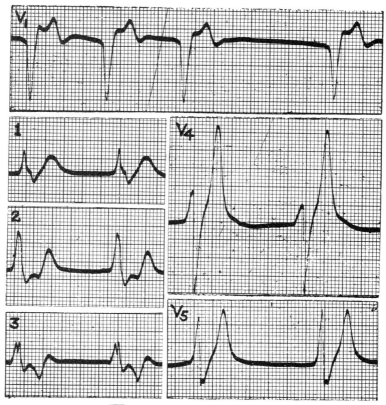

Figure 11.12. ECG recording of a 72-year-old woman with end-stage renal disease. The serum potassium level was 8.1 mEq/L.

2. Calcium

The ventricular recovery time, as represented on the ECG by the QTc interval (Chapter 3), is altered by the extremes of serum calcium levels:

| Deficiency | Hypocalcemia | Prolonged QTc interval |
| Excess | Hypercalcemia | Shortened QTc interval |

The change in the QTc interval is produced by an increase or decrease in the ST segment while the T wave remains relatively normal (Fig. 11.13).[24]

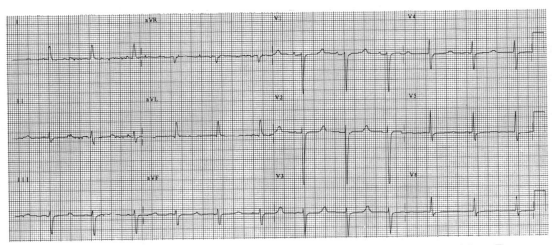

Figure 11.13. ECG recording of a 74-year-old woman with chronic renal failure. The serum calcium level was 7.2 mg/100 ml. The normal range is from 9.0 to 11.0 mg/100 ml.

In *hypocalcemia*, terminal T wave inversion may occur in some leads (Fig. 11.14).

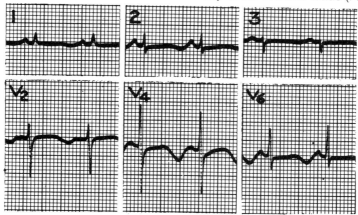

Figure 11.14. ECG recording of a 59-year-old man with hypoparathyroidism. The serum calcium level was 4.2 mg/100 ml.

In *hypercalcemia*, the proximal limb of the T wave abruptly slopes to its peak, and the ST segment may disappear, as illustrated in Figure 11.15.[25] In extreme hypercalcemia, an increase in QRS amplitude, diphasic T waves, and Osborn waves has been described.[26,27]

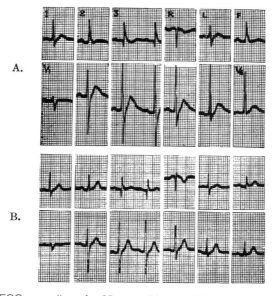

Figure 11.15. ECG recording of a 62-year-old man with hyperparathyroidism before parathyroidectomy with the serum calcium level 15 mg/100 ml (**A**) and after parathyroidectomy with the serum calcium level 10.7 mg/100 ml.(**B**) (From Beck GH, Marriott HJL. The electrocardiogram in hyperparathyroidism. Am J Cardiol 1959;3:411.)

INTRACRANIAL HEMORRHAGE

 Hemorrhage into either the intracerebral or subarachnoid spaces can produce dramatic changes in the ECG, presumably because of increased intracranial pressure (Fig. 11.16).[28-31] Less severe ECG changes occur with nonhemorrhagic cerebrovascular accidents[32]:

a. Precordial T waves becoming widened and usually inverted;
b. Prolonged QTc interval;
c. Bradyarrhythmias.

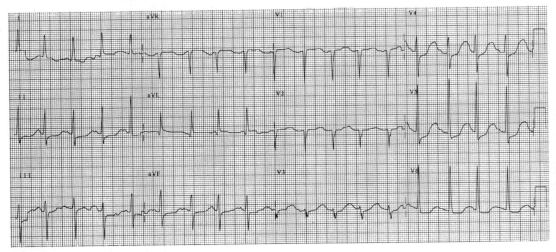

Figure 11.16. ECG recording of a 78-year-old woman with sudden loss of consciousness. Clinical diagnosis is massive intracerebral hemorrhage.

DRUG EFFECTS

Either therapeutic or toxic cardiac effects of various medications can sometimes be detected on the ECG. The term drug effect refers to the therapeutic cardiac manifestations on the ECG, while the term drug toxicity refers to the cardiac arrhythmias caused by the medications (Chapter 22). The level of a drug in blood and tissue at which toxicity occurs can vary widely depending on the underlying pathology, the premedication ECG status, the variations in electrolytes such as potassium, and the presence of other drugs.

1. Digitalis

Digitalis effect occurs because the recovery or repolarization of the myocardial cells occurs earlier, as illustrated in Figure 11.17. This is manifested on the ECG by:

a. "Coved" ST depression;
b. Flattened T wave;
c. Decreased QTc interval.

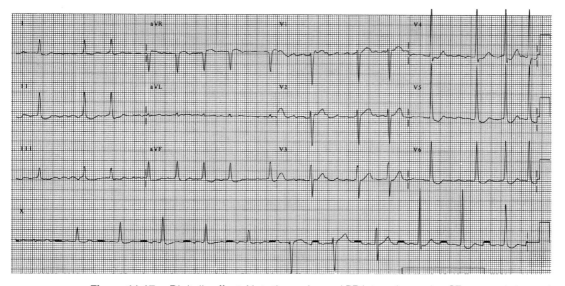

Figure 11.17. Digitalis effect. Note the prolonged PR interval, sagging ST segments in most of the leads, and the short QT interval.

Occasionally, the J point is depressed, mimicking myocardial ischemia (Fig. 11.18). This extreme example of digitalis effect usually occurs only in those leads with tall R waves. Another manifestation of digitalis effect is the vagally mediated slowing of AV nodal conduction (Chapter 22). In sinus rhythm, there is a slight increase in the PR interval within the normal range of <0.20 sec. In atrial flutter and fibrillation, there is a decrease in the ventricular rate within the normal range of >60 beats/min (Chapter 15, "Atrial Flutter/Fibrillation Spectrum").

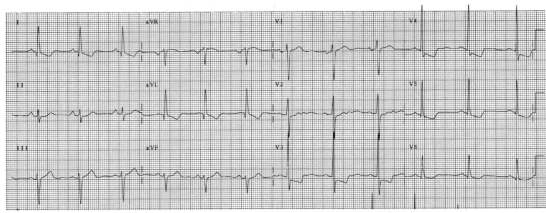

Figure 11.18. ECG recording of a 77-year-old woman with congestive heart failure. The ECG changes, including ST segment depression, developed at the time the digitalis loading dosages were administered.

2. Quinidine and Drugs with Similar Cardiac Effects

In contrast to digitalis, *quinidine* effect is produced by a delay in the recovery or repolarization of myocardial cells. This results in prolongation of the QTc interval, as illustrated in Figure 11.19.[33] Quinidine effect may be summarized as follows:

a. Depressed, widened, notched, and then inverted T waves;
b. Prominent U waves;
c. Prolonged QTc interval;
d. Prolonged QRS complex.

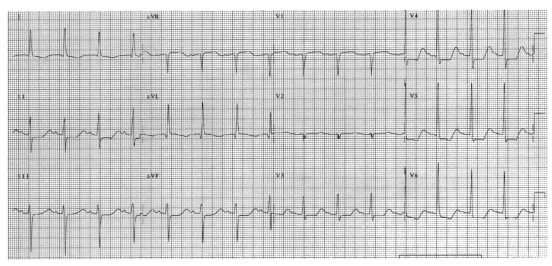

Figure 11.19. ECG recording of a 68-year-old woman with recent acute anterior infarction complicated by ventricular tachycardia. The arrhythmia has been controlled by quinidine, and quinidine effect appears on the ECG.

The QRS complex prolongation occurs only with an extreme quinidine effect, and increased duration of 25–50% is evidence of toxicity (Chapter 22). Life-threatening ventricular tachycardia of the torsades de pointes variety may develop. Quinidine effect is exaggerated by the presence of digitalis. The T wave amplitude is decreased and the U wave amplitude is increased as in hypokalemia (Fig. 11.20).

Drugs with similar antiarrhythmic properties as quinidine, such as procainamide and disopyramide, produce similar effects on the ECG. Amiodarone effect is characterized by even greater prolongation of the QTc interval than is quinidine effect. The phenothiazine group of drugs, which are commonly used in psychiatric disorders, produce ECG changes similar to quinidine effect.[34]

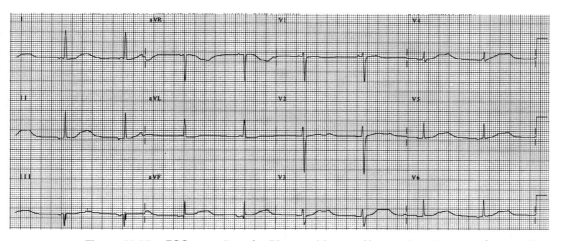

Figure 11.20. ECG recording of a 72-year-old man with recent acute onset of congestive heart failure complicated by atrial fibrillation. Use of digitalis and quinidine converted his rhythm to sinus with evidence of both digitalis and quinidine effect.

HYPERTROPHIC CARDIOMYOPATHY

Cardiomyopathy is a general term applied to all conditions in which the myocardium does not perform normally. Most are caused by myocardial ischemia and infarction and are associated with the ECG changes discussed in Chapters 7–10. *Hypertrophic cardiomyopathy* may occur secondary to right or left ventricular overload (Chapter 4) or as a primary cardiac abnormality. Primary hypertrophic cardiomyopathy may involve both ventricles, only one ventricle, or only a portion of one ventricle. A common localized variety is asymmetrical septal hypertrophy (ASH), which may obstruct the aortic outflow tract during systole, resulting in *subaortic stenosis.*

A spectrum of ECG changes may occur in hypertrophic cardiomyopathy regardless of whether or not the problem is localized to the septum[35,36]:

1. Typical LVH;
2. Marked LAD;
3. Deep, narrow Q waves in the leftward-oriented leads.

These changes are illustrated in Figure 11.21*A.* The R waves may be reciprocally tall in the right precordial leads, as seen in Figure 11.21*B.*

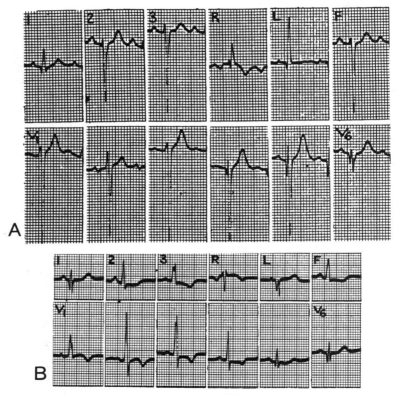

Figure 11.21. Hypertrophic cardiomyopathy. **A.** ECG recording of a 29-year-old, asymptomatic physician. Note the marked left axis deviation (−75°) and prominent but narrow Q waves in leads V4–V6. **B.** Note the deep Q waves in leads I, aVL, and V6 with reciprocal tall R waves in the right chest leads, indicating septal hypertrophy.

PULMONARY ABNORMALITIES

When a pulmonary abnormality creates an increased resistance to blood flow from the right side of the heart, a condition of systolic or pressure overload develops (Chapter 4). This condition has been termed *cor pulmonale* and can occur either acutely or chronically. The most common cause of acute cor pulmonale is pulmonary embolism. Chronic cor pulmonale may be produced by the pulmonary congestion that occurs with left ventricular failure or by the pulmonary hypertension that develops either as a primary disease or secondary to chronic obstructive pulmonary disease. Right atrial enlargement commonly occurs with acute and chronic cor pulmonale. In the acute condition, there is right ventricular dilation. Chronically, there is right ventricular hypertrophy. Since chronic right ventricular hypertrophy is discussed in detail in Chapter 4, only acute cor pulmonale is included here.

Chronic obstructive pulmonary disease is often characterized by *emphysema*, in which the lungs become overinflated. This produces anatomic changes that affect the ECG in unique ways:

Anatomic Changes	ECG Changes
Compression of the heart into a more vertical position	Vertical P wave
Lowering of the diaphragm	QRS axis in the frontal plane
Increased volume of the thorax	Decreased amplitudes of ECG waveforms (low voltage)

The ECG changes of pulmonary emphysema may occur alone or in combination with the changes of right ventricular hypertrophy since emphysema may or may not produce chronic cor pulmonale.

1. Acute Cor Pulmonale

In typical acute cor pulmonale, changes appear in the frontal plane leads which mimic acute inferior myocardial infarction (Chapter 10, "Myocardial Infarction"). Lead III is mostly involved with:

a. An increase in the size of the normal Q wave;
b. Slight ST segment elevation;
c. Shallow inversion of the T wave.

Unlike inferior infarction, there are minimal, if any, changes in leads II and aVF. The size of the S wave is increased in lead I, indicating a rightward shift of the QRS axis as seen in Figure 11.22.[36a]

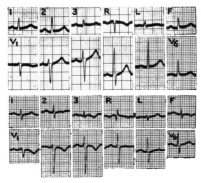

Figure 11.22. The baseline ECG (**A**) was obtained 1 year prior to a documented pulmonary embolism (**B**). Note the rightward shift of the frontal plane axis, the rightward movement of the transverse plane transitional zone, and the inversion of the T waves in leads II, III, aVF, and V1–V3.

In the precordial leads, elevated ST segments and inverted T waves are some-times seen over the right ventricle, while S waves may become more prominent over the left ventricle. The typical changes of RBBB may be apparent in lead V1, as illustrated in Figure 11.23.

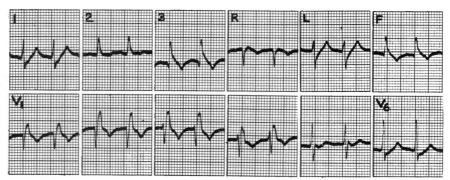

Figure 11.23. Acute cor pulmonale (from a patient with a massive pulmonary embolism). Note the simultaneous inversion of the T waves in the inferior (III and aVF) and anteroseptal (V1–V4) leads and the development of RBBB.

2. Pulmonary Emphysema

The five most typical findings in emphysema have been grouped together[37]:

a. Prominent P waves in leads II, III, and aVF;
b. Exaggerated atrial repolarization (TP) waves producing >0.10 mV ST segment depression in leads II, III, and aVF;
c. Rightward shift of the QRS axis in the frontal plane;
d. Decreased progression of the R wave amplitudes in the precordial leads;
e. Low voltage of the QRS complexes, especially in the left precordial leads.

Figure 11.24 presents a typical example of this combination of ECG abnormalities.

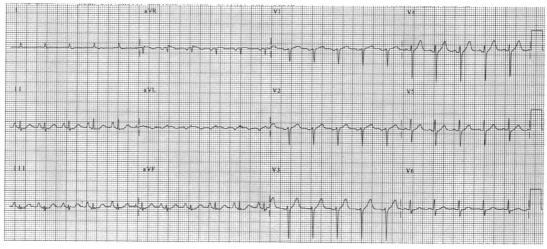

Figure 11.24. ECG recording of a 68-year-old man with severe dyspnea and a chest x-ray diagnostic of advanced pulmonary emphysema.

The QRS axis in the frontal plane is occasionally directly superior (near −90°) rather than directly inferior, as indicated by criterion c above (Fig. 11.25).[38] Thus, the frontal plane QRS axis tends to be vertical in either the superior or inferior direction and seldom inclined much to either side. This occurs because pulmonary emphysema directs the QRS complex posteriorly so that minimal upward or downward deviation will swing the frontal axis from +90 to −90°.

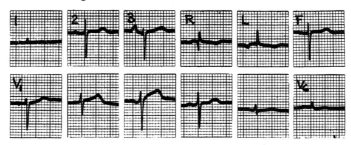

Figure 11.25. ECG recording of a 71-year-old man with pulmonary emphysema. Note the marked LAD (−60°).

Selvester and Rubin have developed quantitative criteria for both definite and possible emphysema[39] as presented in Table 11.1.

Table 11.1[a]

Definite Emphysema	Possible Emphysema
A. P axis > +60° in limb leads	P axis > +60° in limb leads
and either	*and either*
B. 1. R and S amp ≤ 0.70 mV in limb leads	1. R and S amp ≤ 0.70 mV in limb leads
and	*or*
2. R amp ≤ 0.70 mV in V6	2. R amp ≤ 0.70 mV in V6
or	
C. SV4≥RV4	

[a]From Rubin LJ, ed. Pulmonary heart disease. Boston: Martinus Nijhoff, 1984:122.

These criteria achieve approximately 65% sensitivity for the diagnosis of emphysema and 95% specificity for the exclusion of emphysema in normal control subjects and in patients with congenital heart disease or myocardial infarction.[38] This good performance relative to other systems is most likely the result of combining quantitative criteria for frontal plane P wave axis with both frontal and transverse plane QRS amplitude.

GLOSSARY

Cor pulmonale: an acute or chronic pressure overload of the right side of the heart caused by increased resistance to blood flow through the lungs.

Digitalis: a drug, which occurs naturally in the foxglove plant, that is used both to increase the contraction of the cardiac muscle and decrease conduction through the AV node.

Emphysema: a pulmonary disease in which the alveoli are destroyed and the lungs become over-inflated.

Hypercalcemia: abnormally increased level of serum calcium (Ca^{2+}) above 11.0 mg/100 ml.

Hyperkalemia: abnormally increased level of serum potassium (K^+) above 5.0 mEq/L.

Hypertrophic cardiomyopathy: a condition in which the cardiac performance is decreased because the thickened myocardium has decreased contraction capability.

Hypocalcemia: abnormally decreased level of serum calcium below 9.0 mg/100 ml.

Hypokalemia: abnormally decreased level of serum potassium below 4.0 mEq/L.

Hypothermia: subnormal temperature of the body defined as temperature under 36.6 °C or 97.9 °F.

Low voltage: total amplitude of the QRS complex less than 0.70 mV in any limb lead and less than 1.0 mV in any precordial lead.

Myxedema: severe hypothyroidism characterized by a decreased metabolic state and firm, inelastic edema, dry skin and hair, and loss of mental and physical vigor.

Osborn waves: abnormal ECG waveforms caused by hypothermia.

Pericardial sac: the fluid-filled space between the two layers of the pericardium.

Pericarditis: acute or chronic inflammation of the pericardium.

Pericardial effusion: an increase in the amount of fluid in the pericardial sac.

Quinidine: a drug, which occurs naturally in the bark of the cinchona tree, that prolongs myocardial recovery time and protects against some tachyarrhythmias. However, quinidine and other related drugs may also produce tachyarrhythmias by overprolongation of recovery time.

Subaortic stenosis: narrowing of the outflow passage from the left ventricle proximal to the aortic valve sufficient to obstruct the flow of blood.

Thyrotoxicosis: severe hyperthyroidism characterized by an increased metabolic condition, sweating, and protruding eyes.

Torsades de pointes: a variety of ventricular tachycardia resulting from prolongation of the ventricular recovery time. The term is French for "turning of the point."

Total electrical alternans: alternation in the amplitudes of all of the ECG waveforms in the presence of regular cardiac cycle lengths.

REFERENCES

1. Spodick DH. Differential characteristics of the electrocardiogram in early repolarization and acute pericarditis. N Engl J Med 1976;295:523.
2. Bruce MA, Spodick DH. Atypical electrocardiogram in acute pericarditis; characteristics and prevalence. J Electrocardiol 1980;13:61.
3. Spodick DH. Pathogenesis and clinical correlations of the electrocardiographic abnormalities of pericardial disease. Cardiovasc Clin 1977;8(3):201.
4. Bashour FA, Cochran PA. The association of electrical alternans with pericardial effusion. Dis Chest 1963;44:146.
5. Nizet PM, Marriott HJL. The electrocardiogram and pericardial effusion. JAMA 1966;198:169.
6. Dalton JC, Pearson RJ, White PD. Constrictive pericarditis: a review and long term follow-up of 78 cases. Ann Intern Med 1956;45:445.
7. Evans W, Jackson F. Constrictive pericarditis. Br Heart J 1952;14:53.
8. Williams GH, Braunwald E. Endocrine and nutritional disorders and heart disease. In: Heart disease. Philadelphia: WB Saunders, 1980:1825–1853.
9. Vanhaelst L, Neve P, Chailly P, Bastenie PA. Coronary disease in hypothyroidism: Observations in clinical myxoedema. Lancet 1967;2:800–802.
10. Surawicz B, Mangiardi ML. Electrocardiogram in endocrine and metabolic disorders. Cardiovasc Clin 1977;8(3):243.
11. Surawicz B, Mangiardi ML. Electrocardiogram, in endocrine and metabolic disorders. In: Electrocardiographic correlations. Philadelphia: FA Davis, 1977:243–266.
12. Harumi K, Ouichi T. Q-T prolongation syndrome (in Japanese). In: Naika mook. Tokyo: Kinbara, 1981:210.
13. Frank S, Colliver JA, Frank A. The electrocardiogram in obesity: statistical analysis of 1,029 patients. J Am Coll Cardiol 1986;7:295.
14. Starr JW, Wagner GW, Behar VS, Walston A II, Greenfield JC Jr. Vectorcardiographic criteria for the diagnosis of inferior myocardial infarction. Circulation 1974;49:829–836.
15. Okada M, Nishimura F, Yoshino H, Kimura M, Ogino T. The J wave in accidental hypothermia. J Electrocardiol 1983;16:23.
16. Farrokh A, Walsh TJ, Massie E. Amyloid heart disease. Am J Cardiol 1964;13:750.
17. Salerno DM, Asinger RW, Elsperger J, Ruiz E, Hodges M. Frequency of hypokalemia after successfully resuscitated out-of-hospital cardiac arrest compared with that in transmural acute myocardial infarction. Am J Cardiol 1987;59:84–88.
18. Surawicz B. The interrelationship of electrolyte abnormalities and arrhythmias. In: Cardiac arrhythmias: their mechanisms, diagnosis, and management. Philadelphia: JB Lippincott, 1980:83.
19. Krikler DM, Curry PVL. Torsade de pointes, an atypical ventricular tachycardia. Br Heart J 1976;38:117–120.
20. Surawicz B. Relationship between electrocardiogram and electrolytes. Am Heart J 1967;73:814–834.
21. Ettinger PO, Regan TJ, Oldewurtel HA. Hyperkalemia, cardiac conduction, and the electrocardiogram. A review. Am Heart J 1974;88:360–371.
22. Sekiya S, Ichikawa S, Tsutsumi T, Harumi K. Nonuniform action potential durations at different sites in canine left ventricle. Jpn Heart J 1983;24:935–945.
23. Bashour TT. Spectrum of ventricular pacemaker exit block owing to hyperkalemia. Am J Cardiol 1986;57:337.
24. Bronsky D, Dubin A, Waldstein SS, Kushner DS. Calcium and the electrocardiogram. II. The electrocardiographic manifestations of hyperparathyroidism and of marked hypercalcemia from various other etiologies. Am J Cardiol 1961;7:833–839.
25. Nirenburg DW, Ransil BJ. Q-aT$_c$ interval as a clinical indicator of hypercalcemia. Am J Cardiol 1979;44:243–248.
26. Douglas PS, Carmichael KA, Palevsky PM. Extreme hypercalcemia and electrocardiographic changes. Am J Cardiol 1984;54:674–679.
27. Sridharan MR, Horan LG. Electrocardiographic J wave in hypercalcemia. Am J Cardiol 1984;54:672.
28. Burch GE, Meyers R, Abildskov JA. A new electrocardiographic pattern observed in cerebrovascular accidents. Circulation 1954;9:719.
29. Hersch C. Electrocardiographic changes in subarachnoid haemorrhage, meningitis, and intracranial space-occupying lesion. Br Heart J 1964;26:785.
30. Surawicz B. Electrocardiographic pattern of cerebrovascular accident. JAMA 1966;197:913.
31. Shuster S. The electrocardiogram in subarachnoid haemorrhage. Br Heart J 1960;22:316–320.
32. Fentz V, Gormsen J. Electrocardiographic patterns in patients with cerebrovascular accidents. Circulation 1962;25:22–28.
33. Watanabe Y, Dreifus LS. Interactions of quinidine and potassium on atrioventricular transmission. Circ Res 1967;20:434–446.
34. Elisberg EI. Electrocardiographic changes associated with pectus excavatum. Ann Intern Med 1958;49:130–141.
35. Bahl OP, Massie E. Electrocardiographic and vectorcardiographic patterns in cardiomyopathy. Cardiovasc Clin 1972;4(1):95.
36. Spodick DH. Hypertrophic obstructive cardiomyopathy of the left ventricle (idiopathic hypertrophic subaortic stenosis). Cardiovasc Clin 1972;4(1):133.
36a. Sreeram N, Cheriex EC, Smeets JLRM, Gorgels AP, Wellens HJJ. Value of the 12-lead electrocardiogram at hospital admission in the diagnosis of pulmonary embolism. Am J Cardiol 1994;73:298–303.
37. Wasserburger RH, Kelly JR, Rasmussen HK, Juhl JH. The electrocardiographic pentalogy of pulmonary emphysema: a correlation of roentgenographic findings and pulmonary function studies. Circulation 1959;20:831–841.
38. Grant RP. Left axis deviation. An electrocardiographic-pathologic correlation study. Circulation 1956;14:233.
39. Selvester RH, Rubin HB. New criteria for the electrocardiographic diagnosis of emphysema and cor pulmonale. Am Heart J 1965;69:437–447.

III

ABNORMAL RHYTHMS

CHAPTER 12

Introduction to Arrhythmias

The nine features that should be examined in every ECG analysis are presented in Chapter 3 ("Interpretation of the Normal Electrocardiogram"). The two of these that are of primary importance in the evaluation of cardiac rhythm are:

No. 1. Rate and regularity;
No. 9. Identification of the rhythm.

The method for determining the rates of both regular and irregular rhythms should be reviewed before proceeding with this chapter. Normal sinus rhythm, with its rate limit of 60–100 beats/min and its slight irregularity due to respiratory variation, is also presented in Chapter 3. Additional ECG features that are important aspects of many of the cardiac rhythm abnormalities include:

No. 2. P wave morphology;
No. 3. PR interval;
No. 4. QRS complex morphology;
No. 8. QTc interval.

The term *arrhythmia* is very general, referring to all rhythms other than precisely regular sinus rhythm. Even the slight variation in sinus rate caused by altered autonomic balance during the respiratory cycle is termed sinus arrhythmia. The term *dysrhythmia* has been proposed by some as an alternative, but "arrhythmia," meaning "imperfection in a regularly recurring motion," is the commonly accepted term. The presence of an arrhythmia does not necessarily indicate cardiac disease, as indicated by the broad array of abnormal rhythms that commonly occur in healthy individuals of all ages. Arrhythmias are primarily classified according to their rate. Usually, the atria and ventricles have the same rates. However, there are many atrial/ventricular relationships among the cardiac arrhythmias as listed below.

1. The atrial and ventricular rhythms are associated and have the same rate:
   a. The rhythm originates in the atria.
   b. The rhythm originates in the ventricles.
2. The atrial and ventricular rhythms are associated, but the atrial rate is faster than the ventricular rate (the rhythm must originate in the atria).
3. The atrial and ventricular rhythms are associated, but the ventricular rate is faster than the atrial rate (the rhythm must originate in the ventricles).
4. The atrial and ventricular rhythms are independent (*AV dissociation*):
   a. The atrial and ventricular rates are the same (*isorhythmic dissociation*).
   b. The atrial rate is faster than the ventricular rate.
   c. The ventricular rate is faster than the atrial rate.

When the atrial and ventricular rhythms are associated, but have differing rates, the rhythm is named according to the rate of the chambers (atrial or ventricular) from which it originates (e.g., when a rapid atrial rhythm is associated with a slower ventricular rate, the name atrial tachyarrhythmia is used). When the atrial and ventricular rhythms are dissociated, names should be given to both of the rhythms (e.g., atrial tachyarrhythmia with ventricular tachyarrhythmia).

The term *bradyarrhythmia* is used to identify any rhythm with a rate <60 beats/min, and tachyarrhythmia, to identify any rhythm with a rate >100 beats/min. There are also many arrhythmias that do not alter the rate beyond these normal limits. In contrast to the general terms brady- and tachyarrhythmia, the terms brady- and tachycardia refer to specific arrhythmias such as sinus bradycardia and sinus tachycardia.

APPROACH TO ARRHYTHMIA DIAGNOSIS

 The two important aspects of arrhythmias that are basic to their understanding are:

1. Their mechanism;
2. Their site of origin.

The mechanisms that produce arrhythmias are either:

 1. Problems of impulse formation (*automaticity*);
2. Problems of impulse conduction (block or reentry).

PROBLEMS OF IMPULSE FORMATION

Arrhythmias due to problems of automaticity can originate in any cells in the pacemaking and conduction system capable of spontaneous depolarization. Such cells, termed *pacemaker cells*, are present in the:

1. Sinus node;
2. Purkinje cells scattered through the atria;
3. Common (His) bundle;
4. Right and left bundle branches;
5. Purkinje cells in the fascicles and peripheral network.

PROBLEMS OF IMPULSE CONDUCTION: BLOCK

When conduction is slowed, or fails to occur at all, the term *block* is used (e.g., AV block or bundle branch block). Cardiac impulses can be either partially blocked, causing conduction delay (e.g., a prolonged PR interval), or totally blocked, causing conduction failure (e.g., complete AV block). With a partial block of impulses there is no change in rate, but with a total block of impulses a bradyarrhythmia is produced. Either partial or total block can occur at any site within the pacemaking and conduction system.

PROBLEMS OF IMPULSE CONDUCTION: REENTRY

Though conduction abnormalities sufficient to produce block can occur only within the pacemaking and conduction system, uneven or *inhomogeneous conduction* can occur in any part of the heart. This inhomogeneous spread of the electrical impulses can result in reentry of the impulse into an area that has just previously been depolarized and repolarized.[1] Reentry produces a circular movement of the impulse, which continues as long as it encounters receptive cells, resulting in a single *premature beat*, multiple premature beats, a nonsustained tachyarrhythmia, or even a sustained tachyarrhythmia.

MECHANISMS OF ARRHYTHMIAS WITH INCREASED RATES

As indicated above, only a rate >100 beats/min should be considered a tachyarrhythmia. An increase in rate can be produced by two different alterations of impulse formation (automaticity): *accelerated automaticity* or *triggered activation*. The acceleration of automaticity is limited by the maximal rate of impulse formation in pacemaker cells and, therefore, rarely causes a clinically important tachyarrhythmia.

Triggered activation is usually a result of prolongation of the depolarized state and, like inhomogeneous conduction, can produce clinically important reentrant tachyarrhythmias.

ACCELERATED AUTOMATICITY

 Normally, the automaticity of the sinus node exceeds that of all other parts of the pacemaking and conduction system, allowing it to control the cardiac rate and rhythm. This is important because of both the location of the sinus node and its relationship to the parasympathetic and sympathetic components of the autonomic nervous system (Chapter 3). A lower site can initiate the cardiac rhythm either because it usurps control from the sinus role by accelerating its own automaticity or because the sinus node abdicates its role by decreasing its automaticity. The term ectopic is often applied to rhythms that originate from any site other than the sinus node. Cardiac cells function as pacemakers by forming electrical impulses called action potentials via the process of *spontaneous depolarization* (Fig. 12.1). When the automaticity of cardiac cells is severely impaired, the therapeutic use of an artificial pacemaker may be required (Chapter 21, "Artificial Cardiac Pacemakers").

Figure 12.1. Action potential of a pacemaking cell. Sympathetic excess increases (*a*) while parasympathetic excess decreases (*b*) the slope of the slow spontaneous depolarization.

TRIGGERED ACTIVATION

A basic knowledge of the action potential presented in Figure 1.2 is essential to an understanding of this mechanism.[2] In Figure 12.2, there is a small depolarization rebound, or *afterpotential*, immediately following the completion of repolarization. If this rebound becomes large enough to reach a threshold level, it triggers another action potential. Any factor that prolongs depolarization and delays repolarization (e.g., quinidine) encourages the development of afterpotentials. Triggered activation can be the mechanism of clinically important reentrant tachyarrhythmias, as discussed in Chapter 17 ("Ventricular Tachyarrhythmias").

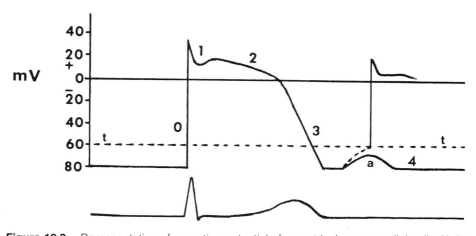

Figure 12.2. Representation of an action potential of a ventricular myocardial cell with its phases *0* through *4* and the corresponding ECG. The 0 mV potential is indicated by the *solid line*, and the threshold potential (*t*) of −60 mV, by the *dashed line*. A small afterpotential (*a*) during phase *4* may reach the threshold potential and "trigger" a second activation of the cell.

REENTRY

There are three prerequisites to the development of reentry:

1. An available circuit;.
2. A difference in the refractory periods of the two limbs in the circuit;.
3. Slow enough conduction somewhere in the circuit to allow the rest of the circuit to recover its responsiveness by the time the impulse returns.

In Figure 12.3, the diagrams represent branching myocardial fibers in three different situations regarding the homogeneity of receptiveness:

1. Both Limbs Are Receptive.   The left and right limbs have completed the recovery process and are in phase 4 (Fig. 12.2) and receptive to the entering impulse (*A*).

2. Both Limbs Are Refractory.   The left and right limbs are still in phase 3 and refractory to being reactivated by the entering impulse (*B*).

3. One Limb Is Receptive and One Is Refractory.   The left limb is refractory (phase 3) and the right limb is receptive (phase 4). By the time the impulse reaches the distal end of the left limb, it is able to reenter because phase 3 has been completed (*C1*). The impulse will continue to cycle within the reentry circuit as long as it encounters receptive cells (*C2*).

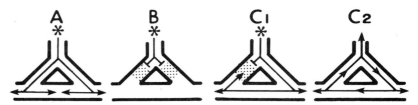

Figure 12.3.   *Asterisks* indicate sites of impulse formation, *arrows* indicate the directions of impulse conduction, *perpendiculars* indicate block of impulse conduction, and *shaded areas* indicate areas that have not completed phase 3 of the activation and recovery process.

An example of the development of a *reentry circuit* in the presence of an accessory AV conduction pathway is presented in Figure 12.4. During sinus rhythm (*A*), both the AV node and the Kent bundle have had time to recover from their previous activation. The premature atrial beat (*B*) encounters persisting refractoriness in the nearby Kent bundle, but receptiveness in the more distant AV node, a situation analogous to that in Figure 12.3, *C1*. This leads to the development of a reentry circuit (*C*) analogous to that in Figure 12.3, *C2*. Reentry circuits vary in size from a local area of myocardial fibers (Fig. 12.3, *C2*) to two cardiac chambers (Fig. 12.4*C*).

Microreentry describes the mechanism when the circuit is too small for its activation to be represented on the surface ECG (Fig. 12.3). The impulses formed by the reentry circuit travel through the adjacent myocardial cells just as they would spread from an automatic or pacemaking site. The P waves and QRS complexes on the ECG represent the passive spread of activation through the atria and ventricles. Microreentry commonly occurs in the AV node (Chapter 16, "Reentrant Junctional Tachycardias") and in the ventricles (Chapter 17).

Macroreentry describes the mechanism when the circuit is large enough for its own activation to be represented on the surface ECG (Fig. 12.4). Cycling of the impulse through the right atrium is represented by a portion of the P wave with the remainder produced by spread of the impulse through the uninvolved left atrium. Cycling of the impulse through the right ventricle is represented by a portion of the QRS complex, with the remainder produced by spread of the impulse through the uninvolved left ventricle. Macroreentry also occurs when the circuit is entirely within either the atrial or ventricular myocardium. Sawtooth-like or undulating ECG waveforms replace discrete P waves (Chapter 15, "Atrial Flutter/Fibrillation Spectrum") or QRS complexes (Chapter 17).

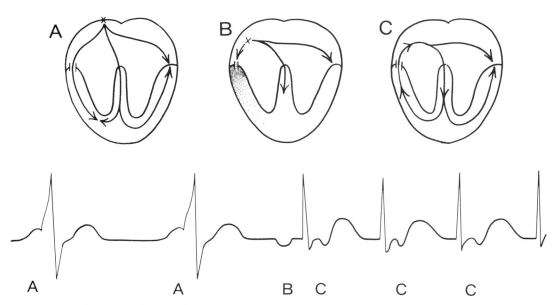

Figure 12.4. *Top*, the presence of a Kent bundle is indicated by the open space between the right atrium and ventricle. *X* indicates the site of the pacemaker: in the sinus node (**A**), in the atria (**B**), and absent (**C**). The *arrows* indicate the direction of impulse conduction. *Bottom*, the corresponding ECG indicating sinus rhythm with ventricular preexcitation (**A**), a premature atrial beat without preexcitation (**B**), and a reentrant junctional tachycardia (**C**). (From Wagner GS, Waugh RA, Ramo BW. Cardiac arrhythmias. New York: Churchill Livingstone, 1983:13.)

IMPORTANCE OF DETERMINING THE TACHYARRHYTHMIA MECHANISM

The mechanism by which a tachyarrhythmia is perpetuated determines the treatment required for its management. Enhanced automaticity can best be terminated by removing the cause of the enhancement. When the enhanced automaticity is originating from the sinus node, the cause is increased sympathetic nervous activity resulting from systemic conditions such as exertion, anxiety, fever, decreased cardiac output, or thyrotoxicosis. When the enhanced automaticity is originating from another location, the most common causes are ischemia and digitalis toxicity. Therefore, enhanced sinus automaticity is terminated by removing the responsible systemic condition, and enhanced nonsinus automaticity is terminated by removing the responsible cardiac condition.

For any reentry circuit to perpetuate itself, the advancing head must not catch up with the refractory tail (Fig. 12.5A). Thus, there must always be a gap of nonrefractory cells between the head and the tail of the recycling impulse. Termination of a sustained reentrant tachyarrhythmia can be produced by:

1. Administering drugs that accelerate conduction of the impulse in the circuit so that it encounters an area that has not yet recovered (Fig. 12.5B). Termination would also result if a drug prolonged the recovery time.
2. Introducing an impulse from an artificial pacemaker that captures part of the reentry circuit, thereby rendering it nonreceptive to the returning impulse (Fig. 12.5C).
3. Introducing a precordial electrical shock, termed *cardioversion*, that captures all receptive parts of the heart, including those in the reentry circuit, rendering the circuit nonreceptive to the returning impulse (Fig. 12.5D).
4. Performing surgical or catheter ablation of one limb of the tissue required for the reentry circuit. For example, ablation of the accessory AV pathway in a patient with ventricular preexcitation (Fig. 12.5E).

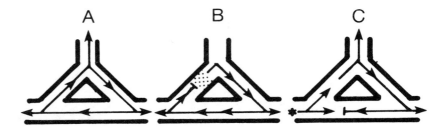

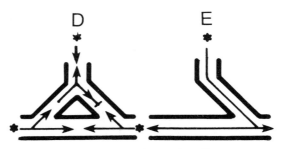

Figure 12.5. The diagram of Figure 12.3 is used to illustrate reentry (**A**) and the four mechanisms of termination (**B–E**). *Asterisks*, *arrows*, *perpendiculars*, and *shaded areas* have the same meanings. The impulse has been cycling within the circle in the direction indicated by the *arrow* on the *curved line* and then spreads out to activate the remainder of the myocardium as indicated by the *arrow pointing leftward*. An impulse formed at the *asterisk to the right* has activated part of the circuit, creating refractoriness and terminating the reentry.

CLINICAL ARRHYTHMIA DETECTION METHODS

The introduction of cardiac care units in the early 1960s stimulated rapid advances in the diagnosis and treatment of cardiac arrhythmias. Patients either with arrhythmias or with a high risk of developing them, because of conditions such as acute myocardial infarction, receive continuous monitoring via a single ECG lead (Chapter 2, "Recording the Electrocardiogram"). A modified lead V1 (MCL$_1$) is commonly used because it provides both a good view of atrial activity and differentiation between right- and left-sided ventricular activity (Fig. 12.6).[3]

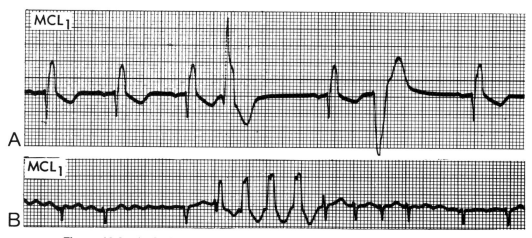

Figure 12.6. In **A**, there is RBBB during sinus rhythm, and both V1 positive (fourth beat) and V1 negative (sixth beat) VPBs (Chapter 17). In **B**, the basic rhythm is atrial fibrillation with most beats conducted normally, but beats four through seven are conducted with RB aberrancy. Note the typical triphasic appearance of the initial wide QRS complex.

DYNAMIC (HOLTER) MONITORING

A method was also developed in the 1960s by Holter for continuous ECG monitoring of ambulatory individuals in their own environment.[4] The technique has been further developed. The patient is attached, via chest electrodes, to a portable tape recorder that records one or two leads for 24 hours. The patient keeps a diary of activities so that symptoms, activity, and rhythm can be correlated. Thus, the individual is monitored during real life situations such as business encounters and pressures, golf or tennis, domestic squabbles, sexual intercourse, driving in traffic, showering, and defecating. Holter monitoring is used to detect and identify any arrhythmic cause of symptoms such as *palpitations*, dizziness, syncope, or chest pain or, alternatively, to rule out arrhythmias as the cause of the symptoms (Fig. 12.7).

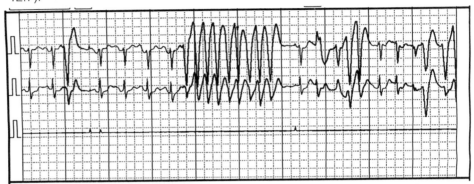

Figure 12.7. Holter recording (as in Figure 8.5) of leads MCL$_1$ and MCL$_5$ revealing VPBs and ventricular tachycardia in a patient with palpitations.

Of 371 monitored patients, 174 (47%) had their symptoms during the 24-hour period of monitoring. However, symptoms coincided with a disturbance of rhythm in only 48 (27%), while the remaining 126 patients (73%) experienced their symptoms when their rhythm was entirely normal. Thus, of the original 371 patients, the Holter gave the answer (symptoms due to arrhythmia or not) in approximately half; but in only about 1 in 8 of the original 371 was arrhythmia the cause of the symptoms.[5]

Holter monitoring is also of value in specific cardiac diseases or situations in which information concerning the heart's rhythm is important for prognosis and management: ischemic heart disease, mitral valve prolapse, cardiomyopathy, conduction disturbances, evaluation of pacemaker function, or Wolff-Parkinson-White syndrome. It may be helpful in the asymptomatic patient in whom an arrhythmia has been detected on routine examination. Holter monitoring may also be of value in assessing the therapeutic effect of antiarrhythmic drugs and adjusting dosages. In this context, however, it is important to realize that there may be spontaneous variation in the frequency of an arrhythmia from day to day of up to 90%[6] and, therefore, there must be a marked and consistent reduction in its incidence before assuming success. The limited span of (usually) 24 hours makes Holter monitoring unsuitable for detecting the infrequent rhythm disturbance.

TRANSTELEPHONIC MONITORING

 The problem of detecting infrequent arrhythmias by Holter monitoring has been largely overcome by transtelephonic monitoring[7,8] in which the patient carries a pocket-sized transmitter and transmits rhythm via telephone when symptoms occur. In this way, there can be more efficient and economical monitoring for days or even weeks if necessary (Fig. 12.8).

HEART RATE 151   T   HEART RATE 154

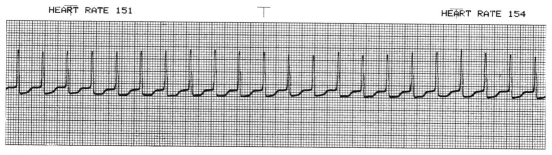

Figure 12.8. ECG recording of a 17-year-old female with a history of palpitations transmits this rhythm strip by telephone immediately following the recurrence of her symptoms.

MEMORY LOOP MONITORS

 It is often clinically important to observe the initiation of the cardiac arrhythmia. This requires a "memory loop," which continually stores the rhythm for a set period of time and then tapes over the stored rhythm.[9] The patient manually activates the permanent recording function as soon as symptoms begin. The immediate period that has been stored on the memory loop is captured to reveal the onset of the rhythm. This system may provide the transition from normal to abnormal brady- or tachyarrhythmias (Fig. 12.9).

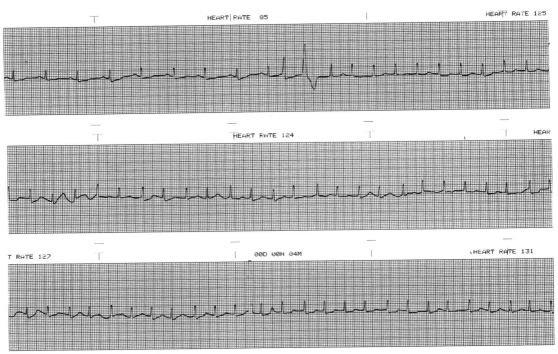

Figure 12.9. A continuous recording of the 30 seconds of rhythm stored by the memory loop monitor preceding manual activation (indicated by the *mark in the middle of the bottom strip*). This 72-year-old man had a history of recurrent shortness of breath and activated his recorder as soon as his symptoms began, 20 seconds after the onset of his supraventricular tachycardia.

INVASIVE ELECTROCARDIOGRAPHIC RECORDING

  The body surface monitoring systems provide access only to the electrical activity from the atrial and ventricular myocardia. Even the atrial activity may be obscured during a tachyarrhythmia because of superimposed QRS complexes and T waves. When the use of alternate body surface sites fails to reveal the atrial activity, either transesophageal or intraatrial recording may be indicated. Figure 12.10 illustrates the ability of both of these techniques to reveal diagnostic atrial activity when none is visible on the body surface.

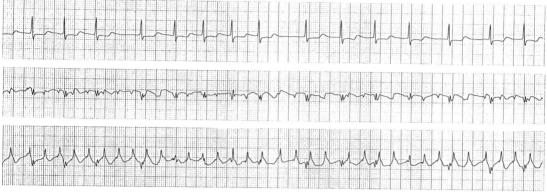

Figure 12.10. Simultaneous recording from surface leads MCL₅ (*top*) and aVF (*middle*), and an intraatrial electrode (*bottom*). An irregularly irregular ventricular rhythm is apparent on lead MCL₅, and intermittent atrial activity can be detected on lead aVF. The diagnosis of a rapid atrial rhythm with variable AV block is confirmed by the intraatrial recording.

Positioning of a multipolar catheter across the tricuspid valve provides direct access to recording from the common or His bundle[10–12] and even the RBB. With a more proximal electrode in the right atrium, simultaneous recording from multiple intracardiac locations is possible, as illustrated in Figure 12.11.

Figure 12.11. Electrograms from the right atrium (*RA*) and His bundle (*HBE*) are presented along with standard leads II and V1. The atrium to His (*A–H*) and His to ventricle (*H–V*) intervals combine to form the PR interval. (From Wagner GS, Waugh RA, Ramo BW. Cardiac arrhythmias. New York: Churchill Livingstone, 1983:117.)

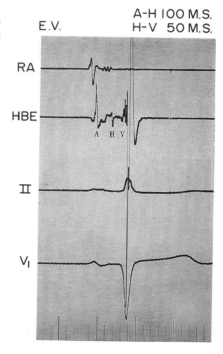

His bundle recording provides partitioning of the PR interval into two components: from the atria through the AV node to the His bundle (AH interval) and from the His bundle to the ventricles (HV interval). This method provides direct identification of the site of AV block (Fig. 12.12.)[13] His bundle recordings have provided proof for many electrocardiographic principles that were originally assumed by deductive reasoning such as:

1. Concealed retrograde VA conduction follows ventricular premature beats which produce compensatory pauses.
2. *Concealed conduction* into the AV node accounts for the irregular ventricular rate during atrial fibrillation.
3. *Aberrant ventricular conduction* of supraventricular premature beats and tachyarrhythmias commonly occurs.
4. Type I AV block with variable conduction times occurs in the AV node, and Type II AV block with fixed conduction times occurs in the His-Purkinje system.

These principles are discussed in Chapters 13 ("Premature Beats"), 15 ("Atrial Flutter/Fibrillation Spectrum"), 18 ("Supraventricular Tachyarrhythmias with Aberrant Ventricular Conduction"), and 20 ("AV Block"), respectively.

A. PROXIMAL BLOCK-A-V NODE

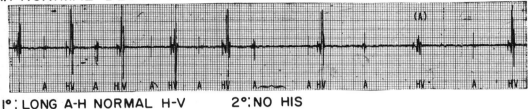

1°: LONG A-H NORMAL H-V   2°: NO HIS
                                    SPIKE

B. DISTAL BLOCK-BUNDLE BRANCHES

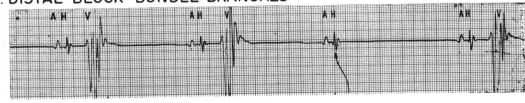

1°: NORMAL A-H LONG H-V   2°: HIS SPIKE
                                    PRESENT

Figure 12.12. His bundle electrograms from two patients with delay and even complete failure of AV conduction. Conduction delays proximal (**A**) and distal (**B**) to the His bundle are indicated by the relationships among atrial (*A*), His (*H*), and ventricular (*V*) spikes. (From Wagner GS, Waugh RA, Ramo BW. Cardiac arrhythmias. New York: Churchill Livingstone, 1983:119.)

INCIDENCES OF ARRHYTHMIAS IN NORMAL POPULATIONS

Many studies have documented high incidences of various arrhythmias in normal individuals of all ages:

1. 134 Normal Infants During the First 10 Days of Life[14]. The maximal heart rate reached 220 beats/min while the minimal rate was 42 beats/min. Atrial premature beats were found in 19 (14%), and sinus pauses occurred in 72%, with the longest pause reaching 1.8 sec.

2. 92 Healthy Children 7–11 Years Old[15]. The fastest rate attained was 195 beats/min and the lowest rate was 37 beats/min. Junctional escape as a result of sinus slowing occurred in 45%. First degree AV block was found in 9 children and second degree AV block in 3. Atrial and ventricular premature beats were found in 21% and sinus pauses in two-thirds of the children.

3. 131 Healthy Boys 10–13 Years Old[16]. Waking maximal heart rates ranged between 100 and 200 beats/min with minimal rates between 45 and 80 beats/min. Maximal sleeping rates were between 60 and 100 beats/min with minimal rates between 30 and 70 beats/min. First degree AV block was found in 8% and second degree AV block in 11%. Single atrial and ventricular premature beats were found in 13 and 26%, respectively.

4. 50 Healthy Women 22–28 Years Old[17]. The waking maximal heart rate ranged between 122 and 189 beats/min with minimal rates between 40 and 73 beats/min. Maximal sleeping rates ranged between 71 and 128 beats/min with minimal rates between 37 and 59 beats/min. Atrial premature beats occurred in 64% and ventricular premature beats in 54%. One woman had one 3-beat run of ventricular tachycardia and two (4%) had periods of second degree AV block.

5. 50 Healthy Male Medical Students[18]. The waking maximal rates ranged from 107 to 180 beats/min with minimal rates between 37 and 65 beats/min. Maximal sleeping rates were between 70 and 115 beats/min with minimal rates of 33–55 beats/min. Half of these young men had sinus arrhythmia sufficient to cause 100% change in consecutive cycles, and 28% had sinus pauses of more than 1.75 sec. Atrial premature beats were found in 56% and ventricular in 50%. Three students (6%) had periods of second degree AV block.

6. 98 Healthy Elderly Subjects 60–85 Years Old with Normal Maximal Treadmill Tests[19]. Sinus bradycardia was found in 91%, supraventricular premature beats in 88%, supraventricular tachycardia in 13%, and atrial flutter in 1%. Ventricular arrhythmias included premature beats in 78%, many with pairs or multiform beats, and ventricular tachycardia in 4%.

7. 20 Male Long Distance Runners 19–29 Years Old[20]. All had atrial premature beats, 70% had ventricular premature beats, and 40% had periods of second degree AV block.

8. 101 Healthy Women[21]. Premature ventricular beats were found in 34%, and complex forms in 10%. Supraventricular premature beats were recorded in 28%, and ventricular premature beats were more frequent in women taking contraceptive pills or thyroid medication.

9. 50 Apparently Healthy Octogenarians[22]. Supraventricular premature beats were found in 100%, with 65% having more than 20 per hour. Supraventricular tachycardia was found in 28%. More than 10 ventricular premature beats per hour were found in 32%, with multifocal beats in 18%.

10. 147 Healthy Swedish Workers 15–65 Years Old[23]. In men under 40 years, 95% had less than three premature ventricular beats per hour, while in those over 40 years, 95% had less than 36 per hour.

SYSTEMATIC APPROACH TO DIAGNOSIS OF ARRHYTHMIAS

 Marriott evolved the following approach to arrhythmia analysis:

> After analyzing the reasons for the mistakes I have made and those that I have repeatedly watched others make, this system is designed to avoid the common errors of omission and commission. Undoubtedly, we make most mistakes because of failure to apply reason and logic, not because of ignorance.

Disturbances of rhythm are most conveniently divided into *supraventricular* and *ventricular*. This corresponds with a simple electrocardiographic difference. Arrhythmias originating in the atrium or *AV junction* (supraventricular), unless complicated by aberrant ventricular conduction (Chapter 18), are characterized by normal QRS complexes, while ventricular arrhythmias produce bizarre QRS complexes with prolonged QRS intervals (Fig. 12.13).

Many disturbances of rhythm and conduction are recognizable at first glance. For example, one can usually spot at once atrial flutter with 4:1 conduction or atrial fibrillation with rapid ventricular response (see Chapter 15). However, if the diagnosis fails to fall into your lap, then the systematic approach is in order. The first step in any medical diagnosis is to know the causes of the presenting symptom. For example, if you want to be a superb headache specialist, the first step is to learn the 50 causes of a headache—which are the common ones, which are the uncommon ones, and how to differentiate between them. This is because "you see only what you look for, you recognize only what you know".[7]

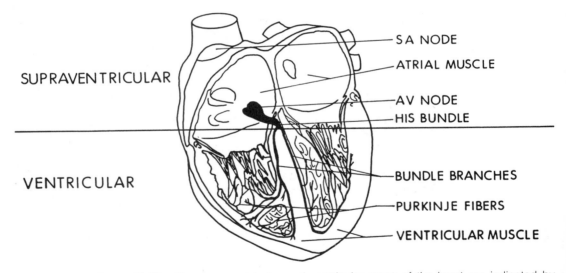

Figure 12.13. The supraventricular and ventricular areas of the heart are indicated by the *line that transects* the pacemaking and conduction system at the distal end of the common bundle.

The steps in the systematic approach are as follows:

1. Know the Causes

The first step is to know the causes of the disturbance of rhythm that confronts you. There are only eight basic kinds of arrhythmias (Table 12.1). Knowing the causes of each of these is part of the equipment that you carry around with you, prepared at a moment's notice to use the knowledge when faced with an unidentified arrhythmia.

Table 12.1. Eight Basic Rhythm Disturbances

1. Early beats
2. Unexpected pauses
3. Tachycardias
4. Bradycardias
5. Bigeminal rhythms
6. Group beating
7. Total irregularity
8. Regular non-sinus rhythms at normal rates

2. Milk the QRS

When a specific arrhythmia confronts you, first milk the QRS. There are two reasons for this. First, it is an extension of the Willie Sutton law. Sutton robbed banks because that was "where the money was." Second, milking the QRS keeps us in the healthy frame of mind of giving priority to ventricular behavior. It matters comparatively little what the atria are doing as long as the ventricles are behaving themselves. If the QRS is of normal duration in at least two leads (Fig. 12.14), the rhythm is supraventricular. If the QRS is wide and bizarre, then you are faced with the decision of whether it is supraventricular with ventricular aberration or ventricular. If you know your morphology, you know what to look for and you will recognize it if you see it.

During the past three decades, the diagnostic morphology of the ventricular complex has come into its own. This began with clinical observation and deduction in which acute coronary care nurses played an important role.[8,11,18,22,24] These observations have been confirmed by electrophysiological studies of Wellens and his colleagues, who found that inspection of the QRS pattern in the clinical tracing afforded the correct diagnosis in 52 of 56 consecutive *wide-QRS tachycardias*.[25] Despite the availability, simplicity, and accuracy of this method, some authorities persist in ignoring its potential.[19,23]

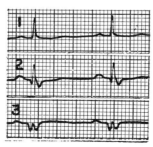

Figure 12.14. In lead I (*1*), the QRS complex appears to be of normal duration, but leads II (*2*) and III (*3*) reveal the true duration to be 0.11 sec.

3. Cherchez le P

If the answer is not afforded by the shape of the QRS complex, the next item to turn to is the P wave. In the past, the P wave has certainly been overemphasized as the key to arrhythmias. A lifelong love affair with the P wave has afflicted many an electrocardiographer with the so-called "P preoccupation syndrome." However, there are times when the P wave holds the diagnostic clue and must be accorded the starring role.

In one's search for P waves, there are several clues and caveats to bear in mind. One technique that may be useful is to employ an alternate lead placement (Chapter 2) with the positive electrode at the fifth right intercostal space close to the sternum and the negative electrode on the manubrium. This will sometimes greatly magnify the P wave, rendering it readily visible when it is virtually indiscernible in other leads. Figure 12.15 illustrates this amplifying effect and makes the diagnosis of atrial tachycardia with 2:1 block immediately apparent. If it succeeds, this technique is a great deal kinder to the patient and safer than passing an atrial wire or an esophageal electrode to corral elusive P waves.

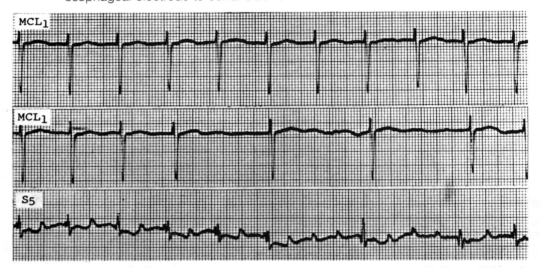

Figure 12.15. The *top strip* does not reveal any definite atrial activity. The *middle strip* shows the effect of carotid sinus stimulation with decreased AV conduction revealing the slightly irregular baseline typical of fine atrial fibrillation. In contrast, there is obvious atrial activity on the *bottom strip*, suggesting sinus rhythm with delayed AV conduction. However, the P waves are halfway between the QRS complexes and, indeed, carotid sinus massage reveals additional P waves concealed within each QRS complex.

Another clue to the incidence of P waves is contained in the Bix rule, named after the Baltimore cardiologist Harold Bix, who observed: "Whenever the P waves of a supraventricular tachycardia are halfway between the ventricular complexes, you should always suspect that additional P waves are hiding within the QRS complex."

In the *top strip* of Figure 12.16, the P wave is halfway between the QRS complexes; therefore, one thinks of the Bix rule. It may be necessary to apply *carotid sinus stimulation* or another vagal maneuver to bring the alternate atrial waves out of hiding. In this case, however, the patient obligingly altered his conduction pattern (*middle strip*) and spontaneously exposed the flutter waves. It is clearly important to know if there are twice as many atrial impulses as are apparent because there is the ever-present danger that the ventricular rate may double or almost double, especially if the atrial rate were to slow somewhat. It is better to be forewarned and take steps to prevent such potentially disastrous acceleration.

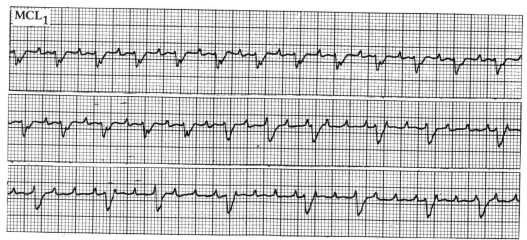

Figure 12.16. The strips are continuous. The *top strip* illustrates the Bix rule, and in the *middle strip* the AV conduction spontaneously decreases, revealing that the atrial rate is twice the ventricular rate.

The "haystack principle" can be of great diagnostic importance when you are searching for difficult-to-find P waves. When you have to find a needle in a haystack, you would presumably prefer a small rather than large haystack. Therefore, whenever you are faced with the problem of finding elusive items, always give the lead with the least disturbance of the baseline (the smallest ventricular complex) a chance to help you. There are some leads that no one would think of looking at to solve an arrhythmia (e.g., aVR), yet the patient illustrated in Figure 12.17 died because his attendants did not know or did not apply the haystack principle and make use of lead aVR. He had a runaway pacemaker at a discharge rate of 440 beats/min with a halved ventricular response at 220 beats/min. Lead aVR was the lead with the smallest ventricular complex, and it was the only lead in which the pacemaker blips were plainly visible (*arrows*). The patient went into shock and died because none of the attempted therapeutic measures affected the tachycardia when all that was necessary was to disconnect the wayward pulse generator.

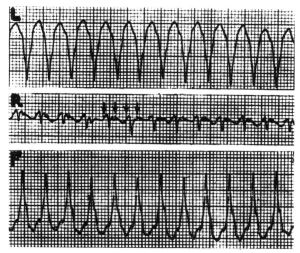

Figure 12.17. Only the prominent wide QRS complexes are visible in leads aVL (*L*) and aVF (*F*). However, in aVR (*R*), where the QRS complexes are much smaller, the extremely rapid rate (460 beats/min) of a "runaway" artificial pacemaker with 2:1 conduction to the ventricles is revealed (*arrows*).

4. Mind Your P's

The next caveat is mind your P's. This means to be wary of things that look like P waves. This particularly applies to P-like waves that are adjacent to the QRS complex that may turn out to be part of the QRS complex. This is a trap for the wary sufferer from the P preoccupation syndrome to whom anything that looks like a P wave is a P wave. Many competent interpreters, given the strip of lead V1 or V2 in Figure 12.18, will promptly and confidently diagnose a supraventricular tachycardia for the wrong reasons. In lead V1, the QRS seems not to be very wide and appears to be preceded by a small P wave. In lead V2, an apparently narrow QRS is followed by an unmistakable retrograde P wave. However, the P-like waves in both of these leads are part of the QRS complex. If the QRS duration is measured in lead V3, it is found to be 0.14 sec. In order to attain a QRS of that width in leads V1 and V2, the P-like waves need to be included in the measurement.

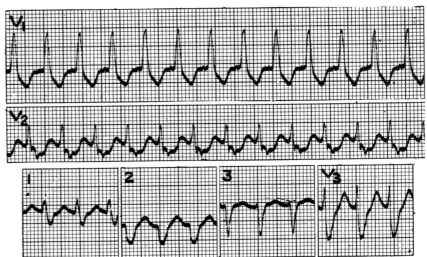

Figure 12.18. The small deflections before (lead V1) and after (lead V2) the large deflections, which are obviously from the ventricles, have the appearances of P waves. However, when the true width of the QRS complexes is revealed in leads I and V3, it is apparent that the small deflections seen in leads V1 and V2 are really almost isoelectric parts of the QRS complexes.

Whenever a regular rhythm is difficult to identify, it is always worthwhile to seek and focus on any interruption in the regularity, a process that can be condensed in the three words "dig the break." It is at a break in the rhythm that you are most likely to find the solution. For example, in the beginning strip of Figure 12.19 where the rhythm is regular at a rate of 200 beats/min, it is impossible to know whether the tachyarrhythmia is atrial or junctional. A third possibility is that the little peak is part of the QRS and not a P wave at all. Further along the strip there is a break in the rhythm in the form of a pause. The most common cause of a pause is a nonconducted atrial premature beat (APB) and the culprit is at the *arrow*. As a result of the pause, the mechanism is immediately obvious. When the rhythm resumes, the returning P wave is in front of the first QRS, and the mechanism is evidently an atrial tachycardia.

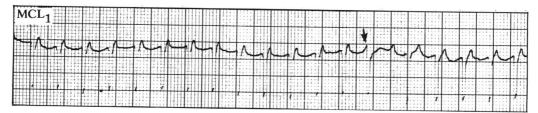

Figure 12.19. At the beginning of the rhythm strip, the small positive waveform could be: (a) a part of a wide QRS complex, (b) a retrograde P wave closely following a narrow QRS complex, or (c) an anterograde P wave with prolonged conduction to a narrow QRS complex. This sequence is broken during the 14th cycle (*arrow*) where the beginning of the small positive waveform is seen preceding the QRS complex and then in the 15th cycle there is no QRS complex. Only at this point is the rhythm revealed to be condition C, an atrial tachycardia with a prolonged PR interval and intermittent complete failure of AV conduction.

5. Who's Married to Whom?

The next step is to establish relationships or ask yourself who's married to whom? This is often the crucial step in arriving at a firm diagnosis. Figure 12.20 illustrates this principle in its simplest form. A junctional rhythm is dissociated from sinus bradycardia. On three occasions there are bizarre early beats with a qR configuration that are nondiagnostic. They could be ventricular premature beats (VPBs), but the fact that they are seen only when a P wave is emerging beyond the preceding QRS tells us that they are "married to" the preceding P waves and establishes them as conducted or *capture beats* with atypical RBBB aberration.

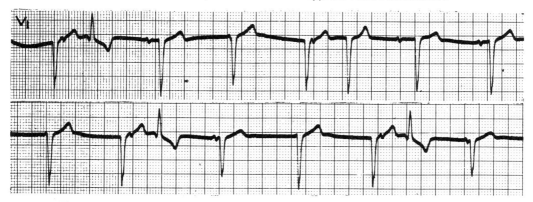

Figure 12.20. The strips are continuous. All of the early QRS complexes, but only some of the later QRS complexes, are preceded by P waves. The use of calipers reveals dissociation between the atria (which have a regular rate of about 50 beats/min) and the ventricles (the later QRS complexes have a regular rate of about 60 beats/min). The presence of P waves prior to each early QRS complex suggests intermittent capture of the ventricular rhythm by the atrial rhythm.

6. Pinpoint the Final Diagnosis

Figure 12.21 illustrates both the previous principle and the final one: pinpoint the primary diagnosis. One must never be content to let the diagnosis rest upon a secondary phenomenon such as AV dissociation, escape, or aberration. Each and all of these are always secondary to some primary disturbance that must be sought out and identified. The illustration was obtained from a patient shortly after admission to a coronary care unit. There were a number of wide, bizarre beats that gave the staff concern. One faction contended that they were ventricular escape beats. The other thought they were conducted, after the longer diastole, with paradoxical critical rate aberration. If you ask yourself, "Who's married to whom?" it becomes immediately obvious that the beats in question are not related to the P waves. For example, look at the PR intervals of the last two anomalous beats in the *second strip* and that of the second anomalous beat in the *top strip*. These three intervals are strikingly different, measuring 0.31, 0.22, and 0.37 sec, respectively. On the other hand, if one measures the RR intervals ending with each of these three beats, they are virtually identical. This indicates that the beats in question are related to the previous QRS complex rather than to the P wave, which in turn identifies them as *escape beats*.

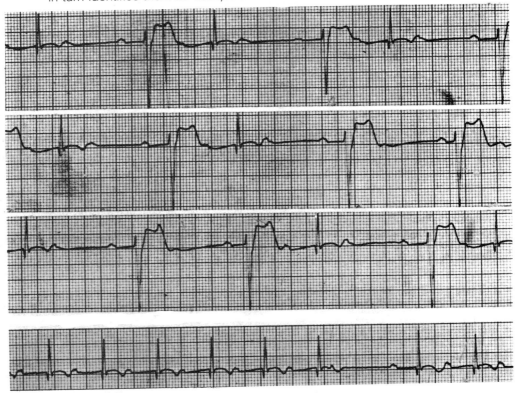

Figure 12.21. The *top three strips* are continuous and the *bottom strip* follows intravenous administration of the antiarrhythmia drug lidocaine. The use of calipers reveals dissociation between the atria (which have a regular rate of about 75 beats/min), and the ventricles (the later wide QRS complexes have a regular rate of about 40 beats/min). The presence of P waves prior to each early narrow QRS complex suggests intermittent capture of the ventricular rhythm by the atrial rhythm. Lidocaine eliminated the independent ventricular rhythm, revealing that the narrow QRS complexes are, indeed, the result of conduction from the atria.

In this case, the nurse, regarding them as VPBs, administered lidocaine and they disappeared. Notice her two mistakes. First, there is nothing "P" about these "VBs." They are late not early beats. Second, one should never treat escape beats. She eliminated them because the lidocaine facilitated AV conduction, leaving no room or need for escape beats. Therefore, by accident she treated the primary disturbance, which was AV block. What she should have done was apply the fifth principle, pinpoint the primary, and treat the block with atropine (if indeed the patient required treatment). With an average rate of over 50 beats/min, the patient may well have been in a satisfactory hemodynamic state and may have required no immediate therapy.

LADDER DIAGRAMS

Ladder diagrams are often helpful for understanding difficult arrhythmias. There are spaces for indicating the atrial (*A*), junctional (*J*), and ventricular (*V*) activation (Fig. 12.22). Additional spaces can be added, as needed, to diagram more complex arrhythmias. The ladder diagram should be constructed directly under, or on a photocopy of, the ECG recording using two sequential stages:

1. Include what you can see (e.g., draw lines to represent the visible P waves and QRS complexes).
2. Add what you cannot see (e.g., connect the atrial and ventricular lines to represent AV or VA conduction and draw lines to represent any missing P waves at regular PP intervals between visible P waves).

Figure 12.22. The format on which ladder diagrams can be constructed: spaces are provided for representing the atrial (*A*), junctional (*J*), and ventricular (*V*) activation.

Figure 12.23 provides an illustration of the use of ladder diagrams to understand a cardiac arrhythmia with various PR intervals and varying QRS morphologies. In the first stage of the diagram, all visible P waves and QRS complexes have been represented. Note the reversed slope representing the premature wide QRS complex, indicating the likelihood that it originated from the ventricles. When the lines representing AV conduction are added in the second stage, the prolonged PR interval following the third P wave is indicated by an angulation to represent a conduction disturbance. The ventricular premature beat must have travelled retrogradely into the junction so that the next sinus impulse found the junction *relatively refractory.*

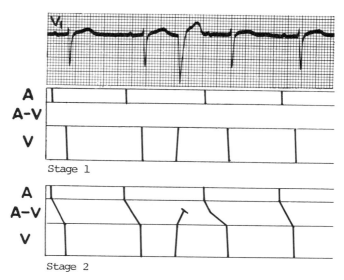

Figure 12.23. The two stages of construction of a ladder diagram: *Stage 1,* use *slanted lines* to include the duration of the obvious waveforms representing both atrial and ventricular activation. The *slanted lines* indicate the presumed direction of spread of activation. *Stage 2,* construct lines in the junctional space to connect the atrial and ventricular lines to represent the presumed direction of the spread of junctional activation. Terminate these lines and cap with short perpendiculars to indicate the presumed failure of impulse conduction.

In subsequent chapters, ladder diagrams will be freely used as a visual aid to understanding mechanisms of arrhythmias. Figure 12.24, *A–D*, presents four examples to indicate how various symbols may be used to represent such phenomena as aberrant ventricular conduction (*A*), junctional rhythms (*B*), ventricular rhythms (*C*), and dissociation between atrial and ventricular rhythms (*D*).

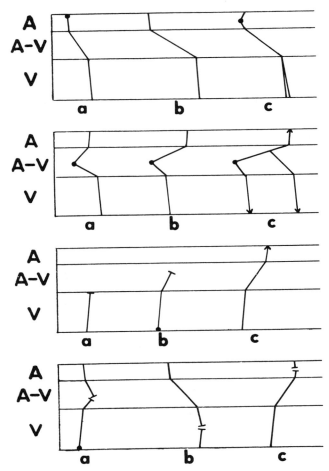

Figure 12.24. **A.** A normal sinus beat (*a*) encounters prolonged AV conduction (*b*) and then is replaced by an atrial beat that encounters both prolonged AV conduction and aberrant ventricular conduction (indicated by the *split line*). A *solid circle* has been added to indicate the site of impulse formation in (*a*) and (*c*). **B.** AV junctional beats with progressively longer retrograde conduction time to the atria: in *a*, the P precedes the QRS, but in *b*, it follows the QRS. In *c*, the retrograde conduction time is so long that a second QRS is generated. An *arrowhead* has been added to indicate the direction of impulse conduction (*c*), but these are not necessary since the direction of the impulse can be indicated by the slope of the line. **C.** Ventricular beats with progressively greater penetration into the AV junction: no (*a*), partial (*b*), and complete (*c*) retrograde VA conduction. **D.** In *a*, there is complete AV dissociation; in *b*, AV conduction results in "fusion" during the QRS complex; and in *c*, VA conduction results in "fusion" during the P wave.

GLOSSARY

Aberrant ventricular conduction: the temporarily abnormal intraventricular conduction of a supraventricular impulse, usually associated with a change in cycle length. Aberrancy differs from "normal" conduction in two ways: (a) the impulse does not travel normally through the ventricular Purkinje system to reach the ventricular myocardium; and (b) it is not the usual conduction pattern for that individual.

Accelerated automaticity: increase in the rate of impulse formation within pacemaker cells.

Afterpotential: also termed afterdepolarization. A small electrical potential that occurs following the completion of repolarization which may produce or "trigger" a second automatic activation of the cell termed triggered activation.

Arrhythmia: any cardiac rhythm other than regular sinus rhythm.

Automaticity: the ability of specialized cardiac cells to achieve spontaneous depolarization and function as "pacemakers" to form new impulses.

AV dissociation: a condition of independent beating of the atria and ventricles caused either by block of the atrial impulse in the AV junction or by interference with conduction of the atrial impulse by a ventricular impulse.

AV junction: the cardiac structures that electrically connect the atria and ventricles normally including the AV node and common (His) bundle and abnormally an accessory AV conduction (Kent) bundle.

Block: either a delay or total failure of impulse conduction through a part of the heart.

Bradyarrhythmia: any rhythm with a ventricular rate <60 beats/min.

Capture beats: atrial impulses that activate the ventricles. The term is used when this interrupts an independent ventricular rhythm.

Cardioversion: application of an electric shock in order to restore a normal heartbeat.

Carotid sinus stimulation: contact with the area in the neck overlying the bifurcation of the carotid artery which contains receptors capable of enhancing parasympathetic nervous activity.

Concealed conduction: conduction of an impulse that is recognizable only by its effect on the subsequent beat or cycle.

Dysrhythmia: a synonym (by usage) for arrhythmia.

Escape beat: a beat from a part of the pacemaking and conduction system which ends a cycle that is longer than the basic cycle.

Inhomogeneous conduction: the wave front of activation spreads unevenly through a part of the heart because of varying refractoriness from previous activation, creating the potential for impulse reentry.

Isorhythmic dissociation: AV dissociation with atria and ventricles beating at the same or almost the same rate.

Macroreentry: recycling of an impulse around a circuit that is large enough for its own activation to be represented on the surface ECG.

Microreentry: recycling of an impulse around a circuit that is too small for its own activation to be represented on the surface ECG.

Pacemaker cells: specialized cardiac cells that are capable of automaticity.

Palpitation: a sensation felt in the chest as a result of ventricular contraction.

Premature beat: a beat that occurs prior to the time when the next normal beat would be expected to appear.

Reentry circuit: a circular course traveled by a cardiac impulse, created by reentry, and having the potential for initiating premature beats and tachyarrhythmias.

Relative refractory: cells that have only partially recovered from their previous activation and are, therefore, capable of slow conduction of another impulse.

Spontaneous depolarization: the ability of a specialized cardiac cell to activate by altering the permeability of its membrane sufficient to attain threshold potential without any external stimulation.

Supraventricular: any cardiac area above the branching of the common bundle and, therefore, capable of initiating a beat that could be conducted normally through the ventricles.

Triggered activation: spontaneous impulse formation produced by early afterdepolarizations.

Ventricular: any cardiac area beyond the branching of the common bundle which is, therefore, is incapable of initiating a beat that could be conducted normally through the ventricles.

Wide-QRS tachycardia: rhythm with a rate over 100 beats/min with QRS complexes at least 0.12 sec in duration.

REFERENCES

1. Hoffman BF, Cranefield PF, Wallace AG. Physiological basis of cardiac arrhythmias. Mod Concepts Cardiovasc Dis 1966;35:103.
2. Rosen MR, Fisch C, Hoffman BF, Danilo P Jr, Lovelace DE. Can accelerated atrioventricular junctional escape rhythms be explained by delayed afterdepolarizations? Am J Cardiol 1980;45:1272–1284.
3. Marriott HJL, Fogg E. Constant monitoring for cardiac dysrhythmias and blocks. Mod Concepts Cardiovasc Dis 1970;39:103.
4. Holter NJ. New method for heart studies: continuous electrocardiography of active subjects over long periods is now practical. Science 1961;134:1214.
5. Zeldis SM, Levine BJ, Michelson EL, Morganroth J. Cardiovascular complaints: correlation with cardiac arrhythmias on 24-hour electrocardiographic monitoring. Chest 1982;78:456.
6. Michelson EL, Morganroth J. Spontaneous variability of complex ventricular arrhythmias detected by long-term electrocardiographic recording. Circulation 1980;61:690.
7. Grodman PS. Arrhythmia surveillance by transtelephonic monitoring; comparison with Holter monitoring in symptomatic ambulatory patients. Am Heart J 1979;98:459.
8. Judson P, Holmes DR, Baker WP. Evaluation of outpatient arrhythmias utilizing transtelephonic monitoring. Am Heart J 1979;97:759.
9. Cumbee SR, Pryor RE, Linzer M. Cardiac loop ECG recording: a new noninvasive diagnostic test in recurrent syncope. South Med J 1990;83:39–43.
10. Damato AN, Lau SH. Clinical value of the electrogram of the conduction system. Prog Cardiovasc Dis 1970;13:119.
11. Goldreyer BN. Intracardiac electrocardiography in the analysis and understanding of cardiac arrhythmias. Ann Intern Med 1972;77:117.
12. Vadde PS, Caracta AR, Damato AN. Indications of His bundle recordings. Cardiovasc Clin 1980;11:1.
13. Pick A. Mechanisms of cardiac arrhythmias; from hypothesis to physiologic fact. Am Heart J 1973;86:249.
14. Southall DP, Richards J, Mitchell P, Brown DJ, Johnston PG, Shinebourne EA. Study of cardiac rhythm in healthy newborn infants. Br Heart J 1980;43:14.
15. Southall DP, Johnston F, Shinebourne EA, Johnston PG. A 24-hour electrocardiographic study of heart rate and rhythm patterns in population of healthy children. Br Heart J 1981;45:281.
16. Scott O, Williams GJ, Fiddler GI. Results of 24-hour ambulatory monitoring of electrocardiogram in 131 healthy boys aged 10 to 13 years. Br Heart J 1980;44:304.
17. Sobotka PA, Mayer JH, Bauernfeind RA, Kanakis C Jr, Rosen KM. Arrhythmias documented by 24-hour continuous ambulatory electrocardiographic monitoring in young women without apparent heart disease. Am Heart J 1981;101:753.
18. Brodsky M, Wu D, Denes P, Kanakis C, Rosen KM. Arrhythmias documented by 24-hour continuous electrocardiographic monitoring in 50 male medical students without apparent heart disease. Am J Cardiol 1977;39:390.
19. Fleg JL, Kennedy HL. Cardiac arrhythmias in a healthy elderly population: detection by 24-hour ambulatory electrocardiography. Chest 1982;81:302.
20. Talan DA, Bauernfeind RA, Ashley WW, Kanakis C Jr, Rosen KM. Twenty-four hour continuous ECG recordings in long-distance runners. Chest 1982;82:19.
21. Romhilt DW, Choi SC, Irby EC. Arrhythmias on ambulatory monitoring in women without apparent heart disease. Am J Cardiol 1984;54:582.
22. Kantelip JP, Sage E, Duchene-Marullaz P. Findings on ambulatory monitoring in subjects older than 80 years. Am J Cardiol 1986;57:398.
23. Orth-Gomer K, Hogstedt C, Bodin L, Soderholm B. Frequency of extrasystoles in healthy male employees. Br Heart J 1986;55:259.
24. Harrison DC. Contribution of ambulatory electrocardiographic monitoring to antiarrhythmic management. Am J Cardiol 1978;41:996.
25. Michelson EL, Morganroth J. Spontaneous variability of complex ventricular arrhythmias detected by long-term electrocardiographic recording. Circulation 1980;61:690.

CHAPTER 13

Premature Beats

Normal sinus rhythm is commonly interrupted by a premature beat (PB). The individual may or may not be aware of the occurrence. The premature beat itself does not cause symptoms, but a palpitation may be felt following the next normal heartbeat. Figure 13.1 illustrates the following sequence of events that occur as a result of a single PB:

1. The PB occurs too early to pump a significant amount of blood.
2. The presence of the PB prevents the occurrence of the next normal beat.
3. There is a pause following the PB until the next normal beat occurs.

A palpitation is caused by the pumping of the excess blood that has accumulated between the two normal beats preceding and following the PB. Premature refers to the early occurrence and beat is short for heartbeat. Other terms are often substituted for these including premature contraction, early beat, extrasystole, premature systole, and ectopic beat.

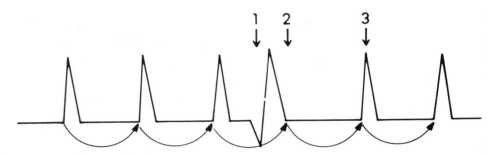

Figure 13.1. The timing of a regular underlying rhythm is indicated by the *curved lines with arrows*. A VPB interrupts this rhythm (*1*), preventing the occurrence of the next normal beat (*2*); however, the following normal beat occurs at the expected time (*3*).

A single PB is potentially the first beat of a sustained tachyarrhythmia (tach). It may be followed by any number of similarly appearing beats with the following terms applied:

Number of Consecutive Beats	Term
1 beat	A premature beat
2 beats	A pair or a *couplet*
3 beats—1 minute continuation	Nonsustained tach
>1 minute continuation	Sustained tach

When a PB follows every normal beat, the term *bigeminy* may be used. When a PB follows every second normal beat, the term *trigeminy* may be used. PBs may originate from any part of the heart other than the sinus node. They are generally classified as *supraventricular premature beats* (SVPBs) or *ventricular premature beats* (VPBs), as indicated in Figure 13.2. This distinction is useful because beats originating from anywhere above the branching of the common bundle (SVPBs) are capable of producing either a normal or abnormal QRS complex, depending on whether they are conducted normally or aberrantly through the intraventricular conduction system. Beats originating from beyond the branching of the common bundle (VPBs) can produce only an abnormally prolonged QRS complex of >0.12 sec because they do not have equal access to both the right and left bundle branches. It should be emphasized that VPBs are always abnormally prolonged, but SVPBs are not always of normal duration.

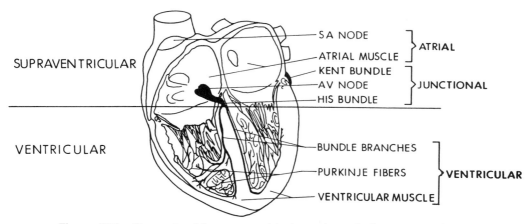

Figure 13.2. The parts of the supraventricular and ventricular areas are indicated. Note the *wide line* connecting the left atrium and left ventricle on the epicardial surface which represents a Kent bundle. (Modified from Netter FH. The Ciba collection of medical illustrations. vol 5. Summit: Ciba-Geigy, 1978:49.)

SVPBs may be either *atrial premature beats* (APBs) or *junctional premature beats* (JPBs). The term junctional is used instead of nodal because it is impossible to distinguish beats originating within the AV node from those originating in another structure located between the atria and the ventricles. Normally, the AV junction consists of only the AV node and the common bundle. Abnormally, however, an accessory AV conduction pathway may also be present.

DIFFERENTIAL DIAGNOSIS OF WIDE PREMATURE BEATS

When SVPBs have abnormally prolonged or wide QRS complexes (>0.12 sec), identification of supraventricular versus ventricular origin may be facilitated by observing the effect on the regularity of the underlying sinus rhythm. In Figure 13.3, the features of the VPB are contrasted with those of the SVPB. If the PB does not disturb the sinus rhythm but merely takes the place of a conducted beat (Fig. 13.3A), then the interval from the conducted beat prior to the PB to the following conducted beat will be equal to two sinus cycles. This interval is termed a *compensatory pause* because the cycle following the PB compensates for the prematurity of the PB, and the sinus rhythm resumes again on schedule.

In contrast, in Figure 13.3B, the sinus rhythm is disturbed by an SVPB. The sinus node is discharged ahead of schedule by the premature impulse, causing the following cycle to also occur ahead of schedule. The pause between these sinus cycles is less than compensatory. However, sometimes when the premature atrial impulse discharges the sinus node, it also suppresses its automaticity. This *overdrive suppression* may delay the formation of the next sinus impulse so long that the pause is compensatory or even longer than compensatory. Thus, the compensatory pause must not be relied upon as the sole indicator of ventricular origin of a wide PB.

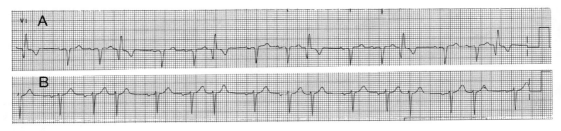

Figure 13.3. The contrasting effects of APBs (**A**) and VPBs (**B**) on the underlying sinus rhythm.

MECHANISMS

PBs may be caused by the three mechanisms indicated in Chapter 12 ("Introduction to Arrhythmias"): enhanced automaticity, triggered automaticity, or reentry. However, triggered automaticity has no practical significance regarding PBs. It is usually difficult to determine the mechanism of PBs unless there are two or more in succession. Fortunately, the mechanism is usually not clinically important unless consecutive abnormal beats are present.

When multiple single PBs occur, and identification of their mechanism is considered clinically important, the following observations of the *coupling intervals* between beats may be helpful:

Observations	Mechanism
There are identical coupling intervals between each PB and the preceding normal beat (Fig. 13.4A).	Reentry
There are not identical coupling intervals between PBs and normal beats, but there are identical intervals between consecutive PBs (Fig. 13.4B).	Enhanced automaticity
There are neither identical coupling intervals between PBs and normal beats nor between consecutive PBs.	Either

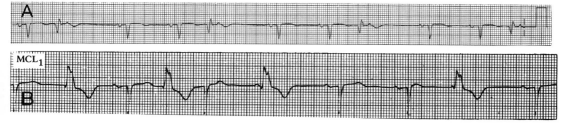

Figure 13.4. The contrasting appearances of VPBs coupled to preceding normal beats (**A**) and coupled to each other (**B**).

ATRIAL PREMATURE BEATS (APBs)

 The usual APB has three features:

1. A premature and abnormal appearing P wave (often labeled P′);
2. A QRS complex similar to that of the conducted sinus beats;
3. A following cycle that is less than compensatory.

As a rule, all of these characteristics are obvious (Fig. 13.5), but no one characteristic is completely reliable. Some common deceptions are:

1. The P′ wave may be unrecognizable because it occurs during the previous T wave.
2. The QRS may show aberrant ventricular conduction.
3. The pause may appear to be compensatory or even longer because of overdrive suppression.

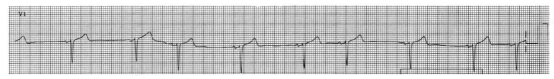

Figure 13.5. Typical APBs occur as the 3rd, 6th, and 9th cycles.

It is extremely rare to have all three of these deceptions appear at the same time. Therefore, with care, one usually has no trouble in identifying the APB. When an APB follows every sinus beat, the result is atrial bigeminy (Fig. 13.6A); when it occurs every third beat, the result is atrial trigeminy (Fig. 13.6B).

When APBs occur very early (a short coupling interval), some parts of the heart may not have had time to complete their recovery from the preceding normal activation. This may result in failure of the premature atrial activation to cause any ventricular activation.

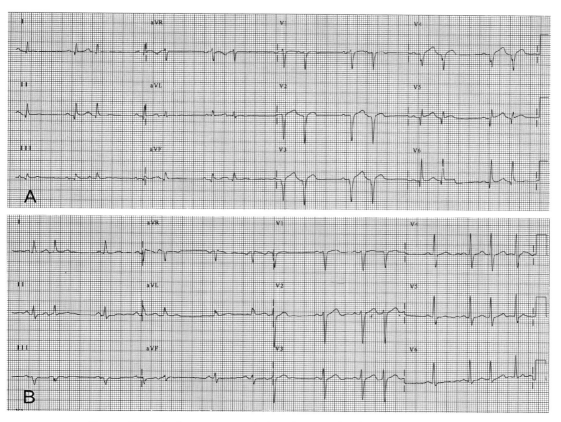

Figure 13.6. In **A**, every normal sinus beat, and in **B** every second normal sinus beat is coupled with constant PP′ intervals to APBs.

Indeed, the most common cause of an unexpected atrial pause is a nonconducted APB (Fig. 13.7). It is better to refer to such beats as "nonconducted" rather than "blocked" because, by definition, block implies an abnormal condition, and APBs fail to be conducted only because they occur so early in the cycle that the AV node is still in its normal refractory period. It is important to differentiate normal (physiologic) from abnormal (pathologic) nonconduction to avoid mistakenly initiating an "antiarrhythmia" treatment. Nonconducted APBs that occur in a bigeminal pattern are particularly difficult to identify. If the premature P waves are not detected, the rhythm will be misdiagnosed as sinus bradycardia.

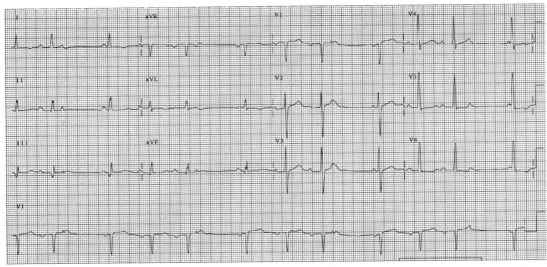

Figure 13.7. After three normal cycles, an APB occurs too early to be conducted to the ventricles. Note that the PR interval decreases following the pause and then gradually increases to exceed the upper limit of normal (0.22 sec), indicating that there is some AV conduction abnormality present.

When very early APBs are nonconducted, the premature P waves may be obscured by the T waves of the preceding normal beats, creating a more subtle atrial bigeminy (Fig. 13.8). If the preceding T waves during the regular sinus rhythm are not available for comparison and the slightly deforming P' waves are not recognizable, the rhythm may be misdiagnosed as sinus bradycardia.

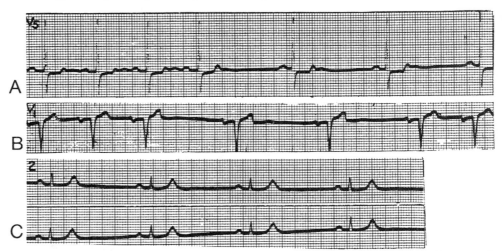

Figure 13.8. In **A** and **B**, the T waves preceding the pauses appear different from usual, but in **C** there are no "usual" T waves available for comparison.

When APBs occur very early in the cardiac cycle of normal beats, they may have other effects on AV conduction, as illustrated in Figure 13.9. In A and B, there is prolonged AV conduction, while in C, there is slightly prolonged AV conduction and also aberrant intraventricular conduction. In A, there are varying coupling intervals (PP' intervals) between normal sinus beats and APBs. When the PP' interval is long, the P'R interval is normal, but when the PP' interval is short, the P'R interval is markedly prolonged. This inverse relationship occurs because of the uniquely long partial refractory period of the AV node: the longer the duration from its most recent activation, the better the node is able to conduct the following impulse and vice versa. This concept is vital to use of the ECG to differentiate between nodal versus Purkinje location of AV block. In B, there are constant PP' intervals and, consequently, equally prolonged P'R intervals.

When an early APB traverses the AV junction, but encounters persistent normal refractoriness in one of the bundle branches or fascicles, aberrant ventricular conduction occurs, as in C. The morphology of the QRS complex is altered, and its duration may be so prolonged that it resembles a VPB. Detection of the preceding P' wave and/or finding that the pause is less than compensatory will usually establish the diagnosis that an APB is present.

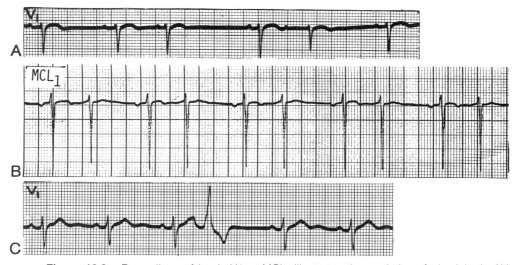

Figure 13.9. Recordings of leads V1 or MCL₁ illustrate other varieties of physiologic AV conduction delays that may occur when the AV node (**A** and **B**) alone, or both the AV node and the right bundle branch (**C**) have not had time to fully recover from their preceding normal activation.

APBs may occur so early that even parts of the atria have not completed their refractory periods. During this time (*vulnerable period*), the APB may initiate a reentrant atrial tachyarrhythmia, as illustrated in Figure 13.10. In this instance, the APB becomes the first beat of atrial flutter/fibrillation (Chapter 15, "Atrial Flutter/Fibrillation Spectrum"). Killip and Gault[1] developed the rule that, when the PP' interval is less than 50% of the previous PP interval, the APB is quite likely to initiate atrial flutter/fibrillation.

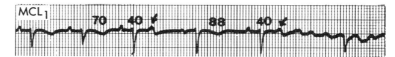

Figure 13.10. The *arrows* indicate two early APBs with PP' intervals of 40 (0.40 sec). The first PP' interval is longer than half the preceding PP interval of 70 (0.70 sec), but the second is shorter than half the preceding PP interval of 88 (0.88 sec), initiating a reentrant tachyarrhythmia.

JUNCTIONAL PREMATURE BEATS (JPBs)

PBs arising in the AV junction may retrogradely activate the atria before, during, or after the ventricular activation, and therefore, the retrograde P wave may be seen preceding or following the QRS complex or it may be lost within it. Upper, mid, and lower are terms based on the relative position of the P wave in relation to the QRS complex which have been used to signify the presumed site of origin within the AV junction (Fig. 13.11A). However, as indicated in B, the P to QRS relationship is also dependent on the relative rates of conduction of the impulse from its origin to the atrial and ventricular myocardia. Therefore, the relationship between the P waves and QRS complexes does not necessarily indicate the level within the junction from which the JPBs originate and the terms (upper, mid, and lower) have been discarded.

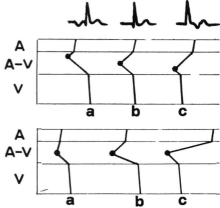

Figure 13.11. Three impulses (a, b, and c) are formed within the AV junction (A-V) in two ladder diagrams. In the *top ladder diagram,* the anatomic site of impulse formation (*solid circle*) varies, but the physiologic conduction velocity is constant, resulting in the P-QRS relationships shown at the *top.* In the *bottom ladder diagram,* the additional influence of variation of the velocity of conduction from the site of impulse formation to the atria and ventricles is illustrated.

The diagnosis of junctional origin of PBs is easiest when a premature normal QRS complex is closely accompanied by an "upside down" P wave (Fig. 13.12). As would be expected, the morphology of the P waves associated with JPBs is markedly different from that of the P waves of normal sinus rhythm. The polarity is approximately opposite, as best seen in a lead with base to apex orientation such as lead II. The P' wave is also inverted in the other inferiorly oriented leads (e.g., aVF), is upright in superiorly oriented leads aVR and aVL, and is almost flat in leftward oriented leads I and V5.

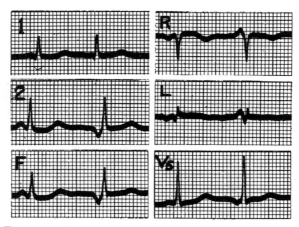

Figure 13.12. The contrasting appearances of P waves originating from the sinus node and the AV junction are illustrated in five of the limb leads and precordial lead V5.

A JPB may be confused with an APB when a premature normal QRS complex is not closely accompanied by an abnormal P wave (Fig. 13.13). In *A*, the normally appearing and normally timed P wave following the premature normal QRS complex indicates a JPB. In *B*, there are no accompanying P waves to provide clues to junctional versus atrial origin of the PBs. Differentiation requires observation of the influence of the PB on the regularity of the underlying sinus rhythm. The sinus rhythm is typically reset by an APB, but not altered by a JPB. The pause following a JPB is, therefore, usually fully compensatory.

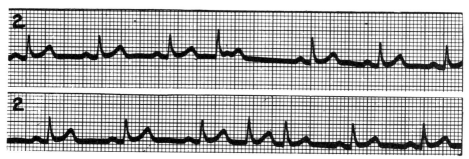

Figure 13.13. *Both panels* are recordings of lead II from the same individual. Note that the regular sinus rhythm "marches through" or is "not reset" by the PBs.

A JPB may be confused with a VPB when the premature QRS is wide (>0.12 sec). The various principles presented in Chapters 17 ("Ventricular Tachyarrhythmias") and 18 ("Supraventricular Tachyarrhythmias with Aberrant Ventricular Conduction") for differentiating supraventricular beats with aberrant intraventricular conduction from ventricular beats may be applied. Figure 13.14 shows JPBs with differing degrees of RBB aberration. The retrograde atrial activation is apparent from the P′ waves following the premature QRS complexes. Although the first premature beat in each strip cannot be distinguished from a VPB, the fact that the second premature beat manifests a lesser degree of the RBBB pattern is a strong point in favor of the aberrant conduction from a JPB.

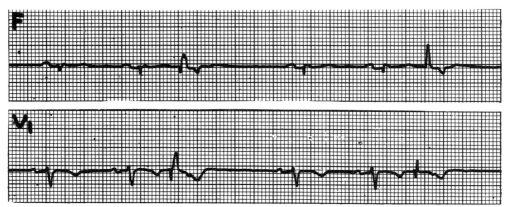

Figure 13.14. The base to apex orientation of lead aVF (*F*) provides the best view of the inverted P waves, and the right versus left orientation of lead *V1* provides the best view of the varying amounts of RBB aberrancy. The combined contributions of both leads confirm the junctional origin of the PBs.

VENTRICULAR PREMATURE BEATS (VPBs)

 The characteristic VPB, as illustrated in Figure 13.15, is represented by a wide and bizarre QRS complex, not preceded by a premature P wave and followed by a fully compensatory pause. However, exceptions to all of these characteristics occur, thereby confounding the distinction of a ventricular versus supraventricular origin of the PB.

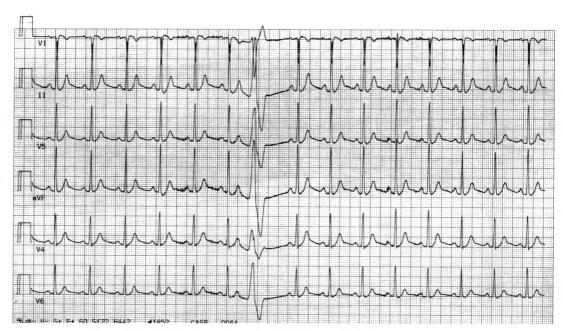

Figure 13.15. The views of a typical VPB from multiple simultaneously recorded ECG leads.

1. Although a VPB is typically wider than 0.12 sec, it may appear to have a normal duration in any single lead because its initial or terminal component is isoelectric. A VPB may even, by coincidence, appear similar to the normal beats on a single lead, as illustrated in Figure 13.16. It is important to consider two or even three simultaneously recorded leads in determining the origin of a PB.
2. A VPB may be preceded by a premature P wave if there is also an APB present.
3. If a VPB is accompanied by an SVPB, the premature P wave of the SVPB may prematurely reset the SA node so that the post-VPB pause is less than compensatory.

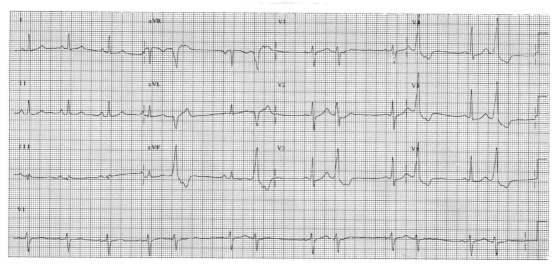

Figure 13.16. Multiple VPBs are obvious in many ECG leads. However, in lead V1, the QRS complexes of the VPBs coincidentally appear very similar to those of the normal sinus beats. If only the lead V1 rhythm strip (*bottom*) was available, the erroneous diagnosis of APBs might be made.

If there is marked variation in the underlying sinus regularity because of sinus arrhythmia, the length of the post-VPB pause may be less than or more than compensatory. Even when the sinus rhythm is regular and there are no APBs, the presence of a compensatory pause requires critical timing of the VPB. It must occur late enough so that it:

1. Does not enter the AV node until that node has recovered from conducting the previous normal beat;
2. Does not enter the SA node until that node has formed the following normal beat.

Figures 13.17–13.19 present examples of VPBs that are not followed by compensatory pauses for various reasons:

1. The VPB Is *Interpolated* Between Consecutive Sinus Beats. When a VPB is extremely premature, it cannot be conducted retrogradely because the AV node has not had time to repolarize from conducting the sinus beat. The following sinus beat can then be conducted to the ventricles. The VPB is interpolated between sinus beats and there is either no pause (Fig. 13.17A) or only the slight pause caused by a prolonged PR interval (Fig. 13.17B).

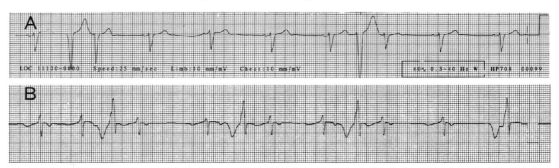

Figure 13.17. Multiple interpolated VPBs are present. In **A**, the following on-time P wave is seen as a bulge at the end of the T wave of the VPB, and the PR interval cannot be determined, but in **B**, the entire P wave is visible, and variable prolongation of the PR intervals (0.22–0.28 sec) is present.

The PR interval of the sinus beat following the VPB is prolonged because the AV node is still partially refractory from its retrograde activation by the VPB. This is an example of concealed conduction because the absence of both a retrograde P wave and resetting of the sinus rhythm indicates that the impulse never reached the atria. The continued "bombardment" of the AV node from both anterograde and retrograde directions prevents its complete recovery. If there is a recurrence of early VPBs, there may be progressively longer and longer PR intervals (Fig. 13.18) until there is complete failure of conduction. Only then is the AV node able to completely recover, as indicated by the normal PR interval of the next sinus cycle. As was discussed above regarding APBs, this is a physiologic "nonconduction" in contrast to pathologic AV block.

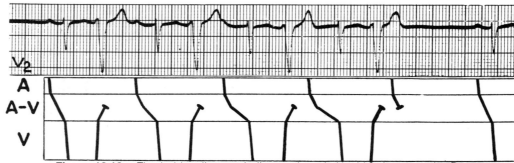

Figure 13.18. The ladder diagram indicates the relationships between the P waves and QRS complexes when both anterograde and retrograde activation prevent full recovery of the AV node.

2. The VPB Resets the Sinus Rhythm. When a VPB occurs late enough to be conducted completely through the AV node, but early enough to enter the SA node before it has formed the following beat, the SA node is reset as though an APB has occurred. The retrograde P wave is usually obscured in the T wave of the VPB, but may be detected in its ST segment, as in Figure 13.19. The pause until the next sinus beat is, therefore, less than compensatory.

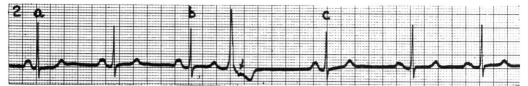

Figure 13.19. The *arrow* points to the retrograde atrial activation by the VPB that resets the sinus node, as indicated by the less than compensatory pause (the *b-c* interval is less than the *a-b* interval).

When a VPB occurs so late that the next sinus P wave has already appeared (Fig. 13.20), the compensatory pause is hardly a pause at all. Only the short PR interval provides the clue that the wide QRS is indeed a VPB. If the PR interval were normal, the diagnosis would most likely be intermittent bundle branch block. The pattern of a normal P wave, short PR interval, and wide QRS complex could also be produced by ventricular preexcitation (Chapter 6, "Ventricular Preexcitation").

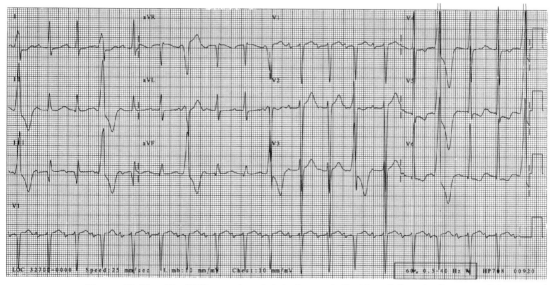

Figure 13.20. The VPBs occur so late in the cycle that they follow the P waves of the normal sinus beats. Note, as in Figure 13.16, that the VPBs appear similar to the normal sinus beats in the lead V1 rhythm strip.

THE RULE OF BIGEMINY

The occurrence of a long cycle (or pause) tends to precipitate reentry following the next normal beat. As discussed in Chapter 3 ("Interpretation of the Next Normal Electrocardiogram"), the ventricular recovery time, as measured by the QT interval, varies with the rate. Therefore, the normal beat that follows a compensatory pause (which follows a VPB) requires a longer recovery time than other normal beats. This longer recovery time creates the potential for reentry of the electrical impulse, resulting in another VPB.[2] A bigeminal pattern occurs with every normal beat followed by a VPB with constant coupling intervals between each pair of normal sinus and premature ventricular beats, as illustrated in Figure 13.21. Ventricular bigeminy may not represent as much of a rhythm abnormality as it suggests. Preventing only the first VPB would prevent them all.

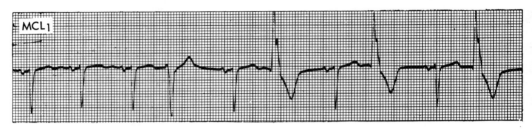

Figure 13.21. The use of lead V1 provides identification of the ventricle of origin of the VPBs. The initial VPB (from the RV) produces a long cycle that precipitates another VPB (from the LV). This pattern continues, resulting in a bigeminal rhythm.

RIGHT VERSUS LEFT VPBs

Figure 13.22 illustrates the contrast between VPBs originating in the right (*right VPBs*) versus the left ventricle (*left VPBs*). The ventricle of origin of ectopic beats can best be recognized in lead V1, which is oriented to differentiate right- versus left-sided cardiac activity (Chapter 1, "Cardiac Electrical Activity"). If the VPB in lead V1 is predominantly positive (*V1 positive*), the impulse must be traveling anteriorly and rightward from its origin in the posteriorly located left ventricle (Fig. 13.22A). If the VPB in lead V1 is predominately negative (*V1 negative*), the impulse must be traveling posteriorly and leftward, usually from its origin in the anteriorly located right ventricle (Fig. 13.22B).[3] However, ischemic heart disease may produce left VPBs with V1 negative morphology (Chapter 17, "Ventricular Tachyarrythmias").

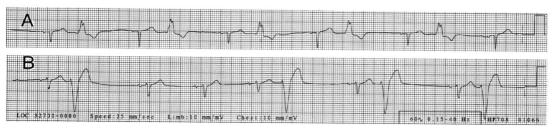

Figure 13.22.   The contrasting appearances of V1 positive (**A**) and V1 negative (**B**) VPBs.

The differentiation between right and left ventricular origin of VPBs is sometimes clinically useful:

1. Left VPBs are more often associated with heart disease, whereas right VPBs are commonly seen in individuals with normal hearts.[4,5]
2. Left VPBs are more likely than right VPBs to precipitate ventricular fibrillation during an acute myocardial infarction.[6]

In a study of over 1000 consecutive patients, there were no instances of ventricular fibrillation in the 249 who manifested only VPBs with a right ventricular pattern in lead MCL$_1$ whereas 82 of 787 (10.4%) with VPBs with a left ventricular pattern developed ventricular fibrillation.

Other morphological features of left VPBs are:

1. Left VPBs usually produce a monophasic (R) or diphasic (qR) complex in lead V1 and a diphasic (rS) or monophasic (QS) complex in lead V6 (Fig. 13.23).
2. If the QRS complex in lead V1 has two peaks (rabbit ears), the left ear is often taller than the right as illustrated in Figures 13.21 and 13.22A.[7]

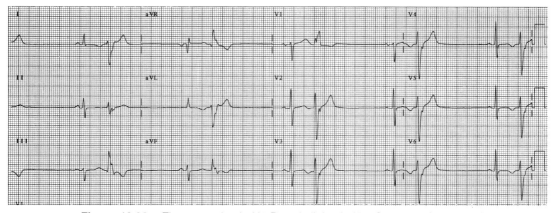

Figure 13.23.   The monophasic V1 R and diphasic V6 rS that typifies the left VPB. Note that the left rabbit ear is atypically shorter than the right.

Other morphologic features of right VPBs are:

1. Right VPBs often have a typical positive morphology in lead V6, but a right axis deviation in the frontal plane and a wide (>0.04 sec) initial R wave in lead V1 (Fig. 13.24).[5,8]
2. Right VPBs tend to show a deeper (rS or QS) complex in lead V4 than in lead V1.[8]

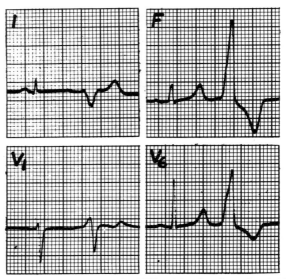

Figure 13.24. The typical morphology of a VPB originating from the right ventricle viewed from limb leads *I* and aVF (*F*) and precordial leads *V1* and *V6*.

MULTIFORM VPBs

When VPBs manifest different QRS morphologies in the same lead (Fig. 13.25), they are termed *multiform VPBs*. Since they are assumed to arise from different foci, they are also called *multifocal VPBs*. It is possible, however, that variation in morphology may result from varying intraventricular conduction rather than from varying sites of origin. Indeed, varying patterns of VPBs have been produced from the same artificially stimulated focus.[9] Therefore, multiform is a more appropriate term than multifocal.

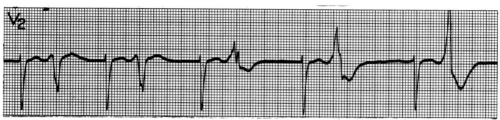

Figure 13.25. The lead *V2* rhythm strip reveals ventricular bigeminy with constant coupling intervals but continually varying (multiform) VPB morphology.

GROUPS OF VPBs

 The definitions of the various groupings of VPBs is provided above. Figure 13.26 illustrates the typical appearances of ventricular bigeminy (A), trigeminy (B), and couplets (C) of VPBs.

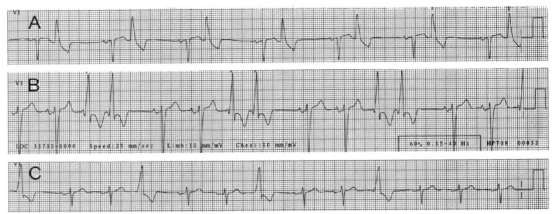

Figure 13.26. The contrasting appearances of the different sequences of VPBs.

In the typical form of bigeminy (Fig. 13.26A), a VPB is substituted for every alternate sinus beat, and each VPB is followed by a compensatory pause. However, when the VPBs are interpolated, a tachyarrhythmia with a bigeminal pattern is produced (Fig. 13.27).

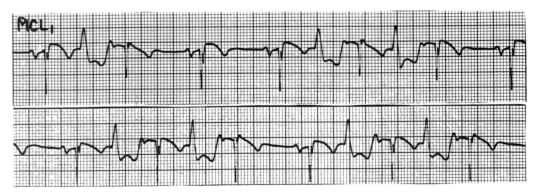

Figure 13.27. A continuous recording of lead MCL₁. The ventricular rate varies from 110 to 140 beats/min during the "tachycardia."

VPBs INDUCING VENTRICULAR FIBRILLATION

When VPBs occur so early that they interrupt the apex of the preceding T wave (Fig. 13.28), they may be ominous.[10] During this early phase of ventricular recovery, there is such inhomogeneity of receptiveness and refractoriness of conduction that the premature impulse may continue to encounter a receptive pathway. The impulse is able to repetitively reenter, thereby producing a tachyarrhythmia, which has been termed ventricular tachycardia of the vulnerable period, ventricular flutter, and coarse ventricular fibrillation. It may terminate spontaneously or progress to typical ventricular fibrillation.

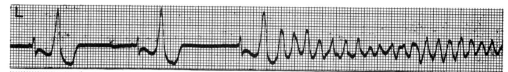

Figure 13.28. A lead aVL (*L*) rhythm strip reveals a bigeminal rhythm produced by very closely coupled VPBs. The VPB that triggers the ventricular flutter has the same coupling interval and morphology as the other VPBs.

The peak of the T wave coincides with the vulnerable period in the cardiac cycle and *R-on-T VPBs* are considered dangerous. Of a series of 48 patients who developed ventricular fibrillation outside the hospital, the initiating beat was an R-on-T VPB in more than two-thirds.[11] Others have also questioned the threat of R-on-T VPBs as compared with later VPBs.[12] One study that carefully documented the VPBs that initiated fibrillation in 20 consecutive patients demonstrated that, in over half, the culpable VPBs occurred after completion of the T wave.[13] Therefore, ventricular fibrillation can be initiated by late VPBs. Surawicz summarizes the situation by concluding that R-on-T VPBs pose a risk of inducing ventricular fibrillation only in the early stages of myocardial infarction, in hypokalemia, and in the presence of a long QT interval.[14]

PROGNOSTIC IMPLICATIONS

VPBs are ubiquitous. Most people have them more or less frequently, and we sometimes find even continuous ventricular bigeminy in apparently normal hearts. They are usually a benign nuisance. During the acute phase of infarction, they appear in 80–90% of patients, but they are also found in the majority of actively employed middle-aged men.[15] Benign VPBs commonly disappear when the sinus rate increases, such as during exercise. The prognostic significance of exercise-induced VPBs is uncertain. VPBs have been reported to occur more readily with isometric than with isotonic (dynamic) exercise.[16]

Many studies have been directed to evaluating the prognostic significance of VPBs during and following acute myocardial infarction. In patients who have survived myocardial infarction, complex VPBs (multiform, couplets) have been shown to increase the risk of sudden death.[17,18] This is in marked contrast to the prognostic importance of similarly appearing VPBs outside the setting of myocardial infarction. In a 7-year follow-up of 72 asymptomatic subjects with frequent and complex ectopy, none died, although a number had angiographically proven significant coronary disease.[19]

Lown's grading system for VPBs[20,21] (Table 13.1) has become a popular frame of reference for gauging the risk of death after myocardial infarction. There is increased risk as the numerical grade advances from 0 to 5. A subsequent study found that consecutive VPBs (grade 4) were associated with a worse prognosis than early, single VPBs (grade 5).[22]

Table 13.1. Lown's Grading System of Ventricular Premature Beats

Grade	Description of VPBs
0	None
1	Less than 30/hour
2	30 or more/hour
3	Multiform
4A	Two consecutive
4B	3 or more consecutive
5	R-on-T

Moss has proposed a simplified two-level system for grading the prognostic significance of VPBs following acute myocardial infarction[23]:

Uniform morphology and late cycle	Low risk	(2-year mortality 10%)
Multiform and/or early cycle	High risk	(2-year mortality 20%)

A study by Califf et al. has documented the relationship between VPBs and left ventricular function in patients with ischemic heart disease.[24] A subsequent study by these same authors failed to find a subgroup of patients with VPBs of any description and good left ventricular function that had a high risk or sudden death.[25] Therefore, VPBs do not appear to be independent predictors of high risk in patients with ischemic heart disease.

GLOSSARY

Atrial premature beat (APB): a P wave produced by an impulse that originates in the atria and appears prior to the expected time of the next P wave generated from the sinus node.

Bigeminy: a rhythm pattern in which every sinus beat is followed by a premature beat.

Compensatory pause: the long cycle length (pause) following a PB completely "compensates for" the short cycle length preceding the PB. This is identified when the interval between the beginning of the P waves of the sinus beats preceding and following a PB is equal to two PP intervals of sinus beats not associated with PBs.

Couplet: two consecutive premature beats.

Coupling intervals: the time durations between the normal sinus beats and premature beats. With APBs, the PP' is the coupling interval, and with JPBs and VPBs the QRS-QRS' is the coupling interval.

Interpolated: occurring between normal beats.

Junctional premature beat (JPB): a P wave and QRS complex produced by an impulse that originates in the AV node, His bundle, or Kent bundle and appears prior to the expected time of the next P wave and QRS complex generated from the sinus node.

Left VPBs: premature beats originating from the left ventricle, usually with a V1 positive morphology, but sometimes with a V1 negative morphology when associated with ischemic heart disease.

Multiform VPBs: premature ventricular beats with two or more different morphologies in a single ECG lead.

Multifocal VPBs: premature beats originating from two or more different ventricular locations.

Overdrive suppression: a decrease in the rate of impulse formation resulting from premature activation of the pacemaking cells.

R-on-T VPB: a VPB that occurs so premature that it occurs during the T wave of the previous beat.

Right VPBs: premature beats originating from the right ventricle, always with a V1 negative morphology.

Supraventricular premature beat (SVPB): either an APB or a JPB.

Trigeminy: a rhythm pattern in which every second sinus beat is followed by a premature beat.

V1 negative: an abnormally wide QRS complex that is predominantly negative in lead V1; sometimes called "LBBB-like."

V1 positive: an abnormally wide QRS complex that is predominantly positive in lead V1; sometimes called "RBBB-like."

Ventricular premature beat (VPB): a QRS complex produced by an impulse originating from the ventricles and appearing prior to the expected time of the next QRS complex generated from the sinus node or other basic underlying rhythm.

Vulnerable period: the time in the cardiac cycle prior to complete repolarization when a reentrant tachyarrhythmia may be induced by the introduction of a premature impulse.

REFERENCES

1. Killip T, Gault JH. Mode of onset of atrial fibrillation in man. Am Heart J 1965;70:172.
2. Langendorf R, Pick A, Winternitz M. Mechanisms of intermittent ventricular bigeminy. I. Appearance of ectopic beats dependent upon length of the ventricular cycle, the "rule of bigeminy." Circulation 1955;11:422–430.
3. Kaplinsky E, Ogawa S, Kmetzo J, Dreifus LS. Origin of so-called right and left ventricular arrhythmias in acute myocardial ischemia. Am J Cardiol 1978;42:774.
4. Lewis S, Kanakis C, Rosen KM, Denes P. Significance of site of origin of premature ventricular contractions. Am Heart J 1979;97:159.
5. Rosenbaum MB. Classification of ventricular extrasystoles according to form. J Electrocardiol 1969;2:289.
6. O'Bryan C. Personal communication, 1981.
7. Gozensky C, Thorne D. Rabbit ears: an aid in distinguishing ventricular ectopy from aberration. Heart Lung 1974;3:634.
8. Swanick EJ, LaCamera F Jr, Marriott HJL. Morphologic features of right ventricular ectopic beats. Am J Cardiol 1972;30:888.
9. Booth DC, Popio KA, Gettes LS. Multiformity of induced unifocal ventricular premature beats in human subjects: electrocardiographic and angiographic correlations. Am J Cardiol 1982;49:1643.
10. Smirk FH, Palmer DDG. A myocardial syndrome, with particular reference to the occurrence of sudden death and of premature systoles interrupting antecedent T waves. Am J Cardiol 1960;6:620.
11. Adgey AJ, Devlin JE, Webb SW, Mulholland HC. Initiation of ventricular fibrillation outside hospital in patients with ischemic heart disease. Br Heart J 1982;47:55.
12. Engel TR, Meister SG, Frankl WS. The "R-on-T" phenomenon; an update and critical review. Ann Intern Med 1978;88:221.
13. Lie KI, Wellens HJ, Downar E, Durrer D. Observations on patients with primary ventricular fibrillation complicating acute myocardial infarction. Circulation 1975;52:755.
14. Surawicz B. R on T phenomenon: dangerous and harmless. J Appl Cardiol 1986;1:39.
15. Hinkle LE Jr, Carver ST, Stevens M. The frequency of asymptomatic disturbances of cardiac rhythm and conduction in middle-aged men. Am J Cardiol 1969;24:629–650.
16. Atkins JM, Matthews OA, Blomqvist CG, Mullins CB. Incidence of arrhythmias induced by isometric and dynamic exercise. Br Heart J 1976;38:465.
17. Moss AJ, Davis HT, DeCamilla J, Bayer LW. Ventricular ectopic beats and their relation to sudden and nonsudden cardiac death after myocardial infarction. Circulation 1979;60:998–1003.
18. Ruberman W, Weinblatt E, Goldberg JD, Frank CW, Shapiro S. Ventricular premature beats and mortality after myocardial infarction. N Engl J Med 1977;297:750.
19. Horan MJ, Kennedy HL. Characteristics and prognosis of apparently healthy patients with frequent and complex ventricular ectopy: evidence for a relative benign syndrome with occult myocardial and/or coronary disease. Am Heart J 1981;102:809.
20. Lown B, Wolf M. Approaches to sudden death from coronary heart disease. Circulation 1971;48:130.
21. Lown B, Graboys TB. Management of patients with malignant ventricular arrhythmias. Am J Cardiol 1977;39:910.
22. Bigger JT, Weld FJ. Analysis of prognostic significance of ventricular arrhythmias after myocardial infarction. Shortcomings of the Lown grading system. Br Heart J 1981;45:717.
23. Moss AJ. Clinical significance of ventricular arrhythmias in patients with and without coronary artery disease. Prog Cardiovasc Dis 1980;23:33.
24. Califf RM, Burks JM, Behar VS, Margolis JR, Wagner GS. Relationships among ventricular arrhythmias, coronary artery disease, and angiographic and electrocardiographic indicators of myocardial fibrosis. Circulation 1978;57:725–732.
25. Califf RM, McKinnis RA, Burks J, Lee KL, Harrell FE Jr, Behar VS, Wagner GS, Rosati RA. Prognostic implications of ventricular arrhythmias during 24 hour ambulatory monitoring in patients undergoing catheterization for coronary artery disease. Am J Cardiol 1982;50:23–31.

CHAPTER 14

Accelerated Automaticity

The arrhythmias presented in this chapter have gradual onsets and terminations because they result from acceleration of automaticity in the cells of the pacemaking and conduction system (Fig. 14.1). Cells termed *pacemakers* have the capability for spontaneous depolarization and are located in the sinus node at various sites in the atria and throughout the His-Purkinje system. Atrial and ventricular muscle cells and AV nodal cells have not been shown to have pacemaking capabilities.

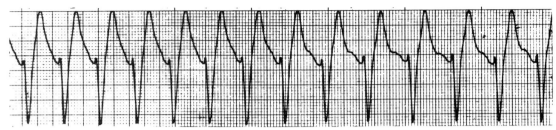

Figure 14.1. During exercise, lead MCL₁ reveals a tachyarrhythmia at a rate of 140 beats/ min with no visible P waves and wide (V1 negative) QRS complexes (0.14 sec). When the activity is stopped, the rate gradually slows and P waves emerge from the ends of each of the T waves, indicating that the rhythm is sinus tachycardia with LBBB. (From Wagner GS, Waugh RA, Ramo BW. Cardiac arrhythmias. New York: Churchill Livingstone, 1983:145.)

The rate of impulse formation is determined by the rate of spontaneous depolarization, and the more superior the location of the pacemaking cell, the more rapidly this occurs. Accelerated automaticity is considered to be a tachyarrhythmia only when the rate exceeds the arbitrary limit of 100 beats/min. Since the upper limit of normal automaticity of the sinus node and atrial cells is 100 beats/min, any acceleration is considered a tachyarrhythmia. The upper limit of normal automaticity is 60 beats/min in the common bundle and 50 beats/min in the bundle branches. Their acceleration is simply called an *accelerated rhythm* until it reaches 100 beats/ min. The pacemaking sites, the terms used for the arrhythmias produced by their acceleration, and their rate ranges are presented in Table 14.1.

Table 14.1

Site	Term	Rate Range (beats/min)
Sinus node	Sinus tachycardia	100–200
Atria	Atrial tachycardia	100–200
Common bundle	Accelerated junctional rhythm (AJR)	60–130
Bundle branches	Accelerated ventricular rhythm (AVR)	50–110

Examples of arrhythmias due to accelerated atrial, junctional and ventricular rhythms are presented in Figure 14.2.

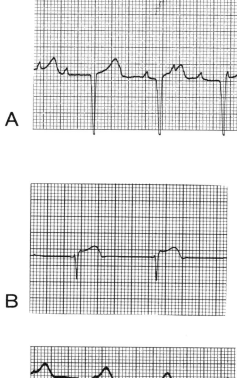

Figure 14.2. Lead V1 recordings of arrhythmias due to accelerated automaticity in three areas of the heart. **A.** A regular atrial rate of 180 beats/min and a slower irregular ventricular rate, indicating an atrial tachycardia with second degree AV block; **B.** A ventricular rate (further monitoring revealed that it was regular) of 65 beats/min with no visible P waves and narrow QRS complexes, indicating AJR; **C.** A regular ventricular rate of 80 beats/min with P waves in the ST segments following wide QRS complexes (0.14 sec), indicating AVR.

Usually, the cardiac rhythm is controlled by the sinus node. However, there are several reasons why the rhythm becomes dominated by the accelerated pacing activity from a nonsinus site. These include:

1. A pharmacologic agent that selectively increases automaticity in lower pacemakers;
2. Blockage of sinus impulses in the AV conduction system, permitting an escape focus in the common bundle to control the ventricular rhythm;
3. Local pathology, especially ischemia, that induces automaticity in the lower areas with pacemaking capability;
4. Local pathology that decreases automaticity within the sinus node.

SINUS TACHYCARDIA

The rate of impulse formation is regulated by the balance between the parasympathetic and sympathetic parts of the autonomic, or involuntary, nervous system. The more superior the location of the pacemaking cells, the greater the autonomic regulation. An increase in parasympathetic activity decreases, while an increase in sympathetic activity increases, the rate of impulse formation. The sympathetic nervous system becomes activated by any condition that requires "flight or fright." The resultant sinus tachycardia is a physiologic response to the body's needs rather than a pathologic cardiac condition. Treatment, therefore, should be directed at correction of the underlying condition and not at suppression of the sinus node itself. Maximal sympathetic stimulation can increase the rate of the sinus node to 200 beats/min or, rarely, 220 beats/min in younger individuals. The rate rarely exceeds 160 beats/min in nonexercising adults.

There is normally one P wave for every QRS complex, but AV conduction abnormalities may alter this relationship. The PR interval is shorter than during normal sinus rhythm because the increased *sympathetic tone* that produces the sinus tachycardia also speeds up AV nodal conduction. The QRS complex is usually normal in appearance, but can be abnormal either because of a fixed intraventricular conduction disturbance (such as bundle branch block, hypertrophy, or myocardial infarction) or because the rapid rate does not permit time for full recovery of the intraventricular conduction system before the arrival of the next impulse (aberrancy). Figure 14.3 demonstrates sinus tachycardia with LBBB. The block is proven to be due to rate-related aberrancy when it disappears during sinus slowing induced by *carotid sinus massage* and returns when the rate gradually increases following the massage.

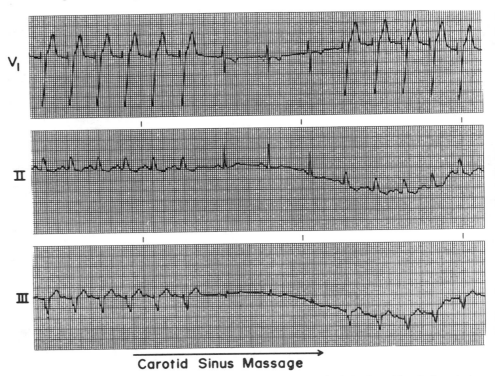

Figure 14.3. Simultaneously recorded leads reveal the gradual slowing of the rhythm during carotid sinus massage (*arrow*). Note that the slowing of the ventricular rate is accompanied by normalization of the QRS morphology, indicating that aberrancy was the cause of the wide QRS complexes during the tachycardia. (From Wagner GS, Waugh RA, Ramo BW. Cardiac arrhythmias. New York: Churchill Livingstone, 1983:140.)

A common clinical problem is the differentiation of sinus tachycardia from the various other supraventricular tachycardias. Interestingly, the other problems of accelerated impulse formation do not mimic sinus tachycardia. Acceleration of an atrial pacemaker is usually accompanied by AV block, and the normal QRS complexes of accelerated junctional rhythm are not preceded by P waves. Figure 14.4 presents true sinus tachycardia in *A* and reentrant supraventricular tachyarrhythmias that appear similar to sinus tachycardia in *B* and *C*. When apparent sinus tachycardia is associated with a prolonged PR interval, one should be suspicious that another tachycardia is present instead. Figure 14.4*B* presents an example of atrial flutter with 2:1 AV block masquerading as sinus tachycardia. An abnormal frontal plane P wave axis also suggests a nonsinus origin of the tachycardia. The inverted P waves preceding each QRS complex suggest an atrial tachycardia in Figure 14.4*C*.

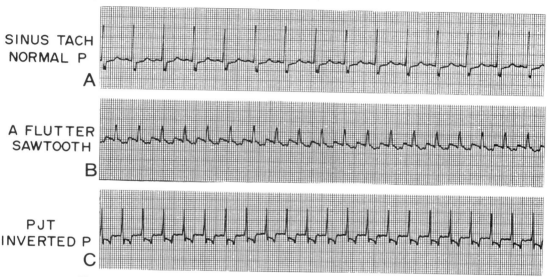

SINUS TACH
NORMAL P
A

A FLUTTER
SAWTOOTH
B

PJT
INVERTED P
C

Figure 14.4. The contrasting appearances of the atrial activity in sinus tachycardia (**A**), atrial flutter (**B**), and reentrant junctional tachycardia (**C**). (From Wagner GS, Waugh RA, Ramo BW. Cardiac arrhythmias. New York: Churchill Livingstone, 1983:176.)

If one can observe the onset and termination of the tachyarrhythmia, the gradual change in rate establishes the diagnosis of accelerated sinus impulse formation (Fig. 14.5*A*). The spontaneous decrease in AV conduction establishes the diagnosis of atrial flutter (Fig. 14.5*B*). A reentrant tachycardia starts and stops abruptly; however, there may be gradual slowing prior to the termination (Fig. 14.5*C*).

If discrete P waves, with anterograde orientation, a short PR interval, and a normal QRS duration are present, the diagnosis of sinus tachycardia is most likely. If the beginning or ending is not available and all of the above characteristics are not present, a diagnostic maneuver or pharmacologic intervention to increase parasympathetic nervous activity may be necessary (Fig. 14.5*B*). Transient slowing without termination during the *vagal maneuver* identifies sinus tachycardia, AV block identifies atrial flutter, and termination identifies junctional reentry. The absence of any change during the vagal maneuver does not permit any diagnostic conclusion. Transesophageal or intraatrial recording may be required when no diagnosis can be made from surface ECG recordings (Fig. 12.10). A summary of the progressive steps toward the diagnosis of an unknown tachyarrhythmia would include:

1. Observe either the onset or the termination.
2. Note the P wave morphology and the PR and QRS intervals.
3. Perform a maneuver to increase parasympathetic activity.
4. Record the atrial activity from the esophagus or right atrium.

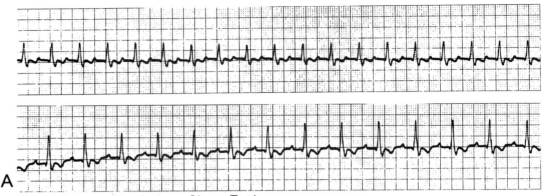

A

Spontaneous Slowing ➔ Sinus Tach

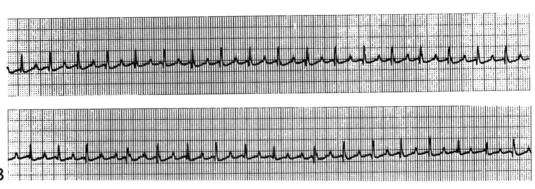

B

Spontaneous Slowing ➔ At Flutter With 2:1 Block

PJT RATE-250

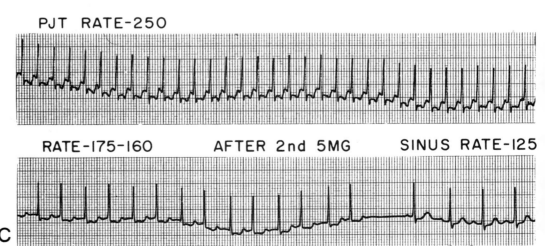

RATE-175-160   AFTER 2nd 5MG   SINUS RATE-125

C

Figure 14.5. The contrasting appearances of the terminations of sinus tachycardia (**A**), atrial flutter (**B**), and reentrant junctional tachycardia (**C**). Note the slowing of the rate of the reentrant junctional tachycardia prior to the sudden termination. (From Wagner GS, Waugh RA, Ramo BW. Cardiac arrhythmias. New York: Churchill Livingstone, 1983:144,179.)

ATRIAL TACHYCARDIAS: PAT WITH BLOCK AND MAT

 There are two commonly occurring varieties of atrial tachycardias due to enhanced automaticity: *paroxysmal atrial tachycardia (PAT) with block* and *multifocal atrial tachycardia (MAT)*. *Digitalis toxicity* is the most common cause of an atrial tachycardia accompanied by AV block. The term *paroxysmal* is inaccurate because it implies a sudden onset and termination. The atrial rate gradually accelerates as digitalis is added or potassium is depleted and then gradually decelerates when the digitalis is withheld or potassium is replaced.[1,2] Digitalis has a parasympathetic effect on both the SA and AV nodes, resulting in sinus slowing and AV block. However, digitalis has a sympathetic effect on other sites with pacemaking capability and thereby enhances automaticity. If the site of this enhancement is above the AV node, the result is the combination of atrial tachycardia with AV block (Fig. 14.6).

K$^+$ 3.1

Atrial Tach:

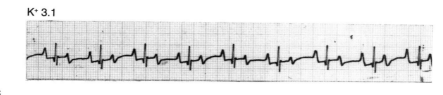

Withheld Digitalis

K$^+$ 4.6

Replaced Potassium

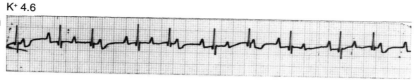

Figure 14.6. The *top rhythm strip* shows a nonparoxysmal atrial tachycardia due to digitalis toxicity in the setting of hypokalemia (K$^+$ = 3.1 mEq/L). The atrial rate is 167 beats/min and there is 2:1 AV block. In the *lower rhythm strip*, digitalis had been withheld and the potassium level increased to 4.6 mEq/L. Note that the atrial rate has now slowed to 136 beats/min, but the 2:1 AV block persists. (From Wagner GS, Waugh RA, Ramo BW. Cardiac arrhythmias. New York: Churchill Livingstone, 1983:138.)

Severe pulmonary disease is the most common cause of irregular atrial tachycardia with multiple differently appearing P waves termed either multifocal or *chaotic atrial tachycardia*.[3] In contrast to the atrial tachycardia of digitalis toxicity, there is no enhancement of the parasympathetic effect on the AV node and, therefore, there is 1:1 AV conduction. MAT is typically a transitional arrhythmia between frequent APBs and atrial flutter/fibrillation. In a series of 31 patients reported by Lipson and Naimi, 20 had preceding APBs and 17 progressed to atrial flutter/fibrillation.[3] In the example of MAT in Figure 14.7, the MAT appeared as acute respiratory failure developed and then regressed as the patient improved.

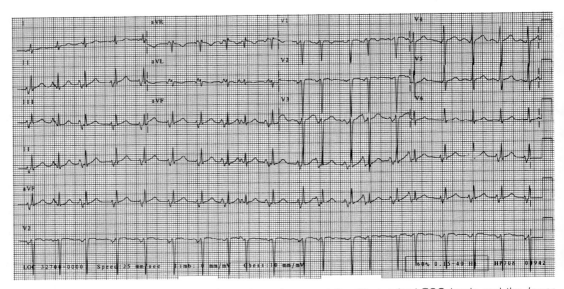

 Figure 14.7. The *top three channels* present the 12 standard ECG leads and the *lower three channels* present 10-sec rhythm strips from leads II, aVF, and V2 recorded simultaneously. Note the multiform P wave morphologies in any single ECG lead.

ACCELERATED JUNCTIONAL RHYTHM (AJR)

If the QRS morphology is normal and dissociation between atrial and ventricular activity is present (*AV dissociation*), the arrhythmia is AJR. It may be necessary to observe a long rhythm strip to document the absence of an A to V relationship. The atrial and ventricular rates are often very similar (*isorhythmia*), and a constant P-QRS relationship may be present for a long time, as in the latter part of Figure 14.8A.

When P waves follow narrow QRS complexes and the rate is <130 beats/min, the most likely diagnosis is AJR with retrograde conduction to the atria (Fig. 14.8B). However, when the rate is between 100 and 130 beats/min, sinus tachycardia with a prolonged PR interval should also be considered. If P waves can be seen clearly on a 12-lead ECG, their direction in the frontal plane should provide differentiation.

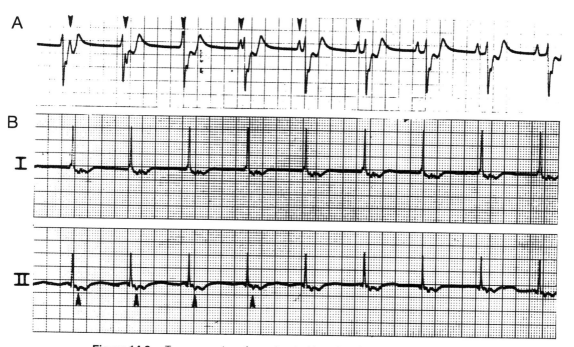

Figure 14.8. Two examples of accelerated junctional rhythm are presented with two varieties of AV relationship: dissociation (**A**) and retrograde conduction (**B**). In the *right-hand aspect* of **A**, a P wave precedes the QRS complex by <0.20 sec, suggesting that sinus rhythm might be present. However, observation of the earlier rhythm reveals that no AV association is present. *Arrowheads* indicate the atrial activity in both examples. (From Wagner GS, Waugh RA, Ramo BW. Cardiac arrhythmias. New York: Churchill Livingstone, 1983:147.)

A regular ventricular rate of >60 beats/min with normal appearing QRS complexes in the presence of atrial fibrillation is diagnostic of AJR. There is dissociation between the reentrant arrhythmia above the AV node and the arrhythmia due to accelerated automaticity below the AV node (Fig. 14.9). This combination of decreased conduction in the AV node and enhanced automaticity in the common bundle is usually caused by digitalis toxicity (Chapter 22, "Drug Toxicity"). If it is unrecognized, additional digitalis will further accelerate the AJR.

Atrial Fibrillation

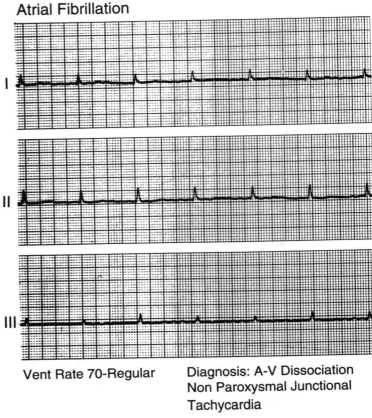

Vent Rate 70-Regular

Diagnosis: A-V Dissociation
Non Paroxysmal Junctional
Tachycardia

Figure 14.9. Simultaneous recording of three leads showing the undulating baseline of atrial fibrillation dissociated from the regular narrow QRS complexes of accelerated junctional rhythm. (From Wagner GS, Waugh RA, Ramo BW. Cardiac arrhythmias. New York: Churchill Livingstone, 1983:149.)

ACCELERATED VENTRICULAR RHYTHM (AVR)

AVR is produced by enhanced automaticity in the bundle branches or the fascicles of the ventricular Purkinje system. This arrhythmia is often given other names such as accelerated idioventricular rhythm (AIVR) or *slow ventricular tachycardia*. Since the pacing rate of these cells located at the distal end of the pacemaking and conduction system is normally very slow, AVR is diagnosed when the rate exceeds 50 beats/min. The most rapid rate of AVR is 110 beats/min, and it rarely exceeds 100 beats/min. AVR most commonly occurs during the early hours of an acute myocardial infarction with reported incidences ranging from 8 to 46%. AVR is also a common manifestation of digitalis toxicity.

AVR occurs either because the sinus rhythm slows and permits the ventricular rhythm to escape (Fig. 14.10A) or because the ventricular rhythm accelerates and usurps control from the sinus node (Fig. 14.10B). When AVR is present, the rates of the sinus and ventricular impulse formation are usually similar, and the dominance of the ventricular pacemaker begins with one or more *fusion beats*.

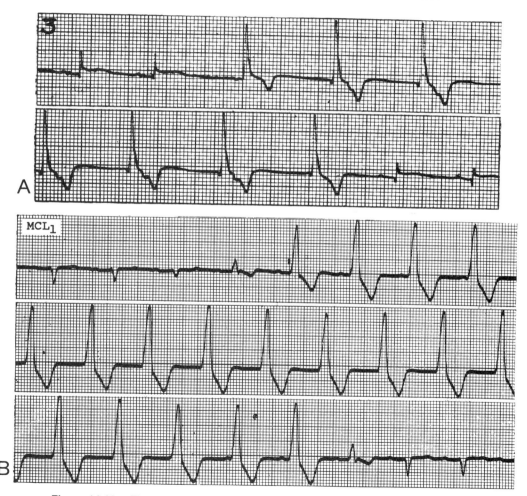

Figure 14.10. The contrasting appearances of an accelerated ventricular rhythm that occur because of slowing of the sinus pacemaker (**A**) and speeding of the ventricular pacemaker (**B**).

AVR, like AJR, commonly occurs when atrial fibrillation is accompanied by decreased AV nodal conduction. This combination of effects on the cardiac rhythm often results from digitalis toxicity. Once the AVR gets under way, it usually proceeds as a perfectly regular rhythm, but sometimes it shows progressive acceleration or progressive slowing until it spontaneously ceases (Fig. 14.11).

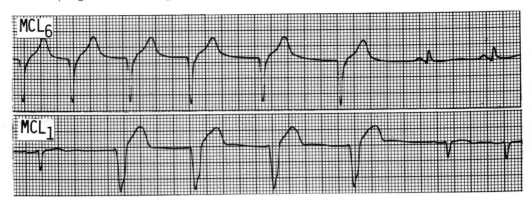

Figure 14.11. Rhythm strips from two patients showing gradual slowing of the accelerated ventricular rhythm leading to resumption of sinus rhythm.

Rarely, the rhythm is quite irregular. In some instances, instead of dissociation between the atria and ventricles, there is retrograde conduction to the atria (Fig. 14.12). AVR is usually benign, even when multiform, and neither affects the blood pressure nor leads to more serious ventricular arrhythmias.[4,5] However, since the normal sequence of atrial and ventricular activation is absent and there is loss of the normal atrial contribution to ventricular filling, AVR may be accompanied by a feeling of weakness or unsteadiness.

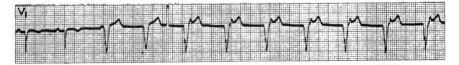

Figure 14.12. Following two beats of sinus rhythm, AVR appears, initially dissociated from the atrial activity (next two beats) and then conducting retrograde to capture the atrial rhythm (the final seven beats).

PARASYSTOLE

Normally, the wave fronts that spread from the most dominant pacemaker activate all of the other cells with pacemaking capability. These cells are repetitively reset and function only as the pacemaker if either the dominant pacemaker fails or their own automaticity is enhanced. However, the advancing wave fronts sometimes fail to enter cells with pacemaking capability. This *pacemaker entrance block* leads to an arrhythmia termed *parasystole*. In contrast to the other arrhythmias in this chapter, the enhanced automaticity is due to protection from normal impulse conduction rather than acceleration of impulse formation. Therefore, rather than a single dominant abnormal rhythm, parasystole is characterized by two competing rhythms.[6,7] Though a parasystolic focus can develop at any location with pacemaking capability, it most commonly occurs in the bundle branches and fascicles of the ventricles.

The *fixed-rate artificial pacemaker* (Chapter 21, "Artificial Cardiac Pacemakers") provides an excellent model of a parasystolic arrhythmia (Fig. 14.13) with the following characteristics:

1. The artificial pacemaker is protected from inhibition by its lack of ability to sense the normal impulse.
2. Spike-like waveforms (*pacemaker artifacts*) occur at the fixed rate of the device.
3. No QRS complex follows the artifact when it occurs at times when the ventricles are refractory from normal activation.
4. A VPB follows the artifact when it occurs after the ventricles have recovered from normal activation.
5. A fusion beat is created when the artifact coincides with a normal QRS complex and both foci capture parts of the ventricles.

There is no constancy of the coupling intervals between normal beats and VPBs as is expected when the cause is reentry. Rather, there is constancy between the *interectopic intervals*: all intervals between VPBs are multiples of the shortest of these intervals. For example, in the second strip of Fig. 14.13, the long interectopic interval equals four times the short interval.

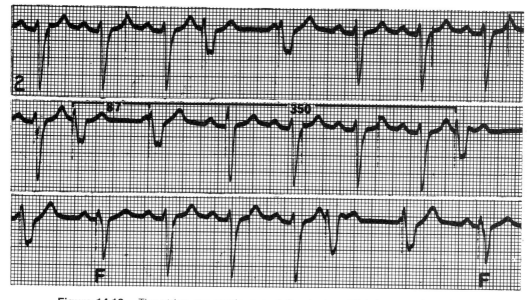

Figure 14.13. The strips are continuous. A fixed-rate artificial pacemaker with an interval of 0.087 sec between impulses is competing with the patient's sinus rhythm. All of the longer interectopic intervals are multiples of the pacemaker's cycle.

In Figure 14.14, the first three VPBs all have different relationships (coupling intervals) to the preceding normal sinus beats, and the interectopic intervals are 1.45 and 1.46 sec, respectively. All subsequent interectopic intervals are multiples of cycles between 1.44 and 1.45 sec. The last beat in the second strip is a fusion beat, upright like the VPBs but narrower, and preceded by a sinus P wave with a long enough PR interval for some conduction into the ventricles.

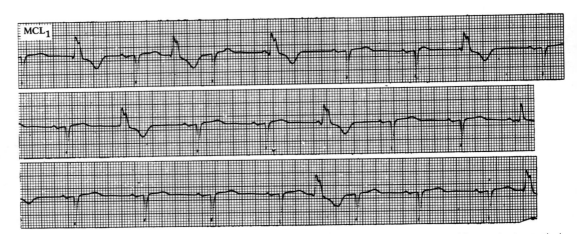

Figure 14.14. The strips are continuous. Multiple VPBs are present with constant morphology, but varying coupling intervals. However, all of the interectopic intervals have a common denominator between 1.43 and 1.56 sec.

GLOSSARY

Accelerated rhythm: the rate is increased above its normal limit.

Chaotic atrial tachycardia: another term used for multifocal atrial tachycardia.

Digitalis toxicity: an arrhythmia produced by the drug digitalis.

Fixed-rate artificial pacemaker: a device capable only of generating cardiac impulses without sensing the patient's own intrinsic rhythm.

Interectopic intervals: the times between consecutive premature beats.

Isorhythmia: the atria and ventricles are beating independently (dissociation), but at very similar rates.

Multifocal atrial tachycardia (MAT): a rapid rhythm produced by pacemakers located at multiple sites within the atria.

Pacemaker: a cell in the heart or an artificial device that is capable of the formation or generation of an electrical impulse.

Pacemaker artifacts: spike-like deflections on the ECG produced by an artificial pacemaker.

Pacemaker entrance block: the failure of a pace-making cell to receive the surrounding cardiac activity. This causes the cell to function as a second pacemaker.

Parasystole: an arrhythmia produced by a cardiac cell that is functioning as a pacemaker without the capability to sense the surrounding cardiac activity.

Paroxysmal: the sudden occurrence of an arrhythmia.

Paroxysmal atrial tachycardia (PAT) with block: a tachyarrhythmia, commonly caused by digitalis toxicity, in which a rapid atrial rhythm is accompanied by failure of some of the impulses to be conducted through the AV node of the ventricles.

Slow ventricular tachycardia: another term used for an accelerated ventricular rhythm.

Sympathetic tone: the relative amount of sympathetic nervous activity as compared to the amount of parasympathetic activity.

Vagal maneuver: an intervention that increases parasympathetic activity in relation to the amount of sympathetic activity.

REFERENCES

1. Lown B, Wyatt NF, Levine HD. Paroxysmal atrial tachycardia with block. Circulation 1960;21:129–143.
2. Geer MR, Wagner GS, Waxman M, Wallace AG. Chronotropic effect of acetylstrophanthidin infusion into the canine sinus nodal artery. Am J Cardiol 1977;39:684–689.
3. Lipson MJ, Naimi S. Multifocal atrial tachycardia (chaotic atrial tachycardia): clinical associations and significance. Circulation 1970;42:397.
4. Denes P, Kehoe R, Rosen KM. Multiple reentrant tachycardias due to retrograde conduction of dual atrioventricular bundles with atrioventricular nodal-like properties. Am J Cardiol 1979;44:162–170.
5. Epstein ML, Stone FM, Benditt DG. Incessant atrial tachycardia in childhood: association with rate-dependent conduction in an accessory atrioventricular pathway. Am J Cardiol 1979;44:498–504.
6. Farshidi A, Josephson ME, Horowitz LN. Electrophysiologic characteristics of concealed bypass tracts: clinical and electrocardiographic correlates. Am J Cardiol 1978;41:1052–1060.
7. Gallagher JJ, Smith WM, Kerr CR, German LD, Sterba R, Sealy WC. Etiology of long R-P' tachycardia in 33 cases of supraventricular tachycardia [Abstract]. Circulation 1981;64(suppl IV):145.

CHAPTER 15

Atrial Flutter/Fibrillation Spectrum

The supraventricular tachyarrhythmias in the *atrial flutter/fibrillation spectrum* are caused by the continuing reentry of an electrical impulse within the atrial myocardium. *Atrial flutter* and *atrial fibrillation* are at the extremes of this spectrum. At the flutter end of the spectrum, the reentering impulse cycles around a single circuit, producing regular uniform "sawtooth-like" waves (*F waves*). At the fibrillation end of the spectrum, the reentering impulse proceeds around multiple circuits, producing irregular multiform waves (*f waves*). The mechanism of these arrhythmias is macro-reentry, as discussed in Chapter 12 ("Introduction to Arrhythmias"). P waves are replaced by F waves representing the continuous activation within the flutter circuit or by f waves representing the continuous activation within the fibrillation circuits.

ATRIAL RATE AND REGULARITY

 The F waves of atrial flutter occur at rates between 200 and 350 beats/min (Fig. 15.1A).[1,2] As the atrial rate increases above 350 beats/min, either the atrial waves have some characteristics of both flutter and fibrillation at a single point in time or there are alternations between F and f waves, and the appropriate term is *atrial flutter-fibrillation* (Fig. 15.1B). Fibrillation varies from coarse to fine. In *coarse fibrillation*, prominent f waves are clearly visible in many leads (Fig. 15.1C), but in *fine fibrillation* there may be no visible atrial activity at all (Fig. 15.1D).

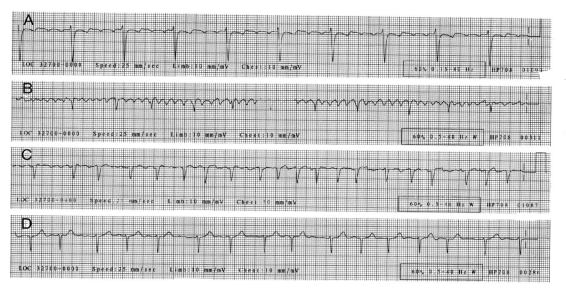

Figure 15.1. The contrasting appearances of four points in the atrial flutter/fibrillation spectrum; flutter (**A**); flutter/fibrillation (**B**); course fibrillation (**C**); and fine fibrillation (**D**).

Some patients may spontaneously change from the flutter to the fibrillation ends of the spectrum, whereas in others such variation occurs only when certain drugs are administered. Digitalis increases the atrial rate toward fibrillation by shortening the refractory periods of myocardial cells in the reentry circuit (Fig. 15.2, *top*). Conversely, drugs such as *quinidine* and *procainamide* decrease the atrial rate toward flutter by lengthening the refractory periods of these cells (Fig. 15.2, *bottom*).

Pre Digitalis

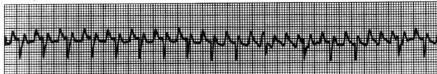

Post Digitalis

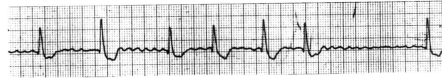

A

On Digitalis – Pre Quinidine

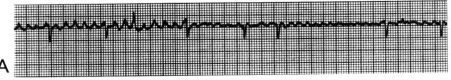

Post Quinidine

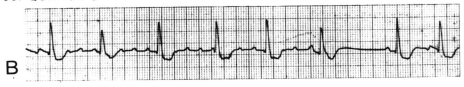

B

Figure 15.2. In **A**, the digitalis accelerates the atrial reentry from flutter to fibrillation and slows the AV conduction. In **B**, the quinidine first slows the atrial reentry from fibrillation to flutter and then terminates it. (From Wagner GS, Waugh RA, Ramo BW. Cardiac arrhythmias. New York: Churchill Livingstone, 1983:159.)

VENTRICULAR RATE AND REGULARITY

 Atrial flutter produces a ventricular rhythm that varies from precisely regular to irregularly irregular; however, fibrillation always produces an irregularly irregular ventricular rhythm. Indeed, when atrial fibrillation is accompanied by a regular ventricular rate, there is dissociation between the atrial and ventricular rhythms. Since the atrial rate may vary dramatically within the flutter/fibrillation spectrum, the ventricular rate may also vary. At times, it may change abruptly from rapid and regular to slow and irregular, incorrectly suggesting a change in the basic underlying atrial rhythm (Fig. 15.3).

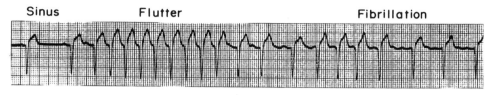

Figure 15.3. After two beats of sinus rhythm, an APB initiates a supraventricular tachyarrhythmia that is initially regular and then becomes irregular. The regular phase is most likely due to flutter at a rate of 200 beats/min with 1:1 AV conduction, and then the irregular phase occurs because the atrial rate speeds to flutter-fibrillation at a rate of 300 beats/min with a slower irregular ventricular rate. (From Wagner GS, Waugh RA, Ramo BW. Cardiac arrhythmias. New York: Churchill Livingstone, 1983:155.)

During atrial flutter, the ratio of atrial to ventricular activation may vary from 1:1 to 2:1 to 6:2 to 4:1 (Fig. 15.4, A–E) so that the ventricles may or may not have a rapid rate. The ratio depends on the capability of the slowly conducting AV node to transport the atrial impulses to the common bundle. When ratios of 1:1, 2:1, or 4:1 remain constant (Fig. 15.4, A, B, and E), the ventricular rhythm is regular. When the ratio is 6:2, the ventricular rhythm is regularly irregular; when the ratio is variable, the ventricular rhythm is irregularly irregular.

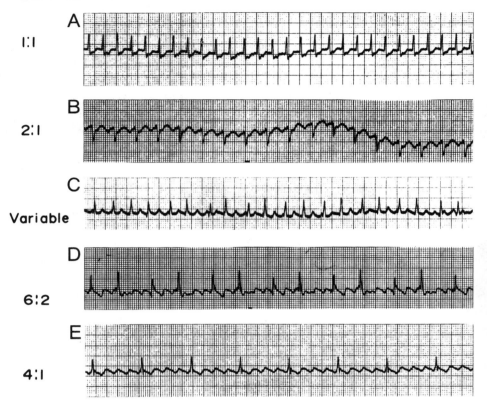

Figure 15.4. Various typical patterns of AV conduction in atrial flutter are shown. **A.** There is 1:1 conduction with a rate of 215 beats/min. **B.** The atrial rate is 300 beats/min and there is a regular ventricular rate of 150 beats/min with a constant relationship between the flutter waves and the QRS complexes. **C.** The atrial rate is 330 beats/min (note the typical flutter waves during periods of increased AV block), and there is a variable, irregular ventricular response. **D.** The atrial rate is 300 beats/min, and there is a regularly irregular ventricular response in a pattern of 6 flutter waves for every 2 QRS complexes. **E.** The atrial rate is 250 beats/min, and there is a 4:1 ventricular response, again with a constant relationship between atrial activity and each ventricular complex. (From Wagner GS, Waugh RA, Ramo BW. Cardiac arrhythmias. New York: Churchill Livingstone, 1983:156.)

When atrial fibrillation is present, the innumerable f waves compete for penetration of the AV node, making it difficult for any impulse to reach the common bundle. Therefore, the ventricular rhythm is slowest at the fibrillation end of the flutter/fibrillation spectrum (Fig. 15.5).[3-5] Typically, a 1:1 AV relationship persists to the upper limit of the atrial rate during exercise or with other conditions that enhance sympathetic stimulation. However, when the atrial rate increases via other mechanisms, such as artificial atrial pacing or a reentrant tachyarrhythmia, the 1:1 AV relationship persists only until the atrial rate reaches approximately 150 beats/min. At higher atrial rates, the physiologic AV nodal conduction delay prevents some of the F waves from reaching the ventricles. As the atrial rate increases further, the ventricular rate decreases because of the competition within the AV node. Changes in the sympathetic to parasympathetic balance can either facilitate or further inhibit AV nodal conduction.

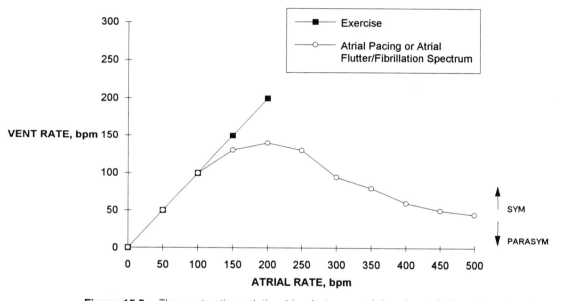

Figure 15.5. The contrasting relationships between atrial and ventricular rates when the atrial rate is accelerated by exercise versus either artificial pacing or the flutter/fibrillation spectrum. With the former, the ventricular rate continues to accelerate with a 1:1 relationship to the limit of the atrial rate. With the latter, the ventricular rate peaks at about 150 beats/min and then decelerates as the atrial rate is increased further. The ventricular rate is also regulated by the balance between sympathetic (*SYM*) and parasympathetic (*PARASYM*) tone as indicated (*arrows*). (From Wagner GS, Waugh RA, Ramo BW. Cardiac arrhythmias. New York: Churchill Livingstone, 1983:9.)

ONSET OF ATRIAL FLUTTER/FIBRILLATION

 Both spontaneous and electrically induced atrial flutter/fibrillation may typically be produced when APBs occur within a narrow range of the atrial refractory period (Fig. 15.6). Thus, the arrhythmia is typically sudden in onset, as are all reentrant arrhythmias.

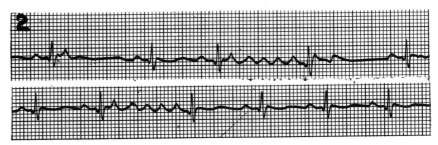

Figure 15.6. The continuous recording documents two 1-sec episodes of atrial flutter.

Like the ventricles, the atria have a vulnerable period, a point in the atrial cycle at which an APB is most likely to precipitate atrial flutter/fibrillation (Fig. 15.7). Killip and Gault have formulated the situation as follows: if the interval from the normal P wave to the premature P wave is less than half of the preceding interval between normal P waves, the premature P wave is within the atrial vulnerable period and may induce flutter/fibrillation.[6]

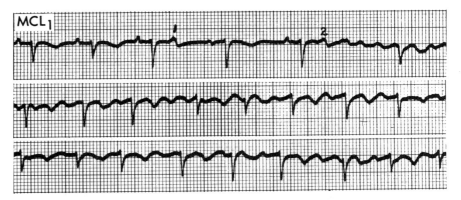

 Figure 15.7. APB *1* occurs after the atrial vulnerable period; however, APB *2* occurs inside the vulnerable period and initiates atrial flutter/fibrillation.

TERMINATION OF ATRIAL FLUTTER/FIBRILLATION

As illustrated in Figure 15.6, atrial flutter/fibrillation may terminate spontaneously. Presumably, the recycling impulse fails to encounter receptive cells and has nowhere to go. When the reentry continues and creates either acute cardiac dysfunction or a chronic clinical problem, some medical intervention may be required. There are two possible treatment strategies:

1. Ignore the flutter/fibrillation and enhance the AV block to slow the ventricular rate.
2. Attempt to terminate the flutter/fibrillation.

Terminating or "breaking" the flutter/fibrillation may be accomplished using either drugs or electrical stimulation. A drug is capable of suddenly terminating the reentrant tachyarrhythmia either by increasing the speed of the recycling impulse so that it encounters only cells that are still refractory or by prolonging the refractory periods of the cells. External electrical stimulation is capable of suddenly breaking the flutter/fibrillation by depolarizing all cardiac cells that are not already in their depolarized state (Fig. 15.8A). The external stimulus eliminates the receptivity to reentry that is required to maintain the tachyarrhythmia. As illustrated in Figure 15.8A, such stimulation is not capable of breaking a tachyarrhythmia produced by enhanced automaticity because it cannot eliminate the enhanced automaticity.

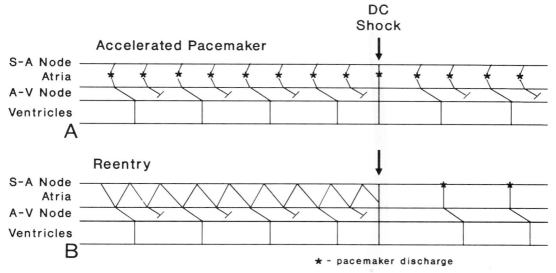

Figure 15.8. Ladder diagrams are used to contrast the expected responses of tachyarrhythmias due to enhanced atrial automaticity (**A**) with those due to atrial macroreentry (**B**). *Asterisks* indicates the site of automaticity and the *arrow* indicates the time of the precordial DC shock. (From Wagner GS, Waugh RA, Ramo BW. Cardiac arrhythmias. New York: Churchill Livingstone, 1983:25.)

When the reentry is orderly, as at the flutter end of the spectrum, it can be suddenly terminated by an external stimulus from an artificial atrial pacing system. Maintenance of the orderly reentry requires that particular areas of atrial myocardium have completed their refractory periods and are receptive to the advancing wave of depolarization. A properly timed external stimulus delivered via a properly positioned electrode produces premature activation of such receptive areas, and the advancing wave front has nothing available to depolarize.

When the reentry is disorderly, as at the fibrillation end of the spectrum, it cannot be terminated by pacing. No particular areas of atrial myocardium are essential for maintenance of a disorderly reentry. Electrical termination requires that stimuli are simultaneously applied to the entire atrial myocardium (Fig. 15.8B). Such premature activation of all potentially receptive areas leaves the advancing wave fronts with nothing available to depolarize. Transthoracic DC shock (*electrical cardioversion*) is capable of terminating the tachyarrhythmias of the entire flutter/fibrillation spectrum.

Table 15.1 summarizes many of the characteristics of the atrial flutter/fibrillation spectrum.

Table 15.1[a]

Atrial rate	200	220	300	360	400	500 +
Ventricular rate	200	180	150	120	100	70
Ventricular rhythm	Regular	Regularly irregular	Regular	Regularly irregular	Irregular	
Name		Flutter	Flutter-fibrillation		Fibrillation	
Stability		Minimal	Moderate		Maximal	
Digitalis decreases AV conduction		Seldom	Sometimes		Usually	
DC shock terminates		Low energy	Intermediate		High energy	
Pacing terminates		Usually	Sometimes		Never	

[a]Modified from Wagner GS, Waugh RA, Ramo BW. Cardiac arrhythmias. New York: Churchill Livingstone, 1983:154.

ATRIAL FLUTTER

  Atrial flutter is relatively uncommon in adults. Its incidence is about one-twentieth that of atrial fibrillation. It is most often found in patients with *ischemic heart disease* and is strikingly rare in *mitral valve disease* compared with atrial fibrillation. Flutter may complicate any form of heart disease, may be precipitated by any acute illness, and often occurs transiently following cardiac surgery. In the first few years of life, flutter is much more common than fibrillation, presumably because fibrillation requires a greater mass of atrial muscle.

CHARACTERISTICS OF THE F WAVES OF ATRIAL FLUTTER

 In the usual variety of atrial flutter, the typical sawtooth pattern of F waves is usually best seen in the inferiorly oriented leads (Fig. 15.9). Indeed, there may be no evidence of atrial activity in the laterally oriented leads such as I and aVL. In the precordial leads, the F waves commonly mimic discrete P waves. The deflections are positive in leads V1 and V2 and negative in leads V5 and V6.

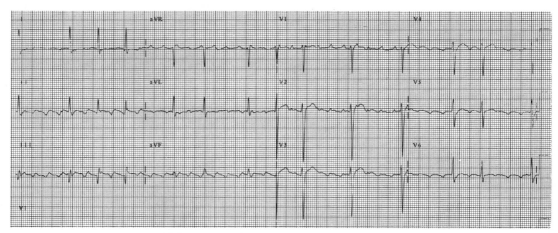

Figure 15.9. ECG recording from a 77-year-old woman on the second day following cholecystectomy.

In a rare variety of atrial flutter, the F waves may be inconspicuous in the limb leads and seen clearly only in precordial leads V1–V3 (Fig. 15.10).

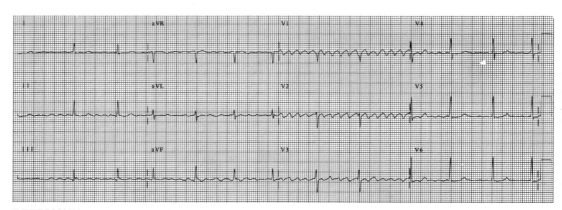

Figure 15.10. ECG recording from a 45-year-old man with a history of recurrent palpitations but no known cardiac disease.

PATTERNS OF AV CONDUCTION

When atrial flutter is untreated, the usual AV conduction ratio is 2:1 (Fig. 15.11*A*) due to the normal refractoriness in the AV node. This rhythm should be termed atrial flutter with 2:1 conduction rather than 2:1 block because the AV node is playing its normal physiological role as a shield protecting the ventricles from the rapid atrial rate. It may be difficult to recognize either of the F waves in each cardiac cycle because one is partially or completely masked by the QRS complex and the other by the T wave. A conduction ratio of 4:1 is also common and often coexists with a 2:1 ratio (Fig. 15.11*B*). The presence of the 4:1 ratio makes the diagnosis of atrial flutter obvious (Fig. 15.11*C*).

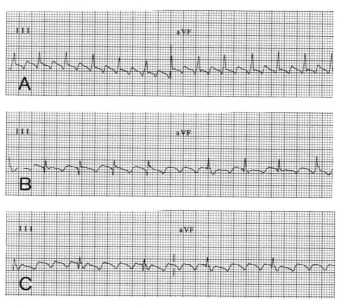

Figure 15.11. Even numbered ratios of AV conduction vary from constant 2:1 (**A**), mixed 2:1 and 4:1 (**B**), and fixed 4:1 (**C**) in three individuals with atrial flutter.

Odd-numbered AV ratios (1:1, 3:1, etc.) are rare. Figure 15.12 presents an example of 1:1 conduction with both atrial and ventricular rates of about 250 beats/min. Such abnormally rapid AV conduction is rarely possible unless an accessory pathway is present (Chapter 6, "Ventricular Preexcitation"). The regular wide QRS complexes without obvious atrial activity often lead to an erroneous diagnosis of ventricular tachycardia.

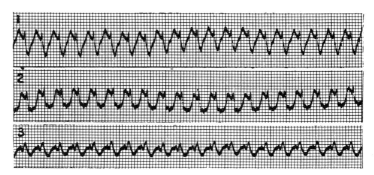

Figure 15.12. Simultaneous recording of three limb leads revealing only a wide-QRS tachycardia. Elimination of the ventricular activity by decreasing the AV conduction would be required to confirm the diagnosis of atrial flutter.

Figure 15.13 presents atrial flutter with the rare 3:1 AV ratio. The diagnosis is obvious in lead II, but lead V1 has the appearance of sinus tachycardia. Instead of one P wave, there are three F waves during each cardiac cycle. The first mimics a P wave, the second is obscured by the QRS complex, and the third appears as a peak in the T wave.

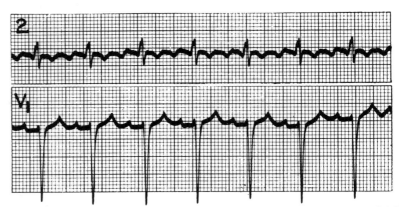

Figure 15.13. Simultaneous recording of two leads reveals the superiority of inferiorly oriented lead II for displaying the F waves.

An interesting feature of atrial flutter is the variety of conduction patterns that may develop because of the interplay at various levels within the AV node.[7] These may produce a regularly irregular ventricular rhythm with a bigeminal pattern (Fig. 15.14). Though all of the atrial impulses enter the AV node, as indicated by the ladder diagram, only two of every three reach the ventricles.

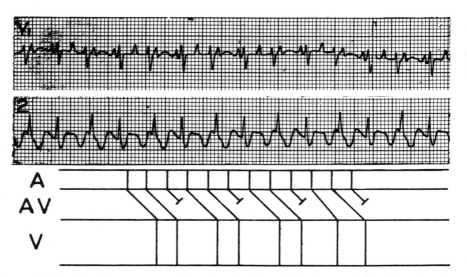

Figure 15.14. Simultaneous recording of two leads provides the capability of constructing a ladder diagram to identify the 3:2 AV conduction pattern.

In Figure 15.15A, prior to sympathetic blockade with propranolol, there is a typical 2:1 AV conduction ratio. With a low level of sympathetic blockade (Fig. 15.15B), one of every two atrial impulses is able to penetrate deeply into the AV node, but only two of every three of these reach the ventricles. The result is a bigeminal ventricular rhythm in which there are six F waves for every two QRS complexes (6:2 AV conduction ratio). A regular ventricular rhythm returns in Figure 15.15C because additional sympathetic blockade allows only one of every four atrial impulses to penetrate through the AV node and reach the ventricles.

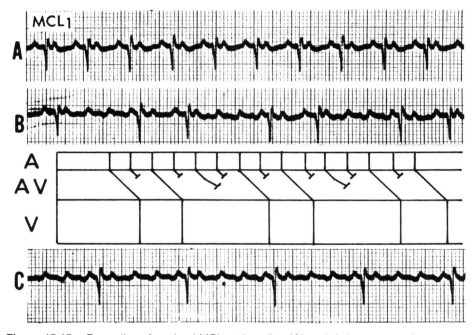

Figure 15.15. Recordings from lead MCL₁ at baseline (**A**) and during progressive sympathetic blockade (**B** and **C**) show progressively decreasing AV conduction. The ladder diagram provides insight into the two levels of block within the AV node that create the intermediate (**B**) 6:2 conduction.

Conduction ratios of 6:1 and higher even-numbered ratios are sometimes produced when there is marked AV block. The differential diagnosis is between conduction with a high AV ratio and complete AV block. Conduction may be assumed when, as in Figure 15.16A, a constant ventricular rate (RR intervals) is accompanied by a constant relationship between atria and ventricles (FR intervals). In contrast, the two rhythm strips in Figure 15.16B present examples of atrial flutter with complete (third degree) AV block as indicated by constant RR intervals accompanied by varying FR intervals.

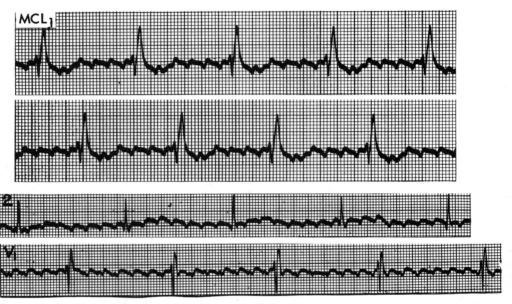

Figure 15.16. The contrast between atrial flutter that is conducted to the ventricles with a high level of block (**A**) and atrial flutter that is not conducted at all (**B**). The QRS complex with RSR′ configuration in lead MCL₁ in **A** is due to RBBB and that in lead V1 in **B** is due to an escape focus in the LBB.

CONCEALED AV CONDUCTION

As discussed above, the atrial rate in the flutter/fibrillation spectrum may be greatly influenced by drugs: accelerated by digitalis and decelerated by quinidine, procainamide, and *lidocaine*. In Figure 15.17, the *top strip* was taken on 1/31 while the patient was receiving digitalis alone. The *bottom strip* was obtained on 2/1, 24 hours after quinidine was begun. The atrial rate slowed from 270 to 224 beats/min, but the ventricular rate increased from 96 to 108 beats/min. This inverse relationship between atrial and ventricular rates (Fig. 15.5) occurs because the more beats that enter the AV node, the fewer are able to completely traverse it and reach the ventricles. The nonconducted atrial impulses are blocked only after they have been able to penetrate some distance into the node. Their concealed conduction depolarizes a part of the AV node, making it refractory to the following atrial impulse.[7]

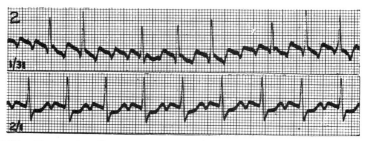

Figure 15.17. The contrasting appearances of atrial flutter before and after quinidine therapy.

When the concealed conduction of the flutter impulses are superimposed upon a minimal degree of AV block, the result can be a much higher apparent level of block, as illustrated in Figure 15.18. The *top strip* shows that with a sinus rate of 62 beats/min the patient has 1:1 AV conduction with only a slightly prolonged PR interval of 0.24 sec (first degree AV block). When consecutive APBs occur, they are not conducted. Then, when atrial flutter develops (*bottom strip*), the consecutive concealed conduction of the multiple F waves keeps the partially penetrated AV node so refractory that none of them get through to the ventricles. Only after the flutter breaks is the AV node able to regain the capability of conducting through to the ventricles. Note that, following the pause, even the first degree AV block is lost and the PR interval is 0.20 sec.

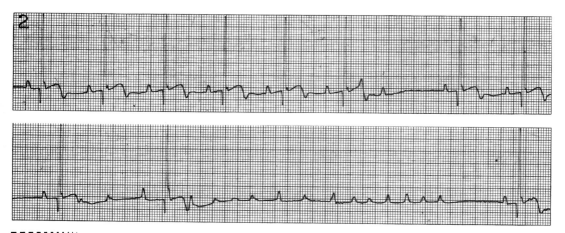

Figure 15.18. Continuous lead II rhythm strip showing the contrasting manifestations of moderate amount of AV nodal block during sinus rhythm (*top*) and during atrial flutter (*bottom*).

ATRIAL FIBRILLATION

 Atrial fibrillation may complicate any cardiac disease and is sometimes seen in the absence of any apparent cardiac disease (*lone fibrillation*).[8] The five most common conditions that produce atrial fibrillation are [9,10]:

1. Rheumatic heart disease;
2. Ischemic heart disease;
3. Hypertensive heart disease;
4. Heart failure of any etiology;
5. Thyrotoxicosis.

Advancing age and increased left atrial size are also related to the development of atrial fibrillation.[11,12] Chronic atrial fibrillation in the elderly often conceals an underlying *sick sinus node*, and such patients frequently have postmortem evidence of narrowing of the sinus node artery and atrophy of the sinus node cells.[13] It is not known whether dysfunction of the sinus node leads to the atrial fibrillation or whether disuse of the sinus node during chronic atrial fibrillation leads to its dysfunction.

 Chronic atrial fibrillation, once established, usually lasts for life. However, occasionally it may revert to sinus rhythm following valvotomy for mitral stenosis.[14] Atrial fibrillation appears during two stages of ischemic heart disease: acute myocardial infarction and chronic heart failure.

CHARACTERISTICS OF THE f WAVES OF ATRIAL FIBRILLATION

 Atrial fibrillation is recognized by irregular undulation of the baseline with an irregularly irregular ventricular rhythm. The undulations may be gross and distinct (Fig. 15.19A), intermediate in form (15.19 B), or barely perceptible (15.19 C). For descriptive purposes, these may be called coarse, medium, and fine atrial fibrillation, respectively. Although the size of the f waves has not been found to correlate with the size of the atria or the type of the heart disease[15], large f waves are unlikely to occur in the presence of a normal-sized left atrium.[16]

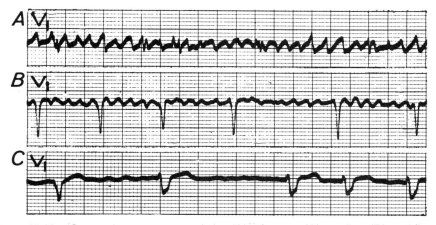

Figure 15.19. Contrasting appearances in lead V1 of coarse (**A**), medium (**B**), and fine (**C**) fibrillation. The example of coarse fibrillation might also be termed flutter-fibrillation.

When there is no recognizable deflection of the baseline, the atrial fibrillation may be inferred from the irregularly irregular ventricular response (Fig. 15.20A). In this fine fibrillation, some baseline undulation may be seen in leads V1–V3 (Fig. 15.20B).

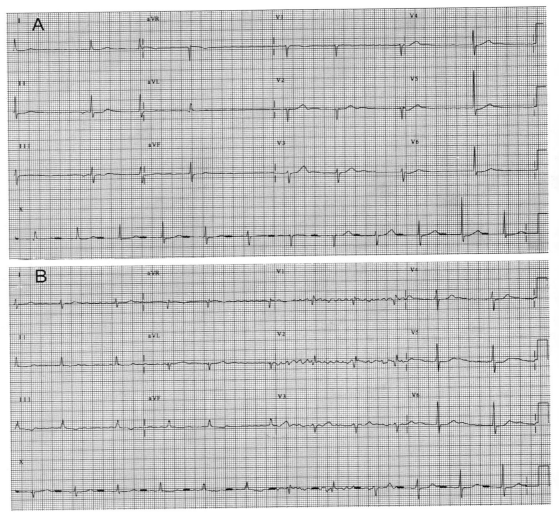

Figure 15.20. ECG recordings of two patients (**A** and **B**) with chronic atrial fibrillation due to long-standing congestive heart failure.

The ventricular rate during atrial fibrillation is variable. If the AV node is normal and its conduction has not been suppressed by digitalis, a sympathetic blocker, or a *calcium antagonist*, rates as high as 200 beats/min may develop (Fig. 15.21*A*). However, if the AV node is diseased or markedly suppressed by drugs, the ventricular rate may be markedly reduced (Fig. 15.21*B*). Unlike the slower, more orderly atrial flutter, atrial fibrillation is not capable of producing a regular ventricular rhythm. Therefore, when both atrial fibrillation and a regular ventricular rhythm coexist, they are independent of each other. Such AV dissociation may occur for two reasons:

1. There is excessive AV block, which creates the need for normal escape from a site in the ventricular Purkinje system (Chapter 20, "Atrioventricular Block").
2. There is normal AV conduction, but interference has developed from enhanced automaticity in the ventricular Purkinje system (Chapter 14, "Accelerated Automaticity").

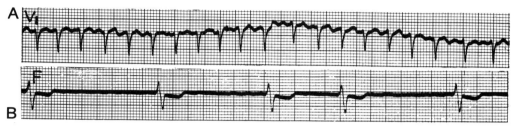

Figure 15.21. The contrast between extremely increased (**A**) and extremely decreased (**B**) AV conduction during atrial fibrillation.

In Figure 15.22, the ventricular rhythm is regular and the rate is in the bradycardia range: 50 beats/min in *A* and 35 beats/min in *B*. The proper terminology would be atrial fibrillation with AV dissociation due to complete AV block and junctional escape. At times, the escape site may be below the branching of the common bundle, producing a widened QRS complex.

Whenever atrial fibrillation is accompanied by a regular ventricular rate, and the patient is receiving digitalis, one should consider the possibility of digitalis toxicity.[17]

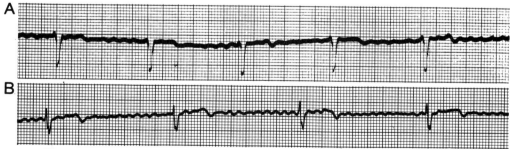

Figure 15.22. Lead III recordings from two patients with atrial fibrillation and AV dissociation due to AV block, with a normal (50 beats/min) (**A**) and with a slow (35 beats/min) (**B**) junctional escape rate.

Additional digitalis could cause acceleration of the junctional or ventricular rhythm, producing AJR or AVR (Chapter 14). In this situation, the atrial fibrillation is accompanied by a regular ventricular rhythm at an accelerated rate. The proper terminology would be atrial fibrillation with AV dissociation due to AJR or AVR.

ATRIAL FLUTTER/FIBRILLATION WITH VENTRICULAR PREEXCITATION

Normally, the AV node is the only electrical pathway connecting the atria and the ventricles. However, as discussed in Chapter 6, some individuals have the congenital abnormality of an accessory AV conduction pathway (Kent bundle). Since this pathway is composed of myocardial cells, these individuals have a bypass of the AV nodal protection that is so important when atrial flutter/fibrillation occurs. The normal inverse relationship between the atrial and ventricular rates illustrated in Figure 15.5 is lost. Instead, the preexcitation pathway permits a direct relationship, thereby allowing for particularly rapid ventricular rates at the fibrillation end of the spectrum. The refractory period of the accessory pathway determines the ventricular rate, and sometimes rates as high as 300 beats/min occur (Fig. 15.23, A and B).[18,19] There is serious danger of ventricular fibrillation developing, either because the descending impulse arrives in the vulnerable phase of the ventricular cycle or because the rapid ventricular rate causes such a low cardiac output that myocardial ischemia results.

It can be extremely difficult, and sometimes impossible, to differentiate atrial flutter/fibrillation with preexcitation from a ventricular tachycardia. At the flutter end of the spectrum, there is often a 1:1 AV ratio and a regular ventricular rhythm (Figs. 15.12 and 15.23, A and B, top). Intermittent irregularity or normal appearing QRS complexes (second strip in B) are indicative of the atrial flutter. At the fibrillation end of the spectrum, there is a less than 1:1 ratio and an irregular ventricular rhythm (bottom two strips in A). Throughout the atrial flutter/fibrillation spectrum, a slow QRS upstroke may be indicative of the delta wave of ventricular preexcitation.

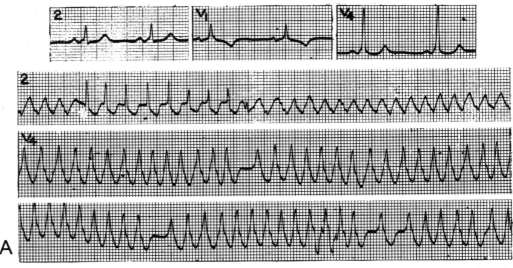

Figure 15.23. ECG recordings of two teenage patients evaluated in the emergency department with complaints of palpitations and weakness. In **A**, there was a previous ECG during sinus rhythm which documented ventricular preexcitation (leads 2, V1, and V4), but no previous ECG was available in **B**. Recording during the tachyarrhythmia from lead V4 in **A** and from lead 1 in **B** are continuous.

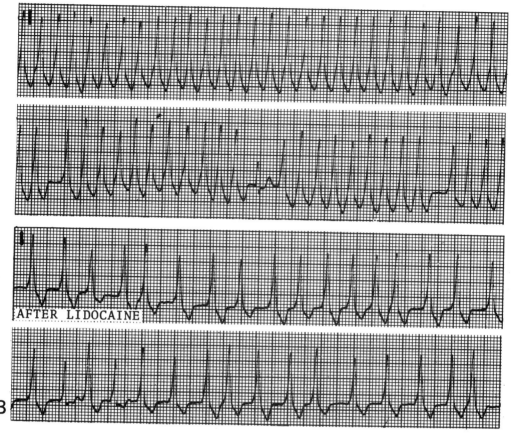

Figure 15.23B

When atrial fibrillation and ventricular preexcitation coexist:

1. The ventricular cycle length may be as short as 0.20 sec, the equivalent of a rate of 300 beats/min (*A* and *B, top strips*).
2. Some ventricular cycles may be more than twice as long as the shortest cycles (*bottom two rhythm strips* in *A*).

This greater than 100% variation in cycle length would represent an extremely unusual degree of irregularity in a reentrant ventricular tachycardia (Chapter 17, "Ventricular Tachyarrhythmias").

Establishing the diagnosis of atrial fibrillation may lead to a serious error in treatment of the tachyarrhythmia. Digitalis has the opposite effect on the ventricular rate when a preexcitation pathway is present than when only the AV node is available for conduction. When atrial fibrillation is present, the ventricular rate is determined by the length of the refractory period of the AV conduction pathway. As noted above, digitalis prolongs the refractory period of the AV node. As discussed in Chapter 11 ("Miscellaneous Conditions"), however, digitalis shortens the refractory period of myocardial cells. Digitalis is, therefore, capable of paradoxically increasing the ventricular rate and inducing ventricular fibrillation when a preexcitation pathway is present.[20]

GLOSSARY

Atrial fibrillation: the tachyarrhythmia at the rapid end of the flutter/fibrillation spectrum produced by macroreentry within multiple circuits in the atria and characterized by irregular multiform f waves.

Atrial flutter: the tachyarrhythmia at the slow end of the flutter/fibrillation spectrum produced by macroreentry within a single circuit in the atria and characterized by regular uniform F waves.

Atrial flutter/fibrillation: the tachyarrhythmia in the middle of the flutter/fibrillation spectrum having some aspects of flutter and some of fibrillation.

Atrial flutter/fibrillation spectrum: a range of tachyarrhythmias caused by macroreentry in the atria which extends from flutter with an atrial rate of 200 beats/min through flutter-fibrillation and coarse fibrillation to fine fibrillation with no atrial activity detectable on the body surface.

Calcium antagonist: a drug that diminishes calcium entry into cells and slows conduction through the AV node.

Coarse fibrillation: prominent f waves in some of the ECG leads.

Electrical cardioversion: use of transthoracic electrical current to terminate a reentrant tachyarrhythmia such as those in the atrial flutter/fibrillation spectrum.

F waves: the regular uniform sawtooth-like atrial activity characteristic of flutter.

f waves: the irregular multiform atrial activity characteristic of fibrillation.

Fine fibrillation: either minute f waves or no atrial activity at all in any of the ECG leads.

Ischemic heart disease: cardiac abnormality caused by decreased blood flow to the myocardium usually because of atherosclerosis with or without superimposed thrombosis in the coronary arteries.

Lidocaine: a compound with local anesthetic properties that is used in treatment of reentrant tachyarrhythmias.

Lone fibrillation: atrial fibrillation occurring in an individual with no evidence of cardiac disease.

Mitral valve disease: either abnormally tight (stenotic) or loose (insufficient) valve between the left atrium and left ventricle.

Procainamide: a compound related to the local anesthetic procaine that is used in the treatment of reentrant tachyarrhythmias.

Sick sinus node: a term that is loosely used clinically to describe any abnormal low sinus rate. These bradyarrhythmias are more likely caused by increased parasympathetic nervous activity than by disease in the sinus node.

REFERENCES

1. Waldo AL, Henthorn RW, Plumb VJ. Atrial flutter—recent observations in man. In: Josephson ME, Wellens HJJ, eds. Tachycardias: mechanisms, diagnosis, treatment. Philadelphia: Lea & Febiger, 1984:113.
2. Wells JL Jr, MacLean WAH, James TN, Waldo AL. Characterization of atrial flutter: studies in man after open heart surgery using fixed atrial electrodes. Circulation 1979;60:665–673.
3. Langendorf R, Pick A, Catz LN. Ventricular response in atrial fibrillation: role of concealed conduction in the atrioventricular junction. Circulation 1965;32:69.
4. Lau SH, Damato AN, Berkowitz WD, Patton RD. A study of atrioventricular conduction in atrial fibrillation and flutter in man using His bundle recordings. Circulation 1969;40:71–78.
5. Moore EN. Observations on concealed conduction in atrial fibrillation. Circ Res 1967;21:201.
6. Killip T, Gault JH. Mode of onset of atrial fibrillation in man. Am Heart J 1965;70:172.
7. Besoain-Santander M, Pick A, Langendorf R. A-V conduction in auricular flutter. Circulation 1950;2:604.
8. Peter RH, Gracey JG, Beach TB. A clinical profile of idiopathic atrial fibrillation. Ann Intern Med 1968;68:1296.
9. Kannel WB, Abbott RD, Savage DD. Coronary heart disease and atrial fibrillation: the Framingham study. Am Heart J 1983;106:389.
10. Morris DC, Hurst JW. Atrial fibrillation. Curr Prob Cardiol 1980;5:1.
11. Henry WL, Morganroth J, Pearlman AS, Clark CE, Redwood DR, Itscoitz SB, Epstein SE. Relation between echocardiographically determined left atrial size and atrial fibrillation. Circulation 1976;53:273–279.
12. Probst P, Goldschlager N, Selzer A. Left atrial size and atrial fibrillation in mitral stenosis: factors influencing their relationship. Circulation 1973;48:1282.
13. Davies MJ, Pomerance A. Pathology of atrial fibrillation in man. Br Heart J 1972;34:520.
14. Zimmerman TJ, Basta LL, January LE. Spontaneous return of sinus rhythm in older patients with chronic atrial fibrillation and rheumatic mitral valve disease. Am Heart J 1973;86:676–680.
15. Morganroth J, Horowitz LN, Josephson ME, Kastor JA. Relationship of atrial fibrillatory wave amplitude to left atrial size and etiology of heart disease. Am Heart J 1979;97:184–186.
16. Bartall H, Desser KB, Benchimol A, Massey BJ. Assessment of echocardiographic left atrial enlargement in patients with atrial fibrillation. An electrovectorcardiographic study. J Electrocardiol 1978;11:269.
17. Kastor JA. Digitalis intoxication in patients with atrial fibrillation. Circulation 1973;47:888.
18. Klein GJ, Bashore TM, Sellers TD, Pritchett EL, Smith EL, Gallagher JJ. Ventricular fibrillation in the Wolff-Parkinson-White syndrome. Circulation 1976;11:187.
19. Grant RP, Tomlinson FB, Van Buren JK. Ventricular activation in the pre-excitation syndrome (Wolff-Parkinson-White). Circulation 1958;18:355.
20. Sellers TD Jr, Bashore TM, Gallagher JJ. Digitalis in the pre-excitation syndrome. Analysis during atrial fibrillation. Circulation 1977;56:260–267.

CHAPTER 16

Reentrant Junctional Tachyarrhythmias

The *reentrant junctional tachyarrhythmias* (RJTs) usually occur in young people without underlying heart disease. Reentry within the AV junction can result in single JPBs or in sustained RJTs. These tachyarrhythmias may be difficult to understand because they originate from the junctional area between the atria and ventricles which is very important electrically but not represented directly on the ECG. Also, the terminology is confusing and the specific tachycardias that occur in the AV junction have only become apparent since electrophysiologic techniques became highly developed.

In susceptible individuals, the occurrence of RJTs has been related to periods of anxiety, excess caffeine intake, and fatigue. The susceptibility to the development of junctional reentry is due to either abnormal impulse conduction within the AV node or the presence of the congenital abnormality of a Kent bundle, which serves as an accessory AV conduction pathway (Fig. 16.1). Usually, the accessory pathway is identified by ECG evidence of ventricular preexcitation during sinus rhythm (Chapter 6, "Ventricular Preexcitation"). The combination of ventricular preexcitation and RJTs is called the Wolff-Parkinson-White (WPW) syndrome.[1]

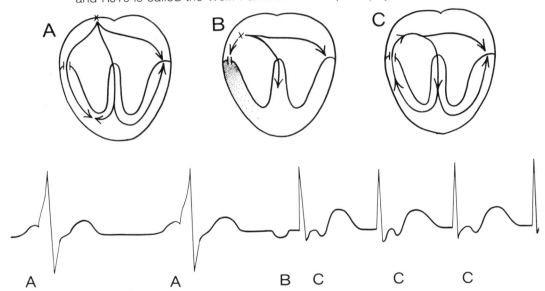

Figure 16.1. The formation and conduction of the cardiac impulse during sinus rhythm (**A**) and an APB (**B**), and the conduction through the various parts of the heart during the sustained tachyarrhythmia (**C**) are shown anatomically (*top*) and electrocardiographically (*bottom*). Sites of impulse formation are indicated by *X*, the directions of impulse conduction by *arrows*, the Kent bundle by an *open space between the right atrium and ventricle*, and persistent refractoriness in the Kent bundle by *shading*. (From Wagner GS, Waugh RA, Ramo BW. Cardiac arrhythmias. New York: Churchill Livingstone, 1983:13.)

However, the accessory pathway may be capable of conduction only in one direction, causing either the ventricular preexcitation or the RJTs to occur without the other:

1. If only anterograde (AV) accessory pathway conduction is possible, there will be preexcitation during sinus rhythm but no RJTs.
2. If only retrograde (VA) accessory pathway conduction is possible, there is no preexcitation during sinus rhythm, but there is potential for RJTs. In this instance, a *concealed AV bypass pathway* is present.

VARIETIES OF RJTs

The mechanism that produces RJTs may be either microreentry totally within the AV node (*AV nodal tachycardia*, Fig. 16.2*A*) or macroreentry including one of the atria, an accessory pathway, one of the ventricles, and the AV node (Fig. 16.2, *B* and *C*). The presence of a second AV conduction pathway creates the potential for the development of reentry circuits in which the impulses travel in either the normal or reverse direction through the AV node and ventricular Purkinje system. The term *orthodromic tachycardia* is used when the impulse proceeds in the normal direction (Figs. 16.1*C* and 16.2*B*), and *antidromic tachycardia* when it proceeds in the reverse direction (Fig. 16.2*C*). A concealed AV bypass pathway is capable only of participating in an orthodromic tachycardia.

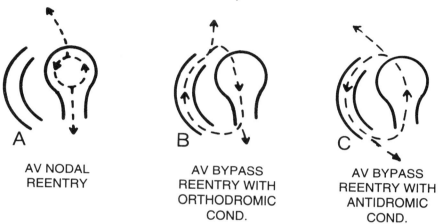

A	B	C
AV NODAL REENTRY	AV BYPASS REENTRY WITH ORTHODROMIC COND.	AV BYPASS REENTRY WITH ANTIDROMIC COND.

Figure 16.2. The Kent bundle (*curved space*) and AV node and common bundle (*bulb-like space*) are represented to indicate the anatomic sites (**A–C**) of the three varieties of RJTs. *Dashed lines* indicate the locations of, and *arrows* indicate the directions of, conduction within the three reentry circuits.

The different terms for the RJTs fall into three categories:

1. Those that apply to the clinical behavior: reentrant, persistent, permanent, incessant, sustained, nonsustained, chronic, relapsing, and repetitive;
2. Those that describe the site of origin: supraventricular, atrial, ectopic, AV nodal, AV bypass, and junctional;
3. Those that describe the mechanism: reentrant, reciprocating, paroxysmal, circus movement, slow-fast, fast-slow, orthodromic, and antidromic.

Table 16.1 presents the classification of the RJTs which are used in this chapter.

Table 16.1

AV Nodal Tachycardia	AV Bypass Tachycardia
Slow-fast AV nodal tachycardia *Fast-slow AV nodal tachycardia*	Orthodromic tachycardia Antidromic tachycardia

CONDUCTION THROUGH THE ATRIA

 Since the AV junction is distal to the atria, junctional reentry produces *retrograde atrial activation* which results in inversion of the P waves as illustrated in Figure 16.1. The P waves, therefore, are negative in the base to apex oriented leads (e.g., lead II).

CONDUCTION THROUGH THE VENTRICLES

Since the AV junction is proximal to the branching of the common bundle, junctional reentry produces supraventricular arrhythmias which result in normal-appearing QRS complexes (Fig. 16.3A) unless the impulses encounter aberrant ventricular conduction. The aberrant conduction may be either the typical variety occurring in the bundle branches or fascicles (Fig. 16.3, *B* and *C*) or an atypical variety occurring in the accessory AV conduction pathway (Fig. 16.3*D*).

1. *Ventricular Purkinje aberrancy* occurs when the impulses generated by AV nodal (Fig. 16.3*B*) or orthodromic (Fig. 16.3*C*) tachycardia encounter abnormal intraventricular conduction because of rate-related delay in the bundle branches or fascicles (Fig. 16.3, *B* and *C*).
2. *Accessory pathway aberrancy* occurs when the impulses generated by antidromic tachycardia reach the ventricular myocardium via the accessory pathway (Fig. 16.3*D*).

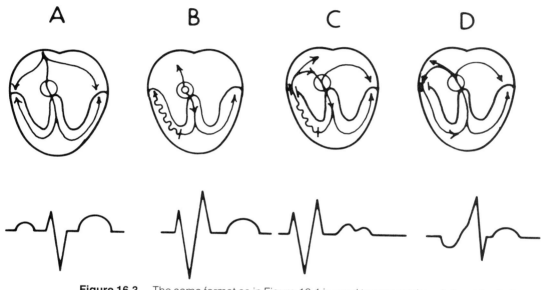

Figure 16.3. The same format as in Figure 16.1 is used to present the relationships between the intracardiac impulse conduction and the surface ECG during sinus rhythm (**A**), AV nodal reentrant tachycardia (**B**), orthodromic tachycardia (**C**), and antidromic tachycardia (**D**). The *circle on the summit* of the interventricular septum represents the AV node, the *small circle within that circle* in **B** represents the microreentry circuit shown in Figure 16.2**A**, and the *wavy lines* in **B** and **C** represent a conduction delay within the right bundle branch.

NATURAL HISTORY OF THE RJTs

 There have been several studies of the follow-up of children with RJTs with and without evidence of ventricular preexcitation.[2-4] A high percentage of neonates with RJTs have evidence of ventricular preexcitation, but many of these have spontaneous resolution during the first year of life. Some lose the capability for anterograde conduction through their accessory AV pathway, but retain the capability for retrograde conduction as evident from recurrent episodes of RJTs. There is a decreasing incidence of evidence of preexcitation among progressively older groups of patients with RJTs.

One study reported that 85% of adults with RJTs did not have evidence of an accessory pathway and that those without pathways were older than those with pathways (55 versus 40 years old).[3] There was also a higher incidence of underlying heart disease in those without accessory pathways (50 versus 10%). These data suggest that there are two groups of patients with RJTs of the AV nodal tachycardia variety:

1. Those with a congenital abnormality of the AV node; and
2. Those with an acquired abnormality of the AV node either as part of a general cardiac disease or as a side effect of drug therapy (e.g., digitalis).

 The natural history of group 1 is probably the same as that of accessory pathways, but the natural history of group 2 is that of general cardiac disease or continued use of the drug.

DIFFERENTIATION FROM OTHER TACHYCARDIAS

 When the QRS complex is normal, RJTs superficially resemble both sinus tachycardia and atrial flutter (with a 2:1 AV conduction ratio). However, when atrial activation is visible, its appearance should be diagnostic since it differs markedly in these three arrhythmias (Table 16.2):

Table 16.2

Arrhythmia	Atrial Activity
RJTs	Discrete retrograde P waves
Sinus tachycardia	Discrete anterograde P waves
Atrial flutter	Regular F waves

The ventricular rate may be helpful because sinus tachycardia rarely exceeds 150 beats/min in an adult, whereas RJTs almost always exceed this rate. Observance of the onset or termination should differentiate sinus tachycardia because the enhanced automaticity gradually accelerates and decelerates in contrast to the abrupt behavior of reentry. The effect of an APB on the tachycardia also may be helpful since it would be expected to reset the sinus rate but either have no effect or terminate the RJTs (Fig. 16.4).

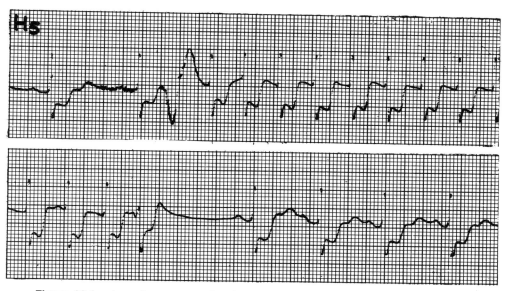

Figure 16.4. A continuous recording from a Holter monitor. A VPB initiates, and an SVPB terminates, a 12-beat run of one of the RJTs.

None of these characteristics differentiates RJTs from flutter, since the ventricular rates are similar and both are caused by reentry. Further observation of the rhythm may be helpful since the 2:1 conduction pattern of atrial flutter tends to be unstable and alternates with a 4:1 pattern providing a clear view of the F waves. When no differentiating features are apparent, even on a full 12-lead ECG, a vagal maneuver such as carotid sinus massage may be indicated (Fig. 16.5). Lown and Levine have provided a comprehensive review of the techniques for performing this intervention safely and effectively.[5]

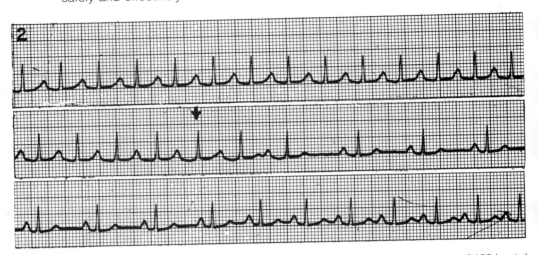

Figure 16.5. A continuous recording of lead II reveals a regular SVT at a rate of 150 beats/min. The diagnosis could be sinus tachycardia, flutter with 2:1 block, or one of the RJTs. Carotid sinus stimulation (*arrow*) produces gradual slowing so that an upright P wave emerges from the T wave, establishing the diagnosis of sinus tachycardia.

The typical responses of RJTs, sinus tachycardia, and atrial flutter to vagal maneuvers are presented in Figure 16.6. The response of sinus tachycardia (Fig. 16.6A) is produced by inhibition of the enhanced automaticity in the sinus node. The atrial flutter itself is unaffected (Fig. 16.6B), but the diagnosis is provided by the increased AV nodal block. At times, slight acceleration of the flutter rate may be observed. The abrupt termination is a typical response of RJTs (Fig. 16.6C). The increase in parasympathetic activity produces termination by prolonging the AV nodal refractory period, thereby eliminating the receptive pathway for the recycling impulse. When there is no response of the arrhythmia to the parasympathetic stimulation, the diagnosis remains uncertain and transesophageal or intra-atrial recording may be indicated.

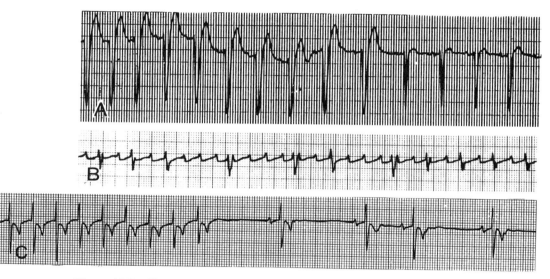

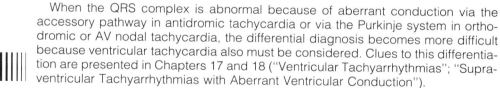

Figure 16.6. The contrasting responses of sinus tachycardia (**A**), atrial flutter (**B**), and RJTs (**C**) to carotid sinus stimulation. (From Wagner GS, Waugh RA, Ramo BW. Cardiac arrhythmias. New York: Churchill Livingstone, 1983:138,161,175.)

When the QRS complex is abnormal because of aberrant conduction via the accessory pathway in antidromic tachycardia or via the Purkinje system in orthodromic or AV nodal tachycardia, the differential diagnosis becomes more difficult because ventricular tachycardia also must be considered. Clues to this differentiation are presented in Chapters 17 and 18 ("Ventricular Tachyarrhythmias"; "Supraventricular Tachyarrhythmias with Aberrant Ventricular Conduction").

DIFFERENTIATION BETWEEN AV NODAL AND AV BYPASS TACHYCARDIAS

 This differentiation becomes most important when the arrhythmia is resistant to conservative treatment and catheter or surgical ablation is being considered. The diagnosis of antidromic tachycardia is facilitated by the delta waves at the onset of the QRS complexes since the ventricles are entered via the accessory pathway, as illustrated in Figure 16.7. Differentiation between the other two RJTs is more difficult. Orthodromic tachycardia may be assumed when there has been preexcitation during sinus rhythm. However, the accessory pathway may be concealed in sinus rhythm if it is incapable of anterograde conduction.

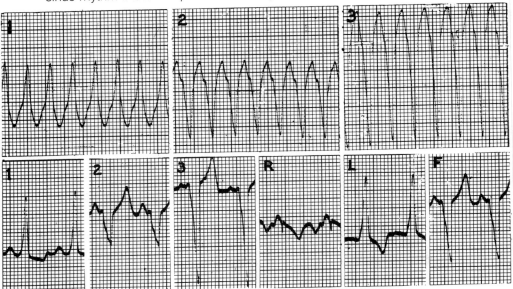

Figure 16.7. A patient presents with a wide-QRS tachycardia (*top*) which could be atrial flutter with 1:1 conduction, antidromic tachycardia, or ventricular tachycardia. The slur on the initial QRS waveform suggests either the flutter or the antidromic tachycardia, and this is confirmed by observing the prominent delta wave after sinus rhythm has returned (*bottom*).

The diagnosis of orthodromic tachycardia is facilitated by observing characteristics that are uniquely present because of the location of the macroreentry circuit[6]:

1. A negative P wave in lead I which suggests that both the left atrium and a left-sided accessory pathway are components of a macroreentry circuit;
2. A sudden decrease in the rate of the tachycardia coincident with the development of aberrant conduction which suggests that both the bundle branch in which the aberrancy has occurred and an accessory pathway on the same side of the heart are components of a macroreentry circuit.

The relationship of the P wave to the QRS complex is also helpful in distinguishing nodal from orthodromic tachycardia. Since its macroreentry circuit includes both an atrium and a ventricle, the P waves and QRS complexes in orthodromic tachycardia cannot occur simultaneously (Fig. 16.8).

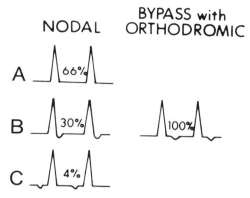

Figure 16.8. A–C. The relationships between P waves and QRS complexes in the various RJTs. The instances of occurrence of the various patterns during AV nodal reentry are presented. All individuals with orthodromic tachycardia had a relatively prolonged QRS-P interval.

Conversely, since the microreentry circuit of AV nodal tachycardia is contained within the AV node, the P waves and QRS complexes must occur either completely or almost simultaneously. Figure 16.9 presents examples of the three varieties of the P wave to QRS complex relationship which may occur with AV nodal tachycardia.

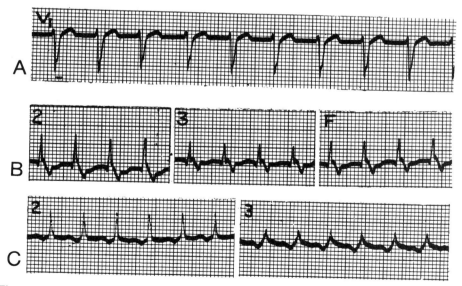

Figure 16.9. A–C. The contrasting P-QRS relationships during the three varieties of the RJTs presented in the same order as in Figure 16.8.

However, as indicated in Figure 16.10, the multiple views provided by a full 12-lead ECG may be required for recognition of the P waves which occur simultaneously with the T waves in orthodromic tachycardia.

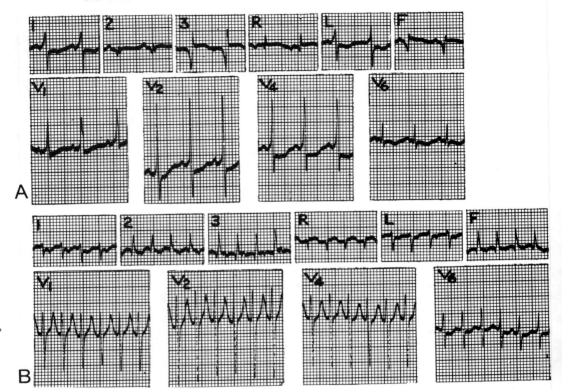

Figure 16.10. Twelve-lead ECGs during sinus rhythm (**A**) and orthodromic tachycardia (**B**). Only the inferiorly oriented leads reveal the retrograde P waves concealed within the T waves which are indicative of an orthodromic tachycardia.

THE TWO VARIETIES OF AV NODAL TACHYCARDIA

 Investigators have demonstrated that the AV node may contain two parallel and independent conduction pathways, one characterized by faster conduction but a longer refractory period and the other by slower conduction but a shorter refractory period.[7] As illustrated in Figure 16.11, these two pathways form the limbs of the microreentry circuit in the two varieties of AV nodal tachycardia:

1. Slow-fast AV nodal tachycardia: The impulse proceeds down the slow pathway and up the fast pathway (Fig. 16.11A).
2. Fast-slow AV nodal tachycardia: The impulse proceeds down the fast pathway and up the slow pathway (Fig. 16.11B).

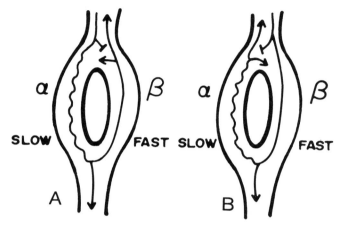

Figure 16.11.   A and B. Schematic diagrams illustrate the contrasting routes of impulse conduction within the slow (alpha) and fast (beta) AV nodal pathways. The slower conduction is represented by a *wavy line*.

The clinical and ECG characteristics of each of these two forms of AV nodal tachycardia are listed in Table 16.3.

Table 16.3.   Dual Pathways of AV Junction

	Slow-Fast	Fast-Slow
Synonyms	Paroxysmal	Persistent, etc.
Initial P'-R	Prolonged	Normal
Incidence	Usual form in adults	Especially in children
Triggered by	APB	Spontaneous; APB; VPB
P' relations	Coincides with QRS	R-P' > P'R

 The distinguishing P wave to QRS complex relationships are illustrated in Figure 16.8. *A* and *B* are typical of the slow-fast form while *C* is typical of the fast-slow form.

SLOW-FAST AV NODAL TACHYCARDIA

This form is common in adults, and may be congenital, but often results from either diseases or drugs that impair AV nodal conduction. The AV nodal reentry is usually triggered by an APB associated with a prolonged PR interval (Fig. 16.12). The premature impulse has found the faster pathway still refractory, but the slower pathway available for its conduction to the ventricles. By the time the impulse reaches the distal AV node, the fast pathway has completed its refractory period and reentry is possible. This process may result in a single JPB, an *echo beat*, or in either nonsustained or sustained slow-fast AV nodal tachycardia. The retrograde P' wave often coincides with the QRS complex since activation of the atria occurs via the fast pathway while activation of the ventricles occurs via the Purkinje system. The P' wave is either entirely invisible on the surface ECG as in Figure 16.8*A* or just emerging from the terminal part of the QRS complex as in Figures 16.8*B* and 16.12.

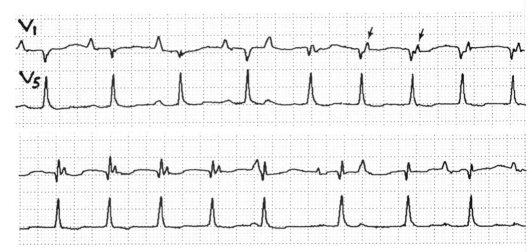

Figure 16.12. Continuous recordings of simultaneous leads V1 and V5. The slow-fast variety of AV nodal tachycardia with its closely following retrograde P waves (*arrows*) is initiated and terminated by APBs.

FAST-SLOW AV NODAL TACHYCARDIA

This is the least common variety of the RJTs in adults. When it does occur it is almost continuously present as indicated by its various names: persistent, permanent, incessant, and repetitive. Since fast-slow AV nodal tachycardia proceeds anterograde down the fast pathway, it does not begin with a prolonged PR interval. The use of the slow pathway for the retrograde limb of the circuit allows for ventricular activation (and even recovery) to be completed prior to atrial activation. Indeed, the retrograde P' wave usually just precedes the following QRS complex (Fig. 16.7).

GLOSSARY

Antidromic tachycardia: an RJT of the AV bypass variety produced by macroreentry in which the impulse recycles sequentially through an accessory AV bypass pathway, a ventricle, the AV node, and an atrium.

AV bypass tachycardia: an RJT produced by macroreentry which includes the AV node along with an atrium, a ventricle, and an accessory AV bypass pathway.

AV nodal tachycardia: an RJT produced by microreentry within the AV node.

Concealed AV bypass pathway: a Kent bundle that is only capable of VA conduction and, therefore, is incapable of producing ventricular preexcitation.

Echo beat: an APB produced by reentry within the AV node.

Fast-slow AV nodal tachycardia: An RJT of the AV nodal variety produced by microreentry in which the impulse travels down the fast pathway and up the slow pathway.

Orthodromic tachycardia: an RJT of the AV bypass variety produced by macroreentry in which the impulse recycles sequentially through the AV node, a ventricle, an accessory AV bypass pathway, and an atrium.

Reentrant junctional tachyarrhythmias: any of the tachyarrhythmias (RJTs) produced by continual recycling of an impulse through structures which are present either normally or abnormally between the atria and the ventricles.

Retrograde atrial activation: spread of the impulse from the AV junction through the atrial myocardium toward the SA node.

Slow-fast AV nodal tachycardia: an RJT of the AV nodal variety produced by microreentry in which the impulse travels down the slow pathway and up the fast pathway.

REFERENCES

1. Wolff L. Syndrome of short P-R interval with abnormal QRS complexes and paroxysmal tachycardia (Wolff-Parkinson-White syndrome). Circulation 1954;10:282.
2. Lundberg A. Paroxysmal tachycardia in infancy. Follow-up study of 47 subjects ranging in age from 10 to 26 years. Pediatrics 1973;51:26.
3. Giardinna ACV, Ehlers KH, Engle MA. Wolff-Parkinson-White syndrome in infants and children. Br Heart J 1972;34:839.
4. Wu D, Denes P, Amat-y-Leon F, Dhingra R, Wyndham CRC, Bauernfeind R, Latif P, Rosen KM. Clinical, electrocardiographic and electrophysiologic observations in patients with paroxysmal supraventricular tachycardia. Am J Cardiol 1978;41:1045–1051.
5. Lown B, Levine SA. The carotid sinus: clinical value of its stimulation. Circulation 1961;23:766.
6. Farre J, Wellens HJJ. The value of the electrocardiogram in diagnosing site of origin and mechanism of supraventricular tachycardia. In: Wellens HJJ, Kulbertus HE, eds. What's new in electrocardiography. Boston: Martinus Nijhoff, 1981:131.
7. Sung RJ, Castellanos A. Supraventricular tachycardia: mechanisms and treatment. Cardiovasc Clin 1980;11:27.

CHAPTER 17

Ventricular Tachyarrhythmias

A ventricular tachyarrhythmia can result from enhanced automaticity in Purkinje cells (Chapter 14, "Accelerated Automaticity") or from reentry occurring in either a localized area (*microreentry*) or in a wider area of myocardium (*macroreentry*).[1-5] Figure 17.1 presents ladder diagrams that illustrate these mechanisms. Only the extremes of the accelerated ventricular rhythm due to enhanced automaticity achieve a rate >100 beats/min, thereby qualifying for the term tachyarrhythmia. The great majority of ventricular tachyarrhythmias have the characteristics of reentry presented first in Chapter 12 ("Introduction to Arrhythmias") and discussed further in Chapters 13 ("Premature Beats"), 14, 15 ("Atrial Flutter/Fibrillation Spectrum"), and 16 ("Reentrant Junctional Tachyarrhythmias"). The reentry may be initiated either by a nonhomogeneous slowing of impulse conduction or the "triggering" effect of early afterdepolarizations.

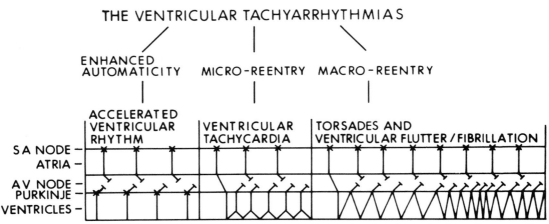

THE VENTRICULAR TACHYARRHYTHMIAS

ENHANCED AUTOMATICITY   MICRO-REENTRY   MACRO-REENTRY

Figure 17.1. In the ladder diagrams, × indicates the site of impulse formation, a *vertical line* indicates normal conduction through the atria or ventricles, a *diagonal line* indicates conduction through the AV node and conduction around a reentry circuit, and a *short perpendicular line* indicates the site of block. (Modified from Wagner GS, Waugh RA, Ramo BW. Cardiac arrhythmias. New York: Churchill Livingstone, 1983:189.)

The arrhythmia called *ventricular tachycardia* is analogous to the AV nodal variety of junctional tachyarrhythmia (Chapter 16) in that it originates from a reentry circuit so small that it is not represented on the ECG. The mechanism of *ventricular flutter/fibrillation* is analogous to that of the atrial flutter/fibrillation spectrum presented in Chapter 15. There are no discrete QRS complexes or T waves, just as there are no discrete P waves in the atrial variety. Torsades de pointes is an atypical form of ventricular tachyarrhythmia which is difficult to classify. There is no analogy elsewhere in the heart. Torsades is probably a macroreentry triggered by early afterpotentials; "reentry" because it abruptly appears and terminates, "macro" because there are no discernible QRS complexes or T waves, and "triggered" because it is caused by conditions which prolong ventricular repolarization.

VENTRICULAR TACHYCARDIA

By definition, ventricular tachycardia (VT) consists of at least three consecutive QRS complexes originating from the ventricles and recurring at a rapid rate (over 100 beats/min). It is considered either nonsustained or sustained, depending on whether it persists for a specified time as defined below. The rhythm of VT is either regular or only slightly irregular.

"The ventricles" refers to any area distal to the branching of the common bundle and includes both the Purkinje cells of the pacemaking and conduction system and the ventricular myocardial cells. The reentry circuit in VT is confined to a localized region and the remainder of the myocardium passively receives the impulses, just as it would if they were originating from an automatic (pacemaking) focus (Fig. 17.1). The QRS complexes and T waves that appear on the ECG are generated from the regions of ventricular myocardium not involved in the reentry circuit.

During VT, the atria may be associated via retrograde activation from the ventricles or dissociated with their own independent rhythm (usually sinus). In either situation, the P waves frequently are lost in the barrage of ventricular cycles since either wide QRS complexes or T waves are occurring constantly. The P waves sometimes may be recognized as bumps or notches in the ventricular cycles. When atrial and ventricular activation are associated, there is a particular V:A ratio such as 1:1, 2:1, 3:2, and so on. More commonly, there is AV dissociation with no relationship between the ventricular and atrial rhythms, as illustrated in Figure 17.2.

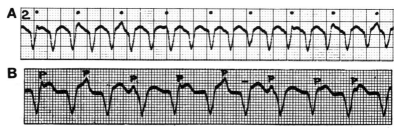

Figure 17.2. In **A** , the regularly occurring P waves are indicated by *dots* ; in **B** , they are indicated by *P*. When no P wave at all is visible, its assumed position has been identified by the regular sequence.

In a given patient, the VPB initiating VT is usually less premature than those occurring in isolation, and the coupling interval is usually longer than the intervals between the ventricular beats during the VT. In one study, the initiating VPB landed before the end of the QT interval in only 13% (Fig. 17.3).[6]

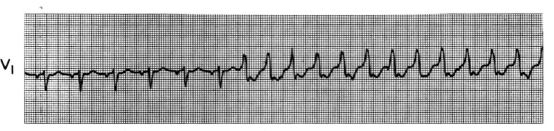

Figure 17.3. The VPB that initiates the VT occurs following the end of the T wave. Its coupling interval with the preceding sinus beat is the same as the intervals between the ventricular beats during the VT. (From Wagner GS, Waugh RA, Ramo BW. Cardiac arrhythmias. New York: Churchill Livingstone, 1983:190.)

ETIOLOGY

VT usually occurs as a complication of severe heart disease but occasionally may appear in individuals with no evidence of heart disease.[7-9] VT was documented in 6% of a series of patients with mitral valve prolapse[10] and has been reported to rarely follow a malignant course in this common minor cardiac abnormality.[11]

The proarrhythmic effect of many antiarrhythmic drugs is manifested by either VT or torsades.[12,13] Those that slow conduction such as flecainide may prolong the QRS complex and convert nonsustained VT into sustained VT; those that prolong recovery time such as quinidine may prolong the QTc and produce torsades (Chapter 22, "Drug Toxicity"). VT is most likely to occur as a proarrhythmic effect in patients with poor ventricular function due to ischemic heart disease.[3]

VT is a major complication of ischemic heart disease, acutely during the early hours of myocardial infarction and chronically following a large infarction. VT may appear almost immediately following complete proximal obstruction of a major coronary artery when there is transmural myocardial ischemia but not yet infarction. It tends to be unstable, often leading to ventricular fibrillation. During the weeks to months following a large infarction, a more stable form of VT may appear. Chronically arrhythmogenic infarcts are typically large enough to decrease left ventricular function and may have other typical anatomic characteristics.[14] One study has reported that in patients with a wide QRS tachyarrhythmia two aspects of the clinical history consistently predicted a ventricular site of origin[15]:

1. A previous myocardial infarction;
2. No preinfarction tachyarrhythmia.

VT also occurs as a complication of various nonischemic forms of cardiomyopathy.[1] The reentry circuit has been localized within the ventricular Purkinje system in many of the patients with idiopathic dilated cardiomyopathy. VT, usually nonsustained, commonly complicates hypertrophic cardiomyopathy, and either nonsustained or sustained VT is usually the first manifestation of arrhythmogenic right ventricular cardiomyopathy.

DIAGNOSIS

The diagnosis of VT would be an easy task if all supraventricular tachyarrhythmias (SVTs) were conducted normally through the ventricles. However, aberrant conduction of supraventricular impulses, via either the bundle branches and fascicles or an accessory pathway, occurs frequently (Chapter 18, "Supraventricular Tachyarrhythmias with Aberrant Ventricular Conduction"). When no P waves are revealed on a standard 12-lead ECG, the details of the QRS morphology may provide differentiation between VT and SVTs.[16–19] The most common sources of error in the diagnosis of VT are listed in Table 17.1.

Table 17.1. Common Sources of Error in Diagnosis of VT

1. Believing that VT cannot be well tolerated
2. Depending on a single lead, especially lead 2
3. Depending on independent atrial activity
4. Putting faith in irregularity
5. Ignoring or neglecting QRS morphology

1. It is commonly believed that VT is associated with greater alteration of the patient's hemodynamics than are SVTs; however, the study by Morady et al. showed this to be a misconception.[20] In a study by Tchou et al., all of the patients with proven VT were hemodynamically stable when first seen.[15] The importance of differentiating VT from SVTs was emphasized by the adverse responses to the calcium channel blocking drug verapamil. Half of the patients received verapamil because of an erroneous diagnosis of an SVT. Many of these patients promptly deteriorated and some required resuscitation. The main factors that determine a patient's tolerance to a tachyarrhythmia from any origin are the ventricular rate, the size of the heart, and the severity of the underlying clinical problem and associated conditions.

2. When observing QRS morphology to differentiate VT from an SVT with aberrancy, it is important to consider the relative values of different ECG leads. Figure 17.4 illustrates the superiority of using lead V1, with its right versus left orientation, rather than lead II, with its base to apex orientation. When abnormally wide QRS complexes have a V1 positive morphology, the differential diagnosis is between VT from the left ventricle (LVT), as seen in Figure 17.4 A, and RBBB (Fig. 17.4 D). When abnormally wide QRS complexes have a V1 negative morphology, the differential diagnosis is between VT from the right ventricle (RVT), as illustrated in Figure 17.4 B, and LBBB.

Lead II may have a similar appearance in LVT and RVT (Fig. 17.4, A and B) and in LBBB and RBBB (Fig. 17.4, C and D). This is one of several reasons why a right chest lead (e.g., MCL₁) is superior to an inferiorly oriented limb lead (e.g., lead II) for rhythm monitoring. Monitoring via at least two leads provides even greater diagnostic accuracy.

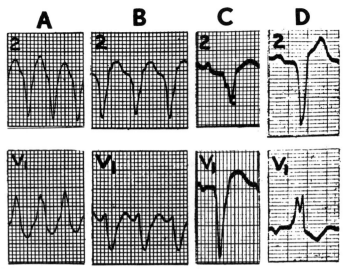

Figure 17.4. QRS complexes either originating in the ventricles (**A** and **B**) or resulting from a bundle branch block (**C** and **D**) have been recorded from lead 2 (*top*) and lead V1 (*bottom*).

3. Identification of independent atrial activity (AV dissociation) eliminates the possibility of an SVT originating from the atria or depending on an accessory pathway, but it does not exclude an SVT originating within the AV node. Figure 17.5 presents an example of an AV nodal tachycardia with left bundle branch aberrancy, confirmed by observing the similarly appearing LBBB during sinus rhythm.

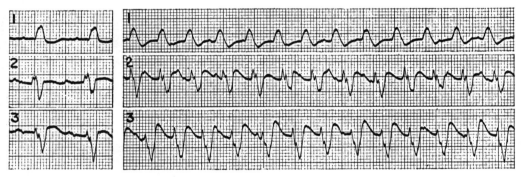

Figure 17.5. Recordings of limb leads *1*, *2*, and *3* during sinus rhythm (*left*) and a tachyarrhythmia (*right*). Note the P waves in leads 2 and 3 which have regular PP intervals but irregular PR intervals.

However, this is the exception. When there is AV dissociation with a wide-QRS tachycardia, the diagnosis of VT is highly probable. In a study by Wellens et al., AV dissociation was identified on the ECG in 32 of 70 patients with VT proven by intracardiac recording and in none of the 70 with an aberrantly conducted SVT.[21]

4. VT has been said to be characterized by slight irregularities of both rate and morphology. However, like all reentrant tachyarrhythmias, VT is usually almost regular. In the study of Wellens et al., there was complete regularity in 55 of the 70 patients with VT and in 65 of the 70 with an SVT.[21] Therefore, the degree of regularity does not help with the differential diagnosis.

The morphology also is usually regular and then the term monomorphic is applied. When an intermittent irregularity of QRS morphology appears, either on time or slightly early, the most likely cause is a breakthrough of conduction of the atrial rhythm to the ventricles. If the atrial breakthrough occurs during a ventricular beat, the result is a *fusion beat*. If it occurs before a ventricular beat has begun, the result is a *capture beat* (Fig. 17.6, *A* and *B*). Fusion is a hybrid QRS morphology in which a portion of the QRS represents the areas of the ventricles activated by the VT and the other portion represents the areas activated by a competing atrial impulse. Capture means that the entire QRS complex represents activation of the ventricles by a competing atrial impulse. If either fusion or capture beats are proven to be present, the diagnosis is almost certainly VT. However, fusion and/or capture beats are seldom seen and then only at the less rapid rates (under 160 beats/min). Indeed, they appeared in only 4 of a series of 33 reported patients with sustained VT.[21]

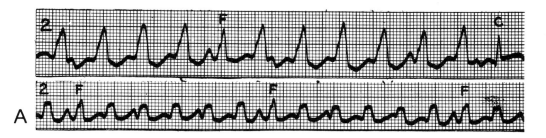

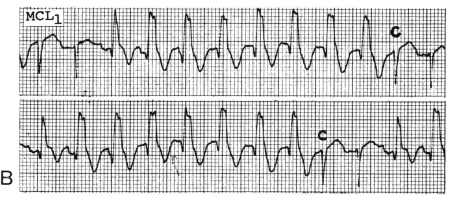

Figure 17.6. In the lead 2 recording in **A** and the MCL₁ recording in **B**, fusion beats are indicated by *F* and capture beats by *C*.

5. During the past 20 years, electrophysiologic studies have provided the capability for using intracardiac recordings to differentiate VT from an SVT with aberrancy. The diagnostic weaknesses of the methods discussed above have been documented.[19,21] The development of drugs such as verapamil, which are often therapeutic with an SVT but life threatening with VT, have made an accurate bedside diagnosis more critical.[22-24] As better clues were sought, it became evident that subtle differences in the shape of the QRS complexes often afforded a reliable indication of their source.[19,21,25,26] The use of QRS morphologic clues for the differential diagnosis of VT versus an SVT with aberrancy is discussed in detail in Chapter 18 and certain important aspects are included below.

The simple measurement of the duration of the wide QRS complexes may provide important diagnostic information, particularly if a recording of that individual's QRS morphology during sinus rhythm is available. Wellens et al. found that in more than half of the examples of VT, the QRS duration is >0.14 sec.[19] Indeed, all 59 patients with QRS duration >0.14 sec had electrophysiologic confirmation of VT. Since the exception would be the individual with an already widened QRS complex during sinus rhythm, a previous rhythm strip is needed before concluding that the diagnosis is VT simply because the QRS duration is >0.14 sec.

In LVT, the lead V1 positive QRS complex usually includes either a monophasic R or a diphasic qR and only occasionally a triphasic rsR. Coronary care nurses were the first to consider the paired peaks of the QRS complex in right-sided chest leads such as V1 or MCL$_1$ (rabbit ears) for determining the origin of wide beats.[27] The initial peak of the positive deflection is considered the left rabbit ear and the second peak is considered the right rabbit ear. Examples are provided in Figure 17.7, A and B, where the taller left rabbit ear suggests that the arrhythmia is VT originating from the left ventricle. However, a taller right rabbit ear does not necessarily indicate an SVT with RBB aberration: the rhythm is just as likely to be LVT. The rS pattern with no Q wave in lead V6 is also typical of LVT. However, it also occurs when the aberrancy of an SVT is produced by LAFB in addition to RBBB.

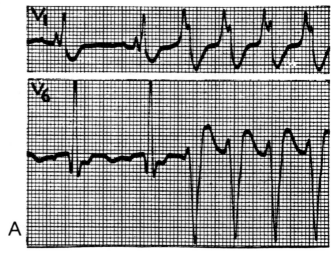

Figure 17.7. In **A**, the origin of a VT is recorded on leads V1 and V6; in **B**, all 12 standard leads are recorded during VT. The left rabbit ear is taller in lead V1 during the tachyarrhythmia in both examples. Note that in **A** the right rabbit ear is taller with RBBB during sinus rhythm.

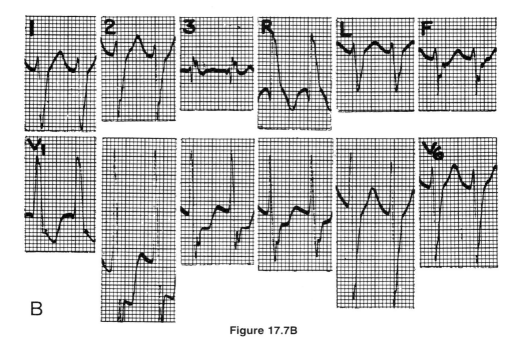

Figure 17.7B

A complete absence of any positive deflection (QS complex) in lead V6 is almost diagnostic of VT originating from either ventricle. There are identical QS patterns in lead V6 in LVT in Figure 17.8 *A* and in RVT in Figure 17.8 *B*.

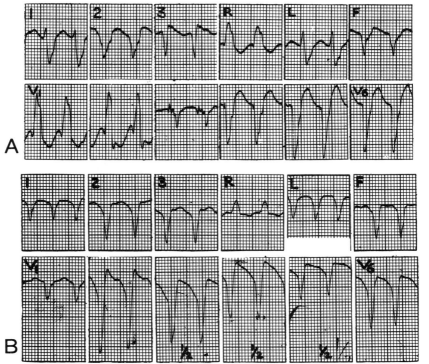

Figure 17.8. Full 12-lead ECGs are recorded in both **A** and **B**. Note that precordial leads V3–V5 are recorded at half standard gain (5 mm = 1.0 mV) in **B**.

Concordance of the predominant direction of the wide precordial QRS complexes is another useful clue. When all of the ventricular complexes from leads V1 to V6 are either positive (*concordant precordial positive*) or negative (*concordant precordial negative*), the diagnosis is most likely VT. Concordant negativity, as presented in Figure 17.8 *B*, is virtually diagnostic of RVT. Concordant positivity (Fig. 17.9) indicates the presence of LVT unless the patient has an accessory AV conduction pathway.

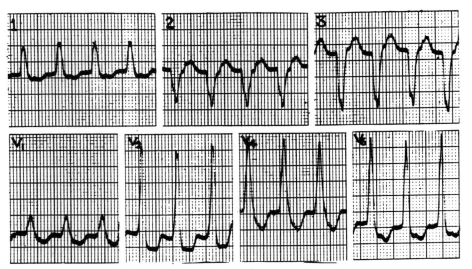

Figure 17.9. Three limb and four precordial leads recorded during the tachyarrhythmia.

Brugada et al. developed two additional morphologic criteria from the precordial leads for the diagnosis of VT (Fig. 17.10)[28]:

1. None of the precordial leads has an RS morphology (Fig. 17.10 *A*).
2. If an RS morphology is present, the interval from the onset of the QRS to the nadir of the S wave is >0.10 sec (Fig. 17.10 *B*).

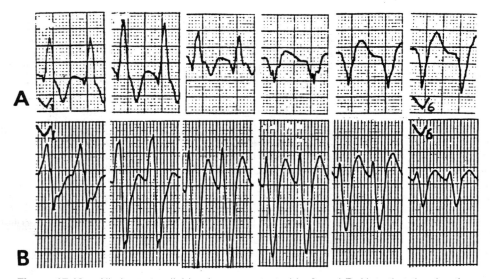

Figure 17.10. All six precordial leads are presented in **A** and **B**. Note that the durations from the onset of the QRS complexes to the nadir of the S waves in **B** vary from 0.11 to 0.12 sec in the various leads.

Rosenbaum described a pattern of QRS morphology which is commonly present in healthy young individuals with RVT.[29] As illustrated in Figure 17.11, there is the typical pattern of LBBB except for:

1. RAD in the frontal plane;
2. A broad initial R wave in lead V1.

With true LBBB, there is neither the greater delay in the posterior-inferior than in the anterior-superior fascicle which would be required to produce RAD nor the left to right septal activation which would be required to produce a prominent lead V1 R wave.

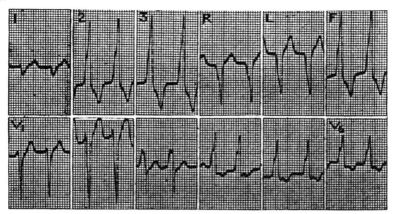

Figure 17.11. All 12 standard leads are recorded.

When monitoring with a single right-sided lead such as MCL$_1$, the morphology of the initial part of the QRS complex may provide sufficient clues to differentiate VT from an SVT with LBBB. Figure 17.12 illustrates the difference between the typical narrow initial R wave of LBBB and the broad initial R wave of RVT. The transition from typical atrial fibrillation with an irregularly irregular ventricular rhythm with LBB aberration (*top strip*) to a more rapid regular tachycardia with wider QRS complexes (*bottom strip*) could be caused by either:

1. Slowing of the atrial rate from fibrillation to flutter with a consequent increase in AV nodal conduction, but a further decrease in conduction via the left bundle branch (increased aberrancy);
2. The development of a second reentrant tachycardia within the RV. The change from a narrow to a broad initial R wave in the middle strip establishes the latter diagnosis. Note the capture beat near the end of the bottom strip.

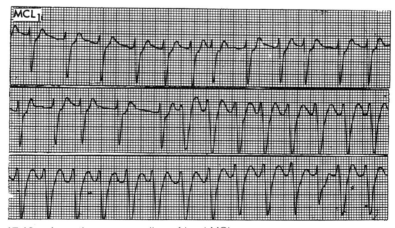

Figure 17.12. A continuous recording of lead MCL$_1$.

Figure 17.13 illustrates schematically the contrast between the initial 0.06 sec of the QRS complexes in LBBB versus RVT with lead V1 negative morphology. LBBB causes a delay in the activation of the left ventricle and, therefore, notching or slurring in the terminal part of the QRS complex. The initial part of the QRS complex represents rapid activation of the RV via the unaffected RBB. This is represented in lead V1 by either a narrow initial R wave or a Q wave with a sharp downstroke which reaches its nadir within 0.06 sec. When the impulse originates from a site of microreentry within the ventricles, there is slow movement of the wave fronts of activation throughout the remainder of the ventricular myocardium and, therefore, notching or slurring may occur in any part of the QRS complex. Such slow conduction is represented in lead V1 by either a broad initial R wave or a slurred or notched Q wave which reaches its nadir later than 0.06 sec.

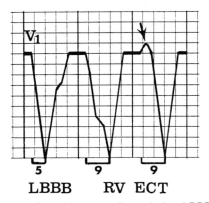

Figure 17.13. A schematic of lead V1 recordings during LBBB and two varieties of RVT. The *arrow* points to the broad initial R wave, and the *brackets* indicate the durations from the onsets of the QRS complexes to the nadirs of the maximal negative waveforms. *5* refers to 0.05 sec, and *9* refers to 0.09 sec.

The slow conduction during VT is also indicated by a slow rise or descent of the initial waveform in lead V6. Drew and Scheinman have observed that if >0.07 sec is required to reach either the peak of the R wave or the nadir of the S wave, the diagnosis is almost always VT (Fig. 17.14).[30]

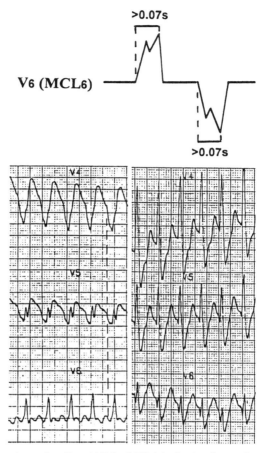

Figure 17.14. The schematic of lead V6 (or MCL$_6$) indicates the method for measuring from the QRS onset to the peak to the R or S wave, and the recordings of leads V4–V6 from two patients illustrate the slow rise of the R wave (*left*) and the slow descent of the S wave (*right*).

An extreme deviation of the QRS axis in the frontal plane into the upper right quadrant between −90 and −180° very seldom is found in aberrantly conducted beats (exceptions include some complex congenital heart lesions and hearts with multiple infarcts). However, often this appears in VT arising from either ventricle (Figs. 17.7 *B* and 17.8, *A* and *B*).[19] The presence of extreme axis deviation is, therefore, strongly suggestive of a diagnosis of VT.

Figure 17.15 summarizes the observations of the various QRS morphologic clues for differentiating VT from an SVT with aberrancy. The perpendicular frontal plane leads I and aVF indicate the axis and the widely separate precordial leads V1 and V6 indicate concordancy. There are seven combinations of QRS morphologies in this quartet of leads which are highly suggestive of a diagnosis of VT. In quartets 3 and 5, both the clues of extreme frontal plane axis deviation, indicated by concordance of negatively oriented QRS complexes in leads I and aVF, and concordance of transverse plane QRS directions, appear. The frontal plane RAD and transverse plane broad initial R wave in lead V1 provide the clues in quartet number 6.

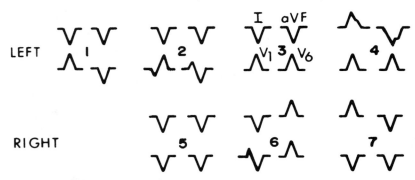

Figure 17.15. Four examples of LVT (*1–4*) and three examples of RVT (*5–7*). Limb leads 1 and aVF and precordial leads V1 and V6 are illustrated schematically in all examples.

All of the above clues owed their original recognition to clinical observation and deduction and were in use for many years before they were confirmed by experimental studies. Their performance in patients with the diagnosis of VT, confirmed by invasive electrophysiologic studies, is presented in Table 17.2.[19,21]

Table 17.2. Diagnosis of Ventricular Tachycardia

	Favoring Ectopy		
V₁	Single peak		15/15
	Taller left rabbit ear		7/7
	QR		16/17
	RS		4/4
V₆	rS		27/31
	QS		17/17
	QR		8/8
	Axis −30− −180°[a]		68/75
	QRS interval >0.14 sec[a]		59/59

[a]Of little use if previous tracing not available.

LEFT VERSUS RIGHT VENTRICULAR TACHYCARDIA

It is generally true that one can distinguish between origination in the right versus the left ventricle by observing whether the QRS complexes are V1 positive or V1 negative. However, important exceptions have been identified by observing the QRS morphology during artificial ventricular pacing[31] and by electrophysiologic identification of the site of origin of clinical episodes of VT. In all 22 individuals with V1 positivity, the VT indeed originated from the left ventricle, but the VT originated from the right ventricle in only 3 of the 20 with V1 negativity (Table 17.3). [32] The ventricle of origin seemed to vary with the condition of the heart: in the 3 individuals with normal hearts, V1 negativity was indeed associated with right ventricular origin, but in all 17 with ischemic heart disease, the VT originated from inside or near the left side of the interventricular septum. It has been hypothesized that areas of infarction sufficiently delay activation of the LV, allowing the RV to be activated earlier and producing V1 negativity.[33] In another series of individuals without heart disease, all of the electrophysiologically investigated VTs with V1 negativity originated from the outflow tract of the right ventricle.[34]

Table 17.3. QRS Morphology/Site of Origin

V₁	LV	RV
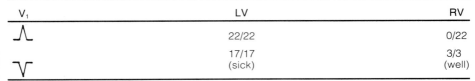	22/22	0/22
	17/17 (sick)	3/3 (well)

VARIATION OF VT DURATION

 VT is usually designated as either *nonsustained VT* or *sustained VT*, depending on whether it persists for longer than 30 seconds.[1] Nonsustained VT has also been defined as lasting less than 1 minute[35] and fewer than 10 beats.[36] Figure 17.16 illustrates two recurrences of VT which satisfy all of these definitions of nonsustained VT.

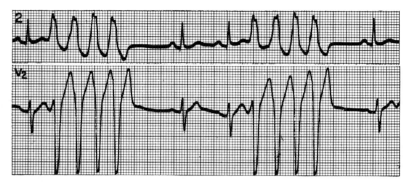

Figure 17.16. Simultaneous recording of leads 2 and V2.

Episodes of nonsustained VT may recur chronically over a period of months to years.[37] However, there are striking differences in incidence and prognosis between RVT and LVT.[38] Those with LVT tend to be older, male, and have diagnosable heart disease, whereas those with RVT tend to be younger, female, and do not have diagnosable heart disease. RVT is more likely to be induced by particular situations such as moderate exercise, emotional excitement, upright posture, or smoking.[39,40] LVT associated with either ischemic or idiopathic cardiomyopathy has also been documented to be exercise induced.[41] RVT associated with arrhythmogenic right ventricular cardiomyopathy is of great clinical importance.[1]

VARIATIONS IN VT APPEARANCE

All of the above examples have been of *monomorphic VT*, but there are also rare examples of *polymorphic VT* due to microreentry. Presumably, there are either two competing microreentry circuits or two different directions of spread of activation from a single circuit. Discrete, wide QRS complexes and T waves are present, and the rate may be regular (Fig. 17.17 *A*) or slightly irregular (Fig. 17.17 *B*). The QRS morphology in all 12 leads should be compared with that seen during sinus rhythm to eliminate the possibility that the rhythm is monomorphic VT with fusion or capture beats.[42] When the polymorphic VT is regular and there are two alternating QRS morphologies with opposite polarity, the term *bidirectional tachycardia* is applied (Fig. 17.17 *A*). This extremely unusual arrhythmia occurred more often when large amounts of digitalis were given.[43]

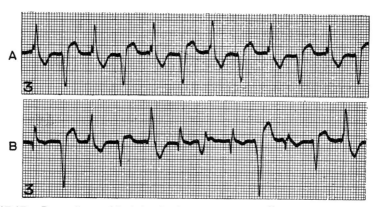

Figure 17.17. Recordings of limb lead 3 from patients **A** and **B**.

TORSADES DE POINTES

This French term translates as "twistings of the points." Torsades is a polymorphic ventricular tachyarrhythmia regarded as intermediate between VT and ventricular flutter/fibrillation.[26,44,45] Torsades is characterized by undulations of continually varying amplitudes which appear alternately above and below the baseline. The wide ventricular waveforms are not characteristic of either QRS complexes or T waves (Fig. 17.18).[46] The rate varies from 180 to 250 beats/min. Torsades is usually nonsustained; however, it may persist for longer than 30 sec, satisfying the definition of a sustained tachyarrhythmia. It may, at times, evolve into ventricular fibrillation.

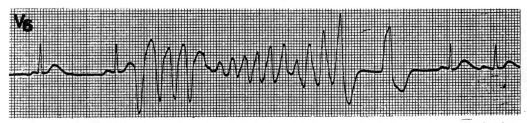

Figure 17.18. A recording of lead V6 rhythm strip from a patient with presyncopal episodes.

Torsades almost always occurs in the presence of prolongation of the QTc interval.[47,48] This may be caused by the proarrhythmic effect of drugs that prolong ventricular recovery time, including quinidine,[49,50] procainamide,[44,48] disopyramide,[51,52] amiodarone, sotalol,[12] phenothiazines, and tricyclic antidepressants.[12] It also occurs with electrolyte abnormalities such as hypokalemia and hypomagnesemia,[12] insecticide poisoning,[53] subarachnoid hemorrhage,[54] congenital prolongation of the QTc interval,[55] ischemic heart disease,[56] and bradyarrhythmias.[3]

VENTRICULAR FLUTTER/FIBRILLATION

 Ventricular flutter/fibrillation is a macroreentrant tachyarrhythmia within the ventricular muscle which is analogous to the atrial flutter/fibrillation spectrum discussed in Chapter 15 (Fig. 17.19). Neither clearly formed QRS complexes nor T waves are present and the rhythm looks similar when viewed right side up or upside down. Immediately following the onset of the reentry, a regularly undulating baseline is present (Fig. 17.19 A, *top*). *Ventricular flutter* looks like a larger version of atrial flutter but it remains regular and orderly only transiently because the cardiac output is too low to provide sufficient coronary blood flow (Fig. 17.19 B, *middle*). There is prompt deterioration toward the irregular appearance of *ventricular fibrillation* (Fig. 17.19 B, *bottom*). Ventricular flutter has been given various names including ventricular tachycardia of the vulnerable period and prefibrillation.

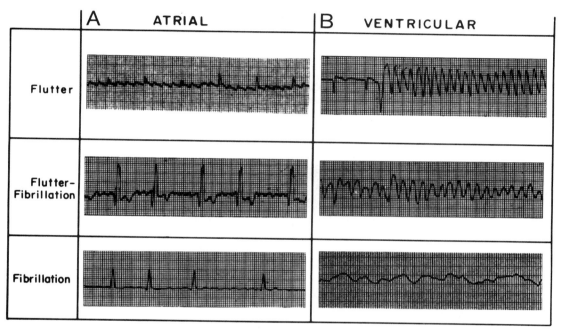

Figure 17.19. The atrial flutter/fibrillation spectrum (**A**) is compared with its ventricular counterpart (**B**). (From Wagner GS, Waugh RA, Ramo BW. Cardiac arrhythmias. New York: Churchill Livingstone, 1983:22.)

CLINICAL OBSERVATIONS

The various factors capable of creating movement along the flutter/fibrillation spectra in the atria and ventricles are presented in Figure 17.20. When the ventricular reentry is electrically induced during cardiac surgery and the coronary blood flow is maintained by an external pump, slow-coarse ventricular flutter may be maintained until it is electrically terminated at the completion of the procedure. When ventricular flutter/fibrillation occurs spontaneously and deteriorates toward the rapid-fine end of the spectrum, the direct relationship between the coarseness of the rhythm and the effectiveness of an electrical shock is used clinically. Beta-adrenergic agents and calcium are commonly used during a ventricular fibrillation-induced cardiac arrest when electrical defibrillation fails to terminate the reentry process.

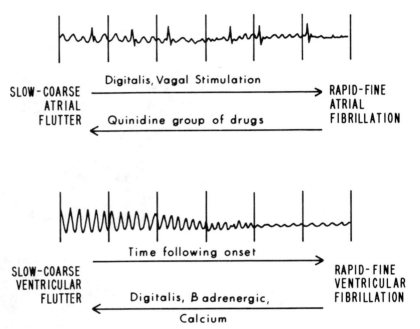

Figure 17.20. Movement in either direction along the flutter/fibrillation spectrum in the atria (**A**) and ventricles (**B**). The *arrows* indicate the direction the various factors tend to affect the rate of the reentry process. (From Wagner GS, Waugh RA, Ramo BW. Cardiac arrhythmias. New York: Churchill Livingstone, 1983:23.)

VENTRICULAR FLUTTER

A common error is mistaking external electrical artifact for ventricular flutter as illustrated in Figure 17.21. This patient mistakenly received emergency treatment for her ventricular arrhythmia. Personnel in critical care units have observed that patients with ventricular flutter may remain apparently stable for several seconds, particularly if they do not have a cardiac disease. They have also learned that a firm blow to the chest may terminate ventricular flutter.[57] It is important that they learn to quickly scan the rhythm strip for continuing regular QRS complexes before initiating the emergency therapy.

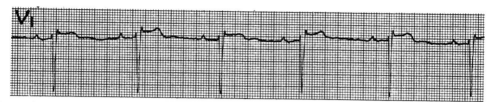

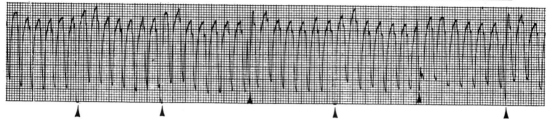

Figure 17.21. Lead V1 from the standard ECG is recorded above monitor lead MCL$_1$. The *arrows* indicate the regularly occurring higher frequency waveforms indicating the locations of the patient's QRS complexes.

VENTRICULAR FIBRILLATION

   Holter recordings that fortuitously capture the onset of sudden death have confirmed that the cause is usually ventricular fibrillation as illustrated in Figure 17.22. The onset is often preceded by one of the varieties of other reentrant ventricular tachycardias.[58,59] In patients receiving continuous bedside monitoring during acute myocardial infarction, the arrhythmias observed just prior to the onset of ventricular fibrillation have been an R-on-T VPB, monomorphic VT persisting for more than 100 beats, monomorphic VT with a rate above 180 beats/min, or polymorphic VT.[60]

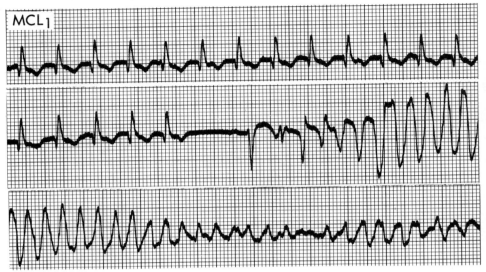

Figure 17.22.   Continuous bedside recording of lead MCL₁ from a patient with cardiac arrest.

GLOSSARY

Bidirectional tachycardia: VT with a regular rate and two QRS morphologies with opposite polarities.

Concordant precordial negative: abnormally wide QRS complexes are predominately negative in all six of the precordial leads.

Concordant precordial positive: abnormally wide QRS complexes are predominately positive in all six of the precordial leads.

Monomorphic VT: VT with a regular rate and consistent QRS morphology.

Nonsustained VT: VT less than 30 sec in duration.

Polymorphic VT: VT with a regular rate but frequent changes in QRS morphology.

Sustained VT: VT at least 30 sec in duration or requiring an intervention to terminate.

Torsades de pointes: a polymorphic ventricular tachyarrhythmia with the appearance of slow polymorphic ventricular flutter with no discernible QRS complexes or T waves. The ventricular activity has constantly changing amplitudes and seems to revolve around the isoelectric line.

Ventricular fibrillation: rapid and totally disorganized ventricular activity with no discernible QRS complexes or T waves.

Ventricular flutter: rapid organized ventricular activity with no discernible QRS complexes or T waves.

Ventricular flutter/fibrillation: the spectrum of ventricular tachyarrhythmias with no discernible QRS complexes or T waves, ranging from gross undulations to no discernible electrical activity.

Ventricular tachycardia: rhythm originating distal to the branching of the common bundle with a rate of at least 100 beats/min.

REFERENCES

1. Shenasa M, Borggrefe M, Haverkamp W, Hindricks G, Breithardt G. Ventricular tachycardia. Lancet 1993;341:1512.
2. Akhtar M, Gilbert C, Wolf FG, Schmidt DH. Reentry within the His Purkinje system: elucidation of re-entrant circuit using right bundle-branch and His bundle recordings. Circulation 1976;58:295.
3. Ben-David J, Zipes DP. Torsades de pointes and proarrhythmia. Lancet 1993;341:1578.
4. Toboul P. Torsade de pointes. In: Wellens HJJ, Kulbertus HE, eds. What's new in electrocardiography. Boston: Martinus Nijhoff, 1981:229.
5. Welch WJ. Sustained macroreentrant ventricular tachycardia. Am Heart J 1982;104:166.
6. Qi WH, Fineberg NS, Surawicz B. The timing of ventricular premature complexes initiating chronic ventricular tachycardia. J Electrocardiol 1984;17:377.
7. Lesch M, Lewis E, Humphries JO, Ross RS. Paroxysmal ventricular tachycardia in the absence of organic heart disease: report of a case and review of the literature. Ann Intern Med 1967;66:950.
8. Pederson DH, Zipes DP, Foster PR, Troup PJ. Ventricular tachycardia and ventricular fibrillation in a young population. Circulation 1979;60:988.
9. Fulton DR, Chung KJ, Tabakin BS, Keane JF. Ventricular tachycardia in children without heart disease. Am J Cardiol 1985;55:1328.
10. Swartz MH, Teichholz LE, Donoso E. Mitral valve prolapse: a review of associated arrhythmias. Am J Med 1977;62:377.
11. Wei JY, Bulkley BH, Schaeffer AH, Greene HL, Reid PR. Mitral-valve prolapse syndrome and recurrent ventricular tachyarrhythmias: a malignant variant refractory to conventional drug therapy. Ann Intern Med 1978;89:6.
12. Campbell TJ. Proarrhythmic actions of antiarrhythmic drugs: a review. Aust NZ J Med 1990;20:275.
13. The Cardiac Arrhythmia Suppression Trial (CAST) Investigators: Preliminary report: effect of encainide and flecainide on mortality in a randomized trial of arrhythmia suppression after myocardial infarction. N Engl J Med 1989;321:406–412.
14. Bolick DR, Hackel DB, Reimer KA, Ideker RE. Quantitative analysis of myocardial infarct structure in patients with ventricular tachycardia. Circulation 1986;74:1266–1279.
15. Tchou P, Young P, Mahmud R, Denker S, Jazayeri M, Akhtar M. Useful clinical criteria for the diagnosis of ventricular tachycardia. Am J Med 1988;284:53.
16. Marriott HJL. Differential diagnosis of supraventricular and ventricular tachycardia. Geriatrics 1970;25:91.
17. Sandler IA, Marriott HJL. The differential morphology of anomalous ventricular complexes of RBBB-type in V1: ventricular ectopy versus aberration. Circulation 1965;31:551.
18. Swanick EJ, LaCamera F Jr, Marriott HJL. Morphologic features of right ventricular ectopic beats. Am J Cardiol 1972;30:888.
19. Wellens HJJ, Bar FW, Vanagt EJ, Brugada P. Medical treatment of ventricular tachycardia, considerations in the selection of patients for surgical treatment. Am J Cardiol 1982;49:186.
20. Morady F, Baerman JM, DiCarlo LA Jr, DeBuitleir M, Krol RB, Wahr DW. A prevalent misconception regarding wide-complex tachycardias. JAMA 1985;254:2790.
21. Wellens HJJ, Bar FW, Lie KI. The value of the electrocardiogram in the differential diagnosis of a tachycardia with a widened QRS complex. Am J Med 1978;64:27.
22. Switzer DF. Dire consequences of verapamil administration for wide QRS tachycardia. Circulation 1986;74(suppl II):105.
23. Dancy M, Camm AJ, Ward D. Misdiagnosis of chronic recurrent ventricular tachycardia. Lancet 1985;2:320.
24. Stewart RB, Bardy GH, Greene HL. Wide-complex tachycardia: misdiagnosis and outcome after emergent therapy. Ann Intern Med 1986;104:766.
25. Vera Z, Cheng TO, Ertem G, Shoaleh-var M, Wickramasekaran R, Wadhwa K. His bundle electrography for evaluation of criteria in differentiating ventricular ectopy from aberrancy in atrial fibrillation. Circulation 1972;45(suppl II):355.

26. Gulamhusein S, Yee R, Ko PT, Klein GJ. Electrocardiographic criteria for differentiating aberrancy and ventricular extrasystole in chronic atrial fibrillation: validation by intracardiac recordings. J Electrocardiol 1985;18:41.

27. Gozensky C, Thorne D. Rabbit ears: an aid in distinguishing ventricular ectopy from aberration. Heart Lung 1974;3:634.

28. Brugada P, Brugada J, Mont L, Smeets J, Andries EW. A new approach to the differential diagnosis of a regular tachycardia with a wide QRS complex. Circulation 1991;83:1649–1659.

29. Rosenbaum MB. Classification of ventricular extrasystoles according to form. J Electrocardiol 1969;2:289.

30. Drew BJ, Scheinman MM. Value of electrocardiographic leads MCL_1, MCL_6 and other selected leads in the diagnosis of wide QRS complex tachycardia. J Am Coll Cardiol 1991;18:1025.

31. Waxman HL, Josephson ME. Ventricular activation during ventricular endocardial pacing. I. Electrocardiographic patterns related to the site of pacing. Am J Cardiol 1982;1.

32. Josephson ME, Horowitz LN, Waxman HL, Cain ME, Spielman SR, Greenspan AM, Marchlinski FE, Ezri MD. Sustained ventricular tachycardia: role of the 12-lead electrocardiogram in localizing site of origin. Circulation 1981;64:273.

33. Josephson ME, et al. Relation between site of origin and QRS configuration in ventricular rhythms. In: Wellens HJJ, Kulbertus HE, eds. What's new in electrocardiography. Boston: Martinus Nijhoff, 1981:200.

34. Buxton AE, Marchlinski FE, Doherty JU, Cassidy DM, Vassallo JA, Flores BT, Josephson ME. Repetitive, monomorphic ventricular tachycardia: clinical and electrophysiologic characteristics in patients with and patients without organic heart disease. Am J Cardiol 1984;54:997.

35. Vandepol CJ, Farshidi A, Spielman SR, Greenspan AM, Horowitz LN, Josephson ME. Incidence and clinical significance of induced ventricular tachycardia. Am J Cardiol 1980;45:725.

36. Josephson ME, Horowitz LN, Farshidi A, Kastor JA. Recurrent sustained ventricular tachycardia. I. Mechanisms. Circulation 1978;57:431.

37. Denes P, Wu D, Dhingra RC, Amat-y-leon R, Wyndham C, Mautner RK, Rosen KM. Electrophysiological studies in patients with chronic recurrent ventricular tachycardia. Circulation 1976;54:229.

38. Pietras RJ, Mautner R, Denes P, Wu D, Dhingra R, Towne W, Rosen KM. Chronic recurrent right and left ventricular tachycardia: comparison of clinical, hemodynamic and angiographic findings. Am J Cardiol 1977;40:32.

39. Vetter VL, Josephson ME, Horowitz LN. Idiopathic recurrent sustained ventricular tachycardia in children and adolescents. Am J Cardiol 1981;47:315.

40. Wu D, Kou HC, Hung JS. Exercise-triggered paroxysmal ventricular tachycardia: a repetitive rhythmic activity possibly related to afterdepolarization. Ann Intern Med 1981;95:410.

41. Mokotoff DM. Exercise-induced ventricular tachycardia: clinical features, relation to chronic ventricular ectopy, and prognosis. Chest 1980;77:10.

42. Cohen SI, Voukydis P. Supraventricular origin of bidirectional tachycardia. Circulation 1974;50:634.

43. Cohen SI, Deisseroth A, Hecht HS. Infra-His bundle origin of bidirectional tachycardia. Circulation 1973;47:1260.

44. Kossmann CE. Torsade de pointes: an addition to the nosography of ventricular tachycardia. Am J Cardiol 1978;42:1054.

45. Smith WM, Gallagher JJ. "Les torsades de pointes": an unusual ventricular arrhythmia. Ann Intern Med 1980;93:578.

46. Strasberg B, Sclarovsky S, Erdberg A, Duffy CE, Lam W, Swiryn S, Agmon J, Rosen KM. Procainamide-induced polymorphous ventricular tachycardia. Am J Cardiol 1981;47:1309.

47. Kay GN, Plumb VJ, Arcciniegas JG, Henthorn RW, Waldo AL. Torsade de pointes: the long-short initiating sequence and other clinical features: observations in 32 patients. J Am Coll Cardiol 1983;2:806.

48. Soffer J, Dreifus LS, Michelson EL. Polymorphous ventricular tachycardia associated with normal and long Q-T intervals. Am J Cardiol 1982;49:2021.

49. Reynolds EW, Vandeer Ark CR. Quinidine syncope and the delayed repolarization syndromes. Mod Concepts Cardiovasc Dis 1976;45:117.

50. Roden DM, Thompson KA, Hoffman BF, Woosley RL. Clinical features and the basic mechanisms of quinidine-induced arrhythmias. J Am Coll Cardiol 1986;8:73A.

51. Nicholson WJ, Martin CE, Gracey JG, Knoch HR. Disopyramide-induced ventricular fibrillation. Am J Cardiol 1979;43:1053.

52. Wald RW, Waxman MB, Colman JM. Torsades de pointes ventricular tachycardia: a complication of disopyramide shared with quinidine. J Electrocardiol 1981;14:301.

53. Ludomirsky A, Klein HO, Sarelli P, Becker B, Hoffman S, Taitelman U, Barzilai J, Lang R, David D, DiSegni E, Kaplinsky E. Q-T prolongation and polymorphous ("torsade de pointes") ventricular arrhythmias associated with organic insecticide poisoning. Am J Cardiol 1982;49:1655.

54. Carruth JE, Silverman ME. Torsade de pointes: atypical ventricular tachycardia complicating subarachnoid hemorrhage. Chest 1980;78:886.

55. Jervell A, Lange-Nielsen F. Congenital deaf-mutism, functional heart disease with prolongation of the Q-T interval and sudden death. Am Heart J 1957;54:59.

56. Krikler DM, Curry PVL. Torsade de pointes, an atypical ventricular tachycardia. Br Heart J 1976;38:117.

57. Lown B, Taylor J. Thump-version. N Engl J Med 1978;283:1223–1224.

58. Kempf FC, Josephson ME. Cardiac arrest recorded on ambulatory electrocardiograms. Am J Cardiol 1984;53:1577.

59. Panadis IP, Morganroth J. Sudden death in hospitalized patients: cardiac rhythm disturbances detected by ambulatory electrocardiographic monitoring. J Am Coll Cardiol 1983;2:798.

60. Bluzhas J, Lukshiene D, Shlapikiene B, Ragaishis J. Relation between ventricular arrhythmia and sudden cardiac death in patients with acute myocardial infarction: the predictors of ventricular fibrillation. J Am Coll Cardiol 1986;8(suppl IA):69A.

CHAPTER 18

Supraventricular Tachyarrhythmias with Aberrant Ventricular Conduction

Aberrant ventricular conduction is the temporary, abnormal intraventricular conduction of supraventricular impulses, usually due to a change in cycle length. Its importance rests firmly on two facts:

1. **It is common**. As Lewis said in 1925, "Aberration is known to be frequent in paroxysmal tachycardia."
2. **It is often overlooked**, with the result that supraventricular arrhythmias are misdiagnosed as ventricular and are treated as such.

Aberration is not a rare curiosity that can be left to the experts in arrhythmias. Almost all physicians occasionally are called upon to diagnose and treat paroxysmal tachyarrhythmias. Therefore, they should know the fundamental difference between supraventricular and ventricular sites of origin. The dilemma arises in those tachyarrhythmias with widened, bizarre QRS complexes which raise the specter of ventricular tachycardia.

TYPE A ABERRATION

 The Circumstances

When any responsive tissue reacts to a stimulus, the reaction is followed by a dormant interval, the refractory period, during which it cannot respond to a similar stimulus. This period of rest is necessary for the tissue to recoup and return to a state in which it can again react normally to the stimulus. Naturally, any such period has a finite, measurable duration, and if the tissue is asked to respond during its refractory period, the response will be absent or at least subnormal. Characteristics of the refractory period differ with different tissues. For example, the bundle branches in the heart usually respond with an "all-or-none" response. That is, if they respond at all, they respond fully and normally. However, the AV node shows a gradual rather than an abrupt improvement in conduction over a relatively long period.

The refractory period of the conducting paths is proportional to the length of the preceding cycle (RR interval). Thus, the longer the cycle and slower the rate, the longer the ensuing refractory period and vice versa. Ventricular aberration can, therefore, result either from shortening of the immediate cycle or from lengthening of the preceding one or from a combination of both (Fig. 18.1).

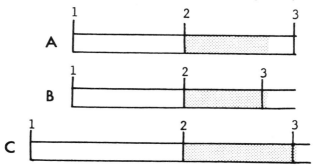

Figure 18.1. In the diagrams, *1*, *2*, and *3* are consecutive beats and the *stippled area* represents the refractory period of some part of the conducting system during the second cycle. **A.** There are two regular cycles with normal conduction. *Beat 3* may become aberrant (*lower two diagrams*) if either the first cycle is lengthened or the second cycle is shortened. Shortening of the cycle (**B**) may bring the beat within the refractory period of part of the conducting system. Lengthening of the preceding cycle (**C**) will prolong the refractory period so that the next beat, though no earlier than before, falls within the now longer refractory period.

There are three forms of aberration (Table 18.1). The common form is due to fascicular refractoriness (Type A). To produce aberration of this type, the obvious ploy is to get an impulse to arrive at the ventricular fascicle before it has recovered from its last activation while it is still in its refractory period. Clearly, the simplest way to achieve this is either to have a supraventricular premature beat or to accelerate the sinus rhythm.

Table 18.1. Forms of Ventricular Aberration and Their Causes

Type A	Fascicular refractoriness
Type B	Anomalous supraventricular activation
Type C	Paradoxical critical rate

Figure 18.2 illustrates right bundle branch block aberration of atrial premature beats. The early impulses have taken the right bundle branch "by surprise" (while it is still refractory) and it has been unable to respond and conduct.

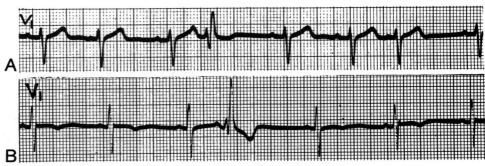

Figure 18.2.   In both **A** and **B**, after three normally conducted beats, an atrial extrasystole arises and its impulse arrives at the RBB while it is still refractory and is, therefore, conducted with RBBB aberration. In **A**, the second and seventh beats are also extrasystoles, but they are less premature and are, therefore, conducted normally.

RBBB aberration is much more common than LBBB aberration. In fact, it is believed that 80–85% of all aberration is of the RBBB type.[1,2] In a relatively sick population, as in a coronary care facility, LBBB aberration assumes greater prominence and accounts for perhaps one-third of the aberrant conduction encountered. In the experimental study of Kulbertus et al.[3], RBBB accounted for a smaller than expected proportion of the aberrancy produced experimentally. By inducing atrial premature beats in 44 patients, they were able to produce 116 different aberrant configurations (Table 18.2), of which RBBB accounted for only 53%.

Table 18.2.   Patterns of Induced Aberration and Their Incidences

RBBB alone	28	i.e.
RBBB + LAFB	21	RBBB = 53%
RBBB + LPFB	12	LAFB = 32%
LAFB alone	17	LPFB = 19%
LPFB alone	10	LBBB = 15%
LBBB	10	Unclassified = 10%
ILBBB	6	
Unclassified	12	
	116	

LAFB, left anterior superior fascicular block; LPFB, left posterior inferior fascicular block; ILBBB, incomplete left bundle branch block.

The Specifics

The first example of ventricular aberration to be published (Lewis, 1910) showed atrial bigeminy with alternating patterns of aberration. A similar situation is shown in Figure 18.3 where the atrial bigeminy is alternately complicated by RBBB and LBBB aberration. Additional points to notice in this tracing include:

1. The increased height of the R wave in lead I and the depth of the S wave in lead V6 in the RBBB beats presumably indicate an associated left anterior fascicular block.
2. The earliest indication of RBBB in lead V1 may take the form of slurring or notching of the upstroke of the QRS and/or shrinkage of the S wave (Fig. 18.3).

The prime importance of aberration is in its mimicry of ventricular ectopy. It is in itself a secondary phenomenon, always the result of some primary disturbance, and never requires treatment. At times, the morphology of the aberrant complex is indistinguishable from an ectopic pattern. At other times, however, the aberrant shapes provide broad hints of their supraventricular origin. In the tachyarrhythmias, the most important differentiation is from ventricular tachycardia, although isolated or paired aberrant beats may have to be differentiated from VPBs at times.

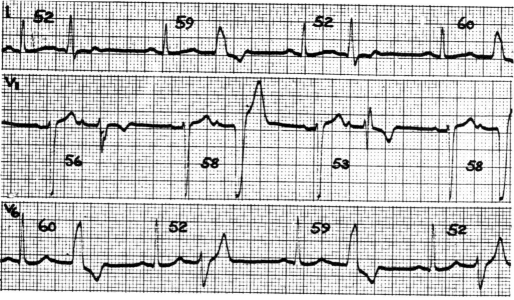

Figure 18.3. Atrial bigeminy with alternating aberration. The shorter extrasystolic cycles end with some form of RBBB aberration, whereas the longer cycles end in LBBB aberration. The beats with RBBB, as evidenced by the slightly increased height of the R wave in *lead 1* and the rS pattern in lead *V6*, also show left anterior fascicular block. In lead *V1*, the first atrial premature beat shows only the earliest sign of RBBB (notching of the terminal upstroke and shrinkage of the S wave).

The first principle in the diagnosis of aberrancy is: do not diagnose it unless there is evidence in favor of it. Despite this often-stated principle, VT is frequently mistaken for SVT with aberration. Ectopy is much more common than aberration and, when you hear hoof beats in this Western World, you do not think first of a zebra: you consider the zebra only if you see its stripes. The positive features in favor of aberration may, therefore, be called the "stripes" of aberration in Table 18.3.

Table 18.3. The "Stripes" of Aberration

1. Triphasic contours
   a. rsR' variant in V_1
   b. qRs variant in V_6
2. Preceding atrial activity
3. Initial deflection identical with that of conducted beats (if RBBB)
4. Second-in-the-row anomalous beat
5. Alternating BBB patterns separated by single normally conducted beat
6. Preexisting BBB with identical QRST pattern

The first four "stripes" are observable in Figure 18.4A in which the two continuous strips contain three clusters of rapid beats. In each cluster, the second beat alone presents a bizarre appearance. It has a triphasic (rsR') RBBB pattern. Its initial deflection is identical to that of the conducted sinus beats and it is preceded by a premature ectopic P' wave. All of these points clinch the recognition of aberration.

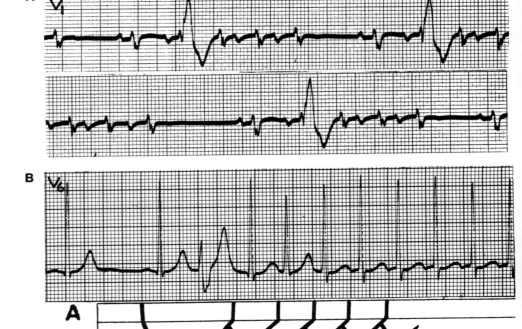

Figure 18.4.   A. The strips are continuous. Three short bursts of supraventricular tachycardia in which only the first beat (second in the row) develops ventricular aberration. **B.** Here the second in the row of rapid beats is probably a ventricular extrasystole initiating a run of reciprocating tachycardia (see ladder diagram).

TRIPHASIC V1/V6 MORPHOLOGY

  The shape of the QRS complex is diagnostic of aberrancy in many cases. The triphasic contours (rsR' in lead V1 and qRs in lead V6) heavily favor the diagnosis of aberration. Figure 18.5A illustrates a junctional tachycardia with RBBB aberration due to digitalis intoxication. The rSR' pattern is virtually diagnostic of the supraventricular origin of the tachycardia.

On the other hand, Figure 18.5B presents a pattern in lead V1 which is nondiagnostic. It could be a left ventricular tachycardia or it could be supraventricular with RBBB aberration. Lead V6, with its little q wave, tall thin R wave, and terminal s wave, is excellent evidence of its supraventricular origin. This patient also had a junctional tachycardia.

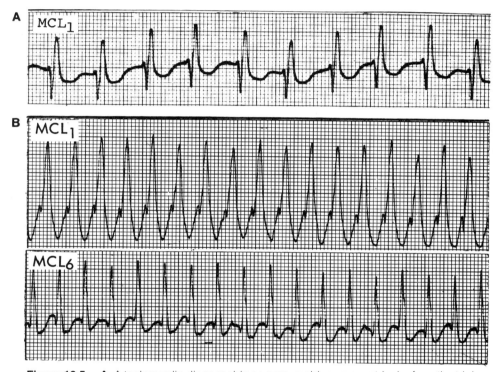

Figure 18.5. **A.** A tachycardia diagnosable as presumably supraventricular from the triphasic (rSR') pattern in a right chest lead (MCL₁). A possible alternative diagnosis is a fascicular tachycardia arising in the LBB. **B.** A tachycardia not identifiable as supraventricular from the right chest lead but readily recognized in a left chest lead (MCL₆) by its triphasic (qRs) contour.

Figure 18.6 presents an example in which the characteristic morphology is seen in both the right and left chest leads. The top strip shows the narrow complexes of a supraventricular tachycardia in lead MCL$_1$. The second strip shows the development of atrial fibrillation during which a lengthened cycle precipitates aberrancy in the following beat ending a shorter cycle (*Ashman phenomenon*).[1] The three aberrant beats have the classical rSR' pattern of RBBB. A narrow, more normally conducted beat is then followed by regularization of the rhythm and the appearance of LBBB aberration. In lead MCL$_6$, three of the more normally conducted beats are followed by four beats manifesting RBBB aberration of the typical qRS form followed again by a single more normally conducted beat and then LBBB aberration. This tracing, therefore, illustrates not only the classical QRS morphology of RBBB aberration in both the left and right chest leads, but also the phenomenon of alternating, bilateral aberration.

Despite the availability of morphological clues introduced during the past 30 years[2,4,5], and more recently confirmed[6-9], many authors persist in ignoring them[10-12]. They continue to give predominant and undue weight to the presence or absence of independent atrial activity. When independent atrial activity (AV dissociation) is evident, it is a most valuable clue. However, it cannot be relied upon for three reasons:

1. Dissociation is present in only a minority of ventricular tachycardias. In one carefully studied series, it was found in only 27 of 100.[13]
2. Even when AV dissociation is present, the independent P waves may be difficult or impossible to recognize in the clinical tracing.
3. Rarely, junctional tachyarrhythmias with bundle branch block may be dissociated from an independent sinus rhythm.

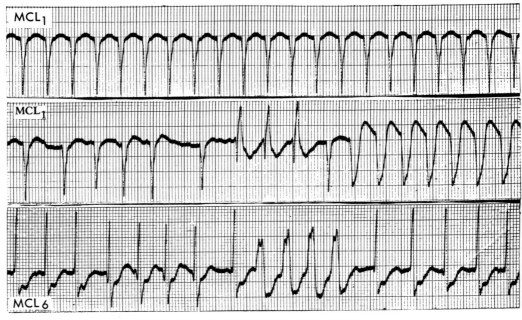

Figure 18.6. The *top strip* shows a regular supraventricular tachycardia. In the *middle strip*, atrial fibrillation develops and aberration of first RBBB and the LBBB type appears. (Note the steep, unhesitating downstroke of the QS complex with the nadir reached in less than 0.06 sec.) In the *bottom strip*, beats 4–7 show RBBB aberration whereas beats 9–12 illustrate LBBB aberration. The RBBB aberration is recognizable from its triphasic configuration in both the right (rSR') and left (qRS) chest leads.

IDENTICAL INITIAL DEFLECTION

There is no reason for an ectopic ventricular impulse to write an initial deflection indistinguishable from that of a normally conducted beat. On the other hand, since normal ventricular activation begins on the left side, pure RBBB does not interfere with initial activation so the initial deflection remains unchanged. Therefore, if the anomalous beat in question has a pattern compatible with RBBB and begins with a deflection identical to that of flanking conducted beats, it is a point in favor of aberration.

PRECEDING ATRIAL ACTIVITY

Sometimes the diagnosis of aberration depends upon the recognition of P waves preceding the abnormal ventricular complex. Figure 18.7 illustrates two bursts of anomalous beats. Careful inspection, however, reveals that each bout of tachycardia is preceded by an accelerating atrial rhythm (P' waves indicated by *arrows*), thereby confirming the diagnosis of aberrant conduction. As the atrial cycle shortens, the refractory period of the left bundle branch is encroached upon and the bundle branch fails to conduct.

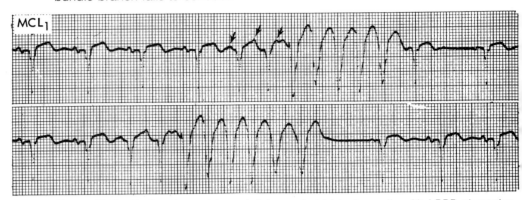

Figure 18.7. Each strip contains a brief run of atrial tachycardia with LBBB aberration. The *arrows* indicate the telltale antecedent P' waves which clinch the diagnosis. Note the momentary shift of the pacemaker following each burst. The returning P wave differs from the sinus P waves.

Figure 18.8 shows another tracing in which the diagnosis of aberration is mainly dependent upon preceding atrial activity. In each of the three strips, the second in a row of rapid beats is anomalous. Is it an aberrant complex because it ends a suddenly shorter cycle? Or is it a VPB initiating a run of reciprocating tachycardia? The morphology is of no assistance. The right rabbit ear is taller than the left; therefore, neither aberration nor ectopy is favored. If the T wave preceding the anomalous complexes is carefully compared with the T waves of the other sinus beats, it becomes obvious that something has been added to the pre-anomalous T waves, a superimposed P' wave confirming the aberration.

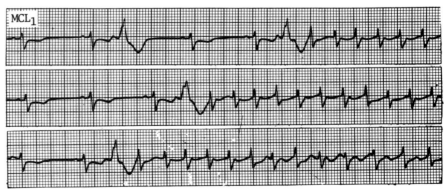

Figure 18.8. Morphologically, the anomalous beats in each strip could be either ectopic ventricular or aberrant. On three occasions, they usher in a run of supraventricular tachycardia; therefore, they could be aberrant (second in the row) or ventricular extrasystoles initiating runs of reciprocating tachycardia. The differentiation is made by observing the slightly positive deformity (P' waves) preceding each anomalous beat and not seen superimposed on the T waves of the other sinus beats.

SECOND-IN-THE-ROW ANOMALY

The reason only the second in a row of beats tends to be aberrant is because it is the only beat that ends a relatively short cycle preceded by a relatively long one. Since the refractory period of the conduction system is proportional to the preceding ventricular cycle length, the sequence of a long cycle (lengthening the subsequent refractory period) followed by a short cycle provides conditions for the development of aberration. However, this cycle sequence is not as diagnostic as one would like, since an anomalous second beat in a row of rapid beats can be a VPB that initiates a run of reciprocating tachycardia (Fig. 18.4*B*).

ALTERNATING BBB PATTERN

When a pattern that could be one BBB is separated from a pattern that could be the other BBB by a single normally conducted beat, as in Figures 18.6 and 18.10B, the presumption is strong that there is bilateral aberration rather than ectopy from alternate ventricles.

PREVIOUS COMPARATIVE TRACING

It is obvious that if one is lucky enough to have a previous tracing available which shows the same anomalous pattern at a time when it was known to be aberrant, one can then identify the pattern in question. In Figure 18.9, the *top strip* shows a tachyarrhythmia which, although the clean downstroke favors LBBB, could represent a right ventricular tachycardia or a supraventricular tachycardia with LBBB aberration. The *bottom strip* is a tracing from the same patient taken one year earlier and it shows an identical QRS complex during an obviously conducted rhythm. This establishes the diagnosis of a supraventricular tachycardia in the top strip.

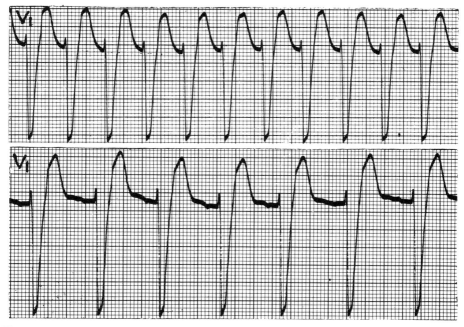

Figure 18.9. During tachycardia, the *top strip* shows wide, bizarre QRS complexes that could represent right ventricular ectopy or LBBB. The sheer downstroke and early nadir favor LBBB. The *bottom strip* was taken 1 year earlier and clearly shows a conducted rhythm with the same QRS morphology, thus confirming the supraventricular origin of the later tachycardia.

VENTRICULAR ABERRATION COMPLICATING ATRIAL FIBRILLATION

 The common form of ventricular aberration frequently complicates atrial fibrillation. It is probably true to say that when a run of anomalous beats interrupts normal intraventricular conduction during atrial fibrillation, it is more likely due to aberration than to coincidental ventricular tachycardia. Because in the presence of atrial fibrillation one cannot invoke preceding atrial activity as an indication of aberrant conduction, one has to rely more heavily than usual on the morphology of the wide complexes to differentiate aberration from ventricular ectopy. Thus, the rsR' pattern in lead V1 or MCL₁ (Fig. 18.10*B*) or the qRs pattern in lead V6 assists in establishing the diagnosis of aberrant conduction.

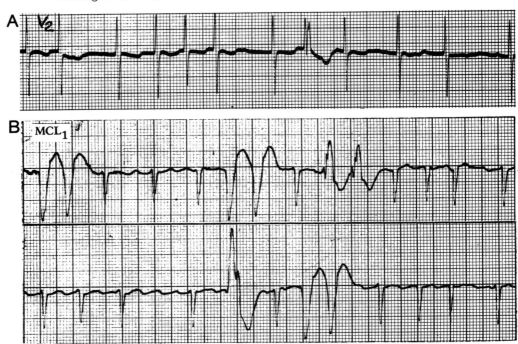

Figure 18.10. **A.** The eighth beat has an RsR' pattern and is undoubtedly aberrantly conducted. Note also that the initial R is virtually identical to the R waves of the flanking conducted RS complexes. **B.** The strips are continuous. In the *top strip*, some beats are conducted with LBBB and others with RBBB aberration. The RBBB aberration is identified by the rsR' configuration whereas the LBBB morphology is of no help and could as well be right ventricular ectopic. In the *bottom strip*, the fifth beat ends in a longer-shorter cycle sequence but is identified as ectopic left ventricular by the taller left rabbit ear configuration.

Gouaux and Ashman[1] first drew attention to the fact that aberrant conduction was likely to complicate atrial fibrillation when a longer cycle was followed by a shorter cycle (Fig. 18.11). When a long-short sequence produces aberration, it is sometimes referred to as the Ashman phenomenon. It is important to keep in mind that this cycle sequence cannot be used to differentiate aberration from ectopy because, by the *rule of bigeminy*, a lengthened cycle also tends to precipitate a ventricular extrasystole (Fig. 18.10*B*). Therefore, a long-short cycle sequence ending with an anomalous complex is as likely to be a VPB as an aberrant beat. Once again, morphological clues become important.

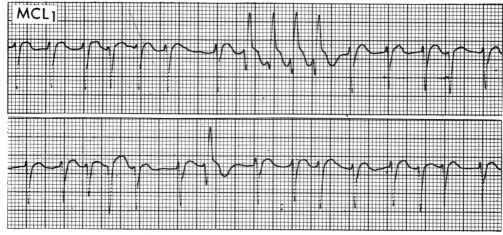

Figure 18.11. Atrial fibrillation with ventricular aberration. The strips are continuous. The run of anomalous beats in the *top strip* begins with the usual longer-shorter cycle sequence and is identified by the rsR′ pattern (RBBB) as aberrantly conducted. In the *bottom strip*, a single aberrant beat ends a longer-shorter sequence.

There are several other minor clues that help to differentiate aberration from ectopy in the presence of atrial fibrillation[4]:

1. The Presence of a Longer Returning Cycle. Ventricular ectopy tends to be followed by a longer returning cycle. This is because many ectopic ventricular impulses are conducted backward into the AV node (concealed retrograde conduction). If this happens, the AV node is left partially refractory by the retrograde invasion so that the next several fibrillatory impulses are unable to penetrate and reach their ventricular destination. Recent work suggests that this clue is of little differential value.

2. The Absence of a Longer Preceding Cycle. As indicated above, a long preceding cycle favors both aberration and ectopy and cannot be used as a differentiating point. On the other hand, the absence of a longer preceding cycle is evidence against aberration and, therefore, favors ectopy (Fig. 18.12*A*).

3. Comparative Cycle Sequences. If an anomalous beat ends a longer-shorter cycle sequence, we have seen that differentiation between aberration and ectopy may be difficult. If an even longer cycle followed by an even shorter cycle ends with a normally conducted beat, the evidence against aberration is strong and the diagnosis of ectopy is favored (Fig. 18.12*B*).

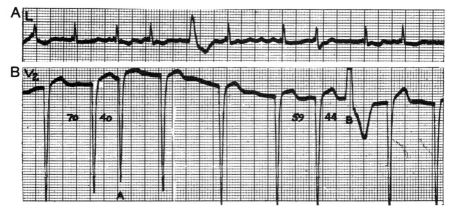

Figure 18.12. Atrial fibrillation with ventricular ectopic beats. **A.** The anomalous beat ends a shorter-longer cycle sequence, identifying it as probably ectopic ventricular. **B.** The anomalous *beat B* ends a longer-shorter cycle sequence, but *beat A*, which is not anomalous, ends an even longer-shorter sequence and is not aberrant. *Beat B* is, therefore, even less likely to be aberrant and is ectopic ventricular.

4. Undue Prematurity. When sufficient AV block is present to ensure that all conducted cycles are relatively long, the sudden appearance of an anomalous beat ending a cycle far shorter than any of the normally conducted beats favors the diagnosis of ectopy (Fig. 18.13A).

5. Fixed or Constant Coupling. This clue is obviously applicable only if several anomalous beats are available for comparison. If the interval between the normally conducted beat and the ensuing anomalous beat is constant to within a few hundredths of a second, ectopy is favored (Fig. 18.13B).

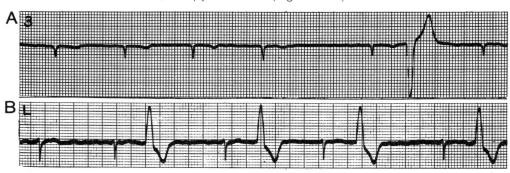

Figure 18.13. Atrial fibrillation with ventricular extrasystoles. **A.** The anomalous beat ends a cycle markedly shorter than any of the conducted beats and is, therefore, most likely ectopic ventricular. **B.** The anomalous beats bear an almost constant relationship to the preceding beats (fixed coupling) and are, therefore, most likely ectopic ventricular.

Figures 18.14 through 18.22 illustrate aberrant conduction occurring in various supraventricular arrhythmias and the pertinent points in diagnosis are dealt with in the respective legends. From a study of these examples, it should be evident that confusion can readily occur and that such confusion can have serious consequences.

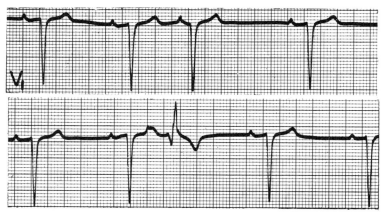

Figure 18.14. Atrial premature beats. The third beat in each strip is an atrial premature beat. In the *top strip*, the ectopic P wave is clearly visible and is followed by unchanged conduction to the ventricles. In the *bottom strip*, the ectopic beat is much more premature (P wave deforms upstroke of T wave) and finds the right bundle branch still refractory so that ventricular aberration of the RBBB type occurs. This beat might easily be mistaken for an ectopic ventricular beat.

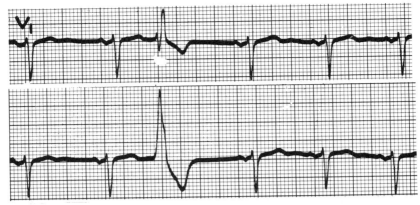

Figure 18.15. Two strips of lead V1 from the same patient. The *top strip* shows an atrial premature beat with ventricular aberration. The *bottom strip* shows a left ventricular premature beat. Note that the aberrant beat has an initial deflection (r) identical with those of flanking sinus beats and a triphasic (rsR′) contour whereas the ectopic ventricular beat is monophasic (R), reaches an early peak and has a slurred downstroke. (From Sandler IA, Marriott HJL. The differential morphology of anomalous ventricular complexes of RBBB-type in lead V1. Circulation 1965;31:551.)

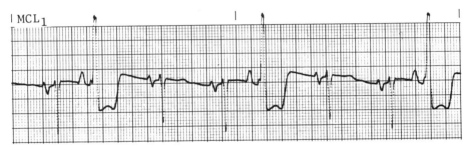

Figure 18.16. Atrial premature beats. The second, fifth, and eighth beats are atrial extrasystoles conducted with a bizarre form of RBBB aberration. Note the larger ectopic premature P waves preceding the aberrant ventricular complexes.

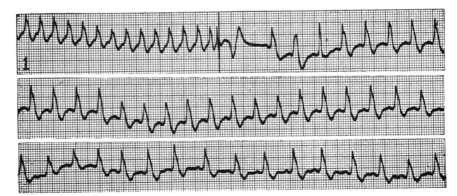

Figure 18.17. Supraventricular tachycardia with ventricular aberration. Continuous strip of lead 1. The record begins with what appears to be a run of ventricular tachycardia. Clinically, at a rate of 245 beats/min, the first heart sound was constant and there were no irregular cannon waves. After procainamide, the paroxysm gives rise to sinus tachycardia in which the preceding P waves are seen at the *end of the bottom strip*. Because the ventricular complexes are identical to those shown during the paroxysmal tachycardia (*beginning of top strip*), there is little doubt that the paroxysm was of supraventricular origin with aberrant ventricular conduction.

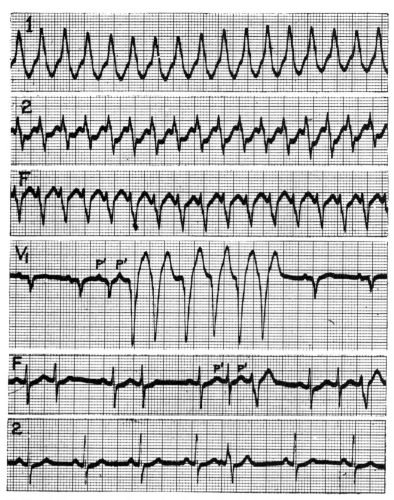

Figure 18.18. Atrial extrasystoles and tachycardia with LBBB aberration. The *upper three strips* show a pattern suggesting ventricular tachycardia. The *lower three strips* demonstrate that the tachycardia is supraventricular with ventricular aberration. The *fourth strip* shows the beginning of a paroxysm which again looks ventricular but is preceded by the onset of rapid ectopic atrial activity (P'), indicating that this paroxysm is probably ectopic atrial with aberrant ventricular conduction. The *bottom two strips* show telltale extrasystoles. In lead 2 (*bottom strip*), there is one bizarre premature beat which is preceded by an ectopic P wave and followed by a pause that is less than compensatory. This is then a supraventricular premature beat with aberration and the aberrant complex is identical to the ventricular complexes during the paroxysm in the upper lead 2 (*second strip*). In lead aVF (*fifth strip*), there are two couplets of atrial bigeminy followed by two triplets of atrial trigeminy. In these triplets, the second premature beat shows ventricular aberration with bizarre complexes identical to the QRS complexes during the paroxysm in the upper aVF lead (*third strip*). All of this adds up to overwhelming evidence that the "ventricular" tachycardia in the *upper three strips* is really supraventricular with aberrant ventricular conduction.

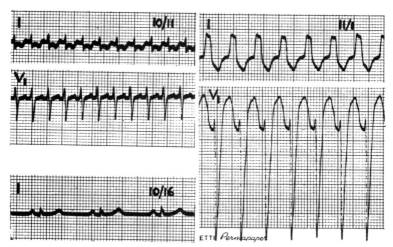

Figure 18.19. Two paroxysms of tachycardia in a boy with no demonstrable heart disease. On the *left*, the paroxysm is unmistakably supraventricular. On the *right*, 3 weeks later, the QRS pattern has altered markedly and now, at a slower rate, represents SVT with LBBB aberration. The first heart sound was constant and lead S_5 demonstrated a P wave in relation to each QRS complex. LBBB aberration developing at a slower rate suggests that the tachycardia was orthodromic using an accessory pathway on the same side as the BBB (*left*). Blocking of the bundle branch on the same side as the accessory pathway lengthens the available circuit and increases the time taken for the reciprocating impulse to complete the circuit, thereby slowing the rate.

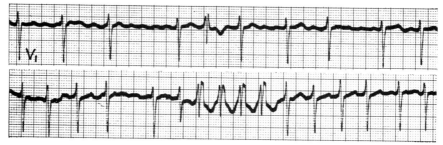

Figure 18.20. Atrial fibrillation with aberrant ventricular conduction. In the *upper strip*, the fifth beat might well be mistaken for an ectopic ventricular beat; however, it is of the RBBB (RSR') form and is more likely an aberrant complex. In the *lower strip*, the fifth beat, which terminates a long diastole, is followed by five aberrant complexes. The first of these shows only minor distortion (slurred upstroke, less deep S wave and an inverted T wave), but the following four beats show an RSR' of RBBB which could readily be mistaken for a short burst of ventricular tachycardia.

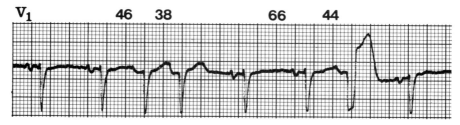

Figure 18.21. Three atrial premature beats, one with LBBB aberration illustrating the importance of the preceding cycle. The third APB ends a cycle of 44 (0.44 sec) and is conducted with LBBB aberration. The second APB ends a shorter cycle of only 38, but is not aberrantly conducted because its preceding cycle was only 46 (compared with 66).

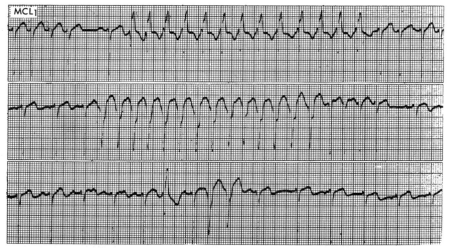

Figure 18.22. Runs of atrial tachycardia with aberrant conduction of the RBBB type in the *top strip* and of the LBBB type in the *middle strip*. In the *bottom strip*, both forms are present, separated by a single, more normally conducted beat. Note the typical rSR' contour for RBBB and the slick downstroke with the slurred upstroke of LBBB.

Figure 18.23 illustrates aberrancy that led to regrettable mistreatment. The *top strip* shows the patient's rhythm on admission: atrial tachycardia with 2:1 AV conduction. He was, therefore, started on digitalis and by the next morning (*second strip*) he frequently manifested 4:1 conduction ratios. Because of this "impairment" of conduction, digitalis was discontinued and quinidine started. The bottom strip was taken the following morning and shows the situation that developed at about midnight and led to night-long erroneous therapy for ventricular tachycardia. In fact, the bottom strip represents atrial tachycardia with 1:1 AV conduction and RBBB aberration. The quinidine, perhaps partly by its antivagal effect, but certainly through its slowing effect on the atrial rate from 210 to 192 beats/min, has enabled the AV node to conduct all of the ectopic atrial impulses. The resulting much-increased ventricular rate from approximately 90 to 192 beats/min produced a dangerous hypotension from which the patient was finally rescued with the combination of a pressor agent and countershock.

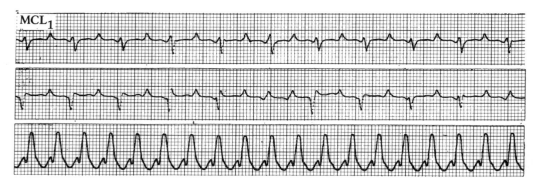

Figure 18.23. The strips are not continuous. On admission, the *top strip* shows atrial tachycardia with 2:1 AV conduction. The next day shows the middle strip shows 2:1 and 4:1 conduction. Twenty-four hours later the *bottom strip* shows a slower atrial rate with 1:1 conduction and RBBB aberration (mistaken and treated for hours as ventricular tachycardia).

In 1958, Rosenblueth documented the effect of atrial rate on normal AV conduction by pacing the atria of normal dogs. He found that, at an average rate of 257 beats/min, the animals developed Wenckebach periods and began to drop beats. At an average rate of 285 beats/min, they developed constant 2:1 conduction. Consider what this means in terms of ventricular rate. At an atrial rate of 286 beats/min, the ventricular rate will be 143 and, if the atrial rate is slowed to only 256 beats/min, the ventricular rate will be 256 beats/min. In other words, by slowing the atrial rate only 30 beats/min, the ventricular rate has increased 113 beats/min. This is why it can be so dangerous to give an atrial-slowing drug like lidocaine, quinidine, or even procainamide in the presence of atrial flutter or fibrillation when the ventricular response is already uncomfortably fast.[14] For example, if atrial flutter at a rate of 300 beats/min is associated with a 2:1 response, producing a ventricular rate of 150 beats/min, and a drug such as lidocaine is administered, the atrial rate may slow to 250 beats/min and AV conduction may increase to 1:1, producing a dangerous ventricular rate of 250 beats/min.

From a therapeutic point of view, an extremely important form of aberration may complicate atrial flutter. Uncomplicated and untreated, atrial flutter usually manifests an AV conduction ratio of 2:1. If digitalis, propranolol, or verapamil is then administered, the conduction pattern often changes to alternating 2:1 and 4:1, producing alternately longer and shorter cycles. At this stage, the beats that end the shorter cycles may develop aberrant conduction (Fig. 18.24). In someone receiving digitalis, this is likely to evoke a diagnosis of ventricular bigeminy and be attributed to digitalis toxicity. The still-needed digitalis is then wrongfully discontinued, when in fact the situation calls for more digitalis to further reduce conduction to a constant 4:1 with a normal ventricular rate, which is always the immediate goal of therapy.

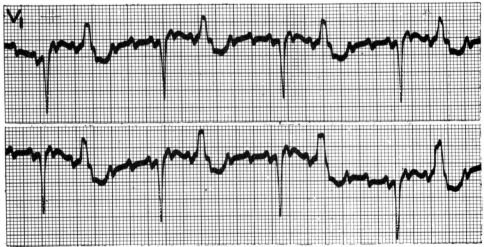

Figure 18.24. Atrial flutter with alternating 2:1 and 4:1 conduction and RBBB aberration of the beats that end the shorter cycles.

There is a striking tendency, not infrequently seen in aberration complicating tachyarrhythmias, for the aberrancy to be bilateral. This is seen in Figures 18.6, 18.10, 18.22, and 18.25. Another intriguing feature shown in these figures is the abrupt switch from one form of aberration to the other, from RBBB to LBBB or vice versa, via a single intervening normally conducted beat. Although unexplained, this phenomenon is sufficiently characteristic to assist in differentiating bilateral aberrancy from bifocal ectopy.

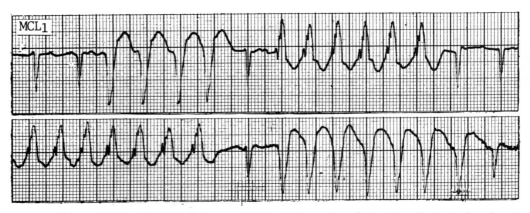

Figure 18.25. Atrial fibrillation and bilateral aberration. Both strips illustrate the abrupt change from one BBB aberration to the other BBB, with a single intervening normally conducted beat.

Most of the examples of aberration that we have seen so far have developed because the ventricular cycle, for some reason, suddenly shortened. At times, we see the same phenomenon appear as the sinus rhythm gradually accelerates. Figure 18.26 presents two examples of slight sinus acceleration in which the cycle gradually shortens until it becomes shorter than the refractory period of one of the bundle branches, whereupon aberrant conduction develops. It will persist until the cycle lengthens enough for normal conduction to occur. The rate at which the BBB develops is known as the *critical rate*, and when such block comes and goes with changes in the heart rate it is known as rate-dependent BBB.

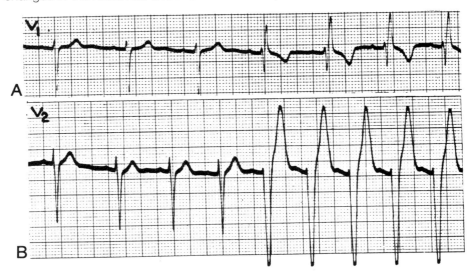

Figure 18.26. Rate-dependent BBB. **A.** From a 19-year-old student nurse. As her sinus rate accelerates and the cycle shortens in response to gentle exercise, progressively increasing degrees of RBBB develop (critical-rate or rate-dependent RBBB). **B.** From a 64-year-old man with severe coronary disease. As his sinus rate accelerates and the cycle shortens, LBBB develops at a critical rate of just over 100 beats/min.

Figure 18.27 presents another example of rate-dependent RBBB.

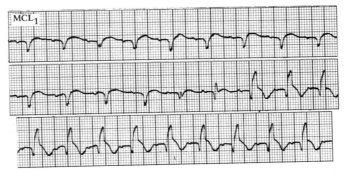

Figure 18.27. Rate-dependent RBBB develops in the *second strip* and continues through the *bottom strip*. As the sinus cycle shortens in the *middle of the second strip*, increasing degrees of RBBB aberration develop. Note that the PR remains constant.

One of the interesting features of rate-dependent BBB is that the critical rate at which the block develops is faster than the rate at which the BBB disappears. In Figure 18.28, as the sinus rhythm accelerates, normal conduction prevails at a cycle of 100 (rate of 60 beats/min) and the cycle at which the BBB develops is 91 (rate of 66 beats/min). However, as the rate slows, the BBB persists at a cycle of 100 (rate of 60 beats/min) and for normal conduction to resume, the cycle must lengthen further to 108 (rate of 56 beats/min).

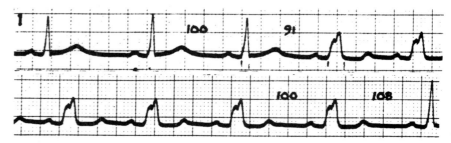

Figure 18.28. Rate-dependent LBBB. Strips are continuous. As the sinus rhythm acceler-ates, LBBB develops when the rate exceeds 60 beats/min (cycle length < 100). For normal conduction to resume, the rate must fall below 60 beats/min (cycle length > 100).

The two reasons for this difference in rate requirement during acceleration and deceleration are difficult to describe:

1. Since the refractory period of the ventricular conduction system is proportional to the length of the preceding ventricular cycle, it follows that as the rate accelerates the refractory periods get shorter and shorter (i.e., the potential for conduction progressively improves and, therefore, there is a tendency to preserve normal conduction). The converse is true as the rate slows.

2. More important, however, is the factor diagrammed in Figure 18.29. The shaded area in the RBB indicates the refractory segment that precludes conduction when the impulse first arrives and causes RBBB aberration. A moment later, the refractory segment has recovered and, when the transseptal impulse that has meanwhile negotiated the LBB approaches it, the RBB is again responsive and the impulse discharges it. For the impulse to travel down the LBB and through the septum requires about 0.06 sec. Thus, the previously refractory RBB is depolarized about 0.06 sec after the beginning of the QRS complex. As far as the RBB is concerned, therefore, its cycle begins about 0.06 sec after the beginning of the RBBB QRS complex. When you measure the cycle length conventionally from the beginning of one QRS complex to the beginning of the next, you are not giving the RBB a fair deal since its cycle did not begin until halfway through the first QRS complex. It follows that for normal conduction to resume, the cycle during deceleration must be longer than the critical cycle during acceleration by about 0.06 sec. This calculation fits nicely with the observed findings in Figure 18.28.

Figure 18.29. Diagram to illustrate one of the two mechanisms responsible for the fact that the critical rate is different during accelera-tion than during deceleration.

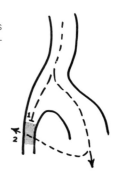

Another way in which the rate dependency of BBB may be revealed is when a sudden lengthening of the ventricular cycle causes the disappearance of a previously present BBB pattern. This is most often seen at the end of the lengthened cycle following an extrasystole. Figure 18.30 shows two examples of this phenomenon. The concept of critical rate is of greater importance in AV block than in BBB but has received even less attention. Analogous to the development of BBB at a given critical rate is the development of AV block when the atrial rate reaches a certain critical level and 1:1 conduction gives rise to Wenckebach periods and, at a somewhat faster rate, to 2:1 conduction. This is more important than critical rate BBB because failure to appreciate the role of rate in determining the AV conduction ratio has often led to unnecessarily aggressive therapy.

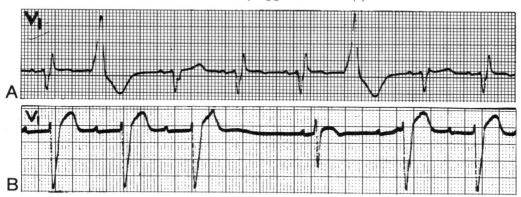

Figure 18.30. Examples of postextrasystolic revelation of rate-dependent BBB. In **A**, after each of the ventricular extrasystoles the returning sinus beat manifests a lesser degree of RBBB than do the sinus beats ending the normal (shorter) sinus cycles. In **B**, after three sinus beats conducted with first degree AV block and LBBB, a nonconducted atrial extrasystole results in a prolonged ventricular cycle at the end of which the returning sinus beat is conducted with a normal PR and normal intraventricular conduction, demonstrating that both the AV delay and the LBBB are rate dependent.

Progressively developing aberration, as in Figures 18.26A and 18.27, must be differentiated from progressive degrees of fusion as a ventricular ectopic rhythm takes over. If fusion develops by degrees, the PR interval must progressively shorten whereas if aberration gradually widens the QRS, the PR is likely to remain constant throughout the various stages of increasing aberrant conduction as seen in Figures 18.26A and 18.27.

TYPE B ABERRATION

The second form of ventricular aberration, Type B (Table 18.1), is due to anomalous activation at a supraventricular level (above the branching of the common bundle) which causes abnormal distribution to the ventricles to produce an aberrant complex. Although not usually included under the heading of ventricular aberration, Wolff-Parkinson-White (WPW) conduction causes this form of aberration. As a result of anomalous activation and conduction (via a Kent bundle) above the ventricles, activation of the ventricles is distorted (Fig. 18.31, *1*).

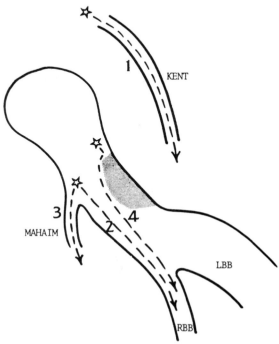

Figure 18.31. Diagram to illustrate the four forms of type B aberration. *1*, Kent-bundle (WPW) conduction; *2*, AV junctional impulse arising from an eccentrically placed focus spreading preferentially down the ipsilateral bundle branch; *3*, junctional impulse arising from an eccentrically placed focus spreading preferentially via a Mahaim tract; and *4*, a junctional impulse arising eccentrically and deflected contralaterally by a patch of diseased tissue.

A much more common form of aberration of this type is seen with AV junctional beats. Since there are innumerable potential pacemaker sites in the common bundle, it follows that most of them cannot be centrally located in the mainstream and, therefore, are situated off to one side. As most junctional pacemakers are eccentrically placed, and since longitudinal insulation between parallel fibers in the common bundle is effective[15], it follows that an impulse arising from such a pacemaker tends to be conducted down its side of the bundle and the corresponding bundle branch sooner than down the contralateral side and branch (Fig. 18.31, 2). The QRS complex registers the pattern of more or less conduction delay on the contralateral side. Such a mechanism obviously has nothing to do with cycle length and refractory periods. If the impulse arises eccentrically and spreads asymmetrically, it is not important whether it is an early, punctual, or late beat. This is why it is almost always the rule for junctional escape beats to show some degree of ventricular aberration. Figure 18.32 presents two examples of minor aberration of junctional escape beats. Although minor aberration is the rule, occasionally it assumes major proportions and can then be mistaken for ventricular ectopy.[16]

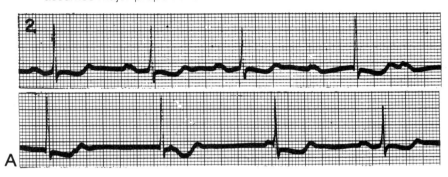
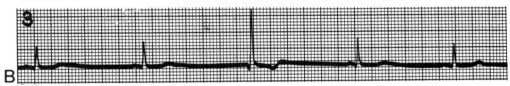

Figure 18.32. Minor aberration of junctional beats. **A.** The two strips are continuous. After three sinus beats showing intra-atrial block and first degree AV block, the fourth sinus impulse is blocked, resulting in four junctional escape beats. Note the slight but definite differences in contour: the junctional beats have small Q waves and taller R waves. **B.** After two conducted beats, the third beat is exactly on time but without benefit of the preceding P wave. Its form is obviously changed, but since it is normally narrow, it probably arises in the AV junction and is conducted with Type B aberration (one obviously cannot absolutely exclude a ventricular septal or fascicular origin).

A similar form of aberrant conduction can be produced if the eccentrically placed junctional pacemaker, situated near the origin of a *Mahaim tract* (Fig. 18.31, 3), delivers at least a part of its impulse via that tract and initiates a distorted QRS complex. Such delivery via Mahaim fibers has been called *preferential conduction.*[17] A similar form of aberration could result if, owing to disease affecting one side of the junction, the impulse were deflected toward the opposite side (Fig. 18.31, 4) and distributed asynchronously via the bundle branches to the ventricles.

TYPE C ABERRATION

The third form of aberration, Type C (Table 18.1), is characterized by the development of abnormal intraventricular conduction only at the end of a lengthened cycle. Since one would expect conduction to be better after a longer diastolic respite, this form is known as *paradoxical critical rate*. It is also sometimes referred to as bradycardia-dependent BBB, but this is unsatisfactory as an inclusive term because it is not always necessary to achieve a rate that merits the designation bradycardia (i.e., under 60 beats/min) for the BBB to develop: normal conduction may be present at a rate of 82 beats/min and the BBB may develop only if the cycle length increases to a point equaling a rate of 68 beats/min as in Figure 18.33.

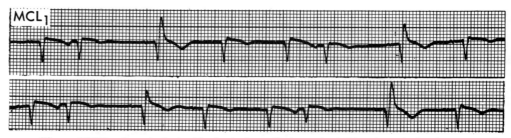

Figure 18.33. Paradoxical critical rate (type C aberration). The sinus rhythm is repeatedly interrupted by atrial extrasystoles. The conducted beats ending the lengthened post extrasystolic cycles all show RBBB whereas the shorter sinus cycles and the even shorter extrasystolic cycles show more normal intraventricular conduction.

So many theories have been advanced to explain this paradoxical phenomenon[18,19] that it is unlikely that any one of them is universally satisfactory. The currently popular explanation invokes a phase 4 phenomenon. It is well known that as a pacemaking cell spontaneously depolarizes during diastole (phase 4), it becomes less and less responsive to extraneous stimuli. To explain the paradoxical development of BBB after a lengthened cycle, it is assumed that Purkinje cells in the bundle branch are functioning as pacemakers and spontaneously depolarizing. Early in diastole, they will respond to and permit passage of an approaching impulse. Later, when depolarization has progressed further, they are unresponsive and conduction is impossible. Such an explanation is plausible, but proof is lacking.[18]

At other times, the paradoxical effect appears to be due to a vagal influence that both slows the rate and impairs conduction through the bundle branch. This, of course, involves the assumption that the subject is an oddity in whom autonomic innervation extends to the bundle branches. Another possibility in some cases postulates a critical level of perfusion to a bundle branch and that perfusion, which is barely adequate at the end of shorter cycles at faster rates, becomes inadequate by the end of the longer diastoles. The primary importance of all forms of ventricular aberration is that they may be confused with, and must be differentiated from, ventricular ectopy. This distinction becomes especially important when one is faced with a wide QRS tachycardia.

DIFFERENTIAL DIAGNOSIS OF WIDE QRS TACHYCARDIAS

Although there are numerous causes of wide QRS tachycardia (Table 18.4), the most commonly encountered problem is the distinction between VT and SVT with aberration. Whereas in the 1970s it was fashionable to mistake SVT with aberration for VT, in the 1980s the trend apparently reversed and it became the vogue to think that VT is SVT with aberration, often despite the presence of compelling clues favoring ventricular ectopy.

Table 18.4. Wide QRS Tachycardias

1. Monomorphous ventricular tachycardia
   a. Automatic
   b. Reentrant
2. Ventricular flutter
3. Dimorphous ventricular tachycardia
   a. Alternating
   b. Bidirectional
4. Polymorphous ventricular tachycardia—including torsades de pointes
5. Antidromic tachycardia
6. AV nodal reentrant tachycardia with "bystander" nodoventricular tract or Kent bundle
7. Any of the "narrow QRS" tachycardias listed in Table 12.1 with aberration or preexisting BBB

Morady[20], aware that many physicians held the mistaken belief that VT could not be hemodynamically tolerated, circulated to 196 physicians the 12-lead tracing of a morphologically typical left ventricular tachycardia in a man who maintained his blood pressure at 140/80 for 2 hours. They were asked for the diagnosis and to state how much they were influenced by the patient's hemodynamic status. Of the subset of physicians who were significantly influenced by the blood pressure, 96% made the wrong diagnosis. Dancy et al.[21] reported 163 paroxysms of VT in 24 patients, all of which were misdiagnosed as SVT with aberration. Twenty of the 24 patients received verapamil, and five of these became seriously hypotensive.

Shortly thereafter, Stewart et al.[22] reported 38 patients with VT of whom 15 (39%) were misdiagnosed and received verapamil. All developed hypotension and in two ventricular fibrillation supervened. Switzer et al.[23] told an even worse tale of similar disasters. Out of 33 wide QRS tachycardias, 28 of which turned out to be VT and the other 5 tachycardias complicating pre-excitation, only 7 had been correctly diagnosed and all had been treated with intravenous verapamil. Fifteen suffered hemodynamic collapse and 11 developed ventricular fibrillation.

In a subsequent survey of over 2500 cardiac nurses in the United States and England, using the same 12-lead tracing that Morady distributed to his physicians, 87% made the diagnosis of SVT with aberration. Of the remaining 13% who made the correct diagnosis, only 5% diagnosed VT because they recognized the telltale morphological clues. The remainder made a lucky guess. Experiences such as these underscore the widespread need for physicians and cardiac nurses to acquire knowledge of the numerous available clues which, when applied systematically, should enable them to arrive at the correct diagnosis in over 90% of the wide QRS tachycardias.[24] To achieve this percentage, one must be familiar with all of the diagnostic criteria, clinical and electrocardiographic. Of all of these, there is no doubt that details of the QRS morphology deserve the most attention.

HISTORICAL ESTABLISHMENT OF MORPHOLOGICAL POINTERS

Beginning in 1965, morphological clues were at first the result of clinical observation and deduction.[2,4,5] Before long, confirmation by electrophysiologists began to emerge. In 1972, Vera et al.[7] evaluated 1100 anomalous complexes during atrial fibrillation and confirmed that the triphasic (rsR') configuration in lead V1 offered 24 to 1 odds in favor of ventricular aberration, whereas a monophasic R or diphasic qR provided 9 to 1 odds in favor of ventricular ectopy.

In 1978 and 1982, Wellens et al.[8,9] analyzed the morphological features of 100 patients with proven VT and 100 with SVT and aberration. They again confirmed the value of triphasic patterns (rsR' in lead V1 and qRs in lead V6) in recognizing RBBB aberration and the monophasic R or diphasic qR with taller left peak (rabbit ear) in lead V1, and the rS and QS configurations in lead V6 as hallmarks of ventricular ectopy. They also introduced several new clues that favored ectopy including the single, symmetrical peak in lead V1, equiphasic QR in lead V1 or V6, and equiphasic RS in lead V1. They also observed that left axis deviation and a QRS duration greater than 0.14 sec favored ventricular ectopy.

Like Vera and coworkers, Gulamhusein et al.[6] examined anomalous beats during atrial fibrillation in 1985 and again confirmed many of the previously recognized clues. Some of the most important findings in the studies of Wellens and Gulamhusein are listed in Tables 18.5 and 18.6. Wellens[25] and Kindwall et al.[26] drew attention to differences in the V1 morphology of LBBB aberration and VT with negative QRS in lead V1. In LBBB, the downstroke is usually steep and the nadir of the QS or rS is reached in less than 0.06 sec, whereas in ectopy the nadir is reached later than 0.06 sec either because of an initial wide r wave, as previously described by Rosenbaum[27] and Swanick et al.[28], or because of a slurred downstroke.

Apart from details of the QRS morphology, the following additional features favoring ventricular ectopy should always be looked for:

1. Concordant positivity in the V leads;
2. Concordant negativity in the V leads;
3. Axis in the right upper quadrant (''no man's land'');
4. QRS interval wider than 0.14 sec[8,9];
5. Fusion beats;
6. Early nonaberrant ventricular capture beats;
7. Independent atrial activity.

Table 18.5. QRS Contours Favoring Ventricular Ectopy[a]

	Wellens[24,25]	Gulamhusein[6]
V1 (tall narrow peak)	15/15 (100%)	84/86 (98%)
V1 (tall narrow peak)	7/7 (100%)	177/187 (95%)
V6 (deep narrow)	27/31 (87%)	189/190 (100%)
V6 (deep narrow)	17/17 (100%)	38/40 (94%)

[a]In each pair of numbers, denominator is number of times contour was encountered; numerator is number of times it was ectopic.

Table 18.6. QRS Contours Favoring Ventricular Aberration

	Wellens[24,25]	Gulamhusein[6]
V1	38/41 (93%)	55/55 (100%)
V6	44/47 (94%)	27/27 (100%)

Key: In each pair of numbers, denominator is number of times contour was encountered, numerator is number of times it was aberrant.

GENERAL APPROACH TO THE DIAGNOSIS OF REGULAR TACHYCARDIAS

    With close attention to clinical detail, the bedside diagnosis of regular tachycardia can be surprisingly accurate. First some principles:

1. The proper posture for the diagnostician at the bedside is to apply the stethoscope to the precordium and eyes to the neck veins simultaneously.
2. Clues to search for are:
   a. The presence or absence of cannon "a" waves or flutter waves in the jugular pulse;
   b. Variation in the intensity of the first heart sound;
   c. Splitting of the heart sounds.
3. Splitting of the sounds is due to ventricular asynchrony whereas irregular cannon waves in the neck and variation in the intensity of the first sound are signs of dissociation between the atria and ventricles.
4. Signs of dissociation are at times more easily identified at the bedside than in the tracing because the independent P waves are often lost in the barrage of ventricular complexes.
5. Dissociation does not prove ventricular tachycardia but it excludes atrial tachycardia and, therefore, makes ventricular tachycardia that much more likely. Dissociation can occur between atrial and AV junctional pacemakers and, if ventricular aberration is also present, the imitation of ventricular tachycardia may be perfect clinically and electrocardiographically.
6. Regular cannon waves (with every beat) may be seen in any SVT or in VT with 1:1 retrograde conduction.

    The electrocardiographic recognition of typical supraventricular tachycardia is easy. The difficulty arises in separating ventricular tachycardia from a supraventricular tachycardia combined with ventricular aberration. In attempting to make this separation, QRS morphology should receive primary attention. If characteristic features are observed, accuracy and speed are both served, but if morphologic clues are absent or equivocal, one must look elsewhere.

    Although the demonstration of dissociation is of considerable diagnostic value, and evidence of it should always be sought, it must not be depended upon. If P waves are not recognizable even in lead V1, more specialized leads may be informative (Chapter 2, "Recording the Electrocardiogram"). A precordial lead known as S_5 may be tried.[29] For this lead, the positive electrode is placed in the 5th right intercostal space close to the sternal border and the negative electrode over the manubrium. If this fails, an esophageal[16,30] or intracardiac[31] lead will almost always be successful in displaying P waves. Alternatively, if a tracing is taken during the administration of procainamide[32] or acetylcholine[33] intravenously, the ventricular rate will often slow under their influence and P waves will become apparent in the now lengthened intervals between ventricular complexes. Such maneuvers, however, are seldom necessary or desirable.

    With these many principles in mind, we can formulate a systematic approach to the regular tachycardia:

    1. First look at the neck veins and listen to the first heart sound with the patient holding his breath. If there are irregular cannon waves in the neck and/or the first heart sound varies in intensity from beat to beat, you have evidence of dissociation and this suggests a ventricular tachycardia. If the first heart sound is of unvarying intensity and there are either no cannon waves or regular cannon waves in the neck, this is evidence against dissociation and the tachycardia is probably supraventricular (exceptions include ventricular tachycardia with retrograde 1:1 conduction and ventricular tachycardia with concurrent atrial fibrillation). If an electrocardiograph is available, do not use carotid sinus or other vagal stimulation until after a tracing has been taken, because if the tachycardia is supraventricular the vagal maneuver may terminate it, leaving no graphic record to document the paroxysm.

    2. Take an electrocardiogram and look at the QRS pattern. If it is normal in contour and duration, the tachycardia is supraventricular. If it is widened and bizarre, the tachycardia may be either ventricular or supraventricular with aberrant

ventricular conduction. If it is widened, study the V1/V6 morphology, observe the frontal plane axis, and look for the other morphological clues. Try to find a lead in which P waves are identifiable and look for fusion beats. If previous tracings are available, look for isolated extrasystoles and compare their pattern with that of the tachycardia.

3. If the diagnosis is still in doubt, try carotid sinus massage or other vagal stimulation. If the tachycardia is supraventricular, this may terminate it. In atrial flutter, vagal stimulation may temporarily halve the rate by increasing the AV conduction ratio from 2:1 to 4:1. If the tachycardia is ventricular, it will usually remain unaffected.[34]

4. If there is still doubt, take a lead S_5. If this is unrevealing, consider passing an esophageal or intracardiac electrode. A satisfactory esophageal or intracardiac lead will always reveal P waves when they are unidentifiable in conventional leads. In practice, however, these invasive techniques are almost never needed and should certainly be avoided whenever possible, especially in patients with acute myocardial infarction.

5. If doubt remains, one may administer procainamide intravenously with appropriate precautions. If the tachycardia is ventricular, this will be a correct treatment. If it is supraventricular, the drug may momentarily block AV conduction and reveal the telltale atrial rhythm between the now more widely spaced ventricular complexes.[32]

6. If facilities for recording His bundle electrograms are at hand and the clinical circumstances warrant the procedure, this technique may provide the only certain means of differentiating ventricular aberration from ectopy.[35]

In summary:

Clinically

1. Look for:
   a. Wide splitting of heart sounds;
   b. Variation in the intensity of the first sound;
   c. Cannon waves.
2. Observe the effect of carotid sinus stimulation.

Electrocardiographically

1. Study the QRS morphology.
2. Identify the P waves:
   a. In the conventional leads, especially II and V1;
   b. In lead S_5;
   c. In the esophageal or intracardiac lead;
   d. During administration of procainamide.
3. Look for fusion beats.
4. Look for isolated extrasystoles or BBB in previous tracings if available.

GLOSSARY

Ashman's phenomenon: the intraventricular conduction of an impulse that completes a short cardiac cycle following a long cycle is likely to be aberrant because the long cycle results in prolongation of depolarization and delay of repolarization.

Critical rate: a cycle length so short that part of the ventricular Purkinje system has not yet recovered from its previous activation, resulting in aberrant conduction of a supraventricular impulse.

Mahaim tract: a rarely occurring congenital anomaly in which Purkinje fibers from the common (HIS) bundle lead into the septal myocardium.

Paradoxical critical rate: a cycle length so long that part of the ventricular Purkinje system has already begun the process of impulse formation and, therefore, conducts the supraventricular impulse so slowly that aberrancy occurs.

Preferential conduction: initial activation of the ventricles via an abnormal part of the special conduction system called Mahaim fibers.

Rule of bigeminy: a VPB is likely to occur following a long cycle because the long cycle results in prolongation of depolarization and delay of repolarization, facilitating reentry of the impulse.

REFERENCES

1. Gouaux JL, Ashman R. Auricular fibrillation with aberration simulating ventricular paroxysmal tachycardia. Am Heart J 1947;34:366.
2. Sandler IA, Marriott HJL. The differential morphology of anomalous ventricular complexes of RBBB-type in lead V1; ventricular ectopy versus aberration. Circulation 1965;31:551.
3. Kulbertus HE, de Laval-Rutten F, Casters P. Vectorcardiographic study of aberrant conduction; anterior displacement of QRS, another form of intraventricular block. Br Heart J 1976;38:549.
4. Marriott HJL, Sandler IA. Criteria, old and new, for differentiating between ectopic ventricular beats and aberrant ventricular conduction in the presence of atrial fibrillation. Prog Cardiovasc Dis 1966;9:18.
5. Marriott HJL. Differential diagnosis of supraventricular and ventricular tachycardia. Geriatrics 1970;25:91.
6. Gulamhusein S, Yee R, Ko PT, Klein GJ. Electrocardiographic criteria for differentiating aberrancy and ventricular extrasystole in chronic atrial fibrillation: validation by intracardiac recordings. J Electrocardiol 1985;18:41.
7. Vera Z, Cheng TO, Ertem G, Shoaleh-var M, Wickramasekaran R, Wadhwa K. His bundle electrography for evaluation of criteria in differentiating ventricular ectopy from aberrancy in atrial fibrillation. Circulation 1972;45(suppl II):355.
8. Wellens HJJ, Bar FW, Lie KI. The value of the electrocardiogram in the differential diagnosis of a tachycardia with a widened QRS complex. Am J Med 1978;64:27.
9. Wellens HJJ, Bar FW, Vanagt EJ, Brugada P. Medical treatment of ventricular tachycardia; considerations in the selection of patients for surgical treatment. Am J Cardiol 1982;49:187.
10. Bailey JC. The electrocardiographic differential diagnosis of supraventricular tachycardia with aberrancy versus ventricular tachycardia. Pract Cardiol 1980;6:118.
11. Pietras RJ, Mautner R, Denes P, Wu D, Dhingra R, Towne W, Rosen KM. Chronic recurrent right and left ventricular tachycardia: comparison of clinical, hemodynamic and angiographic findings. Am J Cardiol 1977;40:32.
12. Zipes DP. Diagnosis of ventricular tachycardia. Drug Ther 1979;9:83.
13. Niazi I, McKinney J, Caceres J, Jazayeri M, Tchou P, Akhtar M. Reevaluation of surface ECG criteria for the diagnosis of wide QRS tachycardia. Circulation 1987;76(suppl IV):412.
14. Marriott HJL, Bieza CF. Alarming ventricular acceleration after lidocaine administration. Chest 1972;61:682.
15. Sherf L, James TN. A new electrocardiographic concept: synchronized sinoventricular conduction. Dis Chest 1969;55:127.
16. Kistin AD. Problems in the differentiation of ventricular arrhythmia from supraventricular arrhythmia with abnormal QRS. Prog Cardiovasc Dis 1966;9:1.
17. Pick A. Aberrant ventricular conduction of escaped beats: preferential and accessory pathways in the AV junction. Circulation 1956;13:702.
18. Gambetta M, Childers RW. Reverse rate related bundle branch block. J Electrocardiol 1973;6:153.
19. Massumi RA. Bradycardia-dependent bundle branch block. A critique and proposed criteria. Circulation 1968;38:1066.
20. Morady F, Baerman JM, DiCarlo LA Jr, DeBuittleir M, Krol RB, Wahr DW. A prevalent misconception regarding wide-complex tachycardias. JAMA 1985;254:2790.
21. Dancy M, Camm AJ, Ward D. Misdiagnosis of chronic recurrent ventricular tachycardia. Lancet 1985;2:320.
22. Stewart RB, Bardy GH, Greene HL. Wide-complex tachycardia: misdiagnosis and outcome after emergent therapy. Ann Intern Med 1986;104:766.
23. Switzer DF, Henthorn RW, Olshansky B, Moreira D, Waldo AL. Dire consequences of verapamil administration for wide QRS tachycardia. Circulation 1986;74(suppl II):105.
24. Wellens HJJ, Kulbertus HE, eds. What's new in electrocardiology. Boston: Martinus Nijhoff, 1981:184–199.
25. Wellens HJJ. The wide QRS tachycardias. Ann Intern Med 1986;104:879.
26. Kindwall E, Brown JP, Josephson ME. ECG criteria for ventricular and supraventricular tachycardia in wide complex tachycardias with left bundle branch morphology. J Am Coll Cardiol 1987;9:206A.
27. Rosenbaum MB. Classification of ventricular extrasystoles according to form. J Electrocardiol 1969;2:289.
28. Swanick EJ, LaCamera F Jr, Marriott HJL. Morphologic features of right ventricular ectopic beats. Am J Cardiol 1972;30:888.

29. Lian, Cassimatis, Hebert. Interet de la derivation precordiale auriculaire S_5 dans le diagnostic des troubles du rythme auriculaire. Arch Mal Coeur 1952;45:481.
30. Copeland GD, Tullis IF, Brody DA. Clinical evaluation of a new esophageal electrode, with particular reference to the bipolar esophageal electrocardiogram. II. Observations in cardiac arrhythmias. Am Heart J 1959;57:874.
31. Vogel JHK, Tabari K, Averill KH, Blount SG Jr. A simple technique for identifying P waves in complex arrhythmias. Am Heart J 1964;67:158.
32. Bernstein LM, Pascale LR, Schoolman HM, Foley EF. Intravenous procaine amide as an aid to differentiate flutter with bundle branch block from paroxysmal ventricular tachycardia. Am Heart J 1954;48:82.
33. Schoolman HM, Bernstein LM, Littman A, Pascale LR. Acetylcholine in differential diagnosis and treatment of paroxysmal tachycardia. Am Heart J 1960;60:526.
34. Hess DS, Hanlon T, Scheinman M, Budge R, Desai J. Termination of ventricular tachycardia by carotid sinus massage. Circulation 1982;65:627.
35. Damato AN, Lau SH. Clinical value of the electrogram of the conduction system. Prog Cardiovasc Dis 1970;13:119.

CHAPTER 19

Decreased Automaticity

When the automaticity of the sinus node is decreased, the result is a bradyarrhythmia originating either from the sinus node itself or from a "lower" site in the pacemaking and conduction system (see Fig. 1.6). When the rhythm originates from the sinus node, the term *sinus bradycardia* is used, and when it originates from a lower site the terms *atrial rhythm, junctional rhythm,* or *ventricular rhythm* are used. These are not truly arrhythmias but rather *escape rhythms* which attempt to compensate for the problem of decreased sinus node automaticity. Figure 19.1 illustrates the various consequences of the slowing of sinus automaticity to < 60 beats/min. The automaticity of the lower site is suppressed while the sinus node is pacemaking normally, but it then returns (escapes) at its own slower rate when the sinus node fails.

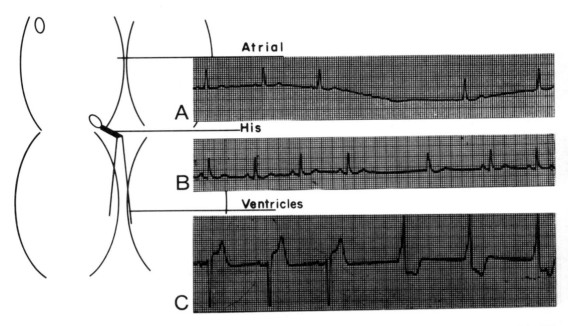

Figure 19.1. Normal escape from an atrial (**A**), His bundle (**B**), or ventricular Purkinje (**C**) site after the sinus impulses have failed to appear. The *small ovals* in the schematic indicate the SA and AV nodes while the common bundle (His) and bundle branches are shown to lead toward the ventricles from the AV node. (From Wagner GS, Waugh RA, Ramo BW. Cardiac arrhythmias. New York: Churchill Livingstone, 1983:4.)

MECHANISMS OF BRADYARRHYTHMIAS OF DECREASED AUTOMATICITY

 There are three causes of decreased automaticity:

1. Physiologic sinus slowing;
2. Physiologic or pathologic enhancement of parasympathetic nervous activity;
3. Pathologic pacemaker failure.

Physiologic Sinus Slowing

Although a rate of < 60 beats/min is technically termed a bradyarrhythmia, it is often a normal variation, especially in well-trained athletes whose heart rates may be as low as the thirties at rest. The rhythm may be either sinus bradycardia or, as shown in Figure 19.2, junctional or ventricular rhythm. Bradycardia is a physiologic reaction to relaxation or sleeping, when the parasympathetic effect on cardiac automaticity dominates over the sympathetic effect. Even in the respiratory cycle there is slowing of the sinus rate, often into the bradycardia range, during the expiratory phase (see Fig. 3.13).

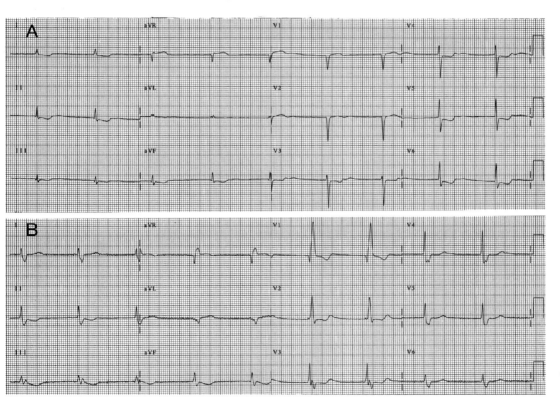

Figure 19.2. Junctional (**A**) and ventricular (**B**) rhythms in which the P waves are obscured by the QRS complexes. The slow rate is typical for impulse formation in the more distal common bundle (**A**) and ventricular Purkinje (**B**) components of the pacemaking and conduction system. The V1 positive QRS complexes in **B** indicate that the escape site is in the left bundle.

Physiologic or Pathologic Enhancement of Parasympathetic Activity

All cells with pacemaking capability are under some influence of the sympathetic and parasympathetic aspects of the autonomic nervous system. This influence is greatest in the sinus node and diminishes in the lower sites. Usually, the changing autonomic balance causes a gradual increase or decrease in the pacing rate. However, many factors are capable of inducing a sudden increase in parasympathetic activity and decrease in sympathetic activity. These factors include:

1. Fright;
2. Carotid sinus massage;
3. Hypersensitivity of the carotid sinus;
4. Straining (i.e., a Valsalva maneuver);
5. Ocular pressure;
6. Increased intracranial pressure;
7. Sudden movement from a recumbent to an upright position;
8. Drugs which cause pooling of blood by dilating the veins.

This is termed a *vasovagal reaction (reflex)* because there is a prominent vascular relaxation component in addition to cardiac slowing, and because it is mediated by the vagus, the principal parasympathetic nerve. Typical bradyarrhythmias which occur suddenly during a vasovagal reaction are presented in Figure 19.3. The combination of these two components of the reflex results in a reduction in cardiac output so severe that it may cause dizziness or even loss of consciousness. This is termed *vasovagal syncope* or fainting. It is typically reversed when the individual falls into a recumbent position, thereby increasing venous return to the heart. When fainting occurs with the individual in the recumbent position, it can usually be reversed by leg elevation.

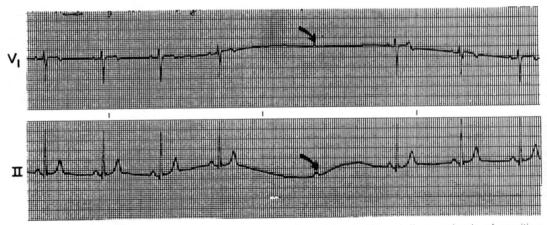

Figure 19.3. In this simultaneous recording of leads *V1* and *II*, an episode of vomiting causes a sudden increase in parasympathetic activity manifested by both slowing of the sinus rate and failure of AV conduction (note the nonconducted P waves indicated by the *arrows*). The increase in parasympathetic activity also suppresses escape pacemakers and the pause is interrupted only by the return of sinus rhythm. (From Wagner GS, Waugh RA, Ramo BW. Cardiac arrhythmias. New York: Churchill Livingstone, 1983:208.)

A single physiologic vasovagal reaction can have severe pathologic consequences if the individual is injured during the fall, or if the required change in body position is not possible. The autonomic reflex itself may become pathologic, resulting in *neurocardiogenic syncope.*[1-3] Repetitive, severe, and sudden episodes of bradyarrhythmias with vasodilation occur and medical interventions are required to prevent serious injury or death.

Pathologic Pacemaker Failure

When a sudden period of complete absence of P waves appears on the ECG, the term *asystole* is used. It is tempting to attribute the problem solely to the sinus node and pathologic pacemaker failure. The term *sick sinus syndrome* is often applied. However, if the problem were limited to the sinus node, there would not be any serious bradyarrhythmia. A 1- to 2-sec pause would be interrupted by escape from a lower site with impulse formation capability (Fig. 19.4).

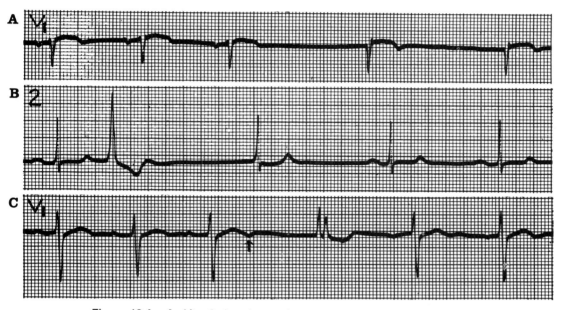

Figure 19.4. **A.** After 3 sinus beats, there is no further evidence of atrial activity, but then two junctional escape beats result. **B.** The pause following a ventricular premature beat ends with junctional escape beat. **C.** After 3 sinus beats, a nonconducted atrial premature beat (*arrow*) provides a cycle long enough for the escape from the ventricular Purkinje system. (From Marriott HJL. ECG/PDQ. Baltimore: Williams & Wilkins, 1987:171.)

Therefore, a prolonged atrial pause is caused by either:

1. Enhanced parasympathetic activity; or
2. Impairment of all cells with impulse formation capability.

Although "sick pacemaker syndrome" would be a more accurate term, sick sinus syndrome is used here because of its general acceptance. Its characteristics are:

1. Bradyarrhythmia at rest;
2. Incapability to appropriately increase the pacemaking rate with increased sympathetic nervous activity;
3. Absence of escape rhythms when the sinus rate slows;
4. Sensitivity to suppression of impulse formation by various drugs;
5. Sensitivity to suppression of impulse formation by a reentrant tachyarrhythmia[4,5] (Fig. 19.5).

Lead II

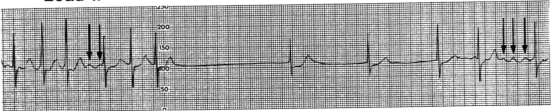

Figure 19.5. In this example of atrial flutter/fibrillation (the *arrow* indicates the atrial waves), the arrhythmia terminated abruptly and was followed by a 2.5-sec pause. All potential atrial, junctional, and ventricular pacemakers were suppressed during the tachycardia. An escape junctional pacemaker eventually emerged. After 3 beats, atrial reentry recurred and atrial flutter/fibrillation reappeared. (From Wagner GS, Waugh RA, Ramo BW. Cardiac arrhythmias. New York: Churchill Livingstone, 1983:210.)

Sick sinus syndrome is a part of the *tachycardia-bradycardia syndrome*[6,7] in which bursts of an atrial tachyarrhythmia, often atrial fibrillation, alternate with prolonged pauses (Fig. 19.6).

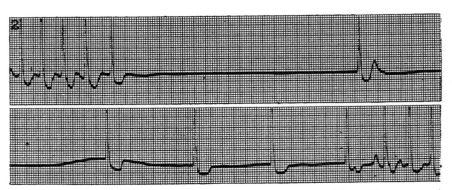

Figure 19.6. An irregular atrial tachycardia stops abruptly and is followed by a 4-sec sinus pause. The junctional rhythm at a rate of 40 beats/min is interrupted by a return of the atrial tachycardia.

Although sick sinus syndrome predominantly affects the elderly, the disease has been recognized as early as the first day of life.[8] Temporary and reversible manifestations of the syndrome can be caused by digitalis, quinidine, beta-blockers, or aerosol propellants. The chronic progressive syndrome was formerly believed to be due to ischemia, but a postmortem angiographic study of the sinus nodal artery confirmed vascular involvement in less than one-third of the 25 subjects with the chronic syndrome.[9] Sick sinus syndrome may result from inflammatory diseases, cardiomyopathy, amyloidosis,[10] collagen disease, metastatic disease, or surgical injury. In many patients, no cause is evident and it is classified as idiopathic. In these patients, it may be part of a sclerodegenerative process also affecting the lower parts of the cardiac pacemaking and conduction system.

Two complications that affect the prognosis of sick sinus syndrome are atrial fibrillation and AV block. During a 3-year follow-up, atrial fibrillation developed in 16% and AV block in 8% of those studied. Atrial fibrillation affected patients treated with AAI pacemakers much less often (4%) than those treated with VVI (22%) models. Furthermore, the incidence of systemic embolism was greater with VVI pacing (13%) than with AAI (1.6%) (Chapter 21, "Artificial Cardiac Pacemakers").[11]

The diagnosis usually can be made from the standard ECG or a 24-hour Holter recording, always carefully correlated with the clinical history. One should be careful not to overdiagnose the syndrome. Pauses of 3 sec or more, although uncommon, do not necessarily indicate a poor prognosis, do not usually cause symptoms, and do not require pacing if the patient is asymptomatic.[12] In some patients, additional more sophisticated tests may be required. One of the best of these is the sinus node recovery time after rapid atrial pacing.[13,14] A sinus node electrogram is useful in recognizing exit block (SA block) as the underlying mechanism.[15] Sinus node disorders probably account for half of the permanent pacemakers implanted in the United States.[16]

SINOATRIAL (SA) BLOCK

 SA block is caused by failure of the impulse to emerge from the sinus node. However, it is often impossible to determine the mechanism responsible for an absent P wave, and SA block is too often loosely and erroneously diagnosed. It should be diagnosed only when a mathematical relationship between the longer and shorter sinus cycles can be demonstrated or when the sinus cycles show the characteristic sequence of a Wenckebach period (Chapter 20, "Atrioventricular Block").

SA block is characterized by the intermittent failure of the impulse to emerge from the SA node, resulting in occasional beats that are completely absent (Fig. 19.7). When no such pattern can be established, "sinus pause" is a useful and appropriate term for the abnormally long cycle, qualified by a statement of its duration (e.g., a 4.5-sec sinus pause).

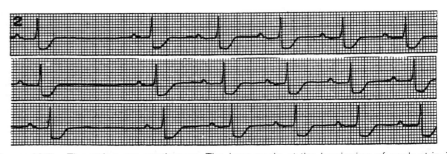

 Figure 19.7. The strips are continuous. The long cycle at the beginning of each strip is due to an absent sinus beat—an entire P-QRS-T sequence is missing.

PERSPECTIVE ON SINUS PAUSES

Sudden sinus pauses are common and important arrhythmias. However, it is often impossible to determine the etiology using the standard ECG or any other clinical test. When the sinus pauses are brief, the differential diagnosis includes sinus node failure, sinoatrial block, and an APB that fails to conduct to the ventricles (Chapter 13, "Premature Beats"). It is often impossible to reach a conclusion because underlying sinus arrhythmia makes it difficult to determine whether the pause is a precise multiple of the PP interval (Fig. 19.7), and the premature P wave is frequently obscured by a T wave (see Figs. 13.7 and 13.8).

When the pauses are prolonged, APBs are not a consideration and failure of all pacemaking cells, rather than only the sinus node, must be considered. The differential between abnormal control of these pacemakers by the autonomic nervous system and abnormality within the pacemaking cells is often difficult to determine. Even the tilt table test may not be helpful because results can be either falsely positive or falsely negative.

When sinus pauses are brief, no clinical intervention is required, and the patient may not be at future risk for either the generalized pacemaker failure or autonomic abnormality that produces prolonged pauses. When sinus pauses are prolonged, it may be necessary to proceed with treatment without differentiating between a neurologic and cardiologic etiology.

GLOSSARY

Asystole: a rhythm synonymous with sinus pause in which there is a period of slowing of the heart rate with neither atrial nor ventricular activity present on the ECG.

Atrial rhythm: a rhythm with a rate less than 100 beats/min with abnormally directed P waves (indicating origination from a site in the atria other than the sinus node) preceding each QRS complex.

Escape rhythms: rhythms that originate from sites in the pacemaking and conduction system other than the sinus node following a pause created by the failure of either the normal sinus impulse formation or atrioventricular impulse conduction.

Junctional rhythm: a rhythm with a rate less than 100 beats/min with an inverted P wave direction visible in the frontal plane leads and normal appearing QRS complexes. The P waves may precede or follow the QRS complexes or may be obscured because they occur during the QRS complexes.

Neurocardiogenic syncope: occurs when an individual experiences vasovagal reactions because of some factor which causes increased parasympathetic or decreased sympathetic nervous system activity. It may be detected using a head-up tilt test.

Sick sinus syndrome: inadequate function of cardiac cells with pacemaking capability, resulting in continuous or intermittent slowing of the heart rate at rest and an inability to appropriately increase the rate with exercise.

Tachycardia-bradycardia syndrome: both rapid and slow rhythms are present. The rapid rhythms tend to appear when the rate slows abnormally while the slow rhythms are prominent immediately following the sudden cessation of a rapid rhythm.

Vasovagal reaction (reflex): sudden slowing of the heart rate by either decreased impulse formation (sinus pause) or decreased impulse conduction (AV block) resulting from increased parasympathetic or decreased sympathetic nervous system activity. The slowing of the cardiac rhythm is accompanied by peripheral vascular dilation.

Vasovagal syncope: loss of consciousness caused by a vasovagal reaction. Consciousness is almost always regained when the individual falls into a recumbent position because this results in increased venous return to the heart.

Ventricular rhythm: a rhythm with a rate less than 100 beats/min with abnormally wide QRS complexes. There may be either retrograde association or AV dissociation.

REFERENCES

1. Abboud FM. Neurocardiogenic syncope. N Engl J Med 1993;328:1117–1120.
2. Fouad FM, Siitthisook S, Vanerio G, Maloney J, Okabe M, Jaeger F, Schluchter M, Maloney JD. Sensitivity and specificity of the tilt table test in young patients with unexplained syncope. Pace 1993;16:394–400.
3. Thilenius OG, Ryd KJ, Husayni J. Variations in expression and treatment of transient neurocardiogenic instability. Am J Cardiol 1992;69:1193–1195.
4. Lown B. Electrical reversion of atrial fibrillation. Br Heart J 1967;29:469.
5. Ferrer MI. The sick sinus syndrome. Mt. Kisco, NY: Futura Publishing, 1974.
6. Kaplan BM, Langendorf R, Lev M, Pick A. Tachycardia-bradycardia syndrome (so-called "sick sinus syndrome"). Am J Cardiol 1973;31:497.
7. Moss AJ, Davis RJ. Brady-tachy syndrome. Prog Cardiovasc Dis 1974;16:439.
8. Ector H, Van der Hauwaert LG. Sick sinus syndrome in childhood. Br Heart J 1980;44:684.
9. Shaw DB, Linker NJ, Heaver PA, Evans R. Chronic sinoatrial disorder (sick sinus syndrome): a possible result of cardiac ischemia. Br Heart J 1987;58:598.
10. Evans R, Shaw DB. Pathological studies in sinoatrial disorder (sick sinus syndrome). Br Heart J 1977;39:778.
11. Sutton R, Kenny RA. The natural history of sick sinus syndrome. Pace 1986;9:1110.
12. Hilgard J, Ezri MD, Denes P. Significance of ventricular pauses of three seconds or more detected on twenty-four-hour Holter recordings. Am J Cardiol 1984;55:1005.
13. Chung EK. Sick sinus syndrome: current views. Mod Concepts Cardiovasc Dis 1980:49;61,67.
14. Gann D, Tolentino A, Samet P. Electrophysiologic evaluation of elderly patients with sinus bradycardia. Ann Intern Med 1979;90:24.
15. Yeh SJ, Lin FC, Wu D. Complete sinoatrial block in two patients with bradycardia-tachycardia syndrome. J Am Coll Cardiol 1987;9:1184.
16. Kaplan BM. Sick sinus syndrome [Editorial]. Arch Intern Med 1978;138:28.

CHAPTER 20

Atrioventricular Block

Atrioventricular (AV) block refers to an abnormality in electrical conduction between the atria and ventricles. The term *heart block* also has been used. Normal AV conduction was discussed in Chapter 3 ("Interpretation of the Normal Electrocardiogram") and the parts of the cardiac pacemaking and conduction system that electrically connect the atrial and ventricular myocardium are illustrated in Figure 3.1. The term *degree* is used to indicate the severity of AV block. Severity can vary from minor (first degree) where all impulses are conducted with delay, through moderate (second degree) where some impulses fail to conduct, to complete (third degree) where no impulses are conducted.

SEVERITY OF AV BLOCK

First Degree AV Block

The "normal" PR interval measures between 0.12 and 0.20 sec. *First degree AV block* is generally defined as a prolongation of AV conduction time (PR interval) to >0.20 sec. In the analysis of records from normal young people, the incidence of a prolonged PR interval is between 0.5%[1] and 2%[2]. In healthy middle-aged men, a prolonged PR interval in the presence of a normal QRS complex does not affect the prognosis and is not related to ischemic heart disease.[3] Figure 20.1 illustrates two examples of first degree AV block: the first is minor, with a PR of 0.24 sec, while the second shows extreme PR lengthening.

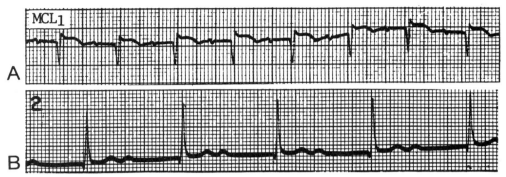

Figure 20.1. Two examples of first degree AV block. **A** is from a patient with an acute myocardial infarction and minor PR prolongation to 0.24 sec. **B** shows marked prolongation to 0.57 to 0.60 sec.

Second Degree AV Block

By definition, *second degree AV block* is present when one or more, but not all, of the atrial impulses fail to reach the ventricles because of impaired conduction. Examples of APBs which fail to conduct simply because they occur early were presented in Chapter 13 ("Premature Beats") (see Figs. 13.7 and 13.8). This is not considered AV block. Figure 20.2 presents an example of on time P waves that fail to conduct to the ventricles.

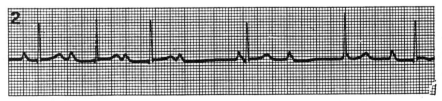

Figure 20.2. The atrial rate is in the normal range with the typical variation of sinus arrhythmia. The PR intervals prior to the 2nd, 3rd, 5th, and 6th QRS complexes are prolonged, indicating first degree AV block. The 4th P wave is not conducted at all, indicating second degree AV block. Note that the interval between the final two P waves is twice the other PP intervals, indicating that a nonconducted P wave is concealed as a slight deformity in the 5th QRS complex.

The block may be intermittent (Fig. 20.3A) or continuous (Fig. 20.3B), and there may be any ratio of P waves to QRS complexes (Fig. 20.4).

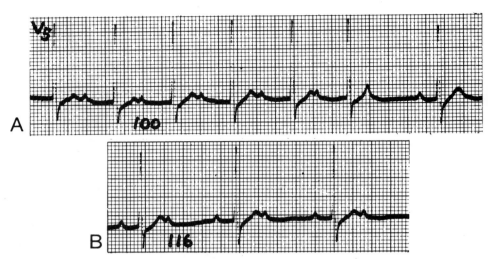

Figure 20.3. In **A**, there is continuous first degree block with intermittent second degree block. In a later recording (**B**) there is continuous second degree block with a 2:1 A:V relationship.

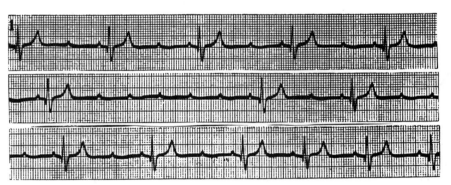

Figure 20.4. There is continuous second degree block, but with A:V relationships varying from 2:1 (*bottom strip*), through 3:1 (*all three strips*), to 7:1 (*middle strip*).

The atrial rate should be considered in determining the clinical significance of second degree AV block. As discussed in Chapter 15 ("Atrial Flutter/Fibrillation Spectrum"), conduction of only some of the atrial impulses is essential for clinical stability in the presence of atrial flutter/fibrillation. Chapter 14 ("Accelerated Automaticity") (see Fig. 14.6) indicates that second degree AV block commonly occurs along with atrial tachycardia, particularly when there is digitalis toxicity. Only when the AV block occurs in the absence of an atrial tachyarrhythmia is it considered the primary aspect of the cardiac arrhythmia (Fig. 20.5). When the second degree AV block accompanies sinus pauses (Chapter 19, "Decreased Automaticity"), the etiology is most likely not within the heart itself, but rather in its autonomic nervous control.

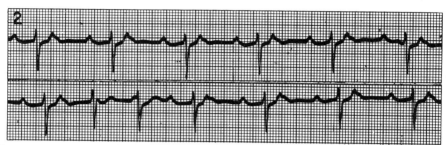

Figure 20.5. The atrial rate is in the tachycardia range (116 beats/min) and the P waves are normally directed in lead 2, indicating that the rhythm is sinus tachycardia. Although the high sympathetic tone that has accelerated the sinus rate would also be expected to enhance AV nodal conduction, both first and second degree AV block are present.

Second degree AV block usually occurs in the AV node[4,5] and is associated with reversible conditions such as acute inferior myocardial infarction or rheumatic fever, or treatment with digitalis, a beta-adrenergic blocker, or a calcium channel blocker. Generally a transient rhythm disturbance, it seldom progresses to complete AV block. However, of one series of 16 children manifesting second degree block, 7 developed complete block.[6] Chronic second degree AV block may occasionally occur in many conditions including aortic valve disease, atrial septal defect, amyloidosis, Reiter's syndrome, and mesothelioma of the AV node.

Third Degree AV Block

When no atrial impulses are conducted to the ventricles, the rhythm is termed *third degree AV block,* and the clinical condition is determined by the escape capability of the more distal Purkinje cells. There is quite adequate junctional escape shown in Figure 20.6A, less optimal ventricular escape in Figure 20.6B, and no escape at all in Figure 20.6C.

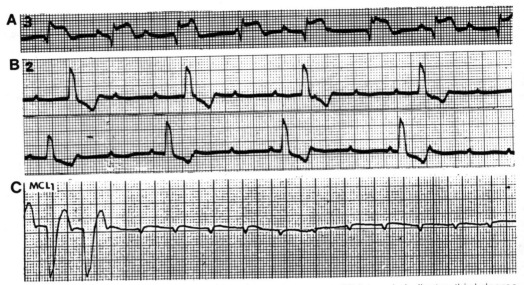

Figure 20.6. **A.** The varying PR interval with constant RR intervals indicates third degree AV block. The QRS complexes are not prolonged, indicating escape from the junction (common bundle). The rate of 70 beats/min indicates acceleration over the typical junctional rate of < 60 beats/min (**B**). There is third degree AV block with ventricular (bundle branch) escape indicated by wide QRS complexes at a regular rate of about 40 beats/min. (**C**). There is third degree AV block with no escape at all, producing prolonged ventricular asystole (cardiac arrest).

Absence of AV conduction may sometimes be accompanied by an accelerated escape rate. Chapter 14 has discussed problems of increased automaticity occurring in the Purkinje cells in either the common bundle or its branches (see Figs. 14.8 through 14.12). AV dissociation is a general term used when there is independent atrial and ventricular activation. It should be considered "AV dissociation due to the AV block" when the only abnormality is the block as illustrated in Figure 20.6B, and "AV dissociation due to a combination of block and interference" when some block is accompanied by an accelerated distal rhythm as shown in Figure 20.6A. There may also be "AV dissociation due to interference alone" as shown in Figure 20.7.

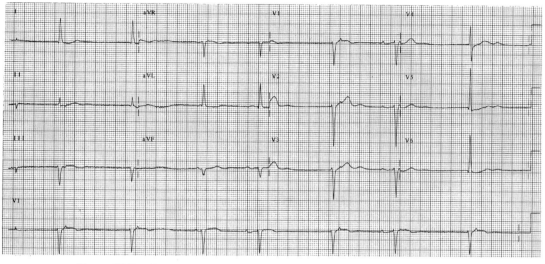

Figure 20.7. A complete 12-lead ECG (*top three channels*) demonstrates sinus bradycardia with marked sinus arrhythmia. When the sinus rate slows to < 45 beats/min, escape from the common bundle (junctional escape) occurs. When the sinus rate accelerates, it captures the ventricles as seen in the 4th and 6th cycles. "AV dissociation due to interference" is seen in the 1st, 2nd, 3rd, 5th, and 7th cycles. Note that when the P waves occur immediately following QRS complexes they are only visible in some of the leads. Lead V1 has been selected for the "rhythm strip" (*4th channel*) because the P waves are most prominent in this lead.

Block in all Purkinje fascicles rather than block at the AV node or in the main bundle is usually the cause of permanent complete AV block.[7–10] This is called bilateral bundle branch block or trifascicular block. Idiopathic fibrosis, termed either Lev's disease or Lenegre's disease, is the most common cause of chronic complete AV block.[7,11] Acute complete block in the AV node results from inferior myocardial infarction, digitalis intoxication, and rheumatic fever.[12] Acute complete block in the bundle branches results from anterior myocardial infarction.[13,14] Complete AV block may be congenital, perhaps caused by maternal anti-Ro antibodies affecting the AV node.[15]

In the presence of chronic bundle branch block, the individual is at some risk of suddenly developing complete AV block. Either the ventricles remain inactive (ventricular asystole) and the patient experiences syncope or even sudden death, or a more distal site takes over and controls the ventricles (ventricular escape). In this event, the atria continue to beat at their own rate and the ventricles beat in a lower tempo or rhythm (Fig. 20.8). This independence (AV dissociation due to AV block) is recognized readily in the recording by the lack of relationship between the slow ventricular complexes and the more frequent P waves. Each maintains its own rhythm without regard for the other.

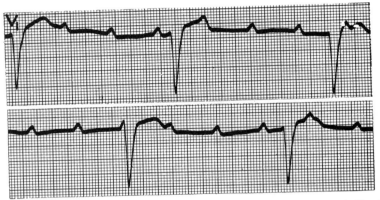

Figure 20.8. Complete AV block. The two strips form a continuous record. The P waves and QRS complexes are independent, with an atrial rate of 96 beats/min and a ventricular rate of 28 beats/min.

Third degree AV block may occur in the presence of any atrial rhythm. Differentiation between second and third degree block is accomplished by considering the relationships between both the adjacent atrial and ventricular waveforms and the consecutive ventricular waveforms. Figure 20.9 presents examples of third degree AV block occurring in the presence of three different atrial tachyarrhythmias: sinus tachycardia (A), atrial flutter (B), and atrial fibrillation (C). Consecutive RR intervals are constant in all of the examples: 2.84, 1.40, and 1.96 sec, respectively. This regularity could be due to either a constant ratio of AV conduction (second degree block), or to an escape rhythm in the absence of any AV conduction at all (third degree block). In A and B, it is obvious that there is no constant AV conduction ratio since the adjacent PR relationships in A and FR relationships in B are quite variable. Since constant AV conduction relationships are impossible with atrial fibrillation, the third degree block can be assumed simply because the RR intervals are constant in C.

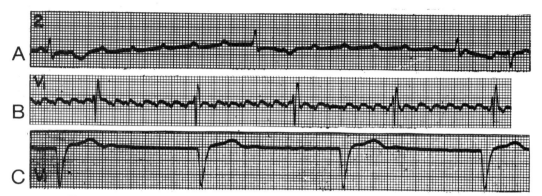

Figure 20.9. Three examples of atrial tachyarrhythmias with third degree AV block and lower escape rhythms. In **A** and **B**, the QRS duration of < 0.12 sec indicates escape from the common bundle, but in **C** the QRS duration of 0.16 sec indicates either escape from the common bundle accompanied by LBBB or escape from the right bundle branch.

LOCATION OF AV BLOCK

As discussed in Chapter 3, AV block can be located in the AV node, the common bundle or the bundle branches. This distinction is important because both the etiology and prognosis are quite different with proximal (AV nodal) versus distal infranodal block. Fortunately, block within the common bundle is extremely rare so that the clinical decision about the location of the AV block is essentially AV nodal versus bundle branch.

There are two aspects of the electrocardiographic appearance of the rhythm which may be helpful in differentiating AV block at the AV nodal versus bundle branch locations: the consistency of the PR intervals of conducted impulses, and the width of the QRS complexes of either conducted or escape impulses. Only the AV node has the capability of varying its conduction time. The Purkinje cells of the common bundle and bundle branches must conduct at a particular rate or not at all. Therefore, when a varying PR interval is present, the AV block is most likely within the AV node. A QRS of normal duration (<0.12 sec) can only occur when the impulse has equal access to both the right and left bundle branches. Therefore, when the AV block is located at the bundle branch level, the conducted or escape QRS complexes must be ≥0.12 sec. The diagnosis is complicated by the possibility of either a fixed bundle branch block accompanying AV nodal block or aberrancy of intraventricular conduction (Chapter 18, "Supraventricular Tachyarrhythmias with Aberrant Ventricular Conduction"). Therefore, a QRS complex of normal duration confirms AV nodal location, but a QRS complex of prolonged duration is not helpful in locating the site of AV block.

CONSIDERATION OF THE AV CONDUCTION PATTERN

When the QRS duration of either conducted or escape beats is within normal limits (<0.12 sec), the location is almost always the AV node. The common bundle would be a possibility, but it is so rarely the site of block that it should not be a clinical consideration. Bilateral bundle location is eliminated by the absence of QRS prolongation. Observations about the patterns of AV conduction discussed below are interesting, but should only be pursued clinically when QRS prolongation (≥0.12 sec) is present. In that situation, the consideration of the conduction patterns is the only means of differentiating an AV nodal from an infranodal (bilateral bundle) location. However, it is only possible to consider the AV conduction patterns when some conduction is present (first or second degree AV block). Therefore, when

the block is complete (third degree) and the escape QRS complexes are wide, no differentiation between AV nodal and infranodal location is possible (Figs. 20.6*B*, 20.8, and 20.9*C*).

AV NODAL BLOCK

The classic form of AV nodal block is the *Wenckebach sequence* in which the PR interval may begin within normal limits but is usually somewhat prolonged. With each successive beat, the PR interval lengthens gradually until an impulse completely fails to conduct and a ventricular beat is dropped. Following the dropped beat, the PR interval reverts to normal, or near normal, and the sequence is repeated. At times, the PR interval may stretch to surprising lengths (0.80, 0.90, or even to more than 1.0 sec). Intervals of 0.50 or 0.60 sec are common.

Progressive lengthening of the PR interval occurs because each successive atrial impulse arrives earlier and earlier in the relative refractory period of the AV node and, therefore, takes longer and longer to penetrate the node and reach the ventricles. This is a physiological mechanism during atrial flutter/fibrillation, but at normal rates it implies impairment of AV conduction.[16] The progressive lengthening usually follows a predictable pattern: the maximal increment of increase in the PR interval occurs between the first and second cardiac cycles, and the increment is less and less between subsequent cycles. This phenomenon leaves its mark on the rhythm of the ventricles. Following the pause produced by complete failure of AV conduction, the RR intervals tend to decrease progressively (Fig. 20.10), and the long cycle (the one containing the nonconducted beat) is less than two of the shorter cycles because it contains the shortest PR interval. This pattern of progressively decreasing RR intervals preceding a pause equal to less than two times the shortest RR interval is only of academic interest with AV nodal block, but a similar pattern of PP intervals may provide the only clue to the presence of sinus exit block (Chapter 19).

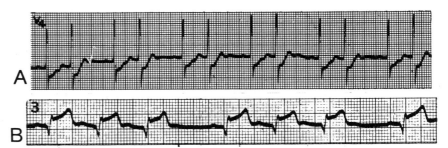

Figure 20.10. Two patients with sinus tachycardia and second degree AV block. In **A**, the 3:2 Wenckebach pattern results in ventricular beats grouped in twos (bigeminy), and in **B** the 4:3 Wenckebach pattern results in ventricular beats grouped in threes (trigeminy).

In summary, there are three characteristic cycle sequences that occur with AV nodal block which can be figuratively referred to as the *footprints of the Wenckebach*: *(a)* the beats tend to cluster in small groups, particularly in pairs, because 3:2 P:QRS ratios are more common than 4:3 which are more common than 5:4, etc.; *(b)* in each group of ventricular beats, the first cycle is longer than the second cycle and there is a tendency for progressive shortening to occur in successive cycles; and *(c)* the longest cycle (the one containing the dropped ventricular beat) is less than twice the shortest cycle (Fig. 20.11).

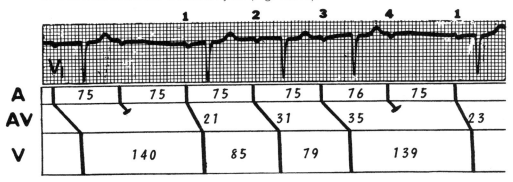

Figure 20.11. Type I second degree AV block showing a classical 4:3 Wenckebach period. Note the following typical features: *1,* even the shortest PR is longer than normal; *2,* the QRS is of normal duration; *3,* the larger PR increment is in the second (*31*) over the first (*21*); *4,* the first cycle (*85*) in the group of three beats is longer than the second (*79*); and *5,* the longest cycle (*139*) is less than twice the shortest (*79*).

The footprints of the Wenckebach are apparent in Figure 20.11, although only the P waves that occur during the long cycles are visible. The beats are grouped in pairs and trios. In three of the four trios, the first cycle is longer than the second cycle and the longest cycles separating the groups are less than twice the shortest cycles.

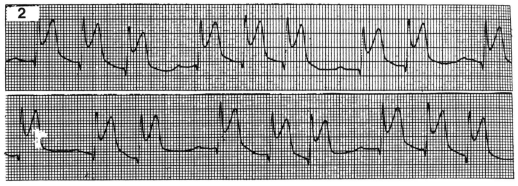

Figure 20.12. A continuous recording of lead 2 from a patient with acute inferior myocardial infarction complicated by AV nodal block.

Figure 20.12 illustrates the typical appearance of second degree AV block appearing in the common clinical setting of an acute absence of blood flow to the AV node.

The reason for the second and third footprints is illustrated in Figure 20.13, an idealized diagram of an AV nodal Wenckebach sequence. The largest increase in PR duration (+12 hundredths of a second) is in the second (34) over the first (22). Thus, although the PR gets progressively longer (22, 34, 39, and 42), it is progressively lengthening by less (+12, +5, and +3). The RR interval is composed of the PP interval plus the incremental increase in the PR interval and, therefore, it progressively decreases from 92 to 85 to 83. The RR interval surrounding the nonconducted P wave (140) is less than twice the shortest cycle (83) because, instead of containing an increment, it contains a PR decrement (−20). The long cycle is, therefore, 80 + 80 − 20 = 140.

A		80	80		80		80		80		80		80		
AV				22		22	12	34	5	39	3			22	
V			140			92		85		83			140		

Figure 20.13. Measurements are indicated in hundredths of a second on this ladder diagram. The regular PP intervals are indicated in level *A*, the abnormal nodal conduction in level *AV*, and the resulting irregular RR intervals in level *V*.

Those are the features of a classical Wenckebach period, but AV nodal block rarely fits this pattern because both the sinus rate and AV conduction are under constant influence of the autonomic nervous system.[17,18] Common divergences from the classical pattern include the following: *(a)* the first increment may not be the greatest; *(b)* the PR intervals may not lengthen progressively; *(c)* the last PR increment may be the longest of all; and *(d)* there may not be any nonconducted atrial beat.[17] The only criterion required to identify the form of AV block which is typical of the AV node is a variation in the PR intervals. The terms *Mobitz type I* or simply *type I* AV block are used when PR interval variation is present. Such variation may occur whenever there are conducted beats and, therefore, with both first and second degree block but not with third degree block.

The earlier an impulse arrives during the AV nodal refractory period, the longer the time required for conduction through to the ventricles. Therefore, the shorter the interval between a conducted QRS complex and the next conducted P wave (*RP interval*), the longer the following conduction time (*PR interval*). This inverse or reciprocal relationship between RP and PR intervals is illustrated schematically in Figure 20.14.

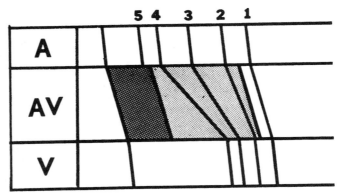

Figure 20.14. The ladder diagram illustrates the effect of progressively earlier entry of atrial impulses (*1–5*) into the AV node (*AV*). The *light stippled area* indicates the node's relative refractory period, during which impulses *2, 3,* and *4* encounter progressively slower conduction. The *dark stippled area* indicates the node's absolute refractory period, during which impulse *5* cannot be conducted to the ventricles.

Figure 20.15 presents an example of this *RP/PR reciprocity*. There is no AV block at all during the first three beats of sinus rhythm. The APB is analogous to impulse 4 in Figure 20.13, and the next three successive sinus beats are analogous to impulses 3 and 2. Only when the sinus beat has a long enough RP interval to avoid the AV node's relative refractory period is it able to be conducted with a normal PR interval. This rhythm should not be considered to be AV block, but physiologic AV nodal delay resulting from the effect of a single APB.

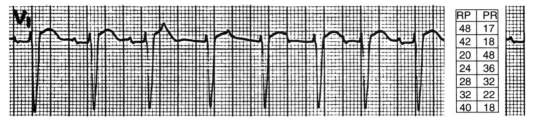

RP	PR
48	17
42	18
20	48
24	36
28	32
32	22
40	18

Figure 20.15. The table of associated RP and PR intervals indicates their reciprocal relationships. The initial cardiac cycle is not included because the RP interval preceding its PR interval has not been recorded.

The need to consider the variability of the AV conduction times to determine the location of AV block is illustrated in Figure 20.16. There is normal sinus rhythm with second degree AV block and RBBB. For the initial complete cardiac cycles, the RP intervals are constant (1.36 sec) and the PR intervals are also constant (0.24 sec). It is tempting to locate the AV block below the AV node because the PR intervals do not vary and there is an obvious intraventricular conduction problem. However, the AV node has not been eliminated because, with a constant RP interval, it would be expected to conduct with a constant PR interval. Only when the conduction ratio changes from 2:1 to 3:2 is a change produced in the RP interval (from 1.36 to 0.56 sec). This shortened RP interval is accompanied by a reciprocally lengthened PR interval (from 0.24 to 0.36 sec), identifying the AV node rather than the ventricular Purkinje system as the location of the AV block.

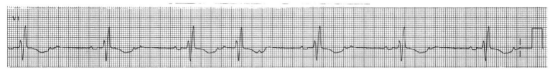

Figure 20.16. The lead V1 rhythm strip provides a clear view of all P waves (rate of 75 beats/min) and location of the intraventricular conduction delay in the right bundle branch.

INFRANODAL (PURKINJE) BLOCK

This much less common location of block is much more serious. It is almost always preceded by a BBB pattern for the conducted beats, and the dropped ventricular beats are due to intermittent block in the other bundle branch.[4,5] Therefore, *infranodol block* is usually due to bilateral BBB. First degree AV block may or may not accompany the BBB, and there is not usually a stable period of second degree AV block. Infranodal block is typically characterized by the sudden progression from no AV block to third degree or complete AV block. Since it occurs in the distal part of the pacemaking and conduction system, no escape rhythm may occur and the patient may experience syncope (*Stokes-Adams attacks*), cardiac arrest, or sudden death.

Unlike the cells in the AV node, those in the Purkinje system have an extremely short relative refractory period. Therefore, they either conduct at a certain time or not at all. Infranodal block is characterized by a lack of PR lengthening preceding the nonconducted P wave, and a lack of PR shortening in the following cycle. This is termed *Mobitz type II* or *type II* AV block. It should be diagnosed whenever there is first or second degree AV block with no change in the PR interval despite a change in the RP interval.

The rhythm in Figure 20.17 should be compared to that in Figure 20.16. Again, there is an intraventricular conduction delay (now LBBB), and the consistent 3:2 AV ratio provides varying RP intervals (from 1.04 to 0.44 sec). However, the PR intervals remain constant at 0.20 sec. Therefore, the AV block is occurring in a location that is incapable of varying its conduction time even when it receives impulses at varying intervals. The PR intervals are independent of, rather than reciprocal to, their associated RP intervals. Type II block is indicative of an infranodal location.

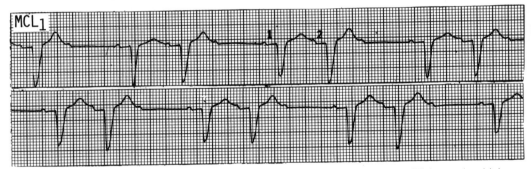

Figure 20.17. The strips are continuous. Numbers *1* and *2* indicate PR intervals which are constant despite being preceded by markedly differing PR intervals.

Figure 20.18 presents another example of type II block. Note that the PR intervals remain unchanged despite longer and shorter RP intervals (i.e., there is no RP/PR reciprocity). The two typical ways by which RP intervals vary are illustrated by this recording: a change in the A:V conduction ratio (from 1:1 to 2:1), and the presence of a VPB.

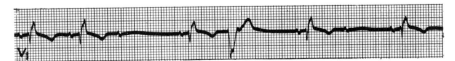

Figure 20.18. Mobitz type II second degree AV block. Two consecutive PR intervals are unchanged before the dropped beat. The conducted beats have a normal PR interval and show RBBB. The 4th beat is a right ventricular premature beat.

A stepwise method for determining the location of the AV block is illustrated in Figure 20.19. This algorithm does not consider the localization of AV block within the common bundle because it is so rare. Such a location should be considered only when a normal QRS duration (step 1) is accompanied by a type II pattern (step 4). Note that steps 2 and 4 may both lead to situations in which it is impossible to determine the location of the block from that particular ECG recording. Additional recordings should be obtained. If these are also nondiagnostic, the patient should be managed as though the block were located in the bundle branches because that has the most serious clinical consequences. This usually requires insertion of a temporary pacemaker which provides time for further studies to determine the location of the AV block. *His bundle electrograms* can be obtained via intracardiac recordings. A prolonged AH interval or the absence of a signal from the His bundle indicates AV nodal location while a prolonged HV interval or absence of a signal from the ventricles following a His signal indicates bilateral bundle location (Fig. 12.12).

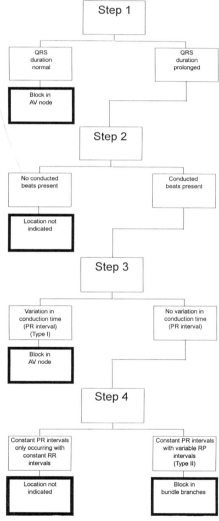

Figure 20.19. The four-step algorithm for identifying the location of AV block from an ECG recording: *Step 1,* consider the QRS duration. *Step 2,* consider whether conducted beats are present. *Step 3,* consider whether there is variation in the conduction times. *Step 4,* consider whether there are constant PR intervals with changing RP intervals. Situations that indicate an end point in the algorithm are indicated by *boxes with accentuated borders.*

GLOSSARY

Atrioventricular (AV) block: a conduction abnormality between the atria and the ventricles. Both the severity and the location should be considered.

Degree: a measure of the severity of AV block.

First degree AV block: atrial impulses conducted to the ventricles with PR intervals > 0.20 sec.

Footprints of the Wenckebach: the patterns of clusters of beats in small groups with gradually decreasing intervals between beats preceding a pause which is equal to less than two times the length of the shortest interval.

Heart block: another term used for AV block.

His bundle electrograms: intracardiac recordings obtained via a catheter positioned across the tricuspid valve adjacent to the common or His bundle. They are used clinically to determine the location of AV block when this is not apparent from the surface ECG recordings.

Infranodal block: AV block that occurs distal or below the AV node and, therefore, within either the common bundle or in both the right and left bundle branches.

Mobitz type I (type I): a pattern of AV block in which there are varying PR intervals. It is typical of block in the AV node that is capable of wide variations in conduction time. Wenckenbach sequences are the classic form of type I block.

Mobitz type II (type II): a pattern of AV block in which there are constant PR intervals despite varying RP intervals. It is typical of block in the ventricular Purkinje system which is incapable of significant variations in conduction time.

RP interval: the time between the beginning of the previously conducted QRS complex and the beginning of the next conducted P wave.

RP/PR reciprocity: the inverse relationship between the interval since the previously conducted beat (RP interval) and the time required for AV conduction (PR interval). This occurs in type I AV block.

Second degree AV block: some atrial impulses are conducted to the ventricles while some fail to be conducted.

Stokes-Adams attacks: syncopal episodes caused by periods of cardiac arrest.

Third degree AV block: none of the atrial impulses is conducted to the ventricles. It is often referred to as complete AV block.

Wenckebach sequence: the classic form of type I AV block that would be expected to occur in the absence of autonomic influences on either the SA or AV nodes.

REFERENCES

1. Johnson RL, Averill KH, Lamb LE. Electrocardiographic findings in 67,375 asymptomatic individuals. VII. A-V block. Am J Cardiol 1960;6:153.

2. Van Hemelen NM, Robles de Medina EO. Electrocardiographic findings in 791 males between the ages of 15 and 23 years; I. Arrhythmias and conduction disorders [Abstract] (Dutch). Ned Tijdschr Geneeskd 1975;23:91.

3. Erikssen J, Otterstad JE. Natural course of a prolonged PR interval and the relation between PR and incidence of coronary heart disease. A 7-year follow-up study of 1832 apparently healthy men aged 40–59 years. Clin Cardiol 1984;7:6.

4. Damato AN, Lau SH. Clinical value of the electrogram of the conduction system. Prog Cardiovasc Dis 1970;13:119.

5. Narula OS. Wenckebach type I and type II atrioventricular block (revisited). Cardiovasc Clin 1974;6:138.

6. Young D, Eisenberg R, Fish B, Fisher JD. Wenckebach atrioventricular block (Mobitz type I) in children and adolescents. Am J Cardiol 1977;40:393.

7. Lenegre J. Etiology and pathology of bilateral bundle branch block in relation to complete heart block. Prog Cardiovasc Dis 1964;6:409.

8. Lepeschkin E. The electrocardiographic diagnosis of bilateral bundle branch block in relation to heart block. Prog Cardiovasc Dis 1964;6:445.

9. Rosenbaum MB, Elizari MV, Kretz A, Taratuto AL. Anatomical basis of AV conduction disturbances. Geriatrics 1970;25:132.

10. Steiner C, Lau SH, Stein E, Wit AL, Weiss MB, Damato AN, Haft JI, Weinstock M, Gupta P. Electrophysiological documentation of trifascicular block as the common cause of complete heart block. Am J Cardiol 1971;28:436.

11. Louie EK, Maron BJ. Familial spontaneous complete heart block in hypertrophic cardiomyopathy. Br Heart J 1986;55:459.

12. Rotman M, Wagner GS, Waugh RA. Significance of high degree atrioventricular block in acute posterior myocardial infarction. The importance of clinical setting and mechanism of block. Circulation 1973;47:257–262.

13. Hindman MC, Wagner GS, JaRo M, Atkins JM, Scheinman MM, DeSanctis RW, Hutter AH Jr, Yeatman L, Rubenfire M, Pujura C, Rubin M, Morris JJ. The clinical significance of bundle branch block complicating acute myocardial infarction. I. Clinical characteristics, hospital mortality, and one year follow-up. Circulation 1978;58:679–688.

14. Hindman MC, Wagner GS, JaRo M, Atkins JM, Scheinman MM, DeSanctis RW, Hutter AH Jr, Yeatman L, Rubenfire M, Pujura C, Rubin M, Morris JJ. The clinical significance of bundle branch block complicating acute myocardial infarction. II. Indications for temporary and permanent pacemaker insertion. Circulation 1978;58:689–699.

15. Ho SY, Esscher E, Anderson RH, Michaelsson M. Anatomy of congenital complete heart block and relation to maternal anti-Ro antibodies. Am J Cardiol 1986;58:291.

16. Brodsky M, Wu D, Denes P, Kanakis C, Rosen KM. Arrhythmias documented by twenty-four hour continuous electrocardiographic monitoring in fifty male medical students without apparent heart disease. Am J Cardiol 1977;39:390.

17. Denes P, Levy L, Pick A, Rosen KM. The incidence of typical and atypical atrioventricular Wenckebach periodicity. Am Heart J 1975;89:26.

18. Narula OS. His bundle electrocardiography and clinical electrophysiology. Philadelphia: FA Davis, 1975:146–160.

CHAPTER 21

Artificial Cardiac Pacemakers

Artificial cardiac pacemakers are most commonly used in the management of symptomatic bradyarrhythmias caused by abnormal cardiac impulse formation or conduction.[1,2] Pacemakers may also be used in patients with tachyarrhythmias when: (*a*) necessary pharmacologic therapy carries a risk of bradyarrhythmias; or (*b*) electrical stimuli are required to stop the tachyarrhythmia. In the latter situation, a device with the added capability of *defibrillation* may be required.[3]

Figure 21.1 illustrates the components of an artificial pacemaking system. Electronic impulses are formed in a device termed a *pulse generator,* which may be located either inside or outside the patient's body. When the rhythm abnormality appears suddenly, an external pacing system may be applied as an emergency procedure.[4] This temporary therapy may be administered via either large electrodes applied to the precordium or small *pacing electrodes* mounted at the end of an intravenous catheter and advanced to the right atrial or ventricular endocardium. Following open heart surgery, temporary epicardial electrodes may be placed on the atria or ventricles. When permanent artificial pacing is required, the device is surgically implanted.

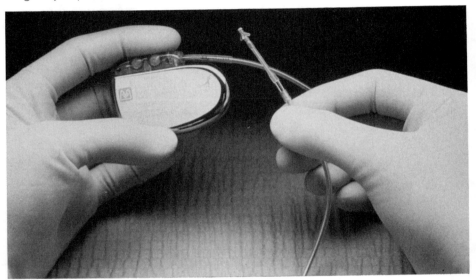

Figure 21.1. The implantable pulse generator is held in the left hand and the pacing electrode in the right. The connecting wire is advanced transvenously so that the tip of the electrode nestles among the trabeculae of the right ventricular endocardium.

EVALUATION OF THE ARTIFICIAL PACEMAKER

 When the cardiac rhythm is initiated by these artificially generated impulses, *pacemaker spikes* can usually be detected on an ECG recording. *Fixed-rate mode* of both of the ventricles (*A*) and the atria (*B*) is illustrated in Figure 21.2.

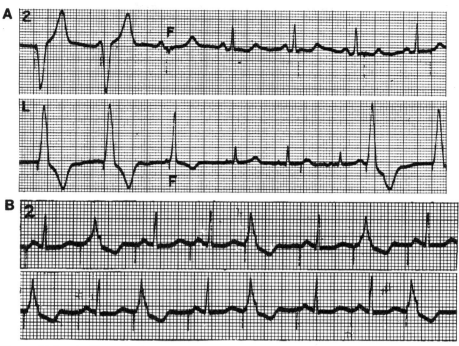

Figure 21.2.   A. Sinus rhythm competing with a fixed-rate pacemaker (V00), resulting in fusion beats (*F*). The regular rhythm of the pacemaker spikes is not disturbed by the natural beats. **B.** Fixed-rate atrial pacemaker (A00) in which each P wave is immediately preceded by a pacemaker spike. The paced rhythm is interrupted by frequent ventricular premature beats that coincide with the next expected P waves so that they look like paced ventricular beats.

As illustrated in Figure 21.3, the amplitude of these spikes varies among leads and might not be apparent on a single lead recording. The amplitude of the pacing spike also depends on the programmed output and the configuration of the pacing system and is increased when unipolar pacing is used.

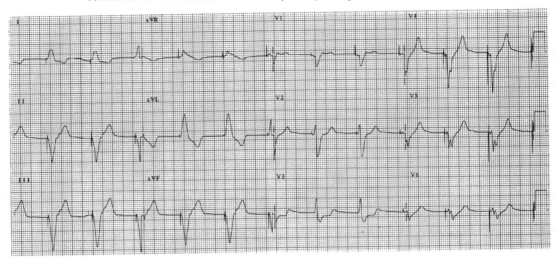

Figure 21.3. The pacing spikes are quite prominent in many leads but minimal in lead aVL and entirely absent in lead V3. If only these leads were observed, there would be no evidence that the rhythm was artificially generated.

Almost all current artificial pacemakers have a built-in standby or *demand mode* because the rhythm disturbances that require their use may occur intermittently.[5] Figure 21.4 illustrates an example of a normally functioning demand pacemaker. In this mode, the device senses the intrinsic impulses and does not generate artificial impulses while the intrinsic rate exceeds that of the pulse generator.

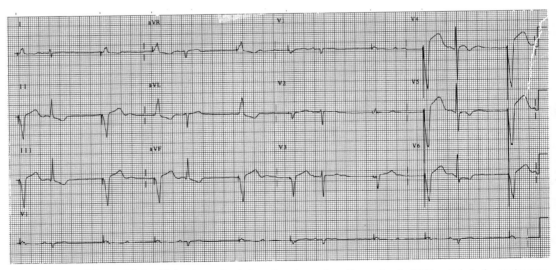

Figure 21.4. There is marked sinus bradycardia with a rate of <40 beats/min (note the two P waves visible in lead V1). The pacemaker cycle length is 1010 msec, resulting in pacemaker capture following each of several single intrinsic beats.

The activity of the demand device may not be detectable on an ECG recording. Only when the bradyarrhythmia (Fig. 21.5) recurs can the activity of the device be observed. The assessment of the ECG recording regarding normal function of the artificial pacing system is dependent on:

1. The patient's rhythm at the time of the evaluation;
2. The type of artificial pacing system;
3. How the pacing system has been programmed;
4. The myocardial location of the pacing electrode.

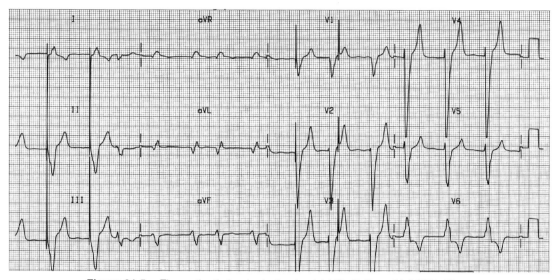

Figure 21.5. The patient's basic rhythm is atrial fibrillation with LBBB. The two consecutive paced beats (at *left*) indicate a pacing interval of 860 msec. After five intrinsic beats at shorter cycle lengths, there is a cycle of >860 msec, and the demand pacemaker recaptures the ventricular rhythm for a single beat. Note that a pacemaker spike occurs following an intrinsic beat (in leads V1–V3) because there was not enough time for sensing to occur (Fig. 21.13).

1. Patient's Rhythm

When a demand mode pacing system is used, the evaluation of its pacing function requires that the sensing function be disarmed if the intrinsic rhythm is faster than the artificial pacemaker. This is accomplished through the use of a magnet, as illustrated in Figure 21.6.

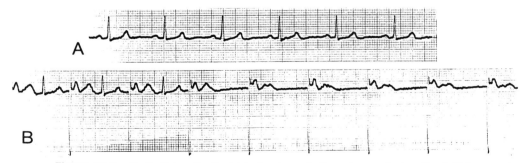

Figure 21.6. In **A,** the patient's intrinsic sinus rhythm at a cycle length of 930 msec is observed. Use of the magnet in **B** disarms the sensing mode, causing the now fixed-rate pacemaker to reveal its ability to capture the ventricles at its 1000 msec cycle length.

With its sensing function disabled, the device functions in the fixed-rate mode. This extrinsic rhythm is then analogous to an intrinsic parasystolic focus (Chapter 13, "Premature Beats"). The ECG recording reveals the competition between the extrinsic and intrinsically generated impulses (Fig. 21.7).

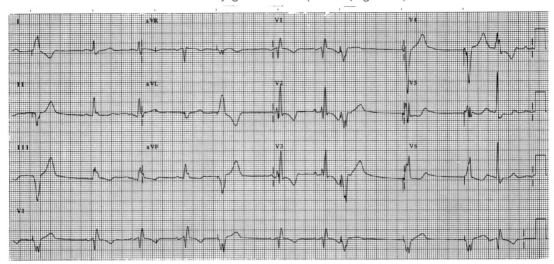

Figure 21.7. A standard 12-lead ECG illustrating a VVI pacemaker functioning in the V00 mode at a cycle length of 1210 msec because of magnetic sensing inhibition (Table 21.1). Note that ventricular capture can occur only when the pacemaker spike occurs after the peak of the T waves.

2. Type of Artificial Pacing System

The three-letter code describing the various pacing modes introduced in 1974 is presented in Table 21.1.[6] For example, a "VVI" mode is the common demand pacemaker that paces the ventricles (V), senses ventricular activity (V), and is inhibited by such sensing (I).

Table 21.1. Types of Pacemakers

	Paced	Sensed	Response
Fixed-rate ventricular	V[a]	0	0
P-triggered ventricular	V	A	T
QRS-triggered ventricular	V	V	T
QRS-inhibited ventricular (demand)	V	V	I
Fixed-rate atrial	A	0	0
Demand A-V sequential	D	V	I
Fixed-rate A-V sequential	D	0	0
Fixed-rate A-V simultaneous	D	0	0
Atrial synchronous, ventricular demand	V	D	D
Universal, fully automatic	D	D	D

[a]V, ventricle; A, atrium; D, both ventricle and atrium; 0, neither chamber; T, triggered; I, inhibited.

The Pacemaker Study Group of the Inter-Society Commission for Heart Disease Resources added two categories to the existing code to describe the pacing system function: programmable functions and special antitachyarrhythmia functions (Table 21.2). For example, a common ventricular demand pacemaker with simple programming of only rate and level of current would be termed "VVI,P."

Table 21.2[a]

Position	I	II	III	IV	V
Category	Chamber(s) Paced	Chamber(s) Sensed	Modes of Response(s)	Programmable Functions	Special Antitachyarrhythmia Functions
Letters used	V-ventricle	V-ventricle	T-triggered	P-programmable (rate and/or output)	B-bursts
	A-atrium	A-atrium	I-inhibited	M-multiprogrammable	N-normal-rate competition
	D-double	D-double	D-double[b] O-none	C-communicating	S-scanning
		O-none	R-reverse	O-none	E-external
Manufacturer's designation only	S-single chamber	S-single chamber	⬇ Comma optional here		

[a]Reproduced with permission from Parsonnet V, Furman S, Smyth NPD, Bilitch M. Optimal resources for implantable cardiac pacemakers. Circulation 1983;68:230A. Copyright 1983 American Heart Association.
[b]Triggered and inhibited response.

If the ventricular demand system also included reverse sensing to detect a tachyarrhythmia (R), multiprogrammability (M), and a burst function to provide rapid stimuli to interrupt the tachyarrhythmia (B), the appropriate code would be "VVR,MB." Usually, there are no markers of the presence of such an antitachycardia device on the ECG recording because it remains in the demand mode until the tachyarrhythmia for which it has been programmed occurs. Figure 21.8 illustrates the normal function of this variety of pacing system.

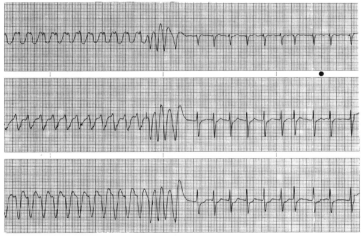

Figure 21.8. Three-channel recording from leads V1 (*top*), V3 (*middle*), and V5 (*bottom*). A burst of three paced stimuli are delivered to the ventricles at a cycle length of 180 msec. This results in polymorphic beats and termination of the monomorphic ventricular tachycardia. The patient then returns to atrial fibrillation with a narrow (<0.12 sec) QRS complex.

The pacing system is chosen to meet the particular needs of the patient. The original units introduced in the 1960s were simple devices with a single fixed-rate mode to pace the ventricles (V00). The demand mode was introduced with sensing capability to prevent interference with the patient's intrinsic rhythm (VVI). Subsequent developments include external programmability, interaction with the patient's underlying rhythm, sensing of the patient's physiological status, AV sequential stimulation, and incorporation of antitachycardia functions. Assessment of whether the pacing system is functioning normally requires knowledge of the specific unit implanted.[7]

3. How the Pacing System Has Been Programmed

The majority of pacing systems currently implanted have programming capability. This is usually achieved through the use of a magnet coupled with a radio frequency transmitter. The programming device is applied on the skin overlying the implanted device. The features that can be programmed vary among manufacturers.[8]

The evaluation of the function of the artificial pacing system on the ECG recording requires knowledge of some of the programmed parameters such as rate and mode of pacing. Many systems include special features such as *hysteresis* (Gr. hysteros = later), which allow the device to be programmed to pace at one rate but to tolerate a lower intrinsic rate before beginning to pace. This function allows the intrinsic rhythm to decrease to a lower rate before pacing at the higher rate is instituted (Fig. 21.9).[9]

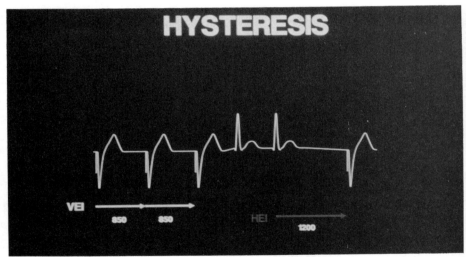

Figure 21.9. A VVI pacemaker is capturing the ventricles at its ventricular escape interval (*VEI*) of 850 msec. The artificial pacemaker is then inhibited by the patient's intrinsic rhythm. There is then a delay of 1200 msec, termed hysteresis escape interval (*HEI*), before the pacemaker is discharged to provide maximal opportunity for the continued dominance of the intrinsic rhythm.

4. Myocardial Location of the Pacing Electrode

The spread of the wave fronts of depolarization within the heart varies, depending on the location of the stimulating electrode. Usually, endocardial electrodes are positioned on the right ventricular endocardium near the apex. This produces sequential right and then left ventricular activation and, therefore, a left bundle branch block pattern on the ECG (Fig. 21.10*A*). When epicardial electrodes are used, they are placed on the left ventricle. This produces sequential left and then right ventricular activation and, therefore, a right bundle branch block pattern on the ECG (Fig. 21.10*B*).

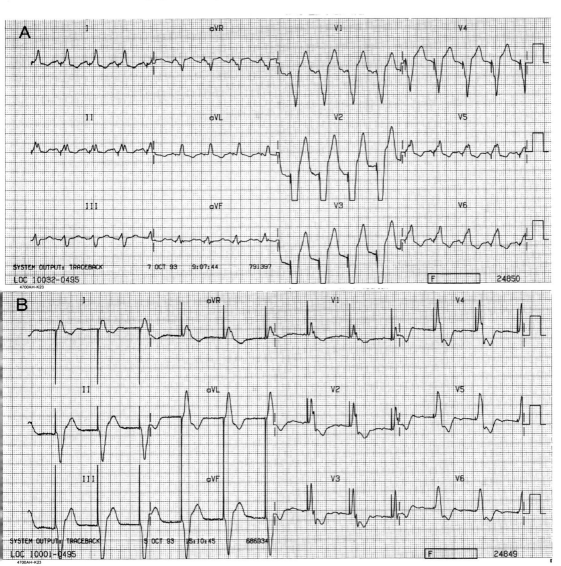

Figure 21.10. Standard 12-lead ECGs illustrate the appearances of the QRS complexes resulting from right ventricular endocardial (**A**) and left ventricular epicardial pacing (**B**). Note the contrasting appearances of the QRS complexes in lead V1, indicating delay over the posterior left ventricle in **A** and over the anterior right ventricle in **B**.

When atrial rather than ventricular pacing is indicated, the endocardial electrode is usually placed on the right atrial appendage. This results in a P wave following the atrial pacing artifact. When both atrial and ventricular pacing are indicated, electrodes are positioned adjacent to both the right atrial and right ventricular endocardial surfaces (Fig. 21.11).

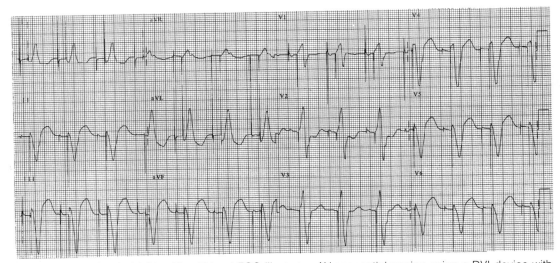

Figure 21.11. The 12-lead ECG illustrates AV sequential pacing using a DVI device with electrodes in the right atrium and ventricle. The cycle length is 760 msec, and the AV interval is 160 msec.

DETECTION OF PACEMAKER MALFUNCTION

 Pacemaker malfunction may be intermittent and, therefore, assessment should include 24 hour ambulatory monitoring and/or exercise testing.

1. Failure to Sense

This problem is apparent when a demand pacemaker functions in a fixed-rate mode (Fig. 21.12). It is most commonly caused by either alteration of the position of an endocardial electrode or scar formation between the electrode and the myocardium. Certain medications can significantly alter the sensing threshold. Correction of this problem may be achieved by programming a lower sensing threshold into the system, but may require repositioning of the electrode.[10]

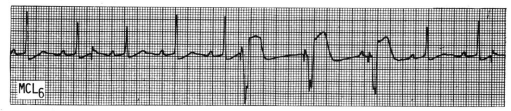

Figure 21.12. Demand pacemaker that intermittently fails to sense. Note the spikes after the second, fifth, and last beats. The pacemaker spike following the fifth sinus beat is slightly later than the other two and, therefore, produces a ventricular response. The pacemaker is inhibited by the other sinus beats.

Since there is some delay between the time of occurrence of an intrinsic cardiac waveform and the time it is sensed by the pacing system, a false indication of sensing failure may be seen on the ECG (Figs. 21.5 and 21.13). Recordings such as this are often misinterpreted as indicating faulty sensing because in many beats the QRS complex contains the pacemaker spike. In Figure 21.13, the pacemaker electrodes are situated within the right ventricle, and the conducted beats indicate RBBB. For the conducted impulse to reach the sensing electrode, it must travel down the LBB and then through the interventricular septum. Since this journey may require about 0.08 sec, a pacemaker spike may be found as late as 0.08 sec after the beginning of the QRS complex without implying failure of the sensing function.[11,12]

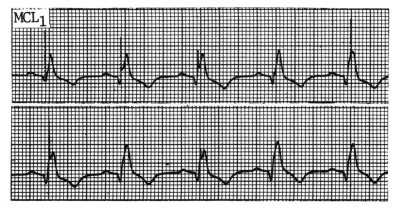

Figure 21.13. Sinus rhythm with RBBB and a normally functioning right ventricular demand pacemaker. Pacemaker artifacts are superimposed on the ventricular complexes as much as 0.08 sec after the beginning of the QRS complex because of the circuitous path taken by the sinus impulse to reach the sensing electrode.

2. Failure to Pace

This is detected by observing a pacing spike that is not followed immediately by the appropriate cardiac waveform. Examples of failure of both atrial and ventricular pacing systems are illustrated in Figure 21.14.

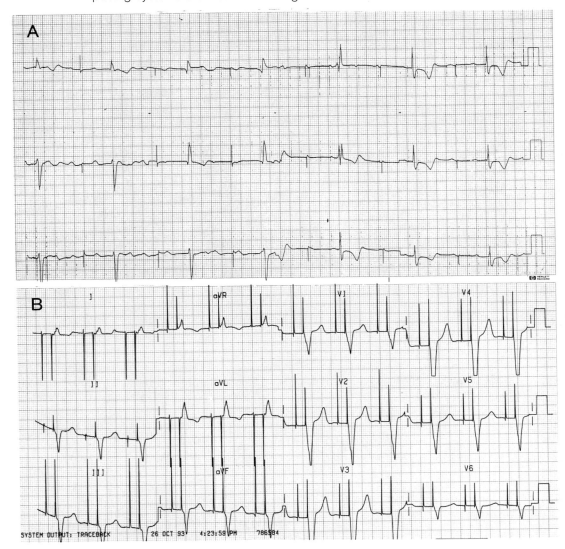

Figure 21.14. In **A,** the VVI pacemaker is sensing appropriately but failing to capture due to a fractured pacing electrode. In **B,** the DDD pacemaker is capturing the ventricles but failing to capture the atria due to migration of the right atrial electrode. Note the absence of P waves following the atrial pacing spikes.

When the threshold for pacing exceeds the programmed output of the pulse generator, failure to pace occurs, which can be life threatening with ventricular pacing. Failure to pace usually occurs early after implantation either due to an increase in the pacing threshold or due to migration of the pacing electrode. When failure to pace occurs late after implantation, fracture of the electrode should be suspected. Most pacemakers are programmed with a wide safety margin between the pacing threshold and the pacing output. When the threshold and output are too close, failure to capture can occur intermittently, for example, with deep inspiration (Fig. 21.15).

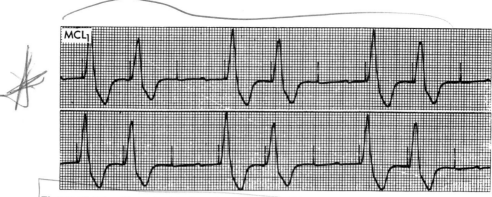

Figure 21.15. Bigeminal rhythm due to the failure of every third pacing stimulus to activate the ventricles.

3. Oversensing

This problem is detected by observing the absence of pacing spikes in the absence of P waves (atrial pacemaker) or QRS complexes (ventricular pacemaker), as illustrated in Figure 21.16. The pacing system is inhibited because it is sensing some electrical activity other than the appropriate cardiac waveform. The other electrical activity may be a T wave, as in Figure 21.16A, or skeletal muscle potentials, as in Figure 21.16B. The problem of *oversensing* is usually benign if the device is sensing another cardiac waveform because it will result only in a bradyarrhythmia. With dual chamber pacing, the atrial component occasionally senses the ventricular T wave, which could produce a type of pacemaker-mediated tachycardia. The problem may be quite serious if the pacemaker is sensing noncardiac electrical activity. Oversensing can usually be readily solved by programming the pacemaker to an increased sensing threshold.[13]

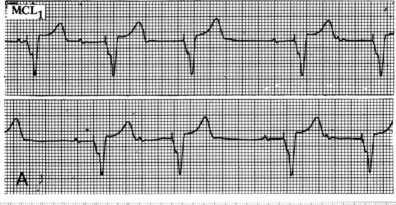

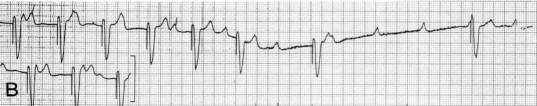

Figure 21.16. **A.** A normally functioning ventricular demand (VVI) pacemaker deceived by T waves. The pacemaker cycle is 0.96 sec, and the longer cycles of 1.38 sec result when the pacemaker senses the preceding T wave. **B.** The unipolar VVI pacemaker is inhibited when the patient does upper extremity exercises, which send skeletal muscle potentials to the implanted device.

4. Pacemaker-induced Tachyarrhythmias

There is always the potential for *pacemaker-induced tachyarrhythmias* with an artificial pacing system because a stimulus occurs during the vulnerable period at the peak of the T wave. With modern pacing systems, this is most unlikely since it would require failure in the pacemaker's sensing system at a time when there was also marked reduction in the patient's threshold for developing a ventricular arrhythmia. Such reduction usually occurs only during an acute myocardial infarction.[14] In a clinical electrophysiology laboratory, high energy pacing stimuli are used to deliberately produce supraventricular or ventricular tachycardia either to establish a diagnosis or to evaluate the efficacy of antiarrhythmia drugs.

5. Pacemaker-mediated Tachyarrhythmias

These arrhythmias are commonly seen with fixed-rate pacemakers, as illustrated in Figure 21.17. The rapid rate is produced by the combined presence of both intrinsic and paced beats. The example in Figure 21.17B presented a difficult diagnostic problem because the patient had intrinsic LBBB, and the pacemaker spikes were invisible on the MCL₁ lead. The diagnosis of *pacemaker-mediated tachyarrhythmia* due to failure of the sensing function required a 12-lead ECG to visualize the pacemaker spikes.

Currently, pacemaker-mediated tachyarrhythmias occur only with dual chambered pacing systems, and the ventricular rates are usually below 150 beats/min

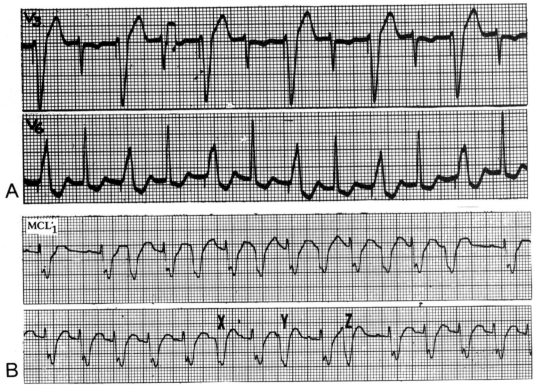

Figure 21.17. **A.** Tachycardia due to interpolated paced beats from a fixed-rate (V00) pacemaker. Both sinus and paced rhythms have a rate of 62 beats/min, producing an interpolated tachycardia at a rate of 124 beats/min. **B.** A ventricular demand (VVI) pacer on standby (the spikes are invisible in this monitoring lead) is intermittently failing to sense. In the *top strip*, a tachycardia is produced by interpolated paced beats in which the spikes are invisible. In the *bottom strip*, the coupling interval of consecutive paced beats (*X, Y, Z*) varies, but the pacing interval is constant.

(Fig. 21.18).[15,16] This arrhythmia occurs because the ventricular paced beat has been able to propagate back through the AV node, thereby producing retrograde atrial activation. The resultant P wave is then sensed via the atrial electrode, thereby initiating a pacemaker-induced ventricular stimulation. The pacemaker is acting as a bypass tract between the atrium and the ventricle. In most cases, the problem can be corrected by careful programming of the various intervals.

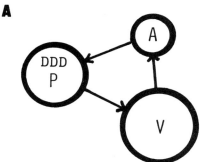

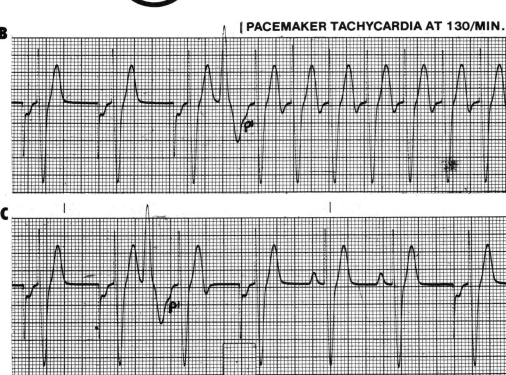

Figure 21.18. **A.** Diagram of the sequence of events in endless loop tachycardia. *A*, atrium; *V*, ventricle; *P*, pacemaker. **B.** Fully automatic (DDD) pacemaker producing endless loop tachycardia in response to a ventricular premature beat. At the *beginning of the strip*, the pacer is operating in the AV sequential mode. The fourth beat is a ventricular extrasystole with retrograde conduction (*P'*). The retrograde P' wave is sensed and, after the preset AV delay of about 0.16 sec, the ventricle is paced. This beat in turn conducts retrogradely and the vicious cycle continues. **C.** The programmable atrial refractory period has been lengthened so that a similar premature beat fails to initiate a tachycardia because the retrograde P' wave now arrives during the atrial refractory period and, therefore, is not sensed. The sixth and seventh beats in this strip show this versatile pacemaker in the ventricular mode (i.e., natural P waves are sensed and the ventricles paced after the preset AV delay).

6. Pacemaker Syndrome

Pacemaker syndrome is a clinical syndrome involving reduced cardiac output, either continuous or intermittent, associated primarily with VVI units where retrograde AV conduction occurs, thereby resulting in reduced cardiac output.[17] An example of such retrograde conduction is presented in leads V1–V3 of Figure 21.10B. Correction may require programming the unit to a slower rate or upgrading the unit to a dual chamber system.

GLOSSARY

Artificial cardiac pacemakers: devices capable of generating electrical impulses and delivering them to the myocardium.

Defibrillation: termination of either atrial or ventricular fibrillation using an extrinsic electrical current.

Demand mode: an artificial pacemaking system with the capability to sense, and be inhibited by, intrinsic cardiac activity.

Fixed-rate mode: an artificial pacing system with the capability only for generating an electrical impulse with no sensing of the intrinsic rhythm.

Hysteresis: delay built into a demand pacemaker to provide a longer period before initiating an impulse following a period of inhibition by the intrinsic rhythm than that between consecutive generated impulses.

Oversensing: abnormal function of an artificial pacemaker in which electrical signals other than those representing activation of the myocardium are sensed and inhibit impulse generation.

Pacemaker-induced tachyarrhythmias: a rapid rate produced by the artificial pacemaker. A paced impulse occurring during the time when the myocardium is vulnerable to induction of a reentrant circuit because it is just emerging from total refractoriness.

Pacemaker-mediated tachyarrhythmias: a rapid rate occurring with a dual chambered pacing system in which some of the beats are intrinsic and some are from the artificial device.

Pacemaker spikes: high frequency signals appearing on an ECG which represent impulses generated by an artificial pacemaker.

Pacemaker syndrome: a reduction in cardiac output caused by activation by an artificial pacemaker that does not produce an optimally efficient sequence of myocardial activation.

Pacing electrodes: in contrast to the electrodes used to record the ECG, pacing electrodes are designed to transmit an electrical impulse to the myocardium. In pacing systems with sensing capability, however, they also transmit the intrinsic impulses to the artificial device.

Pulse generator: the device that produces electrical impulses as the key component of an artificial pacing system.

REFERENCES

1. Furman S, et al. A practice of cardiac pacing. New York: Futura, 1986.
2. Gillette PC, Griffin JC. Practical cardiac pacing. Baltimore: Williams & Wilkins, 1986.
3. Dreifus LS, Fisch C, Griffin JC, Gillette PC, Mason JW. Guidelines for implantation of cardiac pacemakers and antiarrhythmia devices. A report of the American College of Cardiology/American Heart Association Task Force on Assessment of Diagnostic and Therapeutic Cardiovascular Procedures (Committee on Pacemaker Implantation). Circulation 1991; 84:455–467.
4. Wood M, Ellenbogen KA. Bradyarrhythmias, emergency pacing, and implantable defibrillation devices. Crit Care Clin 1989;5:551–568.
5. Barold SS. Modern cardiac pacing. New York: Futura, 1985.
6. Parsonnet V, Furman S, Smyth NPD, Bilitch M (members of the Pacemaker Study Group). Optimal resources for implantable cardiac pacemakers. Circulation 1983;68:227A–244A.
7. Hayes DL. Timing cycles of permanent pacemakers. Cardiol Clin 1992;10:593–608.
8. Bernstein AD, Parsonnet V. Survey of cardiac pacing in the United States in 1989. Am J Cardiol 1992;69:331–338.
9. Lorente P, Davidenko J. Hysteresis phenomena in excitable cardiac tissues. Ann N Y Acad Sci 1990;591:109–127.
10. Barold SS, Falkoff MD, Ong LS, Heinle RA. The third decade of cardiac pacing: multiprogrammable pulse generators. Br Heart J 1981;45:357–364.
11. Castellanos A Jr, Agha AS, Befeler B, Castillo CA, Berkovits BV. A study of arrival of excitation at selected ventricular sites during human bundle branch block using close bipolar catheter electrodes. Chest 1973;63:208–213.
12. Vera Z, Mason DT, Awan NA, Hiliard G, Massumi RA. Lack of sensing by demand pacemakers due to intraventricular conduction defects. Circulation 1975;51:815–822.
13. Kastor JA, Leinbach RC. Pacemakers and their arrhythmias. Prog Cardiovasc Dis 1970;13:240.
14. Castellanos A, Lemberg L. Pacemaker arrhythmias and electrocardiographic recognition of pacemakers. Circulation 1973;47:1382.
15. Vitale N, Santangelo L, Scialdone A, Civitello UF, Mayer MS, Nave C, Vitale P. ECG and arrhythmia in subjects with implanted dual-chamber VDD and DDD pacemakers. Minerva Cardioangiol 1991: 39:111–117.
16. Furman S, Fisher JD. Endless loop tachycardia in an AV universal (DDD) pacemaker. Pace 1982;5:486.
17. Furman S. The present status of cardiac pacing. Herz 1991;16:171–181.

CHAPTER 22

Drug Toxicity

Many of the arrhythmias discussed in the preceding chapters can be caused by the *proarrhythmic effects* of various medications.

DIGITALIS

Digitalis toxicity is manifested by both brady- and tachyarrhythmias because the drug has parasympathetic effects on sinus node automaticity and AV nodal conduction, but sympathetic effects on automaticity from other sites. Digitalis can also cause tachyarrhythmias via the mechanism of reentry and perhaps also triggered automaticity.[1]

Accidental or deliberate overdosage of digitalis produces different toxic effects in individuals with normal hearts versus those with cardiac disease. In the former, digitalis toxicity occurs only with very high blood levels, and the bradyarrhythmias predominate with slowing of the sinus node and advanced AV nodal block.[2] In individuals with cardiac disease, toxicity may develop even with blood levels within the *therapeutic range.* Advanced AV block occurs along with a wide variety of tachyarrhythmias (Table 22.1).

Table 22.1

Excitant	Suppressant	Combined
APBs and VPBs commonly in a bigeminal pattern	Sinus bradycardia	Atrial tachycardia with AV block
Accelerated junctional and ventricular rhythms (AJR and AVR)	Sinus exit block	High degree AV block with AJR or AVR (in the presence of atrial fibrillation)
Ventricular tachycardia	AV nodal block	Double tachycardia (atrial and junctional)
Ventricular fibrillation		

Previously, arrhythmias due to digitalis toxicity were common because the drug was critical for the management of patients with cardiac failure. The recent availability of other positive inotropic agents, potent diuretics, and vasodilators has diminished the use of digitalis and, therefore, the occurrence of digitalis-induced arrhythmias.[3]

EXCITANT ARRHYTHMIAS

 A common manifestation of relatively mild digitalis toxicity is supraventricular or ventricular premature beats appearing in a repetitive pattern. Figure 13.21 presents typical ventricular bigeminy while Figure 22.1 illustrates ventricular trigeminy.

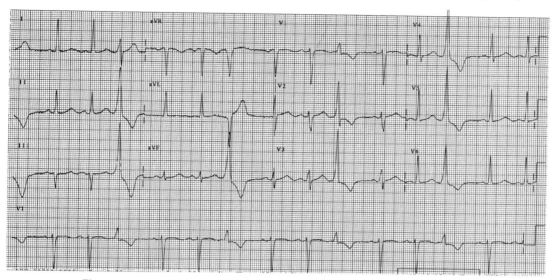

Figure 22.1. A VPB follows every second normal sinus beat. Note the consistent appearance of the VPBs on the lead V1 rhythm strip beneath the recordings of the 12 standard leads.

When ventricular bigeminy occurs in the presence of bundle branch block, the rhythm has the appearance of a wide-QRS tachycardia with alternating QRS morphologies. The term bidirectional tachycardia has been used erroneously since the rhythm is really sinus with multiple VPBs (Fig. 22.2).[4,5] True bidirectional tachycardia is presented in Figure 17.17A. The rhythm appears to be a single regular tachyarrhythmia because the VPBs are interpolated with equal coupling and following intervals.[6]

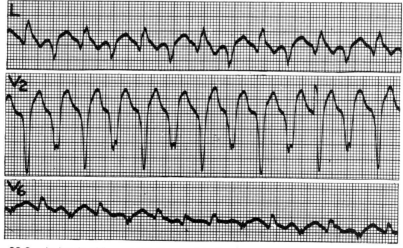

Figure 22.2. In leads aVL and V6, the ventricular complexes are alternately positive and negative. In lead V2, the QRS amplitude alternates, but all of the complexes are negative, indicating LBBB for the conducted beats and right ventricular origin for the VPBs.

Digitalis toxicity commonly causes arrhythmias due to accelerated automaticity. When the acceleration occurs in the atria, the site is probably near the sinus node because the P waves have normal sinus polarity. This tachyarrhythmia is almost always associated with varying ratios of AV block (Fig. 14.6).[7]

AV junctional tachycardia is another common manifestation of digitalis intoxication. Usually, the junctional rate is accelerated above its physiologic upper limit (about 60 beats/min), and the appropriate term is AJR (Fig. 22.3). AV dissociation is produced by the accelerated junctional rhythm, as illustrated by the ladder diagram.

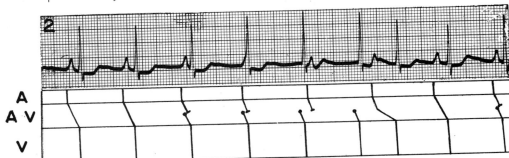

Figure 22.3. Accelerated junctional rhythm (rate of 78 beats/min) replaces sinus rhythm (rate of 70–75 beats/min). The seventh beat is a sinus capture beat conducted with a prolonged PR interval.

Occasionally, the junctional pacemaking sites may be accelerated by digitalis to rates in the tachycardia range. This is most common when large amounts of digitalis are given in an attempt to slow the ventricular rate during atrial fibrillation (Fig. 22.4).

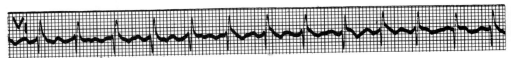

Figure 22.4. AV junctional tachycardia (rate of 140 beats/min) with incomplete RBBB in the presence of atrial fibrillation. Note the regular ventricular rate despite the rapid irregular atrial rhythm, indicating the presence of AV dissociation.

SUPPRESSANT ARRHYTHMIAS

 Digitalis has a suppressant effect both on impulse formation in the sinus node and on conduction out of the node. Figure 22.5 shows both sinus bradycardia and a simultaneous 5:4 exit block out of the sinus node, as illustrated by the ladder diagram (see SA block in Chapter 19, "Decreased Automaticity").

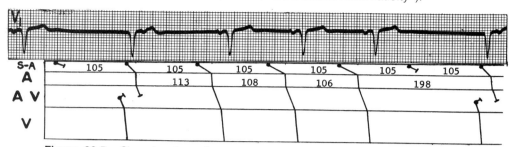

Figure 22.5. Sinus bradycardia complicated by a sinoatrial block with a Wenckebach sequence. The second and last beats are junctional escape beats. A Wenckebach pattern of conduction is inferred from progressive shortening of the atrial (PP) interval (*113, 108, 106*).

Digitalis impairs AV conduction via a parasympathetic effect on the AV node. Therefore, the pattern of conduction disturbance is of the type I variety characterized by variation in the conduction times as indicated by variation of the PR intervals (see Chapter 20, "Atrioventricular Block"). Figure 22.6 presents second degree AV block with a 6:5 AV conduction ratio resulting from digitalis toxicity.

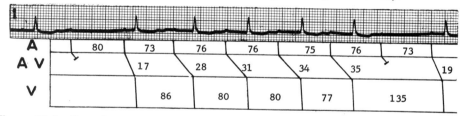

Figure 22.6. Type I second degree AV block. The typical Wenckebach period shows progressive lengthening of the PR interval until the sixth beat is not conducted at all (6:5 AV block).

Figure 22.7 is from a young male who swallowed an unknown number of digoxin tablets in a suicide attempt. As is the case in individuals without cardiac disease, there are suppressant toxic arrhythmias only.[8]

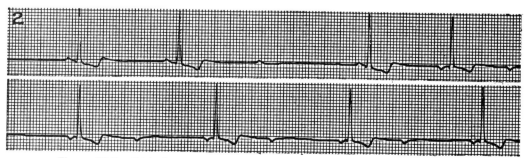

Figure 22.7. Digitalis intoxication. The strips are continuous and are from a young male who swallowed an unknown number of digoxin tablets in a suicide attempt. The sinus rhythm has been slowed to slightly under 50 beats/min. Toward the end of the top strip, an escape pacemaker replaces the sinus rhythm, but 2:1 AV block resumes.

COMBINED EXCITANT AND SUPPRESSANT ARRHYTHMIAS

 One of the most common combinations of excitant and suppressant effects is the combination of atrial tachycardia with AV block, known as PAT with block (Chapter 14, "Accelerated Automaticity"). It is more likely to have multiple P wave morphologies when it occurs in patients with cor pulmonale and hypoxia.[7] Figure 22.8 is an example of multifocal atrial tachycardia (MAT) with AV block.

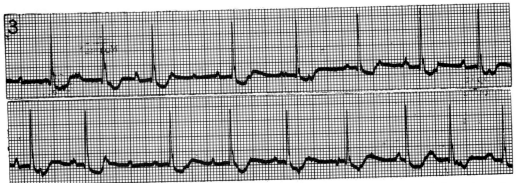

Figure 22.8. The strips are continuous. Note the variable P wave morphology, irregular atrial rhythm, changing AV conduction ratio, and the sagging ST segments characteristic of digitalis effect.

Figure 22.9 shows this combination and also VPBs. The recording is from a 30-year-old female with postpartum cardiomyopathy who was mistakenly given 2 mg of digoxin intravenously. There are digitalis-induced excitant arrhythmias in the atria and ventricles and a suppressant arrhythmia in the AV node.

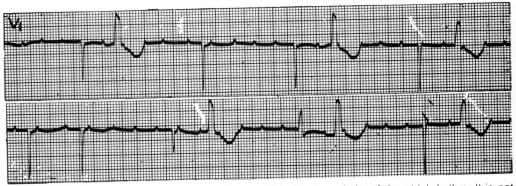

Figure 22.9. The strips are continuous. Note the irregularity of the atrial rhythm. It is not possible to determine if the AV block is second or third degree.

Occasionally, digitalis has a suppressant effect on atrial pacemakers, but an excitant effect on junctional or ventricular pacemakers. This combination is illustrated in Figure 22.10 along with a suppressant effect on AV nodal conduction.

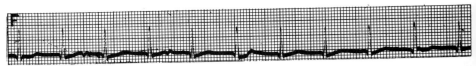

Figure 22.10. There is a regular sinus bradycardia at 55 beats/min and a regular junctional tachycardia at 105 beats/min. Note the shorter RR intervals following the sinus P waves which occur during the second and fourth T waves, indicating sinus capture with prolonged (0.32 sec) PR intervals.

When atrial fibrillation is present, digitalis toxicity is commonly manifested by a suppressant effect on AV nodal conduction and an excitant effect on infranodal pacemakers (Fig. 22.11). This combination of brady- and tachyarrhythmias causes complete AV dissociation.

Figure 22.11. The irregularity of the atrial fibrillation is in contrast to the regularity of the ventricular rhythm. The combination should be termed high degree AV block with accelerated junctional rhythm.

At other times, there is no acceleration of the pacemaking activity of cells in the ventricular Purkinje system. The slow regular junctional or ventricular escape rate allows identification of complete (third degree) AV block (Fig. 22.12). In this example, the excitant component of the digitalis is VPBs coupled with each junctional escape beat, producing a bigeminal rhythm.[9]

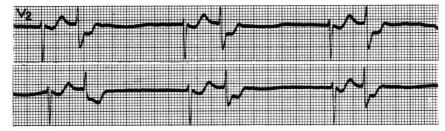

Figure 22.12. The atrial fibrillation is quite fine with no undulation visible in this lead V2 recording. The junctional escape interval is prolonged (approximately 1.5 sec). Note the multiform configuration of the VPBs.

Digitalis toxicity is the most common cause of *double tachycardia,*[10] the simultaneous existence of two independent sites with accelerated automaticity. An example is the simultaneous atrial and junctional tachycardia presented in Figure 22.13. If there was no acceleration of the junctional focus, the atrial tachycardia would be accompanied by high degree AV block.

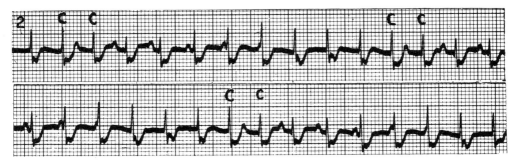

Figure 22.13. The strips are continuous and illustrate simultaneous but independent atrial tachycardia (rate of 172 beats/min) and junctional tachycardia (rate of 154 beats/min). Pairs of atrial capture beats (*CC*) are recognized by slight shortening of the ventricular cycles. Atrial capture is possible only with a prolonged PR interval (first degree AV block).

QUINIDINE AND OTHERS THAT PROLONG THE QTc INTERVAL

 Quinidine effect, which prolongs the QTc interval, is discussed in Chapter 11 ("Miscellaneous Conditions"), and the resultant torsades de pointes type of ventricular tachycardia in Chapter 17 ("Ventricular Tachyarrhymias"). Moore has recently pointed out that QTc prolongation may be produced either by an increased dispersion of action potential recovery (Fig. 22.14B) or by early afterdepolarizations (Fig. 22.14C).[11,12]

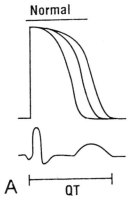

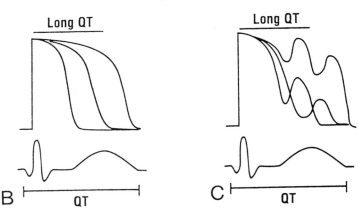

Figure 22.14. The normal temporal dispersion of ventricular recovery and resultant normal QT interval is indicated (**A**). QT interval prolongation produced by an increase in this temporal dispersion (**B**) is contrasted with that produced by early afterdepolarizations (**C**). (From Moore EN. Mechanisms and models to predict a QTc effect. Am J Cardiol 1993;72:6B–7B.)

An example of the torsades de pointes type of ventricular tachycardia is presented in Figure 17.18. Indeed, there is a spectrum of ventricular tachyarrhythmias produced by drugs administered to prevent or terminate atrial, junctional, or ventricular tachyarrhythmias. Many of these only vaguely resemble torsades. They do not always occur in the setting of a prolonged QTc interval. The U wave, discussed in Chapter 3 ("Interpretation of the Normal Electrocardiogram"), is thought to represent ventricular afterdepolarizations, and its accentuation may indicate increased potential for these drug-induced tachyarrhythmias.[13,14] A recent collection of perspectives published as a supplement to the *American Journal of Cardiology* provides basic perspectives regarding these common clinical problems.[15]

GLOSSARY

Double tachycardia: a rapid rate produced by the simultaneous existence of two independent sites with accelerated automaticity.

Proarrhythmic effects: cardiac arrhythmias produced by therapeutic agents that are typically used to prevent or terminate arrhythmias.

Therapeutic range: the blood levels of a pharmacologic agent in which individuals usually experience beneficial effects.

REFERENCES

1. Jackman WM, Szabo B, Friday KJ, Margolis PD, Moulton K, Wang X, Patterson E, Lazzara R. Ventricular tachyarrhythmias related to early afterdepolarizations and triggered firing: relationship to QT interval prolongation and potential therapeutic role for calcium channel blocking agents. J Cardiovasc Electrophysiol 1990;1:170–195.
2. Taboulet P, Baud FJ, Bismuth C. Clinical features and management of digitalis poisoning—rationale for immunotherapy. J Toxicol Clin Toxicol 1993; 31:247–260.
3. Bolognesi R, Tsialtas D, Manca C. Digitalis and heart failure: does digitalis really produce beneficial effects through a positive inotropic action? Cardiovasc Drugs Ther 1992;6:459–464.
4. Cohen SI, Deisseroth A, Hecht HS. Infra-His origin of bidirectional tachycardia. Circulation 1975;47:1260.
5. Morris SN, Zipes DP. His bundle electrocardiography during bidirectional tachycardia. Circulation 1973;48:32.
6. Gavrilescu S, Luca C. His bundle electrogram during bidirectional tachycardia. Br Heart J 1975;37:1198.
7. Agarwal BL, Agarwal BV. Digitalis-induced paroxysmal atrial tachycardia with AV block. Br Heart J 1971;34:330.
8. Vanagt EJ, Wellens HJJ. The electrocardiogram in digitalis intoxication. In: Wellens HJJ, Kulbertus HE, eds. What's new in electrocardiography. Boston: Martinus Nijhoff, 1981.
9. Scherf D, Schott A. Extrasystoles and allied arrhythmias. 2nd ed. London: Heinemann, 1973.
10. Castellanos A, et al. Digitalis-induced arrhythmias; recognition and therapy. Cardiovasc Clin 1969;1:108.
11. Moore EN. Mechanisms and models to predict a QTc effect. Am J Cardiol 1993;72:4B–9B.
12. Roden DM. Current status of class III antiarrhythmic drug therapy. Am J Cardiol 1993;72:44B–49B.
13. Morganroth J. Relations of QTc prolongation on the electrocardiogram to torsades de pointes: definitions and mechanisms. Am J Cardiol 1993;72:10B–13B.
14. Sasyniuk BI, Valois M, Toy W. Recent advances in understanding the mechanisms of drug-induced torsades de pointes arrhythmias. Am J Cardiol 1989;64:29J–32J.
15. Morganroth J, guest ed. QTc interval prolongation: is it beneficial or harmful? Am J Cardiol 1993; 72:1B–59B.

Index

Page numbers in italics denote figures; those followed by "t" denote tables.